AF677572

American Exceptionalism, the French Exception, and Digital Media Law

American Exceptionalism, the French Exception, and Digital Media Law

Lyombe Eko

LEXINGTON BOOKS
Lanham • Boulder • New York • Toronto • Plymouth, UK

Published by Lexington Books
A wholly owned subsidiary of The Rowman & Littlefield Publishing Group, Inc.
4501 Forbes Boulevard, Suite 200, Lanham, Maryland 20706
www.rowman.com

10 Thornbury Road, Plymouth PL6 7PP, United Kingdom

Copyright © 2013 by Lexington Books

All rights reserved. No part of this book may be reproduced in any form or by any electronic or mechanical means, including information storage and retrieval systems, without written permission from the publisher, except by a reviewer who may quote passages in a review.

British Library Cataloguing in Publication Information Available

Library of Congress Cataloging-in-Publication Data

TO COME.
Aesthetics and modernity : essays / by Agnes Heller ; edited by John Rundell. Test test test test test test test test test test test test test.
p. cm.
Includes bibliographical references and index.
ISBN 978-0-7391-4131-1 (cloth : alk. paper) -- ISBN 978-0-7391-4132-8 (pbk. : alk. paper) -- ISBN 978-0-7391-4133-5 (electronic)
1. Aesthetics. 2. Postmodernism. I. Rundell, John F. II. Title.
BH39.H445 2011
111'.85--dc22
2010037457

∞™ The paper used in this publication meets the minimum requirements of American National Standard for Information Sciences Permanence of Paper for Printed Library Materials, ANSI/NISO Z39.48-1992.

Printed in the United States of America

Table of Contents

Chapter One

Introduction

American Exceptionalism, the French Exception, Media Law and Policy

INTRODUCTION: COMPARATIVE COMMUNICATION AND CULTURE

Human societies are by nature communicating entities. From time immemorial, human civilizations and cultures have communicated internally and externally, how they viewed themselves and other civilizations. In other words, these civilizations and cultures have defined, presented, and re-presented themselves either in relation to, or in contradistinction to other civilizations and cultures. They have done this through various forms of visual, oral, and written communication. Collective self-perception—the phenomenon whereby specific politico-cultural collectivities assert their human, ethnic, racial, cultural, and national uniqueness vis-à-vis other politico-cultural collectivities and cultures—is a common trait of humanity. This phenomenon is compounded by the stark, often binary, oppositional distinctions that biology, history, culture, and geography have bequeathed humanity. For example, Ancient Greeks, who perceived themselves as the height of civilization, referred to all non-Greeks as uncivilized "Barbarians." This Greek attitude is summarized by the condescending Greek idiom: "Whoever is not Greek is a Barbarian." The Greeks clearly had an exceptionalist ideology, the belief that they were superior to all other nations and peoples.

The Romans also had a highly developed sense of national exceptionalism. They also called other European and non-European peoples, "Barbarians." The most famous recorded celebration of a nation and people is perhaps *The Aeneid,* an epic poem written by Roman poet, Virgil (70-19 B.C.).

The Aeneid is a panegyric to Roman imperial rule. It recounts the divine origin, global domination, and endlessness of the Roman Empire and its immortal rulers:

> The subject world shall Rome's dominion own,
> And, prostrate, shall adore the nation of the gown.[1]

In the passage from which we get this excerpt, Jupiter (Jove) tells his daughter, Venus, that the global Roman Empire, which shall bring all peoples of the known world—from Africa to India—under its dominion, has the imprimatur, the seal of approval of the gods.

In modern political sociology, the phenomenon of national self-perception, and oppositional self-definition is what Kaplowitz defines as, "how a people sees itself" (vis-à-vis other peoples). He suggests that the construction of a national self-image is an important element of national political culture. In the field of international relations, the construction and representation of national self-image usually takes place in times of uncertainty or flux.[2] Expressions of national self-image can therefore be jingoistic or even xenophobic. They often involve attributing moral virtues to one's nation, culture, and ethnicity, while ascribing immoral, unethical or even evil attributes to other nations, cultures and ethnicities. Though the construction and management of the images of nations and their adversaries is as old as the ancient kingdoms and empires—perhaps the most famous "modern" description of a nation is Tsar Nicholas the First's nineteenth-century description of the Ottoman Empire as the "Sick man of Europe"—that practice was professionalized during World War I when visual propaganda, in the form of posters, demonized opposing powers and reduced them to catchy epithets and clever appellations designed for mass consumption. With the advent of propaganda, and international public diplomacy, the world would never be the same again.

Since national attitudes about nations are disseminated through the means of mass communication, in order to gain insights into, and appreciate the intricacies of civilizations, cultures, nations, and political regimes, it is only natural to compare and contrast their communication systems and regimes. This is especially true of civilizations, cultures, nations, and political systems that are very similar to each other, or are very different from each other. Indeed, modern communication systems have led to a comparative turn in media studies. In effect, invention of the Internet, the interconnection of nations, peoples and cultures, and the explosive growth of innovative information and communication technologies have created a near-seamless, global, networked society in which different conceptualizations of the very notion of the human right to communicate—freedom of expression—has led to conflicts of law. The field of comparative communication studies is concerned with how different nations, cultures, supranational and international jurisdictions manage the regulatory tensions created by the forces of globalization and new communication technologies.

In this age of globalization, multiple innovative information and communication technologies and platforms, national self-image management—the construction and projection of a desired national self-image toward specific national, regional and international publics, through the media in real space and cyberspace—has come to be known in international relations as public diplomacy.

Kaplowitz provides some interesting insights into national self-image construction in contexts of declining international influence and fear of cultural submergence. He states that national self-imagery may be a reaction to unpleasant historical experiences, which are felt to be politically or culturally humiliating and are characterized by fear of a loss of honor, as well as declining international power and influence. He suggests that national self-image is the source of antagonistic or conflictive behavior in international relations because countries that are overly concerned with their national self-image are characterized by "pre-occupation with prestige, fear of humiliation, and concern with declining status."[3] North Korea is a good contemporary example.

National self-image ranges across a spectrum that runs from self-glorification which springs from a perceived, divinely-ordained right of religious or quasi-religious imperial conquest, to a self-ordained secular, pseudo-humanitarian "civilizing mission." The great empires of the world—the Persian Empire, the exceptional Greek Empire, the exceptional Roman Empire, the Byzantine Empire (Eastern Roman Empire) and the Ottoman Caliphate, had an acute sense of divine destiny. The relatively recent, historically speaking, European colonial empires—the British Empire, the French empire, the Spanish and Portuguese colonial empires assigned themselves both religious and secular "civilizing missions." For example, in the nineteenth and twentieth centuries, the British Empire was a master of the art of national self-image construction, projection, and management. British national self-image was grounded in a politico-cultural superiority complex that coincided with the projection of British imperial power and perceived invincibility around the world. Lord Palmerston, the nineteenth-century British Foreign Secretary and Prime Minister, is quoted as saying, that nations have neither permanent friends, nor permanent enemies. They only have permanent interests.[4] This diplomatic aphorism was uttered when Britain was at the zenith of its imperial power. British national self-image was burnished by the instrumentalities of communication, notably British newspapers, British writers, and the British Broadcasting Corporation. Nothing expressed British national self-image like the eighteenth-century nationalistic refrain:

> Rule, Britannia! rule the waves:
> Britons never will be slaves.

Nazi Germany was a regime that gloried in, and exaggerated its racial and cultural superiority. Hitler and his National Socialist (Nazi) Party transformed the hauntingly beautiful melody of Joseph Hayden, which had become a hymn to German unification in the nineteenth century, and later the anthem of the fledgling German republic in the early twentieth century, into the dogmatic, virulently nationalistic anthem:

> *Deutschland, Deutschland über alles*
> *Über alles in der Welt . . .*
> Germany, Germany above all, Above everything in the world . . .

These nationalistic outpourings are essentially statements and restatements of exceptionalism.

Comparative Exceptionalism

While it might be tempting to assume that national exceptionalism has disappeared with the world's great imperial powers, national self-perception, driven by specific national cultural and governmental logics, continues to be a major force in modern international relations. This reality is recognized in international law. Under the 1969 Vienna Convention on the Law of Treaties (VCLT), a nation-state may make "reservations" "when signing, ratifying, accepting, approving or acceding to a treaty, whereby it purports to exclude or to modify the legal effect of certain provisions of the treaty in their application to that State."[5] In other words, states are free to make declarations of exceptionalism; pronouncements to the effect that provisions of certain treaties are at variance with their specific national constitutional traditions, their politico-cultural logics or their national interests.

National Exceptionalism

The United States and France have made reservations to, or asked to be exempted from the provisions of numerous international treaties since World War II. This is due in part to the fact that both countries are self-described "exceptionalist" countries. As we see in chapters 3 and 4, at some point in their history, the United States and France declared that they were unique and "exceptional"; meaning that they were different from other countries, and also from each other. The United States and France have expressed their respective exceptionalist ideologies by highlighting their political and cultural specificities, and ascribing uniqueness to their respective politico-cultural systems. The term "exceptionalism" has been defined as "a theory that a nation, region, or political system is exceptional and does not conform to the norm" (of nationhood).[6] Exceptionalism is by nature oppositional. It comes into play when a self-described exceptional civilization, culture or country sets itself apart from—and in opposition to—the rest of the world. When the United States and France describe themselves as being "exceptional," they are essentially making declarations of difference. Both countries define themselves as being different from each other and from the rest of the world. The term "exceptionalism" is therefore an apt description of the national ideological postures of the United States and France towards the rest of the world. It refers to overt American and French declarations of political and cultural superiority and specificity. Exceptionalism essentially amounts to politico-cultural differentiation. It encapsulates American and French expectations of recognition and respect, if not for their national superiority, at least for their politico-cultural uniqueness. This explains why both nations highlight their political and cultural specificities and ascribe political or cultural uniqueness to their respective systems, vis-à-vis other countries. Two pithy, functionally equivalent theoretical constructs distill and encapsulate American and French perceptions of their respective national uniqueness and specificity: American exceptionalism and *L'Expression française* (the French exception) respectively. While the term "American exceptionalism" is an academic and political buzzword that is at best an unofficial part of the nation's political lingo, its French ideological equivalent, "*l'exception française*" (the French exception) is a statement of French official public policy discourse in a wide range of political and cultural issue areas.

American exceptionalism and the French exception are therefore different, though functionally equivalent ideological worldviews that serve as the philosophical underpinnings of media law, as well as information and communication technology policy in the two countries. In other words, both countries have encoded their political and cultural specificities into their respective media and communications regulatory regimes. As we see in chapters 3 and 4, American exceptionalism is different from the French exception in many respects. American exceptionalism is messianic and isolationist, while the French exception is mostly culturalist, identitarian, and protectionist. American exceptionalism is the proclamation that the United States is a singular nation whose superior democratic system is ordained by God, a system whose unparalleled libertarian values set it apart from the rest of the world. For its part, the French exception is a declaration of Gallic linguistic and cultural specificity. In short, American exceptionalism and the French exception are different, though functionally equivalent worldviews that explain American and French regulation of the media in real space and cyberspace. This volume comprises a number of comparative case studies that describe, explain and illustrate American exceptionalism and the French exception in digital media law and policy.

Exceptionalism as Exemptionalism: The Outsiders Within

Exceptionalism is a paradigm of paradoxes. The stated credo of the United States and France is that their respective political, social and cultural specificities grant them an "exceptional" role in human affairs. Nevertheless they exempt themselves, in whole or in part, from certain international obligations that they believe are contrary to their exceptionalist ideologies.[7] Each country is therefore an integral part of the international communication regime, yet exempts itself from crucial aspects of that regime for purposes of furthering its national interests. The exemptionalist stances of the United States and France are different, and reflect their respective national politico-cultural ideologies. The United States has exempted itself from a number of collective security and human rights agreements while France has sought to carve out for itself and its allies, cultural exceptions in international agreements in order to protect its cultural heritage. The United States and France are therefore "exemptionalist" countries, to borrow the expression of John Gerard Ruggie.[8] Both countries exist in compartmentalized regulatory dualities. They are part of the international communication and human rights regime, and yet they are not of it.

American exemptionalism therefore refers to the phenomenon whereby the United States acts as the main proponent and sponsor of international human rights treaties and conventions only to exempt itself from the provisions of these treaties through either expressing reservations regarding specific treaty provisions, not ratifying some of these treaties at all or not complying with these treaties by declaring that certain provisions of the treaties in question are at variance with American jurisprudence in matters of freedom of expression.[9] The fundamental principle of American exemptionalism is that American constitutional values are qualitatively superior to international human rights values.[10]

Alterity Chic: The French Cultural Exception

The paradox of the French exception is that while France has a universalist, moral philosophical, human rights creed that sprang out of the Revolution of 1789, the country has strenuously insisted on the specificity and uniqueness of the French language, identity, and culture. This posture has become increasingly strident in the face of the global dominance of "Anglo-Saxon" (read American) consumer electronic, cultural industry and information technology products. Furthermore, France was a founding member of the European Union and the Council of Europe, two supranational organizations that are grounded in the "idea" of Europe—a single European market, including a market for media products, and a single European human rights space, yet France has maintained its cultural protectionist creed—*l'exception française*. As a result, France is continually struggling to strike the right balance between the idea of Europe and the French exception. The *Conseil constitutionnel* (the Constitutional Council), the French Supreme Court for constitutional matters, has ruled that while the French legislature seeks to harmonize French laws with European Union Directives in specific issue areas, it must ensure that each transposed law "does not go against a rule or principle inherent in the Constitutional identity of France."[11] Therefore, all French legislation that transpose and domesticate European Union Directives into French law must have a French identitarian imprint that conforms to the French exception.

France has an exemptionalist foreign policy that has been expressed variously as *l'exception culturelle* (cultural exception) or *l'exception française* (the French exception). These politico-cultural expressions crystallize the French government's struggle to maintain the country's perceived distinctive monolithic civilization and monolingual culture in the face of pressures from Anglo-American culture in the post-World War II era.[12] As its name implies, the French cultural exception has been invoked mostly in the field of mass media and culture. Former French Minister of Culture, Jack Lang, was the face of the French Cultural State, and the personification of the politics of culture in the 1980s.[13] Lang told a UNESCO conference in 1982 that France must fight against the flood of American popular culture that was sweeping across the world. He said France had to wage a "real cultural resistance, a real crusade . . . against this financial and intellectual imperialism"[14]

At the international level, the French exception is, like American exceptionalism, an "exemptionalist," phenomenon. France exempts itself from international rules that it perceives to be at variance with its national ideological logic, its self-image, and its cultural specificity. In international multilateral talks, France has often advanced the notion that culture should be exempt from international free trade rules. For example, French cultural exemptionalism came to the fore during the Uruguay Round of the General Agreement on Tariffs and Trade (GATT) talks (1986-1994), where France introduced the concept of cultural exception in international diplomacy.[15] Under the cultural exception, audiovisual services—radio and television programming, as well cinema, music, books, DVDs, and videogames are classified as "cultural products" that are part of the cultural heritage of nation-states. As such, they were not to be considered "goods" like any other marketable goods for purposes of international trade.[16] The international community accepted the cultural exception despite U.S. government objections, and strenuous American movie industry opposition.[17]

Purpose of this book

The aim of this volume is to deploy the concept of exceptionalism as a framework for analysis of media law and policy, using as comparative case studies, American and French resolution of the same or similar problems of human rights and freedom of expression in the digital media. This book therefore describes and explains how the United States and France differentially apply rules and regulations designed to regulate a number of issue areas of media communication in real space, to the realities and specificities of cyberspace, within the framework of their respective exceptionalist logics. The fundamental question addressed concerns what happens when rules and regulations designed to regulate the media in clearly defined, national and regional geographic spaces, are suddenly confronted with the new realities and multi-communication platforms of the interconnected virtual realm of cyberspace. This volume is therefore primarily concerned with exploring and explaining sameness and difference between the United States and France in terms of management of the tensions that arise between freedom of expression and individual rights in salient issue areas of digital communication law and policy. Specifically, it is concerned with how the politico-cultural specificity of the United States and France, two self-described "exceptionalist" countries, affect their respective postures towards freedom of expression on the Internet. The multi-thematic case studies presented in this volume explore and attempt to explain, from a comparative perspective, how both countries deploy their respective exceptionalist ideals as "organizing principles," to borrow the expression of Martin Seymour Lipset,[18] that have led to the emergence of different, culture-specific regulatory solutions to similar Internet communication problems. The volume leaves normative evaluations to the reader. The book makes no overt normative or ethical evaluations about exceptionalism or the freedom of expression regimes of the United States and France.

As we see in chapters 3 and 4, American exceptionalism and the French exception assign civil society and organized interest groups certain roles within each regime. In the United States, civil libertarian and freedom of speech interests have assumed the role of counter-powers whose counter-discourses expose corporate excesses, denounce and resist governmental attempts to restrict freedom of expression in real space and cyberspace. In France, anti-racist, civil society groups are essentially co-powers whose activities promote governmental interests through monitoring, exposing, denouncing, and resisting extreme online speech and expression that is considered objectionable hate speech that is tantamount to illegal group defamation.

Significance of this Book

This book is an exploration of difference, regulatory difference in the domain of freedom of speech and expression. In the realm of politics and culture, certain nations and civilizations "pick" or designate their enemies—usually other nations and cultures that are believed to pose existential threats to their language, culture or prestige—and engage in intellectual, ideological and political battles against these real or imagined enemies. This scenario describes the posture of France vis-à-vis its historic ally and cultural foil, the United States. Though the United States and France are liberal democracies that are part of the Western family of nations, they have a number of cultural and ideological differences. The United States has generally been France's ally in time of war, and its cultural nemesis in time of peace. The result is that both countries have had a rocky cultural relationship since the turn of the twentieth-century. They have had political conflicts over cultural policy, audiovisual media content, and conflicts of law over intellectual property and hate speech hosted on servers based in the United States. In short, the United States and France are similar Western countries separated by different exceptionalist logics.

While there is a wide body of literature on American exceptionalism[19] and the French exception[20] in political science and legal studies, there is a near-total absence of research on comparative exceptionalism, work that compares and contrasts both constructs and uses them as frameworks for the comparative analysis of the legal systems and media regimes of both self-styled exceptionalist countries. American exceptionalism and the French exception have only recently been paired and deployed as comparative analytical frameworks that describe and explain regulation of the traditional media and the Internet in both countries.[21] This book is aimed at filling that void in comparative media studies. Its distinguishing feature is that it advances new interpretations of these two functionally equivalent, to use the formulation of Ralf Michaels,[22] theoretical approaches, and deploys them in novel ways in the analysis of several issue areas of comparative communication law and policy. This comparative approach yields new insights into American and French *Weltanschauungen* (worldviews) on communication, human rights and freedom of expression in real space and cyberspace.

One of the main themes of this volume is that the United States and France have different but functionally equivalent philosophical approaches to freedom of expression. The United States has an "individualist or libertarian view of the world," while the liberal democracies of Europe in general, and France in particular, have a "collective or communitarian view of the world," to use the formulation of Frederick Schauer.[23] Indeed, France is constitutionally, a secular, democratic and social Republic whose national maxim is *Liberté, égalité, fraternité* (Liberty, Equality, Fraternity). In France, the Constitution, including its provisions on freedom of expression, is viewed as "a vehicle for ensuring social rights, community rights, or positive citizen entitlements," as Schauer put it. This kind of constitutional "entitlementality" is frowned upon in the United States, where, "a radically nonjudgmental First Amendment is the natural repository for a culture in which libertarianism, *laissez-faire*, and distrust of government remain the hallmark of a distinctive American ideology."[24]

These differences have led to different procedural and substantive outcomes at the national level, and conflicting postures on international communication issues. These comparative case studies are an attempt to understand the legal mentalities that underpin the exceptionalist postures of the United States and France. The point of these comparative case studies is to explore difference, regulatory difference in the domain of freedom of speech and expression. The book therefore describes and explains how the United States and France approach procedural and substantive problems of Internet law and policy that have been universalized by technological innovations, global interconnectedness, and media convergence.[25] The book invites its readers to understand and even appreciate philosophical and regulatory difference.

In the United States and France, freedom of expression is a fundamental constitutional right. However, the right of freedom of expression is not absolute in both countries. The bundle of communicative rights encapsulated in the expressions "freedom of speech" and "freedom of expression," have to be exercised within the specific politico-cultural contexts of both countries. In other words, these constitutional rights are balanced against other rights and against governmental interests. The fundamental difference between the American and French free speech regimes is their different conceptualization of the role of government in the management of the sphere of freedom of expression. Each country's constitutional "balancing act" is grounded in its specific philosophical and ideological posture towards the communicative freedoms enumerated in its constitution.

In the federal system of the United States, the powers of the Federal government are enumerated. The Supreme Court of the United States has held that "rather than granting general authority to perform all the conceivable functions of government, the Constitution lists, or enumerates, the Federal Government's powers. . . . The enumeration of powers is also a limitation of powers."[26] Therefore, the American Constitution is conceptualized as "a bridle" on the government, to use the expression of political commentator, George Will.[27] Additionally, the Bill of Rights (the first ten amendments to the Constitution) enumerates what the Supreme Court of the United States calls a number of "affirmative prohibitions"[28] against governmental action. The Bill of Rights, which forms the scaffolding of the architecture of freedom in general, and freedom of expression in particular, is a negative charter of expressive liberties, which sets forth certain censorious activities the government is not permitted to engage in since these activities have a tendency to eviscerate the rights of citizens.[29] This ideological edifice is underpinned by an ancient theory of free speech, namely, faith that good—and popular—ideas will ultimately prevail over bad, unpopular ones if the government, that is, the law, creates a level playing field in spaces of public discourse, such that there is a free uninhibited exchange of ideas.

American Exceptionalism and Freedom of Expression

The United States is the land of the First Amendment. As its name implies, the First Amendment was the first bulwark the newly independent United States of America inserted in its Constitution in 1791, to guarantee for its citizens, freedom of speech, freedom of the press, freedom of assembly, and freedom of religion. The First Amendment states:

> Congress shall make no law respecting an establishment of religion, or prohibiting the free exercise thereof; or abridging the freedom of speech, or of the press; or the right of the people to peaceably assemble, and petition the Government for a redress of grievances.[30]

The First Amendment has over the centuries been applied to the specific nature and circumstances of communication that is mediated through multiple technologies and platforms. It has also been applied to a whole gamut of non-mediated symbolic speech and expressive conduct—behavior, actions, and attire that sometimes "speak" louder than words. The words "speech" and "press" are therefore highly elastic legal terms. Freedom of speech involves symbolic, non-verbal, communicative activities that express certain viewpoints or ideas. These communicative activities include wearing arm bands as protest against war,[31] "expressive conduct" like burning the American flag in protest at governmental policies,[32] and "expressive association" like getting together with like-minded individuals to express religious or ethnic pride in public places while excluding people whose conduct expressed undesirable speech.[33] Free speech also includes freedom from forced speech—the right to speak and the right not to speak."[34] The word "press" is an elastic term that covers all kinds of "publications" that provide information to the general public and comment on all matters of "public interest."[35] It also includes the traditional electronic media—broadcasting, cable-casting, satellite communication—and the Internet, which has the same level of free speech protection as the traditional print media.[36] While free speech is not absolute—it is subject to time, place and manner regulations, a principle under which the government can regulate when, where, and how the right of free speech is exercised rather than the content of the speech[37] —American public policy is generally hostile toward all kinds of governmental regulation of, or interference with, mass media and Internet content. The underlying principle of the First Amendment free speech regime is that the greatest threat to freedom of speech and expression is the government, not religion, not political extremists who may misuse or abuse the right of free speech.[38] As a result, the First Amendment expressly forbids Congress—and by extension federal, state and local governments—from infringing on the right of freedom of speech.

The First Amendment essentially makes the United States the epitome of freedom of speech and expression in our interconnected, globalized world. The First Amendment is a unique instrument that is the bedrock of expressive and communicative rights that are without compare. According to Frederick Schauer, the American approach to freedom of expression under the First Amendment is much stronger than that of other Western liberal democracies to the point that the United States is an "outlier," an "exceptional" regime in terms of its protection of freedom of speech and expression under the First Amendment. He suggests that American exceptionalism in matters of freedom of experience may be "the reflection of longer, more extensive American experience with freedom of communication issues."[39] Furthermore, American exceptionalism in matters of freedom of speech and expression is a reflection of the larger phenomenon of American exceptionalism.[40]

This ideological edifice of the First Amendment is underpinned by an ancient theory of free speech, namely, faith that in democratic societies, where there is a free exchange of ideas and discourse, truth as well as good—and popular—ideas will ultimately prevail over falsehood and unpopular ones. The Supreme Court of the United States has analogized faith in the salubrious power of free, open and unfettered social discourse to a "marketplace of ideas:"

> [T]he ultimate good desired is better reached by free trade in ideas--that the best test of truth is the power of the thought to get itself accepted in the competition of the market, and that truth is the only ground upon which their wishes safely can be carried out. That at any rate is the theory of our Constitution. It is an experiment, as all life is an experiment. . . . While that experiment is part of our system I think that we should be eternally vigilant against attempts to check the expression of opinions that we loathe and believe to be fraught with death.[41]

This early admonition is now a settled First Amendment principle. Viewpoint discrimination is prejudicial to the free flow of ideas and information. Actually, an important feature of the American marketplace of ideas is that the rights of the speaker take precedence over the feelings of the listener.[42]

The French Exception and Freedom of Expression

In matters of freedom of expression, the United States and France have different philosophical orientations with respect to regulation of the content of speech and expression in public spaces. France is actually the foil of the United States. France has a positive free speech regime in which the government has a preponderant role in creating a public sphere of democratic freedom of expression. The purpose of governmental surveillance of freedom of expression is to promote national ideals of liberty, fraternity and equality, in short, a culture of ordered "democratic civility." In this sphere, the government decides when and how the right of freedom of expression is to be exercised, and which speakers get to exercise it. The government also gets to decide what kinds of subjects speakers in public spaces may not broach. In other words, the French government is the constitutional content-based regulator of freedom of expression, which engages in viewpoint discrimination for purposes of promoting governmentally-sanctioned truth, and suppressing objectionable speech and expression. This category of speech includes speech that is perceived to be uncivil, defamatory towards ethnic and religious groups, invades individual privacy, undermines the French language and culture, defames public officials, and is prejudicial to human dignity.

In France, the two instruments that have historically protected freedom of expression are the "Declaration of the Rights of Man and of the Citizen of 1789, and the law on Freedom of the Press of 1881. Both documents empower the government to take affirmative steps to regulate the exercise of freedom expression in public spaces on the basis of governmentally-sanctioned truth. France, like most members of the European Union and the 47-member Council of Europe, essentially has a sphere of freedom of expression that van Gerven calls a "marketplace **for** ideas."[43] One of the characteristics of the French marketplace for ideas regime is that the government is the final arbiter of historical truth.[44] In this regard it takes affirmative legal steps to eliminate content that it considers to be abusive of the right of freedom of expression: Holocaust denial, hate speech that targets individuals on the basis of their race, religion, ethnicity, national origin, gender, sexual orientation, and so on. Under the French freedom of expression regime, truth (*exceptio veritatis*) is not necessarily a defense in defamation or invasion of privacy cases. Unfortunately, for every legitimate marketplace, there is a black-market. French and European content-based regulation of hate speech has given rise to a festering "black-market" of intolerance whose stock in-trade is bias-motivated speech and expression against minorities, uttered in spaces of collective socio-cultural manifestations. This kind of intolerant speech—and sometimes violent action—erupts with the fury of a volcano from time to time in situations of crowded anonymity like soccer stadiums and music concerts.[45]

The positive French and Continental European freedom of expression philosophy can be contrasted with the negative, *laissez-faire*, American "market place **of** ideas," regime, which combines several libertarian principles—the commodification of ideas, a Constitutional ban on governmental interference with the dissemination of ideas, information, and discourse, and tolerance of extreme speech.[46] Thus, though the American and French communication law regimes have constitutional provisions protecting freedom of expression, the historico-political contexts, and the exceptionalist postures of each country make the reality of freedom of expression within each jurisdiction different. This volume compares and contrasts the postures of the American and French regimes with respect to a number of controversies involving the digital media in cyberspace.

American Exceptionalism, the French Exception, and Internet Regulation

As we see in chapter 2, the exceptionalist ideologies of the United States and France have left their imprint on the communication law regimes of both countries. This ultimately led to conflicts of law over regulation of the content of the Internet, and its multiple communication platforms. This volume therefore explores the exceptionalist philosophical postures of the United States and France with respect to Internet communication law, using as comparative case studies, the postures of both countries with respect to the following issue areas of media law: 1) Freedom of speech and expression, 2) the media and the privacy rights of public figures in real space and cyberspace, 3) the intellectual property interests of journalists in news articles digitized and stored in searchable electronic databases or published on newspaper websites, 4) the role of organized interest groups in the regulation of Internet content, 5) the international intellectual property issues spawned by Google's Library and Book Search initiatives, whose business models was the digitization and transfer of books from real space to searchable databases in cyberspace, and 6) comparative intellectual property controversies over "gripe" websites and trademark parody law. The comparative case studies in this volume cover these subjects and explore sameness and difference in the exceptionalist media regulation of the United States and France. In short, this volume contextualizes, compares, contrasts, and explains, "authentic national expressions of universal values,"[47] to borrow the expression of Michael Ignatieff. Comparative research that does not set out to make normative evaluations proceeds on the assumption that each freedom of expression regime is grounded in specific politico-cultural contexts and realities. This type of research posture leads to what Pierre Legrand calls respect for "the Other-in-the-law."[48] This is because it takes at least two legal cultures to appreciate and respect difference. Respect for the specificities and intricacies of other politico-cultural and legal systems is an act of intellectual tolerance that gives legal scholars an opportunity, "to grant hospitality to alterity . . . [to recognize the right of] alterity to exist as alterity," as Pierre Legrand put it.[49] This is because comparative legal studies contribute not only to our understanding of our own legal culture and other legal cultures, they also help us appreciate comparative politics. Scholars and students who have knowledge of, and respect for other communication law cultures, have a better understanding and appreciation of their own communication law systems.

The sweeping technological developments and effervescence in information, communication technology and media sectors have elicited different responses from different legal systems and cultures. These case studies analyze how the United States and France, two self-described exceptionalist countries, come to terms with, and use their time-tested, legal and policy values to respond to universal problems posed by new information and communication technologies, and media content. The basic premises of this volume are as follows: Firstly, new information and communication technologies—and the multiple communication platforms they have spawned—are powerful and nimble forces that move faster than the law. As such, they have scrambled the placid surface of settled national and international communication law and policy, and created unprecedented discontinuities in areas as diverse as infrastructures and regulation of the content of the interconnected spaces of the Internet, the international intellectual property protection regime, and international cultural policy. Additionally, the revolutionary changes have led to conflicts of law in several issue areas of communication. In order to navigate these global discontinuities and fluid situations, nation-states, supranational and international organizations have resurrected and re-presented old politico-cultural values and laws designed for real space, and applied them differentially to the new transmedia environment of cyberspace. In the process, the law not only regulates the infrastructures and content of communication, it becomes communication in its own right.[50] Secondly, by its very nature, form and content, communication law is a cultural phenomenon.[51] Put otherwise, communication law is ensconced in national, supranational and international political nexuses. This is part of the series of "contextual matrixes," to borrow the expression of Pierre Legrand, that affect policy logics and influence the outcomes of legal disputes.[52] These comparative case studies are event or issue-specific comparisons that look at how the United States and France use the law to problematize online communication issues, and search for solutions to the perennial problem of freedom of expression in new and evolving media contexts.

Organization of the Book

Revolutionary innovations in information and communication technologies and infrastructures have interconnected the world and spawned a dizzying array of innovative, interlocking multimedia and transmedia platforms that have elicited different regulatory responses from different nations, supranational, and international jurisdictions. The case studies in this volume compare and contrast how the United States and France, two self-described exceptionalist countries, have come to terms with, and used their time-tested regulatory apparatuses to respond to novel global problems posed by new information and communication technologies, and new media content.

This volume is therefore concerned with exploring and explaining sameness and difference in American and French governmental management of the tensions that arise between freedom of expression and governmental and social interests in salient issue areas of digital communication law and policy. The case studies in this volume essentially compare and contrast how different manifestations of exceptionalism affect the contextual and functional "distillations" of American and French law and policy in salient issue areas of communication in real space and cyberspace. The case studies therefore compare and contrast how the United States and France used their different procedural and substantive law regimes to address similar online communication problems posed by innovations in information and communication technology, media convergence, globalization, and the interconnection of global networks and systems.

The basic premises of this volume are as follows: New information and communication technologies—and the multiple transmedia, commercial and cultural platforms they have spawned—are powerful and nimble forces that move at lightning speed while the law plods its way at a glacial pace. This reality has created unprecedented discontinuities in areas as diverse as telecommunications regulation, the human right of communication (freedom of expression), bias-motivated or extreme speech, individual privacy, intellectual property, cultural policy, and so forth, in real space and cyberspace. Additionally, networked global communications have interconnected nations, peoples and cultures, and led to conflicts of law in several issue areas of communication. In order to navigate these global discontinuities and fluid situations, nation-states have re-invented, or re-framed old politico-cultural values and laws designed for real space, and applied them *mutatis mutandis* to the new media environment of cyberspace. In the process, media law has not only acted on the infrastructures, content and participants in the communication process, it has become communication in its own right.[53] The law communicates ideas, values, ideals, morals and social norms.

Furthermore, there is no doubt that by its very nature, form and content, media law is a cultural phenomenon.[54] Put otherwise, communication law is ensconced in national, supranational and international contexts and nexuses of power dynamics. These realities are part of the series of "contextual matrixes," that affect national legal mentalities and influence the outcomes of legal disputes.[55] The case studies are event or issue-specific comparisons that look at how the United States and France use the law to problematize communication issues in real space and cyberspace, and search for solutions to these problems.

Summary of Chapters

Our exploration of exceptionalism in the media begins with an analysis of the politico-cultural context of the media law regimes of the United States and France. Chapter 2 consists of a comparative historical and systemic analysis of media law in the United States and France. It first situates the legal regimes of the United States and France within the "family" of legal systems of the world and explores their basic characteristics and differences. The chapter uses examples of judicial and extra-judicial management of the problem of extreme or bias-motivated speech and expression to illustrate the different postures of both countries towards the same problem—mapping the contours of freedom of speech and expression in real space and cyberspace. It examines 1) the edifice of American freedom of speech and expression under the First Amendment (ratified in 1791), and compares it with 2) the French freedom of expression regime set forth in the Declaration of the Rights of Man and of the Citizen of 1789, and the Law of July 29, 1881 on Freedom of the Press (as amended). The chapter traces the transfer of freedom of speech and expression laws designed for real space to the realities of the dematerialized world of cyberspace.

Chapter 2 shows that in all communicative endeavors, France has a universal, humanistic, moral philosophical approach that lays emphasis on values like human rights, human dignity, civility, solidarity, fraternity, equality, protection of the reputations of individuals, protection of the right to privacy, protection of the physical and moral well-being of children, and so forth. For its part the United States has a market-based media law regime, which combines several libertarian principles—the marketplace of ideas, *laissez-faire* economics, free trade and the free flow of ideas, information, and discourse in real space and cyberspace.[56] In the United States, issues of civility, equality, human dignity, and self-esteem take a back seat to the right of freedom of speech. We shall see that under First Amendment jurisprudence, the rights of the speaker do indeed take precedence over the feelings of the listener, no matter how offensive the speech in question may be.[57]

Finally, chapter 2 introduces American exceptionalism and the French exception, two functionally equivalent ideological constructs that express the politico-cultural worldviews and the ideological postures of the United States ad France. These self-described exceptionalist countries define themselves in opposition to each other, and to the rest of the world and view their cultures, political, social and economic systems as being superior to those of other countries. This chapter traces application of the exceptionalist free speech regime of the United States that was designed for the media in real space, to the realities of the dematerialized media of cyberspace.

The subject matter of chapter 3 is American exceptionalism and its impact on the media law regime of the United States. This chapter explores the regulation of the media in real space and cyberspace under the exceptional First Amendment. The First Amendment makes the United States unique among nations on matters of freedom of speech and expression. Frederick Schauer has described the First Amendment as an exceptionalist document that sets the United States apart from other countries. He notes that "skepticism about the ability of any governmental institution reliably to distinguish the good from the bad, the true from the false, and the sound from the unsound finds its most comfortable home in the First Amendment."[58] This chapter traces application of the exceptionalist free speech regime of the United States that was designed for the media controversies in real space to the dematerialized sphere of cyberspace.

Chapter 4 focuses on *l'exception française* (the French Exception) and media law and policy in France. The French exception is an ideology of differentiation that emphasizes the uniqueness and specificity of French language, culture, and civilization, and defines France in opposition to other countries, specifically, what the French call the "Anglo-Saxon" countries.[59] France is essentially *un état culturel* (a cultural state) in which the government takes a leading role in setting cultural and language policy as well as the creation, management, preservation and promotion of *le patrimoine culturel* (cultural heritage) and *les lieux de memoire* (sites of memory), to use the expression of Pierre Nora.[60] The corollary of the French exception is *l'exception culturelle* (the French cultural exception), a cultural defense mechanism erected against the perceived threats posed by America's ubiquitous mass entertainment, "fast culture," free enterprise religion, and excessive cultural capitalism. All aspects of French society, especially politics, the law, the media, and foreign policy are infused with, and echo the French cultural exception. The Declaration of the Rights of Man and of the Citizen of 1789, which granted the press rather circumscribed freedoms, is the template for the content-based regulation of freedom of expression in France. Under this regime, the government and its accredited non-governmental allies, take affirmative steps to create a democratic "marketplace **for** ideas,"[61] to borrow the formulation of Van Gerven, where officially-sanctioned "truth" on historical occurrences holds sway, and organized interest groups are monitors and co-regulators, with the government, of media content in real space and cyberspace. This chapter focuses on how the French legislature and the French courts transferred the media law regime designed for the media in real space to the new media in cyberspace.

The subject matter of chapter 5 is the conflict between freedom of expression and the privacy rights of public officials in the United States and France. It uses two highly mediated sex scandals involving a president of the United States—the so-called "Clinton/Lewinsky affair"—and a president of France—the so-called *affaire Mitterrand/Anne Pingeot*—respectively, as a springboard for a comparative analysis of the role of the fledgling Internet of the mid 1990s in popularizing and globalizing sex scandals involving both presidents. The chapter discusses how both countries resolve the acute tension between the private sex lives of politicians, the public's right to know about their elected officials, and the media's constitutional right to publish salacious material involving the private lives of these officials. The significance of this chapter lies in the fact that the two "affairs" were the very first time the American and French legal regimes were confronted with the reality of the fledgling network of computer networks—the Internet. In effect, the sexual affair between President Bill Clinton and the White House intern, Monica Lewinsky, was first reported on an online news aggregation site, the Drudge Report in 1998.[62] In France, the new American online multi-communication platform, the Internet, was used to circumvent a 1996 French court order banning a book that was found to have violated late President François Mitterrand's right of privacy.

This comparative study focuses on how the different privacy law regimes of the United States and France dealt with a similar problem—sex scandals involving the president of each country. The outcomes of both scandals reflected the specific exceptionalist conceptualizations of the right of privacy in both countries. While the Lewinsky affair became a major political crisis that led to the historic impeachment and Senate trial of President Bill Clinton, the Mitterrand/Anne Pingeot affair did not become an issue in French politics. While American courts were never asked to rule on the privacy issues involved in the Clinton/Lewinsky affair, French courts and the European Court of Human Rights used the Mitterrand/Anne Pingeot affair to reset the equilibrium between the media's right of freedom of expression and European privacy rights values.

The subject matter of chapter 6 is comparative intellectual property law in the United States and France. The focus is on the early legal disputes that emerged as a result of newspaper companies licensing their archives to commercial database companies for digitization and storage in searchable databases like Lexis/Nexis, without the consent of journalists and freelance writers who contributed to print editions of these collective works. This chapter explores the regulation of collective journalistic works under American and French law, and suggests that some of the problems newspapers and magazines face may be due to their failure to respect the value of the work of their full-time and freelance reporters when the migration from real space to cyberspace began in the late 1990s.

Chapter 7 consists of a comparative analysis of the exceptional role and impact of organized interest groups on Internet content regulation in the United States and France, using as a comparative case study, the impact of the American Civil Liberties Union (ACLU) and two French government-affiliated anti-racist interest groups—*l'Union des Etudiants juifs de France* (the Union of French Jewish Students, UEJF), and *La Ligue International*

Contre le Racisme et L'anti-sémitisme (The International League Against Racism and Anti-Semitism, LICRA)—on the emerging law of the Internet in the United States and France, respectively. The case study analyzes how the two legal systems deal with a similar problem, namely, the role of civil society groups in Internet governance. The premise of this chapter is that laws governing the activities of civil society groups in matters of freedom of expression are functionally equivalent in both countries though the impact and outcomes of these interventions are often different.

Chapter 8 explores the intellectual property disputes engendered in the United States and France by another component of the multi-billion dollar "search" industry—the book search. This is the digitalization, storage, algorithmization, hierarchization, and monetization of millions of copyrighted and public domain works as part of the business model of Google Inc. and other global information and communication technology corporations. This business model, which French scholar, Fréderick Kaplan, calls "linguistic capitalism,"[63] has several intellectual property ramifications. This chapter compares and contrasts how courts in the United States and France managed tensions that arose between Google's unauthorized digitization and transfer of millions of books in English, French and other languages from real space to searchable electronic databases which enriched its search business, and 1) the intellectual property interests of authors and publishers in the works digitalized and stored by Google in "the cloud" (its servers and other infrastructure) as well as, 2) the public interest in maintaining a freely accessible, copyright-free, public domain of published historic works that have been the repository of human knowledge for hundreds of years. This chapter shows that in the Google Books disputes that arose in the United States and France, governmental policy makers and courts in both jurisdictions deployed the respective exceptionalist intellectual property logics of their systems to resolve these unprecedented legal controversies.

Chapter 9 explores how the United States and France negotiate the tensions between intellectual property law and freedom of expression, using as a comparative case study, their different resolution of the problem of trademark parody, involving complaint websites. These so-called "gripe" websites are created by anonymous critics, political opponents, and disgruntled persons with the intent of naming and shaming large corporations into performing certain activities that the registrant of the website finds desirable. "Gripe" websites may also intend to shame the targets of their ridicule into refraining from performing certain other activities that the registrant of the website finds objectionable. Some "gripe" websites are directed at the government, public officials and public figures. As gripe websites have multiplied on the Internet, they have engendered clashes between freedom of expression and the right of corporations to protect their trademarks, reputations, and products from disparagement or trade libel. This chapter explores the statutory and case law governing complaint websites within the framework of the respective exceptional freedom of expression logics of the United States and France. The subject of the chapter is therefore a comparative analysis of French and American application of intellectual property laws designed for real space, to the dematerialized world of cyberspace. The emphasis is on the conflict between protection of trademarks under intellectual property law, and the subversive, unauthorized appropriation of these marks for purposes of creating parody or "gripe" websites under the constitutional right of freedom of expression.

In conclusion, this volume is concerned with what happens when exceptionalist values in the fields of freedom of speech, expression, individual privacy, and intellectual property are transferred from real space to the dematerialized world of cyberspace. It explores what happens when different hitherto discrete, culture-bound legal and philosophical approached to freedom of expression clash in the interconnected world of the Internet The comparative case studies in this volume explore the conflicts of law and policy that arise when American exceptionalist First Amendment values—under which the rights of the speaker take precedence over the feelings of the listener—are transposed from real space to cyber space, and come face to face with the French exceptionalist, moral philosophical freedom of expression posture, under which the dignity and human personhood of the listener generally take precedence over the rights of the speaker. The questions that arise from this conflict of law and culture are significant. The comparative case studies demonstrate that the United States and France are democratic countries that always balance morality, human dignity, group rights, and civility with the right of freedom of expression. However, the outcomes of these balancing acts are influenced by the respective exceptionalist ideologies of both countries. The comparative case studies therefore demonstrate sameness and difference in the exceptionalist media regulatory regimes of both countries.

NOTES

1. Virgil, *The Aeneid*, Book I (19 BCE, 1697), John Dryden (trans). Available at: http://classics.mit.edu/Virgil/aeneid.1.i.html
2. See Noel Kaplowitz, National Self-Images, Perception of Enemies, and Conflict Strategies:
Psychopolitical Dimensions of International Relations," 11 Political Psychology 39, 46-47 (1990).
3. See Noel Kaplowitz, National Self-Images, Perception of Enemies, and Conflict Strategies: Psychopolitical Dimensions of International Relations," 11 Political Psychology 39, 48, 51-52 (1990).
4. Speech to the House of Commons, *Hansard* (March 1, 1848), at: http://hansard.millbanksystems.com/commons/1848/mar/01/treaty-of-adrianople-charges-against#S3V0097P0_18480301_HOC_8
5. *Article 2 (1) (d) (1969),* entered into force on January 27, 1980 (United Nations, Treaty Series, Vol. 1155, p. 331).

6. "Exceptionalism." *Dictionary.com Unabridged (v 1.1)*. Random House, Inc. (2009). Dictionary.com http://dictionary.reference.com/browse/exceptionalism.

7. See John Gerard Ruggie, *American Exceptionalism, Exemptionalism, and Global Governance*, in American Exceptionalism And Human Rights 304, 305 (Michael Ignatieff, Ed. 2005).

8. See John Gerard Ruggie, *American Exceptionalism, Exemptionalism, and Global Governance*, in American Exceptionalism And Human Rights 304, 305 (Michael Ignatieff, Ed. 2005).

9. See Michael Ignatieff, Introduction: American Exceptionalism and Human Rights, In American Exceptionalism and Human Rights. Michael Ignatieff (Ed. 4) (2006).

10. See Michael Ignatieff, Introduction: American Exceptionalism and Human Rights. In American Exceptionalism And Human Rights, Michael Ignatieff (Ed.) 3, 6 (2005).

11. See *Conseil Constitutionnel, Décision n° 2006-540 DC du 27 juillet 2006,Loi relative au droit d'auteur et aux droits voisins dans la société de l'information,* journal officiel du 3 août 2006, p. 11541. (Constitutional Council, Decision No. 2006-540 DC of July 27, 2006, J.O. of August 3, 2006).

12. See Bernard Spolsky, Language Policy 63 (2004).

13. Jacques Rigaud, L'exception Culturelle: Culture Et Pouvoir Sous La Ve République (The Cultural Exception: Culture And Power Under The Fifth Republic) 99 (1995).

14. See Phillip Hollander, Anti-Americanism, Irrational And Rational 385 (1995).

15. See Armand Mattelart, La Mondialisation De La Communication (3rd Ed.) (Globalization Of Communication) 90-91 (2002).

16. See Sophie Meunier, The French Exception, 79 Foreign Affairs 104 (2000). (France's antipathy towards globalization and its Anti-Americanism are intended to preserve French language and culture).

17. See WTO Trips Agreement (1994) (Reprinted in General Agreement on Tariffs and Trade (GATT) Intellectual Property Provisions, Joint Hearing Before The Subcommittee Intellectual Property and Judicial Administration of the House Committee on the Judiciary & The Subcommittee on Patents, Copyrights and Trademarks of the Senate Committee on the Judiciary, 106th Cong. 3d Session 341, 345 (1994); see also generally J. Croome, Reshaping The World Trading System: World Trade Organization (1996). During the Uruguay Round of the multi-lateral General Agreement on Tariffs and Trade (GATT) talks, which were concluded in 1993, the European Community, led by France, insisted on, and obtained an exception that allowed audiovisual services (radio and television programs, as well as movies) to be excluded altogether from the broad General Agreement on Trade in Services (GATS) rules).

18. See Seymour Martin Lipset, American Exceptionalism: A Double-Edged Sword 13 (1996).

19. See generally, Michael Ignatieff (Ed.) American Exceptionalism and Human Rights (2005). See also Seymour Martin Lipsett, *American Exceptionalism Reaffirmed*, in Byron Shafer (Ed.) Is America Different? 16 (1991).

20. See Jacques Rigaud, L'exception Culturelle: Culture Et Pouvoir Sous La Ve République (The Cultural Exception: Culture And Power Under The Fifth Republic) 16 (1995).

21. See Lyombe Eko, American Exceptionalism, the French Exception, Intellectual Property Law, and Peer-to-Peer File Sharing on the Internet, 10 The John Marshall Review Of Intellectual Property Law 93-135 (2010).

22. See Ralf Michaels, The Functional Method of Comparative Law, in Mathias Reimann and Reinhard Zimmermann (Eds.) *The Oxford Handbook of Comparative Law*, 339, 356 (2006).

23. See Frederick Schauer, The Exceptional First Amendment, in *American Exceptionalism and Human Rights* 45 (Michael Ignatieff, Ed., 2005).

24. See Frederick Schauer, The Exceptional First Amendment, in *American Exceptionalism and Human Rights* 46 (Michael Ignatieff, Ed., 2005).

25. See Michel de S.-O.-'E. Lasser, *The Question of Understanding in Comparative Legal Studies: Traditions And Transitions* 197, 215 (Pierre Legrand & Roderick Munday Eds. 2003). (Suggesting that "the point of comparative law is understanding").

26. *National Federation of Independent Business v. Sebelius*, 567 U.S. (2012).

27. See George Will, Conservatives' Consolation Prize, *The Washington Post*, June 28, 2012. Available at: http://www.washingtonpost.com/opinions/george-will-supreme-court-gives-conservatives-a-consolation-prize/2012/06/28/gJQAWyhY9V_print.html
28. *National Federation of Independent Business v. Sebelius*, 567 U.S.(2012).
29. See *Jackson v. Byrne*, 738 F.2d 1443, 1446 (7th cir. 1984).
30. Amendment 1, Constitution Of The United States (1791).
31. *Tinker v. Des Moines Independent Community School District*, 393 U.S. 503 (1969).
32. *Texas v. Johnson*, 491 U.S. 397 (1989).
33. *Hurley v. Irish-American Gay, Lesbian and Bisexual Group of Boston*, 515 U.S. 557 (1995).
34. *Hurley v. Irish-American gay, Lesbian and Bisexual Group of Boston*, 515 U.S. 557 (1995).
35. See *Lovell v. Griffin*, 303 U.S. 444 (1938).
36. *Reno v. ACLU*, 521 U.S. 844 (1997).
37. *Clark v. Community for Creative Non-Violence*, 468 U.S. 288 (1984).
38. See *Reno v. ACLU*, 514 U.S. 844, 885 (1997) (Holding that "...As a matter of constitutional tradition, in the absence of evidence to the contrary, we present that governmental regulation of the content of speech is more likely to interfere with the free exchange of ideas than to encourage it." (Stevens, J.) See also Dan Berkowitz and Lyombe Eko, Blasphemy as a Sacred Rite/Right: "The Mohammed Cartoons Affair" and maintenance of journalistic ideology. 8 Jouralism Studies 779, 782 (2007).
39. See Frederick Schauer, The Exceptional First Amendment, in *American Exceptionalism and Human Rights* 30, 31 (Michael Ignatieff, Ed., 2005).
40. See Frederick Schauer, The Exceptional First Amendment, in *American Exceptionalism and Human Rights* 51 (Michael Ignatieff, Ed., 2005).
41. *Abrams v. United States*, 250 U.S. 616, 630 (1919) (Holmes, J. dissenting).
42. *Snyder v. Phelps*, 562 U.S. (2011), See also *Hustler v. Falwell*, 485 U.S. 46 (1988).
43. See Walter Van Gerven, The European Union: A Polity Of States And Peoples 242 (2005).
44. See UEJF & LICRA v. Yahoo! Inc., Tribunal de grande instance [T.G.I.] [High Court] Paris, May 22, 2000, The Clerk of the Chief Justice Christine Bensoam, (Fr.), available at http://www.juriscom.net/txt/jurisfr/cti/yauctions20000522.htm (Richard Salis, trans.) (Holding that Nazi and Third Reich memorabilia hosted on Yahoo!'s servers in the United States were "an offense to the collective memory of a nation [France]."
45. See Kurt Wachter and Michael Fanizadeh, Racism in Football, Football Against Racism. 44 Un Chronicle 30-39 (2007) (Discussing the Football Against Racism (FARE) Campaign in launched in 14 European countries to combat racist taunts against non-white players in European soccer stadiums).
46. See *Abrams v. United States,* 250 U.S. 616 (1919); *Terminiello v. City of Chicago*, 337 U.S. 1 (1949); See also Lyombe Eko, Many Spiders, One World Wide Web: Towards a Typology of Internet Regulation, 6 Communication Law And Policy 445, 465 (2001).
47. Michael Ignatieff, Introduction: American Exceptionalism and Human Rights. In American Exceptionalism And Human Rights, Michael Ignatieff (Ed.) 26 (2005).
48. See Pierre Legrand, *The Same and the Different, in* Comparative Legal Studies: Traditions and transitions 240, 254 (Pierre Legrand & Roderick Munday eds. 2003).
49. Pierre Legrand, *The Same and the Different, in* Comparative Legal Studies: Traditions And Transitions 240, 254 (Pierre Legrand & Roderick Munday eds. 2003).
50. See generally David Nelken (Ed.) *Law As Communication* (1996).
51. See Pierre Legrand, Fragments On Law-As-Culture 5 (1999).
52. See Pierre Legrand, The Same and the Different, in Pierre Legrand & Roderick Munday (eds.) Comparative Legal Studies: Traditions And Transitions 240, 261 (2003).
53. See generally David Nelken (Ed.) *Law As Communication* (1996).
54. See Pierre Legrand, Fragments On Law-As-Culture 5 (1999).
55. See Pierre Legrand, The Same and the Different, in Pierre Legrand & Roderick Munday (eds.) Comparative Legal Studies: Traditions And Transitions 240, 261 (2003).

56. See *Abrams v. United States,* 250 U.S. 616 (1919); *Terminiello v. City of Chicago*, 337 U.S. 1 (1949); See also Lyombe Eko, Many Spiders, One World Wide Web: Towards a Typology of Internet Regulation, 6 Communication Law And Policy 445, 465 (2001).

57. *Terminiello v. Chicago*, 337 U.S. 1 (1949). See also *Snyder v. Phelps*, 562 U.S. (2011).

58. See Frederick Schauer, *The Exceptional First Amendment, in* American Exceptionalism And Human Rights 29, 46 (Michael Ignatieff, Ed., 2005).

59. See Pierre Rosanvallon, Le Modèle Politique Français (The French Political Model) 109, 112 (2004).

60. See Pierre Nora, Between Memory and History: *Les Lieux de Mémoire* (Sites of Memory): 26 Representations 7-44 (1989).

61. See Walter Van Gerven, The European Union: A Polity Of States And Peoples 242 (2005).

62. See BBC, Scandalous scoop breaks online, January 28, 1998. Available at http://news.bbc.co.uk/2/hi/events/clinton_under_fire/the_big_picture/50031.stm (Last visited July 15, 2009) (Reporting that the Drudge Report published the story after Newsweek killed it).

63. See Frédéric Kaplan, *Nos langues à l'heure du capitalisme linguistique* (Our languages in the age of linguistic capitalism) (2012). Available at: http://www.internetactu.net/2012/04/06/nos-langues-a-lheure-du-capitalisme-linguistique/

Chapter Two

Freedom of Expression in the United States and France

Political, Legal, and Cultural Contexts

As the fledgling network of computer networks that became known as the "Internet" began to be conceptualized and utilized as a cultural platform of multiple utility in the 1990s, Northwestern University in Evanston, Illinois, was at the forefront of institutions of higher learning which foresaw the potential of the Internet as an instrument for the enrichment of the educational experience of its faculty and students. Northwestern University therefore assisted its faculty members to create web pages that would serve as the public faces of the faculty and their academic units on the Internet. The web pages were also expected to connect faculty and students to the burgeoning resources of the fledgling network of computer networks. These web pages were hosted by the information technology services of the institution. Arthur Butz, an associate professor of electrical engineering and computer engineering at Northwestern University, took advantage of the network facilities granted by the university to create a web page that was hosted on the university's servers and linked to other university pages. However, Professor Butz's web page was unorthodox. It was not used to support his electrical engineering courses or connect his students to engineering resources. Rather, he used the web page to propagate his Holocaust denial book, *Historical Revisionism*, in which he questioned the scope, number of victims, gas chambers and other aspects of the World War II era Jewish Holocaust. An uproar quickly ensued. The Jewish community, sections of the mass media, and some students called on Northwestern to discipline Butz for questioning well-established historical facts, and remove his web page from the University's servers.[1] The president of Northwestern University, Henry Bienen, issued a statement in which he emphasized that the views expressed on Professor Butz's web page were the professor's personal views. Bienen said that Northwestern University had a policy of intellectual freedom, that prevented the university from restricting Professor Butz's personal opinions: "The network is a free and open forum for the expression of ideas, including viewpoints that are strange, unorthodox, or unpopular. The network administrators place no official sanctions upon the expression of personal opinion on the network. However, such opinions may not be represented as the views of Northwestern University,"[2] Despite the media and popular uproar, Butz's web page was never removed or censored by Northwestern, and the tenured professor was not terminated because he never expressed his Holocaust denial views in his engineering courses.

The Butz Holocaust denial controversy illustrates the First Amendment free speech regime of the United States. Though the controversy did not take place in a public institution, Northwestern University followed First Amendment content-neutral principles that are applicable to its peer institutions that are state universities. There is ample precedent for First Amendment protection of free speech on university campuses. For example, when a student was expelled from the University of Missouri School of Journalism for distributing cartoons depicting police officers raping the Statue of Liberty and the Goddess of Justice, and containing a headline composed of indecent language describing human sexual functions, the Supreme Court of the United States ordered that the student be reinstated. The court ruled that her expulsion violated the First Amendment because: "state colleges and universities are not enclaves immune from the sweep of the First Amendment" Consequently, the mere dissemination of even offensive and objectionable ideas may not be circumscribed in the name of "conventions of decency."[3]

The United States Supreme Court ruling in *Papish v. University of Missouri Curators* was consistent with the exceptionalist, libertarian free speech regime of the United States, which emphasizes the importance of the right of free speech, in and of itself, and pays scant attention to issues of historical truth and accuracy, civility, and fairness.[4] As we noted earlier, under the exceptionalist First Amendment regime, the right of the speaker almost always takes precedence over the feelings of the listener. Furthermore, the government is not the final arbiter of acceptable speech or even of historical truth.[5] The result is that under the First Amendment, "free speech"—in the broadest sense of the term—takes precedence over metaphysical issues like morality, decency, and human dignity. Freedom of expression also takes precedence over considerations of the negative emotional and psychological impact of speech on those at whom the speech is directed.[6] The U.S. Supreme Court has also held that laws forbidding racial discrimination were not above question: "The First Amendment does not guarantee that other concepts virtually sacred to our Nation as a whole—such as the principle that discrimination based on race is odious and destructive—will go unquestioned in the market-place of ideas."[7]

The Butz affair at Northwestern University, Evanston, Illinois can be contrasted with an identical controversy in France. In 1990, Bernard Notin, a professor of economics, at *Université Jean-Moulin (Lyon-III)* a state university, published a controversial article on Nazi gas chambers in the refereed journal, *Economies et Sociétés.* The article, Professor Notin claimed, was aimed at criticizing mass media trivialization and instrumentalization of the Holocaust for purposes of mass entertainment. The article went on to question the scientific and historic reality of Nazi gas chambers that was presented in mass circulation texts and media programs. Notin was promptly denounced in the French newspaper, *Le Monde,* for publishing "a racist, anti-Semitic, and "revisionist" article. It turned out that Notin was a member of the "scientific advisory committee" of the National Front, a right-wing party in France. Notin's publication was clearly motivated by political considerations. After a hue and cry by the Union of French Jewish Students (UEJF), and disruption of Notin's lectures by UEJF members, *Université Jean-Moulin* authorities summoned Notin to appear before a faculty disciplinary commission. The university cancelled Notin's economics classes, and the French governmental educational authorities suspended him for a year with half pay for publishing a Holocaust "revisionist" article, that contradicted the governmentally-sanctioned "*verité officielle*" (official truth) on the subject, under the pretext of criticizing media trivialization of the Holocaust and Nazi gas chambers.[8] In effect, under French Law (the so-called *Loi Gayssot*), racism, anti-Semitism and xenophobia are criminal offenses. Furthermore, it is a criminal offense to deny or negate the Holocaust (*negationnisme*), or support groups guilty of crimes against humanity as determined by post-World War II military tribunals.[9] Interestingly, the French hate speech law, *la Loi Gayssot,* neither defines nor explains the meaning of the term "xenophobia." Notin ultimately ended up at the *l'Université d'Oujda*, in Morocco, North Africa, an institution which had exchange agreements with the *Université Jean-Moulin (Lyon-III)*, despite the strenuous efforts of the UEJF and other officially accredited anti-racist groups to prevent him from involvement in any teaching activities that may have any direct or indirect connection to his university. Notin was reinstated in the faculty of the *Université Jean-Moulin* after he wrote an apology stating that he did not question the historical facts of the Holocaust.

Notin's case illustrates the French exceptionalist approach to Freedom of expression. The French conceptualize freedom of expression within the framework of a universalistic, moral philosophical worldview that is grounded in the Declaration of the Rights of Man and of the Citizen of 1789. This means that in all communicative endeavors, France lays emphasis on values like human dignity, civility, solidarity, equality, protection of the reputations of individuals, protection of the right to privacy, protection of the physical and moral well-being of children, and so on.[10] In journalistic reporting, these values sometimes take precedence over the truth. It is no surprise, therefore, that French law criminalizes writings, printed matter, drawings, engravings, paintings, emblems, images and other audiovisual material sold or exhibited in public places or meetings, or through any media of audiovisual communication, if the material justifies war crimes, crimes against humanity, or collaboration with the enemy [of France].[11] Furthermore, the law stipulates that it is a criminal offense to use any media outlet to incite discrimination, hatred, or violence toward a person or a group of persons on account of the origin, membership or non-membership of these persons in an ethnic group, a nation, race, or specific religion.[12]

Despite their fundamental philosophical differences on matters of freedom of speech and expression, the destinies of the United States and France have historically been intertwined since the eighteenth century. Perhaps no two countries have influenced the destinies of each other like the United States and France. Though the Framers of the American Constitution were, to use the language of the Supreme Court of the United States, "practical statesmen . . . not metaphysical philosophers,"[13] prone to abstract philosophical speculation, the ideas of French Enlightenment thinkers and political theorists—*philosophes* like Voltaire, Rousseau, Montesquieu, Diderot, and others—influenced the American Revolution. These ideas also influenced the structure and institutions of the republican system of government that emerged from the American Revolution. For its part, the American Revolution of 1776, and the Declaration of Independence greatly influenced the French political scene and helped to trigger the Revolution of 1789. Today, the United States and France are Western liberal democracies separated by their respective exceptionalist ideologies.

The aim of this chapter is to describe and explain the different systemic and politico-cultural contexts of traditional and online media regulation in the United States and France. This contextual analysis serves as the backdrop of the comparative case studies that are the focus of this volume. The question addressed concerns what happens when the contrasting, even oppositional exceptionalist ideologies of the United States and France in the issue area of freedom of expression are brought face to face by the interconnected network of computer networks—the Internet. In other words, this chapter is interested in exploring how the different media law regimes of the United States and France conceptualized and applied their specific logics and ideals of freedom of expression in real space and cyberspace. Before we proceed with this enquiry, we need to survey the political and cultural contexts of the free speech regimes of the United States and France, and explore where they fall within the "families" of legal regimes in the world.

Classification of The Legal and Regulatory Regimes of The United States and France within The World's Legal Families

National law regimes are conceptualized as systems of governance of relationships between political, legislative and judicial actors and institutions in nation-states. National political regimes spring out of, and reflect specific *governmentalities* (mentalities of government), to borrow Michel Foucault's oft-cited neologism. The term "governmentality" refers to the diverse conceptualizations, politico-cultural arrangements, ideologies, institutional logics, rationalizations, and practices of "rulership," or exercise of power.[14] These "mentalities of government" give rise to regimes with specific political and cultural characteristics. That is why we can speak of authoritarian regimes, dictatorial regimes, military regimes, socialist regimes or Islamic regimes.

Comparative law scholars, Zweigert and Kötz suggest that legal systems can be distinguished by their respective philosophies and ideologies.[15] The philosophical orientations, systemic and institutional characteristics of the political and legal regimes of the United States and France are so different that from the perspective of comparative politics, they can be classified as "most-different" regimes.[16] Indeed, comparative law scholars traditionally classify American and French law as belonging to two different "Western" legal traditions, viz, the Anglo-American Common Law,[17] and the Continental European civil or Romanistic Law traditions, respectively.[18]

The American Common Law System

The common law, as practiced in the United States, originated from the British common law system that came to the New World with British settlers in the first part of the seventeenth century. The common law is judge-made law based on the rule of *stare decisis et non quieta movere* (Latin for "let the past decision stand and do not disturb things that are at rest"). The idea is that as they adjudicate legal disputes, judges are expected to follow court precedent. Though the contemporary Americanized form of the rule of precedent originated in the British common law, it has lost some of the iron-clad certainties of its European ancestor.[19] Under the American system, jurisprudence is based upon general principles found in judicial decisions.[20] In the American system, under the doctrine of judicial review, courts have the power to interpret laws and declare statutes unconstitutional. The Supreme Court of the United States has the power to hold acts of other branches of government,[21] as well as the states, unconstitutional.[22] The Court can also review judgments of state courts in cases that fall within the federal judicial power.[23] Under the American system, the Federal Constitution is the supreme law of the land. All federal legislative and administrative enactments, state constitutions, state and local laws that violate the federal constitution, are null, void, and of no legal effect.[24]

The French Civil Law Regime

France is part of the Continental European civil law system, which stands in contradistinction to the Anglo-American common law system. Historically, civil law is grounded in legal codes, which originated with the Romans.[25] Contemporary civil law is generally based on the codification and interpretation of general legal rules and principles of law constructed by legislators.[26] In civil law countries, judges interpret articles of the code in order to arrive at legal decisions in specific cases. Such interpretations do not however, become authoritative legal precedent for subsequent cases. All future cases are based on fresh interpretations of the code without reference to prior judicial interpretations.[27] This statute-law system is different from the case-law system that obtains in the common law countries.[28]

Zweigert and Kötz suggest that *Le Code des Français*, which is also known as Napoleon's *Code civil* of 1804, is the model of the branch of continental European civil law that they call the "Romanistic legal family"[29] In France, the *Code civil* and other legislative enactments in areas as diverse as freedom of expression, individual privacy and defamation are not known for the exactitude, completeness or clarity of their language. Courts therefore have some leeway in interpreting legal provisions in the light of changing society and new technologies.[30] For their part, David and Brierley suggest that French legal rule (doctrine) is related to moral philosophy and is much wider in scope than its Anglo-American equivalent.[31] Some scholars note that the seeming rigidity of precedent and *stare decisis* (in comparison with the more flexible, interpretative French system) is attenuated by the technique of distinguishing cases.[32] A very important difference between the two legal systems is the presumption of innocence of accused persons in criminal law. In the common law adversarial system, under due process principles, an accused person is, in theory, presumed innocent until proven guilty and the burden of proof is on the prosecution. However, this presumption is often negated by pre-trial publicity, especially media reports of arrests that are accompanied by images of the accused. It has become an American tradition for arresting officers to take famous accused persons on "perp walks," a walk around a city block, for purposes of media publicity or political posturing. In such cases, guilt is established journalistically, if not legally.[33] Presumption of innocence is not clear cut in the inquisitorial system of the civil law countries. Over the years, however, the French system has steadily moved away from a presumption of guilt to a presumption of innocence as a result of the diffusion, and domestication of norms and values from the Council of European and the European Union.[34] Under new laws passed in 2000, it is now illegal to show images of an accused individual in handcuffs, or under arrest when that person has not been convicted. Unfortunately, new laws strengthening presumption of innocence infringe on freedom of the press since they make it a criminal offense for the press to publish pictures of a person in handcuffs or shackles without that person's consent, if that person has not been found guilty of committing a crime by a court of law. It is also illegal to seek public opinion about the guilt or innocence of an accused person, or to take pictures of crime scenes if the pictures "violate the dignity of a victim."[35]

The Politico-Cultural Context of Freedom of Speech and Media Regulation in the United States

As we saw earlier, the legal system of the United States emerged from the British common law system that came to North America with the English settlers who created the first official English colonial settlements in the early seventeenth century. The common law is thus an Americanized form of British common law.[36] Under this system, jurisprudence is based upon general principles found in judicial decisions.[37] Though the United States has one of the most elaborate common law systems in the world, most American law is, in fact, statutory law and Constitutional law.[38] Common law is now mostly state law. Under the doctrine of judicial review, courts have the power to review the constitutionality of statutes at the federal, state and local government levels in cases that fall within the federal judicial power.[39] Unlike France, the American Constitution is not a Bill of social or economic rights. As Frederick Schauer notes, the American Constitution is not a "vehicle for ensuring social rights, community rights, or positive citizen entitlements of any kind . . . skepticism about the ability of any governmental institution reliably to distinguish the good from the bad, the true from the false, and the sound from the unsound finds its most comfortable home in the First Amendment." [40] In short, the American Constitution is a libertarian charter under which freedom of speech trumps human dignity, decency, equality, civility, and other social or communitarian values.[41] American law is noted for its uniqueness in matters of freedom of speech and expression. The United States has what Frederick Schauer calls an "exceptional First Amendment." Under these "negative" constitutional provisions, which forbid the government from interfering with freedom of speech, freedom of the press, and freedom of religion, expressive freedom trumps human dignity and other internationally recognized rights. These rights include the right to privacy, culture, information, and so on. Freedom of expression also takes precedence over the reputational rights of public officials and public figures.[42] In the First Amendment scheme of things, the scales are almost always tilted in favor of the speaker, often at the expense of the listener. The

American Congress and federal courts have applied the logic of the First Amendment regime to the online multi-communication platforms and spaces created by the Internet.

The First Amendment and Freedom of Speech

First Amendment jurisprudence is a pragmatic system that is based on the idea that the cardinal function of the law is to guarantee individual freedom of expression, which in turn accomplishes several individual and societal functions in the country's democratic system of government. The United States has a "negative" free speech posture under which the government is perceived as the greatest danger to freedom of expression. As a result, one of the functions of the First Amendment is to limit governmental action with respect to matters of freedom of speech and expression. The First Amendment expressly forbids Congress from infringing on the right of freedom of speech, press and religion:

> Congress shall make no law respecting an establishment of religion, or prohibiting the free exercise thereof; or abridging the freedom of speech, or of the press; or the right of the people to peaceably assemble, and petition the Government for a redress of grievances.[43]

The words "Congress," "speech," and "press" are highly elastic legal terms. The Supreme Court of the United States has held that though the First Amendment expressly bars the American Congress from abridging freedom of speech and of the press, the First Amendment is "made applicable to the states through the due process clause of the 14th Amendment."[44] In other words, what the First Amendment bars Congress from doing, state and local governments are not permitted to do under the fundamental fairness provisions of the Fourteenth Amendment. Over time, the word "Congress" has come to mean all governmental regulatory entities ranging from the United States Congress to municipalities, universities, and local public school boards.

Freedom of speech therefore encompasses a whole range of expressive activities that include symbolic, non-verbal, communicative activities like wearing arm bands to protest an unpopular war,[45] "expressive conduct" like burning the American flag to protest governmental policies,[46] and "expressive association"—getting together with like-minded individuals for purposes of express religious or ethnic pride in public places, while excluding people whose conduct expresses undesirable speech.[47] Free speech also includes freedom from forced speech because the First Amendment guarantees—"the right to speak and the right not to speak."[48]

The word "press" is an elastic term that covers all kinds of "publications" which provide information to the general public, and comment on all matters of "public interest."[49] The term includes the traditional electronic media—broadcasting, cable-casting, satellite communication, as well as the Internet, which the United States Supreme Court has granted the same level of free speech protection as the traditional print media.[50] Nevertheless, the right of freedom of speech is not absolute; it is subject to time, place and manner regulations. This is a constitutional principle under which the government may regulate when, where, and how the right of free speech is exercised rather than the content of the speech.[51] American public policy is generally hostile towards all kinds of governmental regulation of, or interference with media content. One of the functions of these negative, Biblical-style, "thou shalt not" prohibitions imposed on the government by the First Amendment, is to underline a legal and historical presumption against all governmental attempts to censor or impose prior restraints on speech before it has been uttered or published.[52]

In effect, the Supreme Court of the United States has consistently set forth a functionalist perspective of the law of communication. The Court has held that the cardinal function of the First Amendment is to facilitate the emergence of a free and open public space of democratic social discourse analogized as a "marketplace of ideas:"

> the ultimate good desired is better reached by free trade in ideas—that the best test of truth is the power of the thought to get itself accepted in the competition of the market, and that truth is the only ground upon which their wishes safely can be carried out. That at any rate is the theory of our Constitution. It is an experiment, as all life is an experiment. . . . While that experiment is part of our system I think that we should be eternally vigilant against attempts to check the expression of opinions that we loathe and believe to be fraught with death.[53]

Consequently, the Supreme Court of the United States has ruled that the government has an obligation to maintain a non-discriminatory, content-neutral regulatory posture in all matters appertaining to speech and expression—in the widest sense of the word—especially if the intent of the regulation is to suppress objectionable speech or expressive conduct.[54] Thus, under the First Amendment, only content-neutral, narrowly tailored regulation of speech is permissible.[55] The Supreme Court of the United States has also held that all content-based regulations[56] must be subjected to greater legal scrutiny than content-neutral regulations.[57] Therefore, content-based regulations must pass the exacting "strict scrutiny" test, which essentially stipulates that in order to justify content-based speech regulations, the government must show that "the regulation is necessary to serve a compelling state interest and is narrowly drawn to achieve that end."[58] The Supreme Court has also held that all content-based regulations[59] are subject to greater scrutiny than content-neutral regulations.[60] Under the First Amendment, the government is also barred from practicing viewpoint discrimination—favoring a particular point of view or points of view over others in public forums or designated public forums.[61]

American Alterity

The First Amendment certainly makes the United States unique among nations on matters of freedom of speech and expression. It is a Libertarian charter under which freedom of speech trumps dignity, decency, equality, civility, and other social or communitarian values.[62] Indeed, while holding that burning the flag of the United States as a sign of protest against the government was protected symbolic expression, the Supreme Court of the United States held that laws forbidding racial discrimination were not above question: "The First Amendment does not guarantee that other concepts virtually sacred to our Nation as a whole—such as the principle that discrimination based on race is odious and destructive—will go unquestioned in the market-place of ideas."[63]

In sum, freedom of speech and of the press as practiced in the U.S. is exceptional, normative, and, to borrow the expression of Mathew Bunker, "leads us to exercise great caution before silencing viewpoints with which we disagree."[64] Jeffrie Murphy and Jules Coleman define respect for individual free speech rights as a natural or respect-based obligation, "a certain mandatory way in which persons must be treated if their essential humanity is to be respected and preserved."[65] Thus, under the First Amendment, American citizens can bring "claims against certain kinds of interferences"[66] with their rights of freedom of speech. It follows that this fundamental right against government interference cannot be infringed or eviscerated absent a compelling reason to do so.[67] Of course the First Amendment right of free speech does not demand that the government take affirmative steps to promote acceptable speech; it merely forbids the government from injecting itself into the public speech arena and unduly interfering with content that it finds politically or socially objectionable.[68]

Nevertheless, though the First Amendment guarantees substantive free speech, this right is not absolute. It is subject to time, place and manner regulations. This is a principle under which the government can regulate when, where, and how the right of free speech is exercised rather than the content of the speech.[69] Furthermore, certain classes of material are not granted First Amendment protection. Obscenity (material that presents human sexual and scatological (toilet) functions in a highly offensive manner),[70] fighting words (expressions that incite immediate physical reactions), false and deceptive advertisements, advertisements for illegal products and services, libel and slander, indecency (speech that describes human sexual and toilet functions) in over-the-air broadcasting, as well as material that constitutes intellectual property violation, are illegal.

One of the functions of the law is to evaluate the constitutionality of laws that seek to regulate freedom of speech and expression. The Supreme Court of the United States uses the First Amendment, as a measuring rod against which to evaluate the constitutionality of local, state and federal regulation of speech.[71]

In the United States, one function of the law is to guarantee freedom of speech and assembly, and to limit state action and discretion in that domain. In his concurring opinion in *Whitney v. California*, Justice Brandeis stated that the Founding Fathers of the American Republic sought to create a democratic constitutional system in which they believed that:

> the deliberative forces should prevail over the arbitrary . . . that freedom to think as you will and speak as you think are means indispensable to the discovery of political truth . . . that public discussion is a political duty . . . that the path of safety lies in the opportunity to discuss freely supposed grievances and proposed remedies. . . . Recognizing the occasional tyrannies of governing majorities, they amended the Constitution so that free speech and assembly should be guaranteed.[72]

As we saw earlier, the United States has a market-based media law regime which combines several libertarian principles—the marketplace of ideas, *laissez-faire* economics, free trade and the free flow of ideas, information, and discourse.[73] The Constitutional underpinnings of this system include the Commerce Clause, which, in furtherance of the exchange of goods and serves across state lines, rejects regulations that discriminate against interstate commerce.[74] Discriminatory interstate regulations are regulations that impose more burdensome demands on interstate commerce than on other kinds of commerce.[75] Furthermore, in the United States, there can be no governmentally-sanctioned truth, or judicially-approved political viewpoint on any subject, as is the case in France where certain historical interpretations or "truths" touching on the country's "collective memory" bear the government's imprimatur.[76]

The "Occupy Movement," Time, Place, and Manner Regulations

The United States has a system of ordered liberties under which free speech is not absolute. The right of free speech is balanced against other societal rights and governmental interests. The result is that freedom of expression is subject to time, place, and manner regulations, a principle under which the government may regulate where, when, and how the right of free speech is exercised rather than the content of the speech.[77] This principle came to the fore in late 2011 when the so-called "Occupy Wall Street Movement," an organized interest group of mostly white, upper middle-class young people decided to physically seize and occupy public parks and plazas across the United States to protest against what they called the "1 percent" of Americans who controlled most of the wealth of the country. "Occupy" protesters were essentially demanding economic equality. The epicenter of the movement was the Zuccotti Park in New York City, a public access park located a short distance from Wall Street, the place which was, in the minds of the "Occupy" protesters, the metonym for greed, unbridled capitalism, economic injustice, and inequality. Observers around the world watched how the American system dealt with boisterous public dissent.

When the City of New York forcefully evicted the Occupiers after weeks of noisy, controversial protests, the "Occupiers" claimed that their permanent occupation of Zuccotti Park was protected under the freedom of assembly clause of the First Amendment. A court in New York disagreed, ruling that the First Amendment was not absolute. The judge held that the City of New York did not violate the rights of the Occupiers because the rules that were established to maintain cleanliness and safety in the park were reasonable time, place and manner regulations.[78] Evictions of Occupiers in cities around the United States gave rise to a slew of cases heard in federal courts around the country. One of the most interesting "occupy" case was *Occupy Boston v. City of Boston.*[79] In this case the occupiers claimed that the occupation was symbolic speech: "The Occupation is the message." The court disagreed and ruled that the seizure and occupation of a public forum is not protected by the First Amendment. The legal precedent that controlled virtually all the Occupy Movement cases was *Clark v. Community for Creative Non-Violence.* The general legal principle of *Clark* is that the United States is a society of ordered liberties in which the government may impose content-neutral, time, place and manner restrictions on speech/assembly, provided that those restrictions were narrowly tailored to advance a significant government interest, and leave open, ample avenues of communication.[80]

Unprotected Speech under the First Amendment

Since the First Amendment is not absolute, certain categories of speech do not come under its protective umbrella. These classes of speech include: obscenity (material that presents human sexual and toilet functions in a highly offensive manner),[81] fighting words (epithets that incite immediate physical reactions and are said "in your face"),[82] KKK flag-burning that is intended to intimidate,[83] false and deceptive advertising, as well as advertising for illegal products,[84] libel and slander,[85] indecency (speech describing human sexual and toilet functions) in over-the-air broadcasting,[86] and acts that violate copyright[87] are not protected by the First Amendment. By declaring these classes of speech as not being eligible for protection, the law fulfills, in a backhanded fashion, certain crucial social functions—protection of public peace, security, morality, fair competition, promotion of the creative arts and sciences for the betterment of society, and so on.

The United States has a federal system with 51 constitutions (50 state constitutions and the Federal Constitution of the United States). Under the Supremacy Clause of the Constitution of the United States, the Federal Constitution takes precedence over state constitutions. Therefore, any state constitutional provision, state or federal law that contradicts the federal Constitution is null and void.[88] In the United States, the Bill of Rights (the first 10 amendments to the Federal Constitution) is a negative charter of expressive liberties, which enumerates the things that the American government is not permitted to do because these things eviscerate the rights of citizens.[89] The First Amendment focuses on matters of freedom of speech, freedom of the press, freedom of assembly and freedom of religion. The idea behind this free speech regime is that the greatest threat to freedom of speech is the government, not religion, not people who misuse or abuse the right of free speech.[90]

Corporate Personhood Under the First Amendment

One of the most contentious issues in American First Amendment jurisprudence is the personhood of corporations; that is, the problem of treating non-media corporations as "persons" who can exercise the right of freedom of speech and of the press. The dichotomy between "natural or physical persons" (human beings) and "moral persons" (corporations) has been the subject of much ideologically-driven, emotional, and sometimes hyperbolic opinions from anti-corporate and libertarian commentators alike. A few facts are clear: As early as 1819, the Supreme Court of the United States ruled that corporations had constitutional rights that states could not take away.[91] In 1886, the Supreme Court of the United States held that corporations are "persons" entitled to equal protection and due process under the law.[92] Furthermore, the United States Code defines the term "person" as: "an individual, corporation, business trust, estate, trust, partnership, limited liability company, association, joint venture, governmental agency, public corporation, or any other legal or commercial entity."[93] In defamation law, the Court has held that well-known corporations can be classified as public figures (celebrities) who have reputations that can be damaged. These corporations can suffer damage if their products are disparaged. However, in order to collect damages for defamation, these corporations must meet the exacting *New York Times* actual malice fault standard for public figures.[94]

This issue of corporate personhood came up again during the 2008 presidential election. In *Citizen's United v. Federal Election Commission*,[95] a political interest group in Wisconsin wanted to broadcast a film that was highly critical of Democratic Presidential candidate, Hillary Clinton. The group also wanted to advertise the film during television broadcasts in the state. These broadcasts would have violated section 203 of the Bipartisan Campaign Reform Act of 2002, which permitted the Federal Election Commission (FEC) to ban corporations, including, ideological nonprofit interest groups like Citizen's United and trade unions, from engaging in "electioneering communications" (making independent expenditures to support or criticize political particular political candidates in the electronic media) within thirty days of a presidential primary election. Citizen's United sued and the case was appealed all the way to the Supreme Court of the United States. The issue before the Court was whether banning corporate and union "electioneering communications,"—funding of independent political broadcasts that targeted an individual political candidate for defeat or supported a specific political candidate—violated the First Amendment. The Court ruled that banning the "electioneering communications" law violated the First Amendment. Its reasoning was that under the First Amendment, Congress may not fine or jail citizens or associations of citizen who engage in political speech because the First Amendment grants these groups and unions the right to use their money to criticize politicians. As John Fabian Witt puts it, "In the eyes of the law, corporations had long been persons for some purposes and not for others." He notes that while corporations have reputations to protect, and while they can sign contracts, hold property, and speak through agents, they have no right of privacy and certainly cannot marry or run for office.[96]

Freedom of Expression in France: The Politico-Cultural Context of Media Regulation

France is part of the Continental European civil law system. Historically, civil law is grounded in legal codes, which have their origins in the earliest codifications of law in human-size steles and clay tablets such as the *Code of Hammurabi* (1750 BC). The Gallo-Roman nation that became France emerged from the ashes of the collapsed Roman Empire. French legal codes therefore originated from the Roman Empire, which had the most advanced legal system in the ancient world. Contemporary civil law is generally based on the codification and interpretation of general legal rules and principles of law constructed by legislators to regulate specific areas of human activity. The most infamous French code was the *Code noir* (The Black Code) of 1685, an edict that codified all edicts, declarations, decrees and orders that regulated slavery in French colonies and territories of North America and the Caribbean. In civil law countries, judges interpret articles of specific codes in order to arrive at legal decisions in specific cases. Such interpretations do not however, become authoritative legal precedent for subsequent cases. All future cases are based on fresh interpretations of the code without reference to prior judicial interpretations.[97] This statute-law system is different from the case-law system that obtains in the common law countries.[98] French codes that regulate communicational activities include the *Code civil, the Code de la propriété intellectuelle* (the Intellectual Property Code), *le Code du patrimoine* (heritage code) and the *Code pénal* (penal code).

The French legal system is also institutionally different from the American system, which has a hierarchical, pyramidal system whose apex is occupied by the Supreme Court of the United States. In France, historic political discomfort and suspicion of an all powerful, American-style supreme court vested with the responsibility of subjecting lower court decisions to judicial review led to a diffuse system of judicial and constitutional review. In effect, France has three institutions that occupy the highest rung of its judicial system. The *Conseil d'État* (Council of State) is the highest judicial authority, the "supreme court" for administrative matters. The *Cour de cassation* (Court of Cassation) is the highest authority, the "supreme court" for civil and criminal matters—each French jurisdiction is composed of administrative, civil and criminal courts—while the *Conseil constitutionnel* (Constitutional Council) is the highest constitutional authority in France. It is responsible for reviewing all statutes and making determinations whether these statutes conform to the letter and spirit of the French Constitution, including its preamble, the Declaration of the Rights of Man and of the Citizen of 1789, which guarantee freedom of expression and respect for individual privacy within certain bounds.[99] Interestingly, all former presidents of France are *ex officio* life members of the Constitutional Council.[100]

The role of the French president in the judiciary raises issues of separation of powers—at least to non-French observers. Under the Constitution of 1958, the supreme law of the land, the President of the Republic is the guarantor of the independence and authority of the judiciary. He is assisted in this task by the Superior Council of the Magistrature (CSM), which provides advisory opinions to the President of the Republic upon request, appoints and disciplines judges, makes decisions on matters of judicial ethics, and ensures the smooth-functioning of the system of administration of justice.[101] The problem of separation of powers was compounded by the fact that the President of the French Republic chaired the Superior Council of the Magistrature for half a century. However, as a result of former President Nicolas Sarkozy's constitutional reforms of July 2008, the President of the Republic ceased to be the chairman of the CSM. Separation of powers often became problematic when sitting French presidents instituted legal actions again publishers for torts ranging from defamation and invasion of privacy to intellectual property violation. Only once in French history has a French court ruled against a sitting president in a freedom of expression case. That unprecedented decision took place in 2008.[102] Before 2008 French presidents or their families often succeeded in getting courts to ban books, pictures or other forms of expression that mentioned them adversely.[103]

French Secular Republicanism and the "Marketplace For Ideas"

The political culture and freedom of expression regime of France can be traced to the "revolutionary" philosophical ideas about liberty and government that emerged in the Enlightenment and were spread in the eighteenth century by the mostly anti-Catholic *philosophes*.[104] These enlightenment ideas included faith in the power of reason and knowledge, as well as the sovereignty of the people rather than the monarchy and the Catholic Church.[105] These ideas were the chief causes of the French Revolution of 1789, which overthrew the *ancien regime*, abolished the divine rights monarchy, disestablished the Catholic Church, and eliminated Catholicism as the official religion of the state.[106] Today, the official "religion" of France is "secular republicanism."[107] The French Constitution of 1958 (art 1) stipulates that France is a "secular, democratic, social republic." Article II states that: "the official language of the French Republic is French, and its official motto is: *Liberté, Égalité, Fraternité* (Liberty, Equality, Fraternity) the revolutionary slogan-turned-national ideology. This communitarian creed puts a premium on respect for civil discourse, respect for individual and group reputation, state promotion of social equality and civility, cultural homogenization, respect for human dignity, individual privacy, and moral rights over freedom of expression. Under French hierarchical egalitarianism, equality is more important than liberty, and in clashes between freedom of expression and invasion of privacy, individual privacy takes precedence, even over truthful journalistic reporting.[108] Taken as a whole, the French Constitution is a national bill of social rights and equality. It is therefore the vehicle for the valuation of ideas, philosophies, official interpretations of history, granting social and community rights, as well as for ensuring positive citizen entitlements.[109] The French secular republican regime with its content-based, free speech regulatory logic has resulted in what François Furet calls "the supremacy of law over rights."[110]

One of the main tenets of French secular republicanism is that France is a secular nation of culturally homogeneous people.[111] Thus, all persons in France are to be assimilated into the French Republic as *individuals*, with one culture—the French culture—not as members of specific ethnic or religious communities.[112] David Beriss argues that hegemonic, neo-republican notions of France as a culturally unified nation make French culture, rather than race the central tenet of French identity.[113] Through its centralized, bureaucratic policy of *dirigisme* or state capitalism, the French government has taken affirmative steps to promote equality by fostering a "positive" but highly malleable sphere of communication and freedom of expression in which the government can intervene in order to create, in the words of van Gerven, a "marketplace **for** ideas."[114] Under this elastic, content-based ideology, viewpoint discrimination is considered a necessity in a democratic society. As we saw above, from time to time, the French government, with the assistance of anti-racist and other civil society groups, takes affirmative steps to eliminate speech that it considers abusive of the right of freedom of expression from the public sphere.

However, despite its secular creed and historic anti-clericalism, France is culturally a Catholic country. French philosopher, Edgar Morin, has aptly described France as *un état Catho-laique,* (a Catho-secular state).[115] Morin's neologism, *catholaicité* (cathosecularism) aptly describes the reality of France where there is a *de jure* separation of faith and politics, that is, governmental non-recognition of the spiritual, normative, doctrinal, and institutional aspects of the Catholic Church in the political arena. However, there is a parallel *de facto* and *de jure* inseparability between the state and the cultural aspects of Roman Catholicism. In effect, the French state owns and maintains more than 600 churches and cathedrals that are considered *lieux de memoires culturelles* (places of cultural memory).[116] These churches are maintained by the Ministry of Communication and Culture as part of the *partimoine culturel* (cultural heritage) of the country. Even though the number of practicing Catholics in France has continued to decline, these houses of worship have been put at the disposal of the Roman Catholic Church for purposes of public worship. Among the small percentage of French men and women who still practice the Catholic faith, the vast majority ignore the teachings of the Vatican on sexual morality, abortion and birth control. In contemporary France, religion is therefore mostly a cultural phenomenon.

Zweigert and Kötz suggest that *Le Code des Français*, Napoleon's *Code civil* of 1804, is the model of the branch of continental European civil law that they call the "Romanistic legal family"[117] In France, the *Code civil* and other legislative enactments in areas as diverse as freedom of expression, individual privacy and hate speech are not known for the exactitude, completeness or clarity of their language. Courts therefore have some leeway in interpreting legal provisions in the light of changing social realities and new technologies.[118] The pragmatic, fact-based legal exactitude of American common law is contrasted with the systematically-organized, vague, abstract, and elastic "conceptual" formalism of French law.[119]

The Contours of Freedom of Expression in France

While the Gallic, Latin, Catholic culture, and Napoleonic civil law system of France is the foil—the "most different" system, in comparative lingo—of the Protestant, Puritan, Anglo-American common law system, the case studies in this volume approach communication law and policy in both countries from a functional perspective. That is, from the perspective that the laws governing freedom of speech and expression in France and the United States serve different but equivalent functions in the democratic systems of both countries. France is a secular republican democracy in which one of the functions of the law is to protect human dignity, and universal human rights, of which freedom of expression is a fundamental part. The premise is that freedom of expression, within certain limits, is a human right that must be protected by law.

Therefore, in matters of freedom of expression, France has a moral philosophical system under which the constitutional right of freedom of speech is balanced against other constitutional rights, namely, human dignity, privacy, fraternity, equality, reputation and the like. In France, as in the rest of Europe, freedom of expression can be restricted if the government can show that the restrictions are "necessary in a democratic society."[120] Under French law, freedom of the press is rooted in the Declaration of the Rights of Man and of the Citizen of 1789.[121] This declaration, which was one of the cornerstones of the French Revolution, was incorporated into the French Constitution, and became its preamble in 1971. Article XI of the Declaration states that "the free communication of thoughts and opinions is one of the most precious rights of man."[122] However, this clause, is qualified by the next clause which states that people are free to speak, write, and print freely, "*on condition that they answer for any abuse of this freedom*."[123] Furthermore, another article of the Declaration states that: "the exercise of the natural rights of each person has no bounds but those which assure to other members of the society, the enjoyment of these same rights."[124] Despite these noble sentiments, under the political regimes that succeeded each other in the wake of the Revolution of 1789, the law was used to create a system of legalized oppression aimed at protecting authoritarian regimes from criticism. In matters of freedom of expression, the law took precedence over substantive rights. The result is that people have a right freedom of expression but this right is subordinated to, and circumscribed by other governmental and social interests, which essentially eviscerated it.

For close to a century after the Revolution, the French press struggled to exercise the right of freedom of speech and of the press that is set forth in the Declaration. The various regimes that succeeded each other after the French Revolution of 1789 enacted a series of laws regulating the press. For example, between 1814 and 1881, a total of forty press laws were enacted after lengthy and sometimes acrimonious philosophical and metaphysical speculation about the nature and function of the press in post-revolutionary French society. The laws were aimed at controlling the press for purposes of public safety, good morals, individual privacy, the dignity of the Head of State, and social harmony. The general picture that emerges from this historical period is that post-revolutionary French regimes had a vision of a press that was centralized, hierarchical, and elitist, for purposes of singing the governmental tune (commenting on, and communicating governmental policies from the center of power—Paris—to the provinces).[125]

As authoritarian, monarchical and imperial regimes, succeeded each other in the decades after the Revolution, caricature and satirical journalism became the main instruments of journalistic resistance. These artistic and journalistic devices are, to use the expression of Robert Goldstein, part and parcel of a "long-standing tradition of Gallic wit."[126] A series of renowned caricaturists and cartoonists left their mark on the political scene. They included: Honoré Daumier, Paul Gavarni, J.J. Grandville, and others whose works were highly caustic re-constructions and re-presentations of the political, cultural, and social realities of nineteenth-century France.[127] From 1835 to 1881, diverse French regimes were so fearful of caricatures that they imposed a specific regime of censorship on the irreverent and deliberately provocative drawings that skewered the powerful and the mighty. France therefore has a long tradition of freedom of expression through caricatures and cartoons. French cartoons, caricatures, and iconographies have always had political, cultural, and social significance because they have always been purveyors of lessons, shapers of public opinion, creators of stereotypes, and texts that validated political choices.[128] French Cartoons and caricatures are therefore, to quote Deleuze and Guattari, culture-specific, "geo-graphic . . . territorial representations"[129] that are grounded in the centuries-long tradition of French satirical communication.

The Law of July 29, 1881 and Freedom of the Press

The lot of the French press changed dramatically in 1881 with the passage of a series of laws codified as "The Law of July 29, 1881 on Freedom of the Press."[130] The law had a markedly functionalist orientation in that it was designed to manage the tension between freedom of expression, anonymous, anti government publications and objectionable press content. The law set out to solve the legendary historical problem of anonymous tracts and publications that surfaced from time to time even before the Revolution, by requiring, on penalty of a fine or imprisonment, that all written material disseminated in public bear the name and address of the publisher or printer of the material.[131] The Law of 1881 liberalized the free speech regime but enshrined governmental and other controls over the content of speech. For example, article 24 of the Law of 1881 enumerates certain crimes that are likely to be committed by the press or "other means of publication." The law has been amended over the years. Today, it criminalizes writings, printed matter, drawings, engravings, paintings, emblems, images, and other audiovisual material sold or exhibited in public places or meetings, or through any other media of audiovisual communication, if the material justifies war crimes, crimes against humanity, or collaboration with the enemy.[132] Furthermore, the law stipulates that it is a criminal offense to use any media outlet to incite discrimination, hatred, or violence toward a person or a group of persons because of the origin, and membership or non-membership of these persons in an ethnic group, a nation, race, or specific religion.[133] The law further states that those who use media outlets to deny the existence of one or several crimes against humanity—notably the Jewish Holocaust and more recently, the Armenian genocide—committed by an organization declared criminal under the provisions of international law, face criminal prosecution.[134] Additionally, in order to solve the problem of bias-motivated content or hate speech, all public communication or media content directed at people on the basis of their gender, race, religion, national origin, ethnicity, and sexual orientation, as well as speech that justifies or denies genocide or crimes against humanity, is criminalized.[135]

Impact of the Article 10 (Freedom of Expression) Jurisprudence of the European Court of Human Rights

A phenomenon that has had a significant impact on freedom of expression in France is the transfer, transposition and domestication of supranational European law into French law. France is a signatory to the European Convention on Human Rights and Fundamental Freedoms (ECHR) of 1950. It is also a member of the 47-member Council of Europe, the pan-European organization set up to implement the Universal Declaration of Human Rights and the European Convention on Human Rights and Fundamental Freedoms of 1950 in the continental European geo-political space. In the field of freedom of expression law and policy, the most influential European institution is the European Court of Human Rights (ECtHR). The burgeoning Article 10 (freedom of expression) jurisprudence of the ECtHR is the most influential body of human rights and communication law outside the United States. Article 10 of the European Convention on Human Rights states as follows:

> 1. Everyone has the right to freedom of expression. This right shall include freedom to hold opinions and to receive and impart information and ideas without interference by public authority and regardless of frontiers. This article shall not prevent States from requiring the licensing of broadcasting, television or cinema enterprises.
> 2. The exercise of these freedoms, since it carries with it duties and responsibilities, may be subject to such formalities, conditions, restrictions or penalties as are prescribed by law and are necessary in a democratic society, in the interests of national security, territorial integrity or public safety, for the prevention of disorder or crime, for the protection of health or morals, for the protection of the reputation or the rights of others, for preventing the disclosure of information received in confidence, or for maintaining the authority and impartiality of the judiciary.

Since France is a member of the Council of Europe, French courts apply the European freedom of expression standards of the European Court of Human Rights to legal disputes in France. The ECtHR has held that in order to be justified, interference with freedom of expression must be prescribed by law, further a legitimate governmental interests in the protection of the reputation and rights of others, as well as the prevention of crime or disorder. Additionally, if governments plan to interfere with the right of freedom of expression, a determination must be made whether the interference is "necessary in a democratic society."[136]

France, like most countries of the European Union and the Council of Europe, has a government-mediated, content-based, viewpoint discriminatory freedom of expression regime that van Gerven calls a "marketplace **for** ideas,"[137] in contrast to the American viewpoint-neutral "marketplace **of** ideas," free speech system. One of the characteristics of the marketplace for ideas perspective is that it is an interventionist, positive freedom of expression regime where the government actively intervenes in public discourse, and takes affirmative legal steps to eliminate content that is considered abusive of the right of freedom of expression. This is especially true of speech that the government deems prejudicial to human rights and human dignity. In this system, the state uses the law to solve problems of social communication, create a "democratic free speech environment," and protect perceived victims of misuse of the right of freedom of expression.[138] The presumption is that speech deemed objectionable and undemocratic by the government—especially bias-motivated speech or expression that "incites discrimination, hatred or violence against people on the basis of their origin or their membership or non-membership in a specific ethnic group, a nation, a race or a religion, sexual orientation or handicap status," as well as denial of the Holocaust—diminishes the human dignity of its victims. Those who resort to this type of speech abuse—forfeit the right of freedom of expression in the public sphere.[139] Despite this concern for the views and feelings of ethnic and religious minorities, French courts have not entertained attempts by Muslim groups to ban mass mediated speech (especially cartoons) that these groups find objectionable, or disrespectful of Islam. On this score, French courts follow the precedent of the European Court of Human Rights which ruled that Sharia law is incompatible with democracy.[140]

Conclusion

The First Amendment is functionally equivalent to the Declaration of the Rights of Man and of the Citizen of 1789. The First Amendment expresses negative freedoms when it bars Congress from interfering with freedom of speech, freedom of assembly, freedom of the press, and freedom of religion. For its part, the Declaration of the Rights of Man and of the Citizen of 1789 is a qualified, universalist, moral, and philosophical pronouncement of the right to freedom of expression as a human right. Both documents are historic and unprecedented in that they are contextualized solutions to the problem of freedom of expression. This volume compares and contrasts the evolution of freedom of speech and expression in the two countries over the years, using as case studies, the legal and policy postures of both countries in a number of issue areas in offline and online communication. Using the Internet as the focal point for the comparative study of human communication in the United States and France reflects the importance the Internet has assumed as the multi-communication platform par excellence, on which all the media of mass, social and interpersonal communication have converged and serve as the engine of the knowledge economy. Taken together, these case studies demonstrate sameness and difference in the exceptionalist postures of the United States and France with respect to a number of crucial issue areas of communication.

The table below summarizes the main characteristics and logics of freedom of expression in the United States and France. It shows that though the United States and France are different in terms of their regulation of the media, they have functionally equivalent institutions and regulatory instruments in the issue areas of freedom of expression and intellectual property. The only difference between the two systems is in their different conceptualizations of the status of the journalistic profession. France has an historic, bureaucratic tradition of journalistic trade unionism and journalistic accreditation under which the journalistic profession is recognized under the labor code and journalists are issued press cards by *La Commission de la Carte d'Identité des journalistes Professionnels* (The Commission for the Issuance of Identification Cards to Professional journalists, CCIJP). The United States does not have an equivalent national system of journalistic accreditation. The different postures of the United States and France with respect to media regulation in general and Internet regulation in particular may ultimately be a reflection of what Frederick Schauer calls "different stages in the development of the legal and constitutional right to freedom of communication."[141] However, since law is culture, American exceptionalism and the French exception reflect cultural and legal diversity in the conceptualization and regulation of the Internet. They also reflect diversity in the conceptualization of human rights and freedom of expression.

Table 2.1. Freedom of Expression in the United States and France: Characteristics and Logics

Characteristics/Issues	United States	France
Legal Regime	Common Law	Civil Law

Nature of Political Regime	Federal Republic (has one federal and 50 state Constitutions)	Centralized Secular Social Republic (Administrative state)
Exceptionalist Logic	American Exceptionalism	*L'Exception Française* (Cultural State)
Cultural Logic	Anti-establishmentarian	Catho-secular
Instrument of Freedom of Expression	The First Amendment (1791) (Charter of Negative Freedoms) (Marketplace **of** ideas)	Declaration of the Rights of Man (1789); (Charter of Positive Freedoms) Law of July 29, 1881 on Freedom of the Press. (Marketplace **for** ideas)
Regulation of journalistic Profession	None	Journalists have "status" under Labor Code, carry press cards issued by CCIJP.
Philosophy of Intellectual Property	Utilitarian: Copyright Protection granted to creative persons for the betterment of society, has fair use exception.	Romantic: Author's Rights grounded in natural rights: Has economic rights and moral rights. Recognizes parody exception.

NOTES

1. See Pamela Cytrynbaum, Web Entangles NU in Free Speech Debate, Chicago Tribune, December 29, 1996, at 5. Available at: http://articles.chicagotribune.com/keyword/academic-freedom/recent/5.
2. See Statement by Northwestern University President, Henry S. Bienen regarding Associate Professor Arthur Butz and his web page (1997). Available at: http://www.ibiblio.org/team/history/controversy/970107-Butz.html
3. *Papish v. University of Missouri Curators*, 410 U.S. 667 (1973) (Holding that "the mere dissemination of ideas—no matter how offensive to good taste—on a state university campus may not be shut off in the name alone of "conventions of decency").
4. See Frederick Schauer, The Exceptional First Amendment, in American Exceptionalism and Human Rights 29, 56 (Michael Ignatieff, Ed., 2005).
5. *Terminiello v. Chicago*, 337 US 1 (1949).
6. *Hustler Magazine v. Falwell*, 485 U.S. 46, 56 (1988) (Holding that "the fact that society may find speech offensive is not a sufficient reason for suppressing it. Indeed, if it is the speaker's opinion that gives offense, that consequence is a reason for according it constitutional protection"); See also *Terminiello v. Chicago*, 337 U.S. 1 (1949) (Holding that: a "heckler's" veto is illegal and that "a function of free speech under our system is to invite dispute. It may indeed best serve its high purpose when it induces a condition of unrest, creates dissatisfaction with conditions as they are, or even stirs people to anger").
7. *Texas v. Johnson, 491 U.S. 397 (1989).*
8. See *e.g.* Michel Delberghe, *M. Bernard Notin retrouve ses functions d'enseignant à l'université* Lyon-III (Bernard Notin regains his position as instructor at University of Lyon-III), Le Monde, January 16, 1993 at 14 (reporting that French economics professor Bernard Notin was disciplined by the French educational authorities for publishing a refereed journal article questioning the scientific basis of gas chambers).

9. See Art 9, *Loi du 29 juillet 1881 sur la liberté de la presse, modifiée par Loi No. 90-615 du 13 juillet 1990 tendant tendant à réprimer tout acte raciste, antisémite ou xenophobe (Loi Gayssot), J.O. du 14 Juillet 1990.* (Art 9, Law of July 29, 1881 on Freedom of the Press, amended by Law No. 90-615 of July 13, 1990, aimed at suppressing all racist, anti-Semitic and xenophobic acts).

10. See Art. I, Charter of Fundamental Rights of the European Union, Official Journal of the European Communities, 2000/C 364/1 (2000). Available at: http://www.europarl.europa.eu/charter/default_en.htm

11. See art 24, Law of July 29, 1881 On Freedom of the Press (as amended).

12. Id.

13. *Industrial Union Dept., AFL–CIO v. American Petroleum Institute* , 448 U. S. 607, 673 (1980) (Rehnquist, J., concurring).

14. See Michel Foucault, Dits Et Écrits 1954-1988, Tome III. (Sayings and Writings of Michel Foucault, 1954-1988) Vol. III. 655, 720-721, 820 (1994). See also Michel Foucault, The Hermaneutics of the Subject, Lectures at the Collége De France, 1981-1982 252 (2005) (Arnold Davidson, Ed., Graham Burchell, trans. Palgrave, 2005) (2001). See also Jean-Francois Bayart, L'etat En Afrique (The State in Africa) 99 (1989).

15. See Konrad Zweigert and Hein Kötz, An Introduction to Comparative Law 38 (3rd Ed. trans Tony Weir, 1998).

16. See John Gerring, Case Study Research 139 (2007).

17. French scholars generally call the legal system that operated in Great Britain, the United States, Australia, Canada, New Zealand, and most former British colonies, the "Anglo-Saxon" system. See e.g. Boris Starck, Henri Roland & Laurent Boyer, Introduction Au Droit (Introduction To Law) 110 (2000).

18. See Konrad Zweigert & H. KÖTZ, An Introduction To Comparative Law 69-75 (Tony Weir trans., Clarendon Paperbacks 3rd Ed. 1998) (1984) (Classifying legal systems into seven families: Romanistic, Germanic, Nordic, Common Law, Socialist, Far Eastern, Islamic, and Hindu). See also René David & John E.C. Brierly, major Legal Systems Of The World 33 (3rd Ed. 1985) (This legal family includes Latin and Germanic legal traditions).

19. See René David & John E.C. Brierly, major Legal Systems of the World 33 (3rd Ed. 1985) (Courts in the United States, including the Supreme Court of the United States, are not bound to observe their own precedents).

20. See Oliver Wendell Holmes, The Common Law (1881).

21. See *Marbury v. Madison*, 5 U.S. 137 (1803).

22. See *Fletcher v. Peck,* 10 U.S. 87 (1810).

23. See *Martin v. Hunter's Lessee*, 14 U.S. 304 (1816).

24. Art. VI, Clause 2, Constitution of the United States.

25. See Id. at 3.

26. Id. at 333-358 (3rd Ed. 1985)

27. John Crabb, The French Civil Code (1977) AT 9.

28. See Konrad Zweigert And Hein Kötz, Introduction To Comparative Law (3rd Ed.) (Tony Weir, trans.) 90 (1998).

29. See Konrad Zweigert And Hein Kötz, Introduction To Comparative Law (3rd Ed.) (Tony Weir, trans.) 74 (1998).

30. See Konrad Zweigert And Hein Kötz, Introduction to Comparative Law (3rd Ed.) (Tony Weir, trans.) 91 (1998).

31. Id. 359 (The continental European legal rule "is linked to moral theology rather than to procedure."

32. See Boris Starck, Henri Roland & Laurent Boyer, Introduction Au Droit (Introduction to Law) 110-111 (2000).

33. A good example is Dominique Strauss-Kahn, Managing Director of the International Monetary Fund who was arrested and accused of rape. The prosecution latter dropped the case when it was found that the alleged victim was less than truthful. See e.g. Philip Messing et al., Strauss-Kahn Hotel Sex Case Delayed for Tests, Maid ID'd him in Line up. *New York Post*, May 16, 2011.

34. See Art. 48, European Charter of Fundamental Rights, Art 6 (2) European Convention on Human Rights and Fundamental Freedoms (1950). See also Jean-Michel Bezat, La loi sur la présomption d'innocence est définitivement adoptée (Law on presumption of innocence adopted), Le Monde, June 1, 2000 at 7 (The new law strengthens presumption of innocence but restricts newsgathering by journalists.)

35. See Art. 97, loi no 2000-516 du 15 juin 2000 renforçant la protection de la présomption d'innocence et les droits des victimes (Art. 97, Law no 2000-516 of June 15, 2000 Reinforcing Protection of the Presommption of Innocence and the Rights of Victims) J.O. No. 138 of June 16, 2000. See also Art. 35 ter, Loi du 29 juillet 1881 sur la liberté de la presse (Art 35 ter, Law of July 29, 1881 on Freedom of the Press) J.O. of September 22, 2000.

36. Id. René David & John E.C. Brierly (Courts in the United States, including the Supreme Court of the United States, are not bound to observe their own precedents.)

37. See Oliver Wendell Holmes, The Common Law (1881).

38. See Donald Gillmor And Jerome Barron, Mass Communication Law, 5th Ed., (1997). See also, M. Roeder, The Doctrine of Moral Right: A Study in the Law of Artists, Authors and Creators, 53 Harvard Law Review 554 (1940).

39. *Marbury v. Madison*, 5 U.S. (1 Cranch) 137 (1803); *Fletcher v. Peck,* 10 U.S. 87 (1810); *Martin v. Hunter's Lessee*, 14 U.S. 304 (1816).

40. See Frederick Schauer, *The Exceptional First Amendment*, *in* American Exceptionalism And Human Rights 29, 46 (Michael Ignatieff, Ed., 2005).

41. See Frederick Schauer, *The Exceptional First Amendment*, *in* American Exceptionalism And Human Rights 29, 45 (Michael Ignatieff, Ed., 2005).

42. See Frederick Schauer, *The Exceptional First Amendment*, in Michael Ignatieff (Ed.) American Exceptionalism and Human Rights 29, 32-40 (2005).

43. Amendment 1, Constitution Of The United States (1791).

44. See *Gitlow v. New York*, 268 U.S. 652 (1925).

45. *Tinker v. Des Moines Independent Community School District*, 393 U.S. 503 (1969).

46. *Texas v. Johnson*, 491 U.S. 397 (1989).

47. *Hurley v. Irish-American Gay, Lesbian, and Bisexual Group of Boston*, 515 U.S. 557 (1995).

48. *Hurley v. Irish-American Gay, Lesbian, and Bisexual Group of Boston*, 515 U.S. 557 (1995).

49. See *Lovell v. Griffin*, 303 U.S. 444 (1938).

50. *Reno v. ACLU*, 521 U.S. 844 (1997).

51. *Clark v. Community for Creative Non-Violence*, 468 U.S. 288 (1984).

52. *New York Times v. United States*, 403 U.S. 713 (1971).

53. Abrams v. United States, 250 U.S. 616, 630 (1919) (Holmes, J. dissenting).

54. See *United States v. O'Brien*, 391 U.S. 367 (1968).

55. See *Ward v. Rock Against Racism*, 491 U.S. 781 (1989).

56. Content-based regulations are regulations that approve of certain kinds of speech and frown on others based on the ideas, opinions or viewpoints expressed by the speakers. (*Turner Broadcasting System v. The FCC*, 512 U.S. 622 (1994)).

57. These are regulations that are applicable to all speakers irrespective of their point of view (See *Police Department of Chicago v. Mosley, 408 U.S. 92* (1972) (statute banning all picketing, except labor picketing was ruled unconstitutional).

58. See *Simon and Schuster, Inc. v. Members of the New York State Crime Victims Board*, 502 U.S. 105 (1991) (quoting *Arkansas Writers' Project Inc. v. Ragland*, 481 U.S. 221 (1987)).

59. Content-based regulations are regulations that approve of certain kinds of speech and frown on others based on the ideas, opinions or viewpoints expressed by the speakers. *Turner Broad. Sys. v. The FCC*, 512 U.S. 622 (1994). *See also* Ward v. Rock Against Racism, 491 U.S. 781 (1989).

60. These are regulations that are applicable to all speakers irrespective of their point of view. See *Police Dept. of Chicago v. Mosley*, 408 U.S. 92 (1972) (statute banning all picketing, except labor picketing was unconstitutional content-based regulation subject to First Amendment strict scrutiny).

61. See *Rosenberger v. Rectors of the University of Virginia*, 515 U.S. 819 (1995).

62. See Frederick Schauer, *The Exceptional First Amendment*, *in* American Exceptionalism and Human Rights 29, 45 (Michael Ignatieff, Ed., 2005).

63. *Texas v. Johnson,* 491 U.S. 397 (1989).

64. See Matthew D. Bunker, *Critiquing Free Speech: First Amendment Theory and the Challenge of Interdisciplinarity* 8 (2001) (discussing theories of the First Amendment including Marketplace Theory).

65. Jeffrie G. Murphy & Jules L. Coleman, *Philosophy of Law: An Introduction to Jurisprudence* 86 (rev. Ed., Westview Press 1990).

66. Id.

67. Id. at 87.

68. *R.A.V. v. City of St. Paul*, 505 U.S. 377, 382 (1992) ("[The] First Amendment generally prevents government from proscribing speech . . . because of disapproval of the ideas expressed.") (citation omitted).

69. *Clark v. Community for Creative Non-Violence*, 468 U.S. 288 (1984).

70. *Miller v. Cal.*, 413 U.S. 15 (1973) (setting forth the Miller test which states that in order to declare material obscene, the trier of fact (jury) must ascertain: 1. Whether the average person, applying contemporary community standards, would find that the work, taken as a whole, appeals to the prurient interest; 2. Whether the work depicts/describes, in a patently offensive way, sexual conduct or excretory functions specifically defined by applicable state law, 3. Whether the work, taken as a whole, lacks serious literary, artistic, political, or scientific value.

71. See *Simon and Schuster, Inc. v. Members of the New York State Crime Victims Board*, 502 U.S. 105 (1991) (quoting *Arkansas Writers' Project Inc. v. Ragland*, 481 U.S. 221 (1987)) (Finding that a regulation is content-based and subjecting it to strict scrutiny).

72. *Whitney v. California*, 274 U.S. 357, 375-377 (1927), Brandeis, J. (concurring).

73. See *Abrams v. United States,* 250 U.S. 616 (1919); *Terminiello v. City of Chicago*, 337 U.S. 1 (1949); See also Lyombe Eko, Many Spiders, One World Wide Web: Towards a Typology of Internet Regulation, 6 Communication Law and Policy 445, 465 (2001).

74. Article I, § 7. Constitution of the United States.

75. See *Dean Milk co. v. City of Madison*, 340 U.S. 349 (1951) (regulations that discriminate against interstate commerce violate the Commerce Clause unless they are designed to protect noneconomic goals such as health and safety. See also *Boston Stock Exchange v. State v. State Tax Commission* (state taxes that discriminate against interstate commerce violate the commerce Clause).

76. See *UEJF & LICRA v. Yahoo! Inc.*, Tribunal de grande instance [T.G.I.] [Superior Court] Paris, May 22, 2000, The Clerk of the Chief Justice Christine Bensoam, (Fr.), *available at* http://www.juriscom.net/txt/jurisfr/cti/yauctions20000522.htm) (Holding that Nazi, Third Reich, and other German World War II era memorabilia and relics hosted servers in California and displayed on Yahoo! Auctions, directly contravened French Penal Code provisions against hate speech and hate symbols, and constituted "an offense to the collective memory of a nation [France]").

77. *Clark v. Community For Creative Non-Violence*, 468 U.S. 288 (1984).

78. *In the Matter of Waller v. The City of New York* , 112957/11, NYLJ 1202532602387, 1 (Sup., NY, 2011)

79. Civ. No. 11-4152-G (2011).

80. 468 U.S. 288, 293 (1984). See also Ward v. Rock Against Racism, 491 U.S. 781, 798 (1989).

81. *Miller v. California*, 13 U.S. 15 1973

82. *Chaplinsky v. New Hampshire*, 315 U.S. 568 (1942).

83. *Virginia v. Black*, 538 U.S. 343 (2003).

84. *Village of Hoffman Estates v. Flipside*, 455 U.S. 489 (1982).

85. *New York Times v. Sullivan*, 376 U.S. 254 (1964).

86. *FCC v. Pacifica Foundation,* 438 U.S. 726 (1978).

87. *MGM v. Grokster*, 545 U.S. 913 (2005).

88. Article VI, clause 2, Constitution of the United States.

89. See *Jackson v. Byrne*, 738 F.2d 1443, 1446 (7th cir.1984).

90. See *Reno v. ACLU*, 514 U.S. 844, 885 (1997) (Holding that "As a matter of constitutional tradition, in the absence of evidence to the contrary, we present that governmental regulation of the content of speech is more likely to interfere with the free exchange of ideas than to encourage it." (Stevens, J.) See also Dan Berkowitz and Lyombe Eko, Blasphemy as a Sacred Rite/Right: "The Mohammed Cartoons Affair" and maintenance of journalistic ideology. 8 Jouralism Studies 779, 782 (2007).

91. *Dartmouth College v. Woodward,* 4 Wheaton 518 (1819).

92. *Santa Clara County v. Southern Pacific Railroad*, 118 U.S. 394 (1886) (holding that corporations have equal protection under the law); *Smyth v. Ames*, 169 U.S. 466, 528 (1898) (Holding that corporations have due process rights under the law).

93. Electronic Signatures in Global and National Commerce Act, 15 U.S.C. §7006 (8) (2002).

94. *Bose v. Consumers' Union,* 466 U.S. 485 (1984) (Holding that in order for public figure corporations to collect damages, they must show that the defendant published the defamatory statement with knowledge of falsity or with a reckless disregard of whether the statement was true or false (quoting *New York Times v. Sullivan,* 376 U.S. 279 (1964)).

95. *Citizen's United v. Federal Election Commission,* 558 U.S. 50 (2010).

96. See John Fabian Witt, Debunking a Progressive Constitutional Myth; or, How Corporations Became People, Too. (2012). Available at: http://balkin.blogspot.com/2012/10/debunking-progressive-constitutional.html.

97. John Crabb, The French Civil Code (1977) AT 9.

98. See Konrad Zweigert and Hein Kötz, Introduction to Comparative Law (3rd Ed.) (Tony Weir, trans.) 90 (1998).

99. See Constitution of October 4, 1958. Available at: http://www.assemblee-nationale.fr/english/8ab.asp (The Declaration of the Rights of Man and of the Citizen of 1789 is complemented and completed by the Preamble of the Constitution of 1946, which provides certain egalitarian, economic and social guarantees, as well as the Charter of the Environment of 2004, which makes environmental protection a constitutional issue).

100. See Art. 56 of the Constitution of October 4, 1958. Available at: http://www.assemblee-nationale.fr/english/8ab.asp

101. See Arts. 64 & 65, French Constitution of 1958. Available at: http://www.legifrance.gouv.fr/html/constitution/constitution2.htm#titre2

102. See Sophie Louet, *Nicolas Sarkozy débouté, sa poupée vaudou reste en vente* (Nicolas sarkozy's case dismissed. His Vodoo doll remains on sale). Le Point.FR, October 29, 2008. Available at: http://www.lepoint.fr/actualites/nicolas-sarkozy-deboute-sa-poupee-vaudou-reste-en-vente/1037/0/286725 (Reporting that the Tribunal de grande instance de Paris had dismissed a suit by President Nicolas Sarkozy against a French publisher, seeking to ban a satirical biography of the president that was accompanied by a voodoo doll and pins that could be used to stab the president in effigy. No French court had ever ruled against a sitting French president before.)

103. See Lyombe Eko, Anup Kumar, and Qingjiang Yao, To Google or not to Google: The Google Digital Books Initiative and the Exceptionalist Intellectual Property Law Regimes of the United States and France, 15 *Journal of Internet Law* 11 (2012) (Reporting that late President François Mitterrand's family succeeded in convincing a court to issue a permanent injunction against distribution of a book that allegedly invaded the late president's privacy).

104. See Thomas Paine, In, Edmund Burke, Reflections on the Revolution In France, & Thomas Paine, The Rights of Man 333 (Dolphin, 1961).

105. See Alexis De Tocqueville, The Old Regime and the French Revolution 6 (1855) (trans. Stuart Gilbert (Doubleday, 1955).

106. Id.

107. See Maurice Larkin, Religion, Politics and Preferment in France Since 1890, 5 (1995).

108. See Bernard Spolsky, Language Policy 65 (2004) (Suggesting that under the Jacobin government, equality was more important than liberty).

109. See Frederick Schauer, The Exceptional First Amendment, in Michael Ignatieff (Ed.) American Exceptionalism and Human Rights 46 (2005).

110. See François Furet, Revolutionary France: 1770-1880, at 537 (Antonia Nevill trans., Blackwell Books 1992) (1988).
111. See David Beriss, Culture as Race and Race-as-Culture, in Herrick Chapman And Laura Frader (Eds.), Race in France 115 (2004).
112. See Herrick Chapman and Laura Frader, Race in France, in Herrick Chapman and Laura Frader (Eds.), Race in France 1-2 (2004). See also Lyombe Eko, New Media, Old Regimes: The Historical and Ideological Foundations of French and American Regulation of Bias-Motivated Speech and Expression on the Internet, 28 Loyola International and Comparative Law Review 101-156 (2005), and also Jonathan Laurence and Justin Viasse, Integrating Islam: Political and Religious Challenges in Contemporary France XIII (2006) (Stating that the French political system recognizes only individuals, not groups).
113. See David Beriss, Culture as Race and Race-as-Culture, in Herrick Chapman and Laura Frader (Eds.), Race in France 115 (2004).
114. See Walter Van Gerven, The European Union: A Polity of States and Peoples 242 (2005).
115. See Edgar Morin, *Le trou noir de la laicité* (The black hole of secularism) 58 *Le Débat* 38 (1990).
116. See Pierre Nora, Between Memory and Reason: *Les Lieux de Mémoire* (Sites of Memory), 26 Representations 7, 16 (1989).
117. See Konrad Zweigert and Hein Kötz, Introduction to Comparative Law (3rd Ed.) (Tony Weir, trans.) 74 (1998).
118. See Konrad Zweigert And Hein Kötz, Introduction to Comparative Law (3rd Ed.) (Tony Weir, trans.) 91 (1998).
119. See Pierre Legrand, Fragments on Law-As-Culture 75 (1999).
120. Hachette Filipacchi Associés v. France, decision no. 71111/01, § 58 ECHR 2007, available at: http://cmiskp.echr.coe.int/tkp197/view.asp?action=html&documentId=818892&portal=hbkm&source=externalbydocnumber&table=F69A27FD8FB86142BF01C1166DEA398649 (last visited February 1, 2009).
121. Article XI, Declaration of the Rights of Man and of the Citizen (1789).
122. Article XI (Declaration adopted August 26, 1789).
123. Id. (emphasis added).
124. Id. Articles 4&5.
125. See Lucien Jaume, Entre droit de l'État et droits de la société : le choix de Tocqueville, *Electronic Journal of Constitutional History* (2005). Available at: http://hc.rediris.es/06/articulos/html/Numero06.html?id=15
126. See Robert Goldstein, Censorship of Political Caricature In 19th Century France 39 (1989).
127. See Oliver Larkin, Daumier, Man of His Time 1 (1966).
128. See Pierre Legrand, Le Droit Comparé (Comparative Law) 21 (1999).
129. See Gilles Deleuze And Félix Guattari, *Mille Plateaux* (One Thousand Plateaux) 222-223 (1980).
130. See *Loi du 29 Juillet 1881 Sur la liberté de la presse* (Law of July 29, 1881, Law on Freedom of the Press) J.O. of July 30, 1881, at.4201 (as amended).
131. See art 2, *Loi du 29 Juillet 1881 Sur la liberté de la presse* (Law of July 29, 1881, Law on Freedom of the Press) J.O. of July 30 1881, at 4201 (as amended).
132. See art 24, Law of July 29, 1881 On Freedom of the Press (as amended).
133. Id.
134. Id. Art. 24bis
135. See art 2, *Loi du 29 Juillet 1881 Sur la liberté de la presse* (Law of July 29, 1881 on Freedom of the Press) J.O. of July 30, 1881, at 4201 (as amended).
136. See *Lehideux and Isorni v. France*, European Court of Human Rights, No. 55/1997/839/1045 of September 23, 1998. Publication 1998-VII, no. 92.
137. See Walter Van Gerven, The European Union: A Polity Of States and Peoples 242 (2005).

138. See also Caroline Uyttendaele & Joseph Dumortier, Free Speech on the Information Superhighway: European Perspectives, 16 J. Marshall journal of Computer & Information Law 905 (1998).

139. See arts. 24 & 24 bis, *Loi du 29 Juillet 1881 Sur la liberté de la presse* (Law of July 29, 1881 On Freedom of the Press) J.O. of July 30, 1881, at 4201 (as amended).

140. See *Refah Partisi and others v. Turkey*, No. 41340198, 41342198, 41343198, and 41344198 (2003).

141. See Frederick Schauer, The Exceptional First Amendment, in American Exceptionalism and Human Rights 29, 56 (Michael Ignatieff, Ed., 2005).

Chapter Three

American Exceptionalism and Internet Law

American Exceptionalism

American exceptionalism is the ideological lens through which the United States sees itself as the global beacon of freedom and democracy. It is also the lens through which the United States sees the rest of the world.[1] The worldview of the Framers of the Constitution of the United States was fundamentally different from the worldview of the drafters of the French Declaration of the Rights of Man and of the Citizen of 1789. As we see in chapter 4, the French Revolution was triggered in part by the ideas and ideals of the *philosophes* and influential men of letters. That was not the case in the United States. The Supreme Court of the United States has noted that the Framers of the American Constitution were not metaphysicians and theoreticians given to philosophical speculation.[2] They were not, the Court said, "mere visionaries, toying with speculations or theories, but practical men, dealing with the facts of political life as they understood them, putting into form the government they were creating, and prescribing in language clear and intelligible the powers that government was to take."[3]

Frederick Merck suggests that the United States has historically been a nation with a sense of mission.[4] This mission has evolved over the years from the burning desire of the settlers of the New World to redeem the Old World by sheer example, to freedom of religion, independence, protecting the individual from governmental interference with equality of religion, freedom of speech, press and assembly through the Bill of Rights, the end of slavery, civil rights and so on. Even as this mission metamorphosed, the unchanging fact was that, as Merck puts it, "In all these enlargements of mission, the Goddess of Liberty holding aloft her light to the world seemed to Americans to be, in reality, themselves."[5] American national self-image is therefore grounded in a superiority complex nourished by an ideological narrative whose main tenet is that the United States is the leader of the "free world," the global beacon of freedom and democracy. This historic, providential, and messianic narrative has come to be known as "American exceptionalism."[6] The narrative of American exceptionalism is rooted in the political and religious philosophy of the 17th century Puritan settlers of New England.[7] George McKenna suggests that New England Puritanism sowed the seeds of American exceptionalism because the Puritans believed that New England was a biblical "'City Upon a Hill' whose providential mission entitled it to God's special protection. . . . New Englanders were God's new chosen people, a prophetic army, a model to the world."[8] McKenna suggests that this "patriotic romance" exerted a powerful influence on the emerging American nation. Larry Witham has written that stirring sermons preached by New England Preachers from "pulpits of sedition," against the British colonial administration, as well as "sermonic pamphlets" written by Thomas Paine and others, stoked the flames of the American Revolution.[9] Yankee migration to other parts of what was to become the United States diffused this unquestioned politico-religious patriotism: "Yankee patriotism simply assumed that everything authentically American was built on the foundation of Reformation Protestantism of the kind nurtured in New England."[10] Puritan ideals permeated the American Revolution. The Founding Fathers of the American Republic conceptualized the United States as a new republican constellation in the eighteenth-century "sky" of divine rights kings and absolute monarchs. The stars in the American flag are symbolic representations of this emerging reality. In keeping with the Puritan "sacred mission," of the country, the United States considered itself a beacon of liberty; the Biblical "Salt for all mankind . . . the Light of the World . . . and the City Upon a Hill that cannot be hid."[11]

After independence, the emerging American political parties had exceptionalist ideals. The Whig Party, one of the ancestors of the Republican Party, was called the "Ghost of Puritanism," while an influential journalistic advocate of the Democratic Party advanced a variant of exceptionalism, "manifest destiny," in the *Democratic Review*.[12] Manifest destiny was the notion that the United States was destined by "the God of Heaven," "Providence" to occupy the whole of North America, create a free continent-wide confederated republic, spread the fruits of liberty, civilization, and religion, and "manifest the excellence of divine principles to mankind."[13] In time, the ideology and mission of manifest destiny evolved into an internationalist ideology that appropriated the original mission of the Puritans of the New World—America was the beacon of freedom that would save not only the Old World, but the whole world through exemplary democratic republican governance. American manifest destiny had morphed subtly into American exceptionalism. Alexis de Tocqueville, the astute observer of American democracy, described the components of American exceptionalism in his classic work, *Democracy in America*. He stated that the United States differed qualitatively from the Divine rights monarchies of eighteenth-century Europe because of its unique origins in austere New England Puritanism, its personal freedoms, distinctive political institutions and religiosity.[14] The *laissez-faire,* free enterprise economic system of the United States is a legacy of exceptionalism. The main tenet of contemporary American exceptionalism is that American laws and democratic system are unique and unparalleled in human history.[15] All American presidents—from George Washington through Abraham Lincoln to Teddy Roosevelt, Franklin Delano Roosevelt, Ronald Reagan, George W. Bush, and even Barack Obama have used exceptionalist rhetoric in their foreign and domestic policy pronouncements.[16] For example, President Theodore Roosevelt, who had a messianic view of the role of the United States in global affairs, expressed American exceptionalism in the first part of the twentieth century:

> We, here in America, hold in our hands the hope of the world, the fate of the coming years; and shame and disgrace will be ours if in our eyes the light of high resolve is dimmed, if we trail in the dust the golden hopes of men. . . . The worth of our great experiment depends upon its being in good faith an experiment—the first that has ever been tried—in true democracy on the scale of a continent, on a scale as vast as that of the mightiest empires of the Old World.[17]

The political manifestation of American exceptionalism is "Americanism," an ideology that is expressed in terms of "anti-statism, individualism, populism, and egalitarianism."[18] Michael Hunt ascribes a nationalistic underpinning to America's foreign policy ideology when he describes it as "the quest for greatness coupled with the promotion of liberty."[19] For his part, former Secretary of State Henry Kissinger summarized America's foreign policy ideology as a policy which reflected the "uniqueness of America's mission as an exemplar of liberty . . . the moral superiority of democratic foreign policy."[20] Indeed, the United States has always believed that it had been blessed with a "unique and ultimately superior dispensation" that precludes it from entangling itself lightly in international treaties.[21] Today, the United States considers itself as the "leader of the free world," whose exceptional mission is to spread freedom and democracy to all parts of the world.[22]

American "Exemptionalism"

The corollary of exceptionalism is what John Gerard Ruggie calls "exemptionalism."[23] This is the notion that self-described, exceptionalist countries usually exempt themselves from international treaties or provisions of international treaties that they perceive to run counter to their exceptionalist ideologies or exceptional constitutional values. The United States has had an exemptionist policy in international affairs since the end of World War I. American exceptionalism is illustrated by the country's stance towards the Post World War I Treaty of Versailles, and the League of Nations that was formed in an effort to maintain peace through collective security. Despite the fact that President Woodrow Wilson spearheaded the post-war collective security arrangements, the United States did not join the League of Nations because the Senate exempted the United States from certain provisions of the Treaty of Versailles of 1919, as well as the collective security arrangements concluded within the framework of that treaty. American non-adherence led to the collapse of the League of Nations.

After World War II, the United States was instrumental in launching the post–World War II international human rights regime as the instrument for the universalization of American constitutional values of freedom, while simultaneously resisting any reciprocal influence from the international community.[24] American exceptionalism was apparent in the negotiations that led to the adoption of the United Nations Universal Declaration of Human Rights in 1948. Mrs. Eleanor Roosevelt, Chairwoman of the United Nations Commission on Human Rights, and Representative of the United States to the U.N. General Assembly, was one of the principal architects of the Universal Declaration of Human Rights. When the Declaration was adopted, she hailed it as a "Magna Carta" for the world. However, she insisted that the Declaration was neither a treaty nor a binding international legal agreement. According to Eleanor Roosevelt and the United States government, the declaration was certainly **not** "a statement of law or of legal obligation" that would bind the United States, or its European allies.[25] The United States did not want to be bound by the principles of the Universal Declaration of Human Rights, which would have required it to end institutionalized racial discrimination and segregation that was the law of the land in certain parts of the United States. The United States therefore exempted itself from the provisions of the declaration, essentially reducing it to a non-binding hortatory sermon intended for consumption by the "rest of the world." Roosevelt's stance fatally compromised the very foundations of the Declaration of Human Rights and sowed the seeds of disrespect for human rights that are still evident in the 21st century.

The exceptionalist/exemptionalist posture of the Roosevelt administration has continued ever since as a characteristic of American foreign policy. The United States has led the world in promoting human rights by negotiating international human rights conventions and treaties, only to exempt itself from their provisions through either expressing reservations regarding specific provisions, not ratifying some treaties or not complying with them under the theory that American constitutional values are superior to international human rights values.[26] The result is that since the end of World War II, communication between the United States and the international community has been a one-way affair, for the most part. International communication and human rights policy has generally diffused from the United States to the international community. Very few policies transfers have diffused from the international community to the United States.

While American exceptionalism has always been a feature of American foreign policy, it came to the fore in the 1970s during diplomatic negotiations leading up to United Nations General Assembly adoption of the International Covenant on Civil and Political Rights, and subsequent ratification of the Covenant by UN member-states. In effect, the United States objected to a number of articles of the Covenant, specifically, articles 19 and 20, which state:

1. Everyone shall have the right to hold opinions without interference.
2. Everyone shall have the right to freedom of expression; this right shall include freedom to seek, receive and impart information and ideas of all kinds, regardless of frontiers, either orally, in writing or in print, in the form of art, or through any other media of his choice.
3. The exercise of the rights provided for in paragraph 2 of this article carries with it special duties and responsibilities. It may therefore be subject to certain restrictions, but these shall only be such as are provided by law and are necessary:

a. For respect of the rights or reputations of others;
b. For the protection of national security or of public order, or of public health or morals.

ARTICLE 20

1. Any propaganda for war shall be prohibited by law.
2. Any advocacy of national, racial or religious hatred that constitutes incitement to discrimination, hostility or violence shall be prohibited by law.[27]

The United States let it be known that it interpreted these provisions as making freedom of speech and expression subservient to the maintenance of law and order, prevention of defamation, suppression of the advocacy of bias-motivated communication or hate speech against specific national, religious or ethnic groups, as well as the abolition of propaganda for war, this international stance flew in the face of the 'exceptionalist" First Amendment. As a result, when the United States ratified the Covenant, it specifically exempted itself from these and other vague and overbroad provisions. At any rate, since human rights treaties are considered non-self executing under American law,[28] it appears that signature and ratification of the International Covenant on Civil and Political Rights of 1966 was nothing but an exercise in public diplomacy.[29]

American Exceptionalism and Human Rights

Frederick Schauer calls the United States the "recalcitrant outlier" of the international human rights regime. He suggests that the United States has made values of health, privacy, safety, civility, respect and dignity subservient to "the paramount constitutional concerns with freedom of speech and freedom of the press."[30] The result is that the United States has a rights tradition that is more protective of speakers' rights than any other legal tradition in the world. Several explanations have been advanced for American exceptionalism in international affairs. The United States has a traditional judicial wariness about laws from the United Nations and other international institutions, "a perceived need to safeguard the special features and protections of the U.S. Constitution from external interference," as John Gerard Ruggie put it.[31] There are claims that exceptionalism is a manifestation of a concerted American attempt to minimize international human rights constraints on its sovereignty. It is also said that American exceptionalism reflects the desire for a "messianic" moral leadership of the world, as well as the existence of politico-legal institutions designed by the Founding Fathers to insulate citizens from governmental and foreign treaty encroachments on their liberties. Additionally, strong domestic political constituencies opposed to international legal entanglements that are viewed as constrains on the freedoms of Americans ensure that the United States maintains a skeptical attitude towards other legal systems and regimes. Schauer suggests that differences between the United States and Europe in matters of freedom of speech may simply reflect different stages in the development of the constitutional rights and the legal trappings of the right of freedom of speech.[32] For his part, Michael Ignatieff suggests that the United States has maintained an exceptionalist human rights posture because exceptionalism ensures that as the world's sole hegemon, the United States, can engage with the international human rights system on its own terms.[33] The most notable and unprecedented instance of counter-diffusion of human rights policy occured in the wake of the Mohammed cartoons controversy of 2005/2006.[34] In effect, for the first time in American history, the Obama administration put its imprimatur on U.N. resolutions condemming the "defamation of religion." This was a radical departure from American exceptionalism.

American Exceptionalism and Regulation of the Internet

The invention of the Internet, a "system of systems" or network of computer networks exchanging information in self-contained packets,[35] and invention of the World Wide Web at the European Center for Nuclear Research (CERN),[36] created a virtual, interconnected, interactive, global, multi-communication sphere with multiple platforms. The United States took a decidedly exceptionalist posture towards the fledgling network of computer networks when Congress passed the Scientific and Advanced Technology Act of 1992.[37] This act authorized the National Science Foundation "to foster and support access by the research and education communities to computer networks which may be used substantially for purposes in addition to research and education in the sciences and engineering." The act encouraged partnerships between the research community, the government and industry to revitalize information technology.[38] This law essentially opened up the non-military parts of the Internet, which had hitherto been the domain of academic researchers and computer science enthusiasts, to commercial, educational, cultural, economic, social, entertainment, and other activities. Juan Rogers argues that the Internet developed out of America's unique (exceptionalist) governmentality of science; the "knowledge triangle" of collaboration between federal government research and development programs, academia, and the telecommunications and computer industries.[39] It is interesting that when Congress officially regulated the network of networks that had come to be known as the "Internet," within the framework of the Telecommunications Act of 1996, it defined the "Internet" as: "the international computer network of both Federal and non-Federal interoperable packet switched data networks."[40] Later, we shall see that as the Internet diffused to the rest of the world, the United States played a key role in setting up the regulatory architecture of the new communication sphere for the rest of the world.

The Communications Act of 1934 regulates the telecommunications system and the electromagnetic spectrum (the airwaves) in the United States. The fundamental premise of the Communications Act is that the airwaves belong to the people, therefore regulation of telecommunications and broadcasting in the United States must be carried out in the "public interest, convenience and necessity."[41] Furthermore, due to the scarcity of the broadcast spectrum, the federal government regulates over-the-air broadcasting (radio and television) more stringently than cablecasting and direct broadcast satellites, which do not have the same physical constraints.[42]

Early in the 1990s, American courts ruled that the Internet should be regulated within the framework of the Commerce Clause,[43] and soon thereafter, the Supreme Court of the United States transferred the Commerce Clause and First Amendment regulatory regimes of the United States to the virtual world of the Internet.[44] Under this regime, the Internet has the same level of freedom as the print media. That is to say, the government may not impose a regime of prior restraints or censorship on the Internet unless the regulation furthers a substantial government interest that has nothing to do with the suppression of freedom of expression. The Internet has since become a fundament instrumentality of interstate and international commerce. However, the Federal Communications Commission (FCC) does not have the authority to impose net neutrality[45] as a way of regulating the broadband network management practices of Internet Service Providers "traffic-shaping" that give priority to certain types of Internet traffic while slowing down other types of traffic like peer-to-peer file-sharing and pornography.[46] Taken together, these measures have led to a market-based system in which the telecommunications network of networks is dominated by a few big multinational telecommunications, information and communication technology corporations. However, the Internet is the seed-bed of innovation that has seen the emergence of a dizzying array of start-ups.

American Exceptionalism and the Internet Domain Name System

In another exceptionalist move, the United States Department of Commerce transferred management of the Domain Name System (DNS) of the Internet to a non-profit corporation, the Internet Corporation for Assigned Names and Numbers (ICANN). The government wanted the Internet Domain Name System to be managed under principles of stability, competition, bottom-up coordination, and representation.[47] ICANN was created to operate the activities of the Internet Assigned Numbers Authority (IANA), an American organization responsible for the central coordination and management of key parts of the architecture of the global Internet, including domain names, number resources and Internet Protocol (IP) assignments. As the Internet diffused to all parts of the world within the framework set forth by IANA and ICANN, the new multi-communication platform came to be seen as an instrument of American geo-political, geo-strategic, and cultural domination.[48] For example, as the Internet grew, and Russia felt threatened by it, President Vladimir Putin issued the "Information Security Doctrine of the Russian Federation." Its aim was to "thwart the desire of some countries to dominate and infringe upon the interests of Russia in the world information space and to oust it from the external and internal information markets."[49]

Russia was not the only country that felt threatened by the Internet. French ambivalence, hostility, and eventual lukewarm embrace of the Internet is a thematic thread that runs through this book. Many other countries shared these misgivings about American domination of the Internet. Over the years, the international community has made attempts to break what was perceived to be America's stranglehold on the Internet through control of ICANN, and the Internet's root server system. The phrase "Internet governance" was used unsuccessfully to advance the notion of shared international governance of the Internet Root Server System. These ideas were prevalent during World Summits on the Information Society (WSIS) organized by the International Telecommunications Union in Geneva and Tunis, Tunisia.[50]

Internet governance was also a major issue at the World Conference on International Telecommunications (WCIT), which was held in Dubai in 2012. The conference, whose aim was to arrive at new International Telecommunication Regulations (ITRs) aimed at "facilitating global interconnection and interoperability of telecommunication facilities and to promoting the harmonious development and efficient operation of technical facilities," was supposed to result in a global treaty enshrining new International Telecommunication Regulations (ITRs). Such an agreement was necessitated by developments in the field of information and communication technologies. The conference did not end in a consensus. A number of countries insisted that issues of "Internet governance"—and that has become shorthand for international control of the architecture and content of the Internet—be included in the treaty. Even though the new International Telecommunication Regulations (ITRs) adopted by the conference clearly state that these new ITRs do not address content-related aspects of telecommunications, many countries, including the United States, refused to sign the final treaty that came out of WCIT 2012. They felt that the new International Telecommunications Regulations had strayed into governance and content issues when they should have been confined to infrastructural rules and regulations. In effect, the United States and other countries believed that even a benign provision against unwanted bulk electronic mail (spam) could be used to block other categories of objectionable Internet content.[51]

The posture of the United States in the face of these challenges has been exceptionalist. The United States has actively promoted the goals of WSIS conferences—diffusion of the Internet around the world, the right of universal access to the Internet, and bridging of the digital divide between the rich and poor countries of the world, but it has resolutely resisted the so-called "co-regulatory" approach that would have required the United States to share control and management of the critical parts of the architecture of the Internet as demanded by China, Russia, and other countries.[52]

Transferring Exceptional First Amendment Values to the Internet: *Reno v. ACLU*

While Congress granted the Internet implicit First Amendment protection under the Communications Decency Act (CDA) of 1996, it was a case challenging another aspect of the CDA that enabled the Supreme Court of the United States to bring the Internet within the ambit of the First Amendment on the same level as the traditional print media. As pornography and other material appealing to prurient tastes began its massive migration from real space to the Internet, Congress wrote two provisions into the CDA with the intended of protecting minors from harmful online content. These provisions criminalized 1) the knowing transmission of obscene and indecent material to minors under eighteen years of age, and 2) the knowing transmission of material that describes in patently offensive terms, sexual or excretory activities or organs.[53] Several organized interest groups including commercial pornographers, filed suit challenging the constitutionality of these two provisions.[54] The U.S. District Court for the Western District of Pennsylvania issued an injunction against enforcement of both provisions of the act on the grounds that they violated the First Amendment by reason of their vagueness and over-breadth.[55] The Government appealed to the Supreme Court of the United States. The issue before the Court was whether the two contested provisions of the Communications Decency Act violated the freedom of speech guaranteed by the First and 14th Amendments. The Court held that they did, and ruled that the two provisions in question were an imprecise, content-based, blanket restriction that had the potential of censoring speech that adults had a constitutional right to receive and impart.[56] The Court, however, allowed the government to investigate and prosecute obscenity and child pornography on the Internet. The main outcome of this case is that the Court ruled for the first time that the Internet had full First Amendment protection. Due to the global nature of the Internet, the Court essentially globalized America's exceptional free speech values.[57] The United States has since developed a market-based Internet regulatory regime, which combines several libertarian principles— the marketplace of ideas, *laissez-faire* economics, free trade and the free flow of information.[58]

Internet Service Provider Liability for Third Party Content

Once the Internet showed promise as a vibrant platform for First Amendment activities, Internet and computer service providers were faced with threats of legal action for the material they made available through providing Internet access to their customers, or liability for material they hosted on their servers. Some parties thought some of the material on the fledgling Internet was illegal, morally objectionable, or violated their intellectual property rights. Threats of legal action against the Internet and other computer service providers posed a serious threat to the fledgling network of computer networks. In order to remedy the situation, Congress acted by defining computer service providers who hosted unedited bulletin boards or other forums as distributors of publications like libraries or bookstores, which carry all kinds of books whose content they have no knowledge of.[59] Congress granted Internet Service Providers and computer service providers immunity from legal action under section 230 of the Communications Decency Act of 1996, which states in part:

> (1) **Treatment of publisher or speaker**
> No provider or user of an interactive computer service shall be treated as the publisher or speaker of any information provided by another information content provider.[60]

In this act, Congress essentially granted American Internet Service Providers (ISPs) immunity from liability for providing access to, or hosting objectionable or even illegal third party Internet content if they did not participate in the production of the content or were not aware of it. The contours of this immunity have been defined and affirmed in a number of cases. In *Zeran v. America On Line (AOL)*, the 4th Circuit held that Section 230 immunized computer service providers like AOL from liability for information that originated with third parties.[61] In *Carafano v. Metrosplash.com, Inc.*, the 9th Circuit held that "an 'interactive computer service' qualifies for immunity as long as it does not also function as an 'information content provider' for the portion of the statement or publication at issue."[62] In *Blumenthal v. Drudge*, a court held that America Online (AOL) was immune from liability under section 230 of the Communications Decency Act despite contracting with, and promoting the activities of, a gossip columnist and rumor monger, absent evidence that AOL "had some role in writing or editing the material" in the gossip column.[63]

American Exceptionalism and Electronic Commerce

As the Internet became an increasingly popular multi-communication and commercial platform the United States continued to define its perimeters through regulation. The United States soon placed its exceptionalist imprint on the Internet in the issue area of electronic commerce or online business. In 1997, the Clinton-Gore administration offered the world a mercantilist vision and framework for the expansion and regulation of communication in the increasingly commercialized online environment. This market-based "Framework for Electronic Commerce" contained an appeal to governments around the world to assume a minimalist regulatory posture towards electronic commerce.[64] This *laissez-faire* regulatory model bore the hallmarks of American exceptionalism. It was grounded on several libertarian principles, namely, First Amendment protection of speech and expression,[65] free trade,[66] the market place of ideas,[67] the free flow of information,[68] as well as the free flow of goods and services across state lines and international borders under the Commerce Clause of the U.S. Constitution.[69] The aim of the framework was to create a seamless global electronic economy in which the fluid flow of goods, services, information, intellectual property goods, and capital would be the norm.[70] Under this exceptionalist framework, the role of governments would be limited to creating an enabling regulatory environment that would facilitate commerce on the Internet. Needless to say, countries around the world did not flock to this American conceptualization of Internet regulation. Many nation-states opted for their own models. A thread that runs through this volume is that France declined to follow the exceptionalist posture of the United States, opting instead to transfer *l'exception française* to the Internet and its multiple platforms.

American Exceptionalism and Electronic Signatures

Transformation of the Internet into a global information, multi-communication and e-commerce space in the 1990s led to a need for increased security—defined as confidentiality, integrity, and availability of computer systems and databases.[71] One solution to the problem was the use of electronic or e-signatures in communications and electronic commerce. Electronic signatures range from typed e-mail signatures to digital signatures (a unique string of numbers or characters, or a combination of both) that are linked to another series of numbers generated through complex mathematical algorithms or operations made possible by encryption technology.[72] The Clinton-Gore framework for Electronic Commerce discussed above anticipated legislation on electronic signatures. Software and infrastructures would ensure the security and reliability of Internet banking transactions, data protection, messaging, individual privacy, and authentification. The policy of linkage of information and communication technologies with the free market was advanced by the Clinton administration, was officially endorsed by the United Nations, and transferred to the rest of the world within the framework of the work of the United Nations Commission on International Trade Law (UNCITRAL). Harmonization of the international electronic commerce and electronic signature regimes therefore took place within the auspices of the UNCITRAL, because it was a specialized agency of the United Nations. This agency was set up in 1966 to promote the progressive harmonization and unification of international trade law.[73] In effect, the major industrialized and emerging economies of the world realized that in order for electronic commerce and network security to be a global reality, all countries had to harmonize their different, often contrasting network technologies and security regimes. Pursuant to this mandate, UNCITRAL transferred international trade law designed for real space to the dematerialized reality of cyberspace. It set out to bring the multi-billion dollar global electronic commerce industry within the ambit of international trade law through the transfer of two model laws—the UNCITRAL Model Law on Electronic Commerce,[74] and the UNCITRAL Model Law on Electronic Signatures—to countries around the world.[75] As the leading member and active participant in UNCITRAL

Working Groups, the United States was instrumental in drafting and transferring the UNCITRAL Model Laws to other countries. The provisions of these model laws essentially globalized the *laissez-faire,* neo-merchantilist values of the Commerce Clause of the Constitution of the United States.[76] Nevertheless, the model laws were only recommendations. They were not binding under international law. However, the fact that they were adopted as U.N. General Assembly resolutions gave them a cachet of international legitimacy. Most of the provisions of these laws have been transferred to countries around the world.[77]

The Electronic Signatures in Global and National Commerce (E–Sign) Act

In 2000 Congress passed the Electronic Signatures in Global and National Commerce (E–Sign) Act, which stipulated that the United States would "[t]ake a nondiscriminatory approach to electronic signatures and authentication methods from other jurisdictions."[78] The E–Sign law incorporates principles of the UNCITRAL Model Law on Electronic Signatures that are consonant with American law and interests. The E-Sign law explicitly mentions UNCITRAL and gives the Secretary of Commerce the responsibility of actively promoting the model law around the world.[79] This total acceptance of a United Nations' model law is so unusual that one could conclude that the United States had jettisoned its traditional suspicion of international agreements; that is to say, its exceptionalism, and harmonized its electronic commerce laws with the UNCITRAL model laws. However, on closer examination, it is clear that the E–Sign Act did not represent legal or policy transfers from the United Nations to the United States. The reverse is true. The Act transferred American free trade values from real space to cyberspace and globalized them.

The E-Sign Act also represents a departure from classic American exceptionalism in the issue area of electronic signatures. In contrast to what we have seen in the field of human rights, the United States took the lead in drafting the Model Laws on E-Commerce and Electronic Signatures, successfully lobbied for them to be adopted by United Nations General Assembly resolutions, and proceeded to modify American law to bring it abreast of the norms set forth in the UNCITRAL model laws. The American E-Sign Act that emerged from this process essentially harmonized American electronic signature laws with international norms, which are . . . essentially American. The United States was able to accomplish this feat for several reasons. Due to its technological advantage—the basic infrastructure and core protocols of the Internet were invented within the framework of the research and development initiatives of the Advanced Research Projects Agency of the United States Department of Defense. The United States therefore controls the Internet Root Server system, while American hardware and software are the bedrock of the infrastructures, networks, electronic commerce, electronic security, and the multi-media, business, financial, cultural, economic, social and entertainment platforms, and databases of the Internet.

These realities made the United States the dominant country in the Working Groups that drafted the UNCITRAL Model laws. It can be argued that in the domain of electronic commerce and electronic signatures, the United Nations and its specialized agency, UNCITRAL play only, to borrow David Nelken's expression, "mediating institutional roles"[80] between the United States and the rest of the world. The United Nations was simply an instrument for the globalization of America's free-market Internet regulatory regime. The cooperative posture of the United States on matters of electronic commerce and electronic signature regulation stands in stark contrast to its unilateralism in matters of human rights and the environment.

Additionally, America's *laissez faire* e-commerce posture has a national security exception with regard to electronic signature encryption technology.[81] Despite the fact that the United States has eased restrictions on the export or re-export of strong encryption technology that can be used in e-commerce and other activities,[82] the Russian Federation, China and other countries still face major restrictions on importing and re-exporting American strong encryption technology due to American national security reasons. Indeed, export or re-export from the United States of virtually all strong encryption technology that performs an "information security function," still has to be licensed or specifically approved by the Department of Commerce,[83] and the Department of the Treasury.[84] American companies that intend to make such technology available to their foreign workforce are required to obtain governmental approval. This has led to differences of opinion between the computer industry and the United States government over restrictions on the export of encryption technology[85] that drives the instrumentalities of electronic commerce and electronic signatures. The industry is especially unhappy about restrictions that have removed American strong data-encryption technologies beyond 56-bit encryption from the open international market.[86] Thus, United States participation in the UNCITRAL process demonstrates exceptionalism and a high sense of national self-interest, since the U.S. promotes global harmonization of electronic commerce and electronic signatures while it jealously guards its electronic signature technologies, its sovereignty and its markets.[87]

American Exceptionalism and Computer-Generated Pedopornography

There is a fundamental conceptual difference between the United States and the international community with regard to the crucial issue of the distinction between real human children that are the subject of pedopornography (child pornography) and virtual, computer-generated "video game" children developed by pornographers through computer animation and artificial intelligence, and used as virtual avatars or actors in certain types of pedopornography. The problem is compounded by the fact that producers of artificial pedopornography may or may not use images of real children as their models. The United Nations Convention on the Rights of the Child and its Optional Protocol on the Sale of Children, Child Prostitution and Child Pornography are silent on the issue due to its novelty. Computer-generated child pornography and the graphics, animation and artificial intelligence technologies that drive it are relatively new, and evolve rapidly. The presumption of the international community seems to be that child pornography of all kinds causes moral and psychological harm and is therefore illegal. Inasmuch as such material can lead to a loss of innocence and premature sexualization of children, or can be used to entice children to engage in sexual activities, they violate the human rights standards of the Convention on the Rights of the Child. As part of its exceptionalist posture, the United States has not ratified the United Nations Convention on the Rights of the Child, though it has signed the non-binding Optional Protocol on the Sale of Children, Child Prostitution, and Child Pornography. Certain provisions are thought to violate the First Amendment and other Constitutional Provisions.

The Council of Europe makes no distinction between real and virtual pedopornography. In the European Council Framework Decision On Combating the Sexual Exploitation of Children and Child Pornography, the Council calls on member countries to criminalize depictions of "a real person *appearing* to be a child involved or engaged in" child pornography unless that person is eighteen years of age or older.[88] Furthermore, the Council called on all its member-states to criminalize virtual or computer-generated child pornography, which includes "realistic images of a *non-existent child* involved or engaged in sexually explicit conduct."[89]

For its part, the United States regulates Internet content within the framework of its First Amendment free speech jurisprudence. Under the First Amendment, "free speech"—in the widest sense of the term—takes precedence over metaphysical issues like morality, decency, and human dignity.[90] It also takes precedence over considerations of the negative impact of speech on those to whom the speech is directed.[91] Under the First Amendment, pedopornography is a form of speech because the mass media are the major platforms for its production, dissemination, and storage. The question is whether such "speech" is legal. By failing to ratify the United Nations Convention on the Rights of the Child, the United States suggests that its domestic child pornography regulations under the First Amendment are superior to the international child protection regime. America's exceptionalist disdain for certain policies from the United Nations and other international jurisdictions is still evident in domestic law.[92]

In 2003, in the case *Ashcroft v. Free Speech Coalition*, the Supreme Court of the United States ruled that the Child Pornography Prevention Act (CPPA) of 1996, which had criminalized virtual or computer-generated pedopornography was unconstitutional. In effect, organized interest groups, led by the adult pornography industry (The Free Speech Coalition) had challenged the CPPA's constitutional validity. The issue before the Court in *Ashcroft v. Free Speech Coalition* was whether the CPPA violated free speech under the First Amendment. The Supreme Court of the United States said it did and decided that only pedopornography that utilized real children was illegal under the First Amendment. In a decision that reinforced American exceptionalism in matters of freedom of expression, the Court said that non-obscene,[93] computer-generated "video game" images and computer animations of artificial "children" engaging in sexual acts with adults or with other children were protected by the First Amendment. This stunning decision essentially decriminalized realistic "video game-style" pedopornography that did not involve real children. The Court's decision may have compromised United States support for, and participation in global law enforcement activities against computer-generated pedopornography since international treaties are subject to the provisions of the Bill of Rights.[94] Additionally, America's exceptionalist conceptualization of "harm" is also very evident in this decision. The idea is that since video-game "children" cannot be harmed, computer-generated pedopornography is harmless "speech." As noted above, American First Amendment exceptionalism pays scant attention to issues of morality, decency and human dignity.

American Exceptionalism and Intellectual Property

American exceptionalism is very pronounced in the field of intellectual property. It also manifests itself in two forms: 1) American copyright jurisprudence is grounded in a unique incentive philosophy set forth in the Constitution of the United States, and 2) the copyright regime is inextricably linked to the country's First Amendment freedom of speech regime that has been described as exceptional.[95] This linkage is realized through a series of limitations on exclusive copyright monopolies. In effect, American exceptionalism in copyright is expressed in utilitarian terms: the Constitution of the United States stipulates that the function of copyright is: "To promote the progress of science and useful arts, by securing for limited times to authors and inventors the exclusive right to their respective writings and discoveries."[96] Conceptualization of the institution of copyright as an instrument for the betterment of society is what Richard Posner calls "the incentive purpose" of copyright.[97] Indeed, Posner suggests that in the Anglo-American tradition, copyright was historically granted to authors for limited periods because of governmental antipathy towards granting monopolies.[98] William Roeder aptly summarized copyright theory and law in the United States when he said: "[C]opyright in America, as limited by statute, was designed to protect only the exploitative value of creation; its protection is not granted to the creator as such, but to the owner, the person having the power to exploit the creation."[99] The Copyright Act of 1976 focuses first and foremost on the subject matter of copyright, granting protection to "original works of authorship fixed in any tangible medium of expression."[100] Though American law recognizes authors as repositories of copyright,[101] the underlying principle of copyright law is not so much validation of the institution of the author, his or her rights, and his or her role in the cultural life of society—as is the case in France—but utilitarian "bettermentality," the benefits that ultimately accrue to society from granting copyright protection to creative persons.[102] The Supreme Court of the United States has held that the ultimate objective of copyright is to "stimulate artistic creativity for the general public good."[103] The Court reiterated this utilitarian or public good justification of copyright in *Feist Publications Inc. v. Rural Telephone Service Co:* "[T]he primary objective of copyright is not to reward the labor of authors, but [t]o promote the Progress of Science and useful Arts."[104] The *Feist* Court ultimately rejected the existential, Biblical, "sweat of thy brow" principle,[105] which had granted copyright to facts and directly linked copyright to the labor expended by authors. Furthermore, as Lange and Powell suggest, by its very nature and subject matter, copyright touches on, and coexists rather harmoniously with expression protected by the First Amendment: "the stuff from which intellectual property interests are spun is also the stuff of First Amendment interests."[106] In order to underline the link between copyright and freedom of expression, the Supreme Court of the United States has held that the Framers of the Constitution intended for copyright to serve as "the engine of free expression."[107] Therefore, American copyright law has substantial exceptionalist free speech dimensions that are expressed in terms of fair use. This fundamental principle is set forth in the fair use provision of the Copyright Act of 1976:

> the fair use of a copyrighted work, including such use by reproduction in copies or phono records or by any other means specified by that section, for purposes such as criticism, comment, news reporting, teaching (including multiple copies for classroom use), scholarship, or research, is not an infringement of copyright.[108]

Fair use is also an affirmative defense in circumstances where existing works are appropriated for purposes of creating new, transformative, critical works. Parody is a notable category of transformative works protected by the First

Amendment because it is a vehicle for politico-social criticism.[109] This is one instance in which freedom of speech clearly takes precedence over exclusive copyright. However, fair use is only an affirmative defense available to the fair use claimant who is accused of infringing on exclusive intellectual property rights.[110] Fair use is an important limitation on the copyright monopoly. In order to make a determination whether a fair use claim is valid, Federal courts employ these four fair use factors set forth in the Copyright Act of 1976:

1. the purpose and character of the use, including whether such use is of a commercial nature or is for nonprofit educational purposes;
2. the nature of the copyrighted work;
3. the amount and substantiality of the portion used in relation to the copyrighted work as a whole; and
4. the effect of the use upon the potential market for or value of the copyrighted work.[111]

As a result of American exceptionalism in intellectual property law, the country has had to reconcile its philosophical orientations with the need to harmonize its laws with the international community in this interconnected, global environment. The first major steps at aligning American law with international intellectual property regime took place within the framework of the World Intellectual Property Organization (WIPO). The first piece of major harmonizing legislation under the WIPO regime was the Digital Millennium Copyright Act of 1998 (DMCA),[112] through which the United States harmonized certain provisions of its laws for purposes of implementing the WIPO Copyright Treaty of 1996. Furthermore, the United States passed the Copyright Term Extension Act of 2006 (CTEA)[113] to increase the duration of copyright protection for newly created works by twenty years, as well as to lengthen the duration of copyright protection for works published under the Copyright Act of 1976. When the CTEA was challenged, the Supreme Court of the United States held that one of the purposes of enacting the CTEA was to harmonize American law with the European Union directive harmonizing the term of protection of copyright that had been passed ten years earlier.[114] The court ruled that this harmonization did not violate the American Constitution.

American governmental support for international policy transfer and harmonization took place over the objection of academic and other interest group litigants who saw modification of American copyright law for purposes of participating in international intellectual property harmonization initiatives as being contrary to American intellectual property law and First Amendment specificity. When these intellectual property interest groups lost the battle against copyright term extensions—and by extension international intellectual property harmonization—they opened another front in the battle. In *Luck's Music Library, Inc. & MovieCraft, Inc. v. Gonzales,* record company and other interest group litigants challenged the constitutionality of section 514 of the Uruguay Round Agreement Act (URAA), which had restored, under pressure from the European Union, the copyright of foreign works that had already fallen in the public domain in the United States.[115] The issue before the Federal District Court for the D.C. Circuit was whether section 514 of the URAA violated the Copyright Clause, and the First Amendment guarantee of freedom of speech. The argument of the plaintiffs was that by reaching into the public domain and removing works that could serve as the basis of other works, Congress was acting against its constitutional mandate "to promote the progress of science and the useful arts by securing for limited Times to Authors and Inventors the exclusive Right to their respective Writings and Discoveries."[116] Additionally, the plaintiffs argued that the URAA violated First Amendment guarantees of freedom of speech and due process of law. In other words, the United States District Court for the District of Columbia had to decide whether the section of the law in question violated American exceptionalism with respect to First Amendment protections granted to material in the public domain. The *Luck's Music* court rejected the arguments of the plaintiff music companies on the grounds that section 514 of URAA did not violate the Copyright Clause, and did not interfere with the First Amendment rights of the plaintiffs since they could still avail themselves of the fair use provisions of the Copyright Act.[117] In other words, the courts stated that section 514 had not trampled American exceptionalism under foot. On appeal, the United States Court of Appeals, District of Columbia reviewed the case *de novo* and affirmed on other grounds.[118]

The First Amendment, International Intellectual Property Harmonization and the Public Domain

Meanwhile, parallel legal action challenging section 514 of URAA commenced in the United States District Court for the District of Colorado the same year *Luck's Music* was decided. In *Golan v. Ashcroft,*[119] the court dismissed claims that section 514 of URAA violated the Copyright Clause, the First Amendment, and the Due Process Clause of the 14th Amendment. On appeal, the 10th Circuit Court of Appeals affirmed. In *Golan v. Gonzales*, (Gonzales had replaced Ashcroft as Attorney General) the U.S. District Court for the District of Colorado ruled that Congressional action in removing material from the public domain was not unprecedented.[120] The 10th Circuit Court of Appeals reversed in part, finding that section 514: "has altered the traditional contours of copyright protection in a manner that implicates plaintiffs' right to free expression"[121] and remanded for constitutional scrutiny. On remand, the issue before the United States District Court was whether the plaintiffs' asserted First Amendment interests in using works in the public domain that had been removed by section 514 of URAA passed constitutional scrutiny. The court ruled that section 514 of the 1994 Uruguay Round Agreements Act, which brought foreign works of authorship that had fallen into the public domain back into the zone of protected works, violated the First Amendment because by restoring the copyright of works in the public domain, section 514 took away the right of the plaintiffs to use the works in the public domain that they had been exploiting.[122] The 10th Circuit reversed, stating that Congress should be given latitude to decide this issue, given its foreign policy implications. The court held that section 514 did not violate the First Amendment because it was narrowly drawn to further the substantial government interest of protecting the interests of American copyright holders in the international intellectual property arena.[123]

Golan appealed to the Supreme Court of the United States. The issue before the Court was whether section 514 violated the Copyright Clause and the First Amendment. The Court said it did not. It held that Congress acted properly when it essentially extended the duration of copyright of foreign works that had fallen into the public domain after the expiration of a full copyright term either in the United States or the country of origin. The Court held that: "The text of the Copyright Clause does not exclude application of copyright protection to works in the public domain."[124] In this case, the Supreme Court of the United States boldly ruled in favor of harmonization of international intellectual property law when it ruled that restoration of copyright protection in the United States to foreign works that had fallen in the public domain and had became available for the taking free of any charge, did not violate either the Copyright Clause of the Constitution or the First Amendment: "In aligning the United States with other nations bound by the Berne Convention, and thereby according equitable treatment to once disfavored foreign authors, Congress can hardly be charged with a design to move stealthily toward a regime of perpetual copyrights."[125] If anything, the Court ruled the Act ensured protection of the interests of American intellectual property holders under international intellectual property law. Through this ruling, the Court essentially put paid to American-style intellectual property "free-for-all" that harkened to the worst days of American intellectual property isolationism in the twentieth century.

American exceptionalism is the political and ideological framework that has shaped American media law and policy in real space and cyberspace. It is therefore the key to understanding American political and cultural postures towards other countries' free speech regimes, especially when these countries apply their own values of freedom of speech and expression on the interconnected, global network of networks—the Internet. Taken together, the comparative case studies in this volume demonstrate that there are indeed similarities and differences in the exceptionalist postures of the United States and France, in a number of crucial issue areas of media law as it is applied in real space and cyberspace. The case studies also show that tensions and conflicts of law have arisen from time to time between the French and American legal regimes over issues of jurisdiction as both countries have sought to resolve legal disputes that have trans-territorial origins and impact.

NOTES

1. See Deborah L. Madsen: American Exceptionalism 16 (1998).
2. *Industrial Union Dept., AFL–CIO v. American Petroleum Institute*, 448 U. S. 607, 673 (1980) (Rehnquist, J., concurring).
3. *National Federation of Independent Business v. Sebelius*, 567 U.S. (2012) (citations omitted).
4. See Frederick Merck, Manifest Destiny and Mission in American History 3 (1966).
5. See Frederick Merck, Manifest Destiny and Mission in American History 4 (1966).
6. See generally, Michael Ignatieff (Ed.) American Exceptionalism and Human Rights (2005). See also Seymour Martin Lipset, *American Exceptionalism Reaffirmed*, in Byron Shafer (Ed.) Is America Different? 16 (1991).
7. See Deborah L. Madsen: American Exceptionalism 16 (1998).
8. See George Mckenna, The Puritan Origins Of American Patriotism 19, 32, 36-37 (2007).
9. See Larry Witham, A City an a Hill: How Sermons Changed the Course of America History 60-71 (2007).
10. See George Mckenna, The Puritan Origins of American Patriotism 42 (2007).
11. See George Mckenna, The Puritan Origins of American Patriotism 104-106 (2007).
12. See John O'Sullivan, *Annexation*, in 17 United States Magazine and Democratic Review (1) (July-August 1845) at 5-10.
13. See George Mckenna, The Puritan Origins of American Patriotism 104-106 (2007).
14. See Alexis De Tocqueville, Democracy in America 191-195 (Henry Reeve, trans. Alfred A. Knopf (1980) (1835, 1840).
15. See generally, Louis Hartz, The Liberal Tradition in America: An Interpretation of American Political Thought since the Revolution. See also Ronald J. Schmidt, Jr. In the Beginning, all the world was America: American Exceptionalism in New contexts, in Oxford Handbook of Political Theory 281-296 (2006).
16. See George Mckenna, The Puritan Origins of American Patriotism 144, 203, 244, 339, 353 (2007).
17. See Theodore Roosevelt, Address at Carnegie Hall (Mar. 20, 1912), in George B. Lockwood, Americanism 148 (1921).
18. See Seymour Martin Lipset, *American Exceptionalism Reaffirmed*, in Byron Shafer (Ed.) Is America different? 16 (1991).
19. See Michael Hunt, Ideology and U.S. Foreign Policy 17, 42 (1987).
20. See Henry Kissinger, Diplomacy 372 (1994) (suggesting that the United States has historically viewed itself as the very picture of freedom. As such, the country did not want to embrace the morally inferior international system).
21. Id. at 376.
22. Elizabeth Borgwardt, A New Deal For The World: America's Vision For Human Rights (2005).
23. See John Gerard Ruggie, *American Exceptionalism, Exemptionalism, and Global Governance*, in American Exceptionalism And Human Rights 304, 305 (Michael Ignatieff, Ed. 2005).

24. See John Gerard Ruggie, *American Exceptionalism, Exemptionalism, and Global Governance*, in American Exceptionalism And Human Rights 304, 305 (Michael Ignatieff, Ed. 2005).

25. See Christopher Blakesley, Edwin Firmage, Richard Scott & Sharon Williams, The International Legal System 698 (2001).

26. See Michael Ignatieff, Introduction: American Exceptionalism and Human Rights. In American Exceptionalism and Human Rights, Michael Ignatieff (Ed.) 3, 6 (2005).

27. Arts. 19 & 20, International Covenant on Civil and Political Rights, G.A. res. 2200A (XXI), 21 U.N. GAOR Supp. (No. 16) at 52, U.N. Doc. A/6316 (1966), 999 U.N.T.S. 171, *entered into force* Mar. 23, 1976.

28. See Christopher Blakesley, *Autumn of the Patriarch: The Pinochet Extradition Debacle and Beyond*, J. of Crim. L. & Criminology 1 (2001) (stating that treaties that condemn conduct as criminal are non-self executing, that is, they need an act of Congress to take effect upon ratification).

29. See Christof Heyns & Frans Viljoen, The Impact of the United Nations Human Rights Treaties on the Domestic Level 9 (2002) (suggesting that many states ratify international human rights treaties for reasons of public diplomacy).

30. See Frederick Schauer, The Exceptional First Amendment, in Michael Ignatieff (Ed.) American Exceptionalism and Human Rights 29, 30, 42 (2005).

31. See John Gerard Ruggie, *American Exceptionalism, Exemptionalism, and Global Governance*, in American Exceptionalism and Human Rights 304, 305 (Michael Ignatieff, Ed. 2005).

32. See Frederick Schauer, The Exceptional First Amendment, in Michael Ignatieff (Ed.) American Exceptionalism and Human Rights 56 (2005).

33. See Michael Ignatieff, Introduction: American Exceptionalism and Human Rights. In American Exceptionalism And Human Rights, Michael Ignatieff (Ed.) 12-22 (2005).

34. See Lyombe Eko, New Media, Old Regimes: Case Studies in Comparative Law and Policy 161 (2012).

35. See National Telecommunications And Information Administration, United States Department Of Commerce, Arpanet Host-To-Host Access and Disengagement Measures 2-3 (1978). See also, Department of Defense, Dod Science and Technology Success Stories (1998) (Technologies developed by the Department of Defense, namely, packet-switching, Transmission Control Protocol/Internet Protocol (TCO/IP) paved the way for the World Wide Web.)

36. See Tim Berners-Lee, The World Wide Web, A Personal History available at: http://www.w3.org/people/Berners-lee/ See also European Organization for Nuclear Research (CERN) http://www.public.web.cern.ch/public/ACHIEVEMENTS/web.html.

37. See Scientific and Advanced Technology Act of 1992, 42 U.S.C. 1862 (a) (1992).

38. See Scientific and Advanced Technology Act of 1992, 42 U.S.C. 1862 (a) (1992).

39. See Juan Rogers, Internetworking and the Politics of Science: NSFNET in Internet History, 14 The Information Society 213 (1998).

40. Telecommunications Act of 1996, 47 U.S.C. 47 USC § 230(f) (1) (1996).

41. Communications Act of 1934 (as amended by the Telecommunications Act of 1996), 47 U.S.C. §214, 336 *et seq* (1934).

42. *Red Lion Broadcasting Co. Inc. v. FCC*, 395 U.S. 367 (1969).

43. See *American Library Association v. Pataki*, 969 F. Supp. 160 (S.D.N.Y, 1997). See also Robert J. Posch, Another Win For Internet Self-regulation, 60 Direct Marketing 64 (1997).

44. See Reno v. ACLU, 521 U.S. 844 (1997).

45. See Net Neutrality, the *New York Times*, December 22, 2010 (Defining net neutrality as the notion that "companies providing Internet service should treat all sources of data equally. It has been the center of a debate over whether those companies can give preferential treatment to content providers who pay for faster transmission, or to their own content"). Available at: http://topics.nytimes.com/topics/reference/timestopics/subjects/n/net_neutrality/index.html.

46. *Comcast Corp. v. FCC*, 600 F. 3d 642 (D.C. Cir 2010)

47. See Memorandum of Understanding Between the U.S. Department of Commerce and the Internet Corporation for Assigned Names and Numbers ("ICANN") (Nov. 25, 1998). Available at: http://www.law.stanford.edu/program/centers/ttlf/law/us/it/

48. See e.g. Claude Robinson, Cyberspace as backyard for the new 'Monroe Doctrine', JAMAICA OBERVER, November 13, 2005. Available at: http://www.jamaicaobserver.com/columns/html/20051112T140000-0500_92354_OBS_CYBERSPACE_AS_BACKYARD_FOR_THE_NEW__MONROE_DOCTRINE__.asp (Stating that Tunis WSIS conferences was an attempt to "dilute U.S. control of the Internet").

49. Information Security Doctrine of the Russian Federation, No. Pr-1895. "Approved" by Vladimir Putin, President of the Russian Federation, September 9, 2000.

50. See generally, ITU, World Summit on the Information Society (WSIS). Available at: http://www.itu.int/wsis/index.html. See also Milton Meuller, Ruling The Root:Internet Governance and the Taming of Cyberspace 73, 211 (2004).

51. Article 5B, Final Acts of the World Conference on International Telecommunications (2012). Available at: http://www.itu.int/en/wcit-12/Pages/documents.aspx

52. See Yves Poullet, *Internet Governance: Some Thoughts after the two WSIS, in* IF1P International Federation For Information Processing: The Information Society, Innovation, Legitimacy, Ethics And Democracy In Honor Of Professor Jacques Berleur S.J., 201-224 (Philippe GouJ.O.n, et al., eds. 2007).

53. Communications Decency Act, 47 U.S.C § 223 (a) (1) (B) (ii) and 223 (d).

54. *American Civil Liberties Union v. Reno,* 929 F. Supp. 824 (Ed. Pa. 1996).

55. Id.

56. *Reno v. ACLU* 521 U.S. 844, 874 (1997).

57. See Douglas W. Vick, *Exporting the First Amendment to Cyberspace: The Internet and State Sovereignty, in* Media And Globalization 3 (Nancy Morris & Sylvio Waisbord, Ed., 2001) (Suggesting that the U.S. Supreme Court decision in *Reno v. A.C.L.U.* essentially globalized the First Amendment).

58. See Lyombe Eko, Many Spiders, One World Wide Web: Towards a Typology of Internet Regulation, 6 Communication Law and Policy 445, 465 (2001) (Suggesting that the United States has a neo-merchantilist model of Internet regulation).

59. *Smith v. California*, 361 U.S. 147 (1959).

60. 47 USC § 230(c) (1-2).

61. 129 F.3d 327 (4th Cir. 1997).

62. 339 F.3d 1119, 1123 (9th Cir. 2003).

63. 992 F. Supp. 44, 50 (D.D.C. 1998).

64. See William J. Clinton and Albert Gore, Jr., A Framework for Electronic Commerce 5 (1997) (This *laissez-faire* approach would be global, mercantilist, decentralized, contractual, competitive, transparent and protective of intellectual property).

65. See Reno v. ACLU, 521 U.S. 844 (1997).

66. See Adam Smith, An Inquiry into the Nature and Causes of the Wealth of Nations 175-176, 194 (1776) (Trade is the source of law, order, good government).

67. *Abrams v. United States,* 250 U.S. 616 (1919) (The United States is a Marketplace of ideas where truth and falsehood wrestle and truth carries the day).

68. See ART. 19, Universal Declaration of Human Rights, U.N. Doc A/RES/217 A (III) (1948).

69. See Article 1, § 8, Constitution of the United States.

70. See Armand Mattelart, The Information Society 138 (2000) (Suggesting that the aim of the information society is to facilitate "frictionless capitalism").

71. See Charles Pfleeger & Shari L. Pfleeger, Security in Computing 9, 589 (3d Ed.) (2002).

72. *See* Gregory Passman, *The Electronic Age is almost Upon* Us, 229 N.Y. L. J. 1 (2003).

73. G.A. Res. 2205 (XXI), UN GAOR, 21ST Session, U.N. Doc A/RES/2205 (XXI) (1966).

74. G.A. Res. 51/162, UN GAOR 51st Session, Supp. No. 17, annex, U.N. Doc, A/RES/51/162) (1996); See also Daya Kishan Thusu, International Communication 265 (2000) (Electronic commerce is the "production, advertising, sale and distribution via electronic networks, specifically the Internet").

75. G.A. Res. 56/80, UN GAOR 85th Session, Supp. No. 17, annex, U.N. Doc. A/RES/56/80 (2001) (The very definition of the term "electronic signatures" is problematic and varies from country to country. The definition is part of the analysis. Suffice it to say at this juncture that electronic signatures are numbers generated as part of data security, by special software

using complex algorithms. These paperless instruments are used to authenticate business transactions).

76. United States Constitution, Article 1, § 8. cl. 3.

77. See Lyombe Eko, Anup Kumar and Qingjiang Yao, Google This: The Great Firewall of China, The IT Wall of India, Google Inc. and Internet Regulation, 15 the *Journal of Internet Law* 3 (2012).

78. 15 U.S.C. §§7001, 7031(a) (D) (2000).

79. Electronic Signatures in Global and National Commerce Act, 15 U.S.C § 7031(a) (2) (A) (2000) (The Secretary of Commerce is asked to adopt principles from the UNCITRAL Model Law on Electronic Commerce to remove paper-based obstacles to electronic transactions).

80. See David Nelken, Comparatists and Transferability, in Comparative Legal Studies: Traditions and Transitions (Pierre Legrand and Roderick Munday, Eds.) 437, 454 (2003) (Suggesting that the "mediating role of institutions" be taken into consideration in evaluating the success of legal transfers between countries).

81. See F. Lynn McNulty, *Encryption's Importance to Economic and Infrastructural Security*, 9 Duke J. Comp. & Int'l L. 427 (1999); see also Christopher F. Corr, *The Wall Still Stands! Complying with Export Controls on Technology Transfers in the Post-Cold War, Post 9/11 Era,* 25 HOUS. J.INT'L L. 441,448-489 (2003) (Suggesting that even though export controls have been eased, exporters of encryption technology are still subject to strict control. The Russian Federation was not on the list of European countries to which encryption technologies could be exported or re-exported without a license).

82. Revisions to Restrictions on Encryption Technology, 65 Fed.Reg.62600, 62,600-02 (October 19, 2000); see also David Sanger, U.S. Relaxes the Limits on Exports of High-Speed Computers, New York Times, July 2, 1999 at A4 (Reporting that President Bill Clinton had eased some restrictions on super computer exports to Russia and China).

83. See Department of Commerce, Export Administration Regulations: Encryption Clarifications and Revisions, 15 C.F.R. Parts 734,740, 742, 748, 770 and 774 (2003) (The Bureau of Industry and Security of the Department of Commerce regulates the export and re-export of encryption and other "dual use" products, that is software, computer code and other technical information that appears on Commerce Control List."). See also the International Emergency Economic Powers Act, 50 U.S.C. § 1701 et seq.

84. The Trading with the Enemy Act, 50 U.S.C.App. 5; and the International Emergency Economic Powers Act, 50 U.S.C § 1701 et seq.(giving Treasury Department's Office of Foreign Assets Control authority to control financial and commercial transactions involving specific foreign countries).

85. See *Craig Matsumoto, Crypto confab to debate U.S. move on exports*, Electrical Engineering Times, January 18, 1999 at 4 (Reporting that data security experts were frustrated at the Clinton Administration restrictions despite easing of some 56-bit encryption rules); see also John Simons, U.S. to relax restrictions on Encryption Technology, Wall Street journal, September 16, 1999 at B6.

86. See Neil Munro, The Unhappy but Beneficial Coexistence of the FBI and the Tech Elite, 44 Communications Of The ACM 15 (2001) (Reporting on the relationship between governmental security agencies which want to restrict encryption and other high technology exports).

87. See George Soros, Open Society xv (2000) (Suggesting that the United States is willing to enter into multilateral arrangements that open world markets and protect American vested interests but the U.S. is unwilling to make compromises that affect its own internal affairs).

88. European Council Framework Decision 2004/68/JHA, On Combating the Sexual Exploitation of Children and Child Pornography, 2003 J.O. (L.13/44), art. 1.

89. Id.

90. *Papish v. University of Missouri Curators*, 410 U.S. 667 (1973) (Holding that "the mere dissemination of ideas—no matter how offensive to good taste—on a state university campus may not be shut off in the name alone of 'conventions of decency'").

91. *Hustler Magazine v. Falwell*, 485 U.S. 46, 56 (1988) (Holding that "the fact that society may find speech offensive is not a sufficient reason for suppressing it. Indeed, if it is the speaker's opinion that gives offense, that consequence is a reason for according it constitutional

protection"); See also *Terminiello v. Chicago*, 337 U.S. 1 (1949) (Holding that: "a 'heckler's' veto is illegal and that 'a function of free speech under our system is to invite dispute.' It may indeed best serve its high purpose when it induces a condition of unrest, creates dissatisfaction with conditions as they are, or even stirs people to anger.")

92. See e.g. *Lawrence v. Texas*, 539 U.S. 558 (2003) (Decrying the use of legal outcomes in two European countries to support striking down sodomy laws in the U.S. Scalia, J. (dissenting)); See also Printz, v. U.S. 521 U.S. 898, 935 (1997) (Scalia, J) dissenting.

93. In *Miller v. California*, 413 U.S. 15, 24-25 (1973), the Supreme Court of the United States stated that for material to be declared obscene, and therefore not protected by the First Amendment, juries must ascertain "whether the average person, applying contemporary community standards, would find that the work, taken as a whole, appeals to the prurient interest, whether the work depicts/describes, in a patently offensive way, sexual conduct or excretory functions [2] specifically defined by applicable state law, whether the work, taken as a whole, lacks serious literary, artistic, political, and scientific value."

94. Under *Reid v. Covert*, 354 U.S. 1, 16-17 (1957) (Holding that treaties are subject to the Bill of Rights).

95. See Frederick Schauer, The Exceptional First Amendment, in American Exceptionalism and Human Rights 29, 56 (Michael Ignatieff, Ed. 2005).

96. U.S. Constitution, Art. 1 §8, cl.8.

97. See Richard Posner, The Constitutionality of the Copyright Term Extension Act: Economics, Politics, Law, and Judicial Technique in *Eldred v. Ashcroft.* 143 The Supreme Court Review 143 (2004).

98. See Richard Posner, The Constitutionality of the Copyright Term Extension Act: Economics, Politics, Law, and Judicial Technique in *Eldred v. Ashcroft.* 143 The Supreme Court Review 147 (2004).

99. See William Roeder, *The Doctrine of Moral Right: A Study in the Law of Artists, Authors and Creators*, 53 HARV.L.REV. 554, 555 (1940).

100. 17 U.S.C. § 102(a).

101. *Community for Creative Non-Violence v. Reid,* 490 U.S. 730, (1989) ("As a general rule, the author is the party who actually creates the work, that is, the person who translates an idea into a fixed, tangible expression entitled to protection. . . . If the work is for hire, 'the employer or other person for whom the work was prepared is considered the 'author' and owns the copyright unless there is a written agreement to the contrary").

102. See *Fogerty v. Fantasy, Inc.*, 510 U.S. 517, 524 (1994) (Holding that "the primary objective of the Copyright Act is to encourage the production of original, literary, artistic, and musical expression for the good of the public.").

103. *Sony Corporation of America v. Universal City Studios*, 464 U.S. 417 (1984).

104. 499 U.S. 340 (1991) (quoting *Accord Twentieth Century Music Corp. v. Aiken* (citations omitted)).

105. The so-called "sweat of thy brow principle" comes from Genesis 3:19 in which after Man's fall in the Garden of Eden, God tells Adam and Eve that the land was cursed because of their sin and that: "Out of the Sweat of thy Brow Shalt Thou Eat Bread."

106. See David L. Lange and H. Jefferson Powell, No Law: Intellectual Property in the Image of an Absolute First Amendment X, XI, 171 (Stanford Univ. Press 2009).

107. *Eldred v. Ashcroft*, 537 U.S. 186, 219 [Ginsburg, J., quoting *Harper and Row, Inc v. Nation Enterprises, Inc.*, 471 U.S. 539, 558 (1985) and asserting that "copyright's purpose is to promote the creation and publication of free expression".

108. Copyright Act of 1976 (as amended) 17 U.S.C §107.

109. *Campbell v. Acuff-Rose Music*, 510 U.S. 569 (1994) (Holding that a commercially successful music parody was fair use); see also *Warner Brothers, Inc. v. American Broadcasting Corporation, Inc.*, 720 F.2d 231, 242 (2d. Cir. 1983) (Holding that a TV show parodying Superman is protected); and also *Elsmere Music, Inc. v. National broadcasting Company, Inc.*, 623 F.2d. 252, 253 (2d. Cir. 1980) (Holding that *Saturday Night Life* TV parody of the song, "I Love New York" was protected).

110. See David L. Lange and H. Jefferson Powell, No Law: Intellectual Property in the Image of an Absolute First Amendment 52 (Stanford Univ. Press 2009).

111. Copyright Act of 1976 (as amended) 17 U.S.C §107.
112. See Public Law 105-304 (H.R. 2281) codified as 17 U.S.C. § 512 (1998).
113. See Sony Bono Copyright Term Extension Act, 17 U.S.C. §§ 302, 304 (2006).
114. *Eldred v. Ashcroft*, 537 U.S. 186, 193 (2003).
115. *Luck's Music Library, Inc. & MovieCraft, Inc. v. Gonzales* 407 F.3d 1262 (D.C. Cir. 2005).
116. Article 1, §6, cl.8, Constitution of the U.S.
117. *Luck's Music Library, Inc. v. Ashcroft,* 321 F. Supp. 2d 107, 118–19 (D.D.C. 2004).
118. *Luck's Music Library Inc, and MovieCraft, Inc., v. Gonzales*, 407 F.3d 1262 (D.C. Cir. 2005).
119. *Golan v. Ashcroft*, 310 F.Supp.2d 1215 (D. Colo. 2004).
120. *Golan v. Gonzales* No. Civ. 01–B–1854, 2005 WL 914754 (D. Colo., Apr. 20, 2005).
121. *Golan v. Gonzales*, 501 F.3d 1179 (10th Cir. 2007).
122. *Golan v. Holder,* No. 01-cv-01854-LTB (COD., 2009).
123. *Golan v. Gonzales* 609 F. 3d 1076 (2010).
124. See *Golan v. Holder*, 565 U.S. (2012).
125. See *Golan v. Holder*, 565 U.S. (2012).

Chapter Four

The French Exception (*L'Exception Française*) and Media Law

The French Exception: Historical and Political Context

In 1997, the French government and several anti-racist and human rights groups jointly filed criminal charges against Robert Faurisson, a Professor at the University of Lyon, for allegedly posting Holocaust denial material that went against governmentally-sanctioned truth, on a website hosted in the United States. When the case came to trial, Faurisson claimed that French courts had no jurisdiction over Internet content hosted on servers in the United States. The *Tribunal de Grand Instance de Paris* disagreed, holding that material published anywhere on the Internet fell under the jurisdiction of French courts if the material could be accessed by French citizens, using search engines located on French territory.[1] This ruling created a sort of French "*jurisdiction sans frontières*" (jurisdiction without borders), and paved the way for the application of French exceptionalist logic to Internet content around the world.

This ruling exemplifies the French philosophical posture towards the Internet. France has always branded itself as a unique thinking culture, a civil, mature civilization, whose appreciation of the finer things of life—the aesthetic, the literary and cultural, moral philosophical values, and universal humanism—stands in stark contrast to the crass commercialism, excessive materialism, and "fast culture" of the "Anglo-Saxon" (read Anglo-American) culture. This statist, French politico-cultural and ideological posture is what has come to be known as *L'exception française* (the French exception), an ideology and declaration of difference that emphasizes the uniqueness and specificity of the French language, culture, and civilization, and defines France in opposition to other countries.[2] The French exception is what Pierre

Legrand calls: "Traditional faith in the greatness and destiny of France."[3] The French exception also refers to the reified, centralized, statist linguistic, cultural, political, economic, social, intellectual, cinematic, artistic, viticultural, and culinary difference between France and the rest of the world.[4]

The intellectual culture of France has been, first and foremost, a millennium-long labor of difference, a continuous travail of cultural differentiation. French philosophy is thus a philosophy of difference. It is grounded in what Thomas Carlyle called "an enlightened philosophism."[5] This neologism suggests a worship of abstract philosophical speculation for its own sake. The message that is thundered by the lofty insights, counter-intuitive aphorisms, cold, clear-eyed rationalism, high minded speculations, ever present polemics, moral indignation, and clever turns of phrase of French philosophy is this: "France is different, get over it!" The French exception is the French government's struggle to maintain the country's monolithic civilization and monolingual culture in the face of pressures from Anglo-American culture.[6] Therefore, French intellectuals have advanced the notion that respect for the specificities, intricacies and even vicissitudes of their politico-cultural and legal system is an act of intellectual tolerance that gives legal scholars from other cultures, an opportunity, as Pierre Legrand succinctly put it, "to grant hospitality to alterity . . . [to recognize the right of] alterity to exist as alterity."[7]

Contemporary manifestations of the French exception are grounded in the French Constitution, which proclaims that France is an "indivisible, secular, democratic, and social Republic. . . . The language of the Republic shall be French. . . . The motto of the Republic shall be 'Liberty, Equality, Fraternity.'"[8] In the modern global, interconnected world, the French exception promotes the *rayonance* (the spreading abroad) of French culture, while protecting it at home from perceived threats posed by the "Anglo-Saxon" (Anglo-American) media, Internet, and popular culture. This cultural differentiation comes into focus, and has maximum effect when, to borrow the expression of Miriam Feldblum, France is "juxtaposed against other national models."[9] France prides itself in what Hewlett calls its "paradigmatic reputation in the arts, intellectual life and culture generally."[10] This *exception culturelle* (cultural exception), which Rigaud has described as the "very prescriptive, official, institutionalized aspect of culture" is unique to France. It is a French "categorical imperative"[11] which confers on the French state, a greater role and responsibility in the management, funding, and promotion of all things cultural—from architecture, culinary and circus arts, to haute couture (high fashion)—than in any other democratic country.[12] Indeed, *l'exception culturelle* infuses all aspects of society, especially politics, law, and the media. Furthermore, the French exception is a nationalistic exceptionalism. With more than a *soupçon* of jingoism, President Charles de Gaulle called *l'exception française:* "*une certaine idée de la France ou elle n'est réelle-*

ment elle-même que quand elle est au premier rang" (a certain idea of France where she is her real self only when she is at the forefront [of international leadership]).[13] The French exception has led to a policy of cultural protectionism and greatly influenced the country's language and media law regimes.

The Paradox of the French Exception

The French exception is an ideology of politico-cultural differentiation, a declaration of radical cultural alterity, and a pronouncement of French cultural otherness that is intended to cast France as the glorious, mature, critical, intellectual, revolutionary, humanitarian, cultural, and political foil of a certain effervescent upstart, the United States.[14] Through the French exception, the French elite—intellectuals, politicians, the culture industry, and the media establishment—glory in French otherness, and defiantly, even snobbishly proclaims that French culture is radically different from other cultures. The French exception is therefore a call for acceptance and respect for an alterity that defines itself in opposition to other cultures.

By emphasizing its civilizational, linguistic, and cultural distinctness from an undifferentiated "Western culture," while being a full-fledged member of the major institutions of the Western World, the French exception creates a paradoxical situation where France is of the "West," and yet she is different from the rest of the West. France is a member of the European Union and the Council of Europe, two supranational organizations that have had a profound influence on human rights, freedom of expression, and culture in Europe. The paradox is that France has sought to strike a balance between its *francité* (Franchness) and its *Européenité* (Europeaness). This dilemma is especially acute in the field of mass mediated culture where France seeks to protect its culture from the American cultural, technological and media juggernaut, while at the same time transposing European Union Directives into French law, and opening itself to legal and policy transfers from the international human rights regime of the United Nations. Nevertheless, even when it transposes and domesticates Council of Europe policies and European Union Directives, France has always insisted that the transposed European laws have a French "constitutional identity." The French exception thus demands an emphasis on French difference within a European sameness.

The French Exception and Language Policy

The ethno-culturalism of l'*exception française* explains the skeptical and generally critical political and cultural posture of France towards the United States. It also explains early French cynicism towards the Internet and other innovative "Anglo-Saxon" instrumentalities of communication. *L'exception française* has therefore been increasingly framed as a tool for the defense of the French language and culture against global "Anglo-Saxon cultural hegemony."[15] French language laws and policies mandate the elimination of popular English expressions, restrictions on the use of English in advertising and on Internet web pages hosted in France, the establishment of quotas for English language content in the French media, and promotion of French language and culture in the Francophonie, the organization of French-speaking countries.[16] This is all sustained by an active policy of linguistic substitution whereby neologisms are invented to replace English words and expressions spawned by new technologies. For example, the words "*courier éléctronique*" and "*courriel*," has been invented to replace "electronic mail and e-mail."[17] The French government states that its language policies are exceptional and global. Instruction in, and use of the French language in all domains of life has been raised to the level of a human right, a constitutional "*droit au français*" (right to French) right to communicate and be communicated to in French.[18]

This laser-like pre-occupation with preserving the glories of the French language and culture has transformed France into a cultural state without cultural diversity. Indeed, one of the main tenets of French secular republicanism is that France is a secular nation of culturally homogeneous people.[19] All residents of France are required to assimilate into the French Republic as *individuals*, with one culture—the French culture—not as members of specific ethnic or religious communities.[20] This governmentally-directed cultural assimilation officially rejects multiculturalism and renounces overt, non-French, ethnic, religious and other national cultural affiliations and symbols. Compound descriptors of hyphenated citizenship like "African-American," "Italian-American" or Native American—are unacceptable in France. For a nation that has over the course of its long history been composed of diverse ethnicities and languages: Gauls, Franks, Basques, Bretons, Celts, Normans, Alsatians, Corsicans, Arabs, Africans, Romanians, etc, constitutionalization of French as the national language, and the government's active policy of assimilation for purposes of avoiding multi-culturalism and the *communautarisation* (communitarianization) which is believed would follow in its wake, make France one of the least linguistically and culturally diverse countries in the world.

The French Exception and Freedom of Expression

The French freedom of speech regime is the result of centuries of power struggles between political groups and factions, as well as centuries of governmental suppression of the press, and control of its content. These political and social power struggles culminated in the French Revolution of 1789, which swept away most of the vestiges of the absolutist *ancien regime* but left its bureaucratic over-centralization intact. The Revolution was the crystallization of philosophical and humanitarian ideals rooted in natural law doctrines,[21] the philosophical liberalism of the eighteenth-century Enlightenment, and specifically the ideas of the *philosophes*: Voltaire,[22] Rousseau,[23] Diderot,[24] Montesquieu, [25] and others.[26] This philosophical bag of ideas was embodied, for the first time, in the most important pronouncement of the French Revolution, the Declaration of the Rights of Man and of the Citizen, of August 26, 1789. One of the main characteristics of the Declaration is that it had very pronounced humanistic, moral, and universalistic values. This revolution spawned what Jacques Derrida described as an "ethico-political" culture[27] in which a human rights ethic features prominently.

However, in matters of freedom of expression, the Declaration of the Rights of Man and of the Citizen granted rather circumscribed freedoms. Though the Declaration guarantees freedom of speech and of the press—"the free communication of thoughts and opinions is one of the most precious rights of man"[28] —that right is qualified by the next clause which states that people are free to speak, write, and print freely, "on condition that they answer for any abuse of this freedom."[29] Furthermore, the Declaration states that: "the exercise of the natural rights of each person has no bounds but those which assure to other members of society, the enjoyment of these same rights."[30] Thus, under French law, people have inalienable rights but these rights are subordinated to national security interests. In France, national security is, and has always been the first freedom. The result is that the almost one-hundred-year Revolution resulted in a highly-centralized political culture marked by what François Furet calls "the supremacy of the law over rights."[31]

The Declaration of the Rights of Man and of the Citizen of 1789, together with the preamble to the French Constitution of 1946, which completes it through a statement of political, economic and social principles and rights, are incorporated by reference in the French Constitution of 1958, which is the supreme law in France.[32] Therefore, in contemporary France, the Constitution is the vehicle for the valuation of ideas, philosophies, official interpretations of history, ensuring social and community rights, and positive citizen entitlements.[33]

The French Exception and Anti-Americanism

A common feature of the French exception is anti-Americanism, an intellectual discourse of the French intelligentsia that Philippe Roger defines as "the long struggle to differentiate *us* [French] from *them* [Americans] that has mobilized, for more than a century, a large part of French intellectual energies."[34] Since the late nineteenth century, when French public opinion viewed the United States with "a reticent fascination," to borrow the expression of Jacques Portes,[35] America has been framed as the cultural "Non-self," the foil of the French Cultural Self. In effect, under the French exception, France casts itself as the glorious, mature, intellectual, revolutionary, humanitarian, cultural, and political opposite of the effervescent upstart, the United States, whose contribution to human civilization is limited to a narcotizing, consumerist, fast culture.[36]

The French exception is therefore grounded in the logic of the century-long politico-cultural rivalry between France and the United States. The Spanish-American war of 1898, which French intellectuals and the French press perceived as an "Anglo-Saxon" attack on the Latin "cultural community" by the new, "imperialist power" on the other side of the Atlantic, kicked off this rivalry.[37] The result was the impetus for anti-Americanism, an intellectual and ideological posture which French journalist, Guy Scarpetta, described as a "disease which consists of not being able to affirm our (French) identity except through setting ourselves against the United States."[38] At the turn of the twentieth century, anti-Americanism was expressed by phrases like *le péril américain* (the American peril), and *l'américanisation du monde* (Americanization of the world).[39] A wistful sense of the decline of French culture, influence and prestige around the world at the same time that American economic, military and cultural power were in the ascendant, animated anti-Americanism and French cultural differentiation in the early and mid twentieth century.[40]

Therefore, despite its near single-minded focus on French cultural and linguistic specificity, the French exception has a strong undercurrent of anti-Americanism. After the Second World War, when the United States launched the Marshall Plan to reconstruct Europe, some of its programs were considered instruments of American cultural imperialism.[41] The French Communist Party newspaper, *l'Humanité* complained about "the marshallization" and "coca-colonization of France."[42] In effect, a section of the French population, led by the French Communist Party, claimed that American post-World War II cultural diplomacy—specifically the propaganda aspects of the Marshall Plan, amounted to American self-serving "denigration of French cultural accomplishments and intellectual traditions."[43] Additionally, many French intellectuals were suspicious of American motives, disdainful of American materialism, and repulsed by American propaganda films that presented stereotypical images of "The American Way of Life" and offered French people simplistic recipes for attaining that "American Dream."[44]

Though the French still view the United States with a nuanced, "reticent fascination,"[45] the French exception has a strong undertone of what Dennis Ager calls, cultural "Americanophobia" (fear of domination by American culture) and specifically, fear of American English dilution of French as a unique language, and vehicle of Gallic culture.[46]

Anti-Americanism is therefore an intellectual tradition, a narrative against the very "idea" of America, a country that some French intellectuals believe "passed directly from savagery to barbarity, without transiting through civilization"; a country that has posed an existential cultural threat to Europe in general, and France in particular, for more than a century.[47] Anti-American discourse is grounded in what Roger calls a "visceral defense of the French way of life" against the American "counter-civilization" and mass culture. Cultural anti-Americanism does not necessarily manifest itself as animosity felt towards Americans; the enemy is perceived as the amorphous and ubiquitous American hegemonic mass culture.[48] French anti-Americanism is therefore intellectual and cultural resistance to a perceived "*péril americain*" (American peril). This expression was used to describe what was considered American economic and commercial imperialism; an unconventional imperialism that the French feared would lead to "Americanization of the world." [49]

At its most basic, anti-Americanism is intellectual and cultural resistance against *l'américanisme* (Americanism) a selective, negative expression of the cultural values and institutions that the French elite believe to be the very essence of American national identity, and civilization; the so-called "American way of life." To the French elite, Americanism is known for its "non-civilization," and "fast culture" (a play on "fast food").[50] The contemporary manifestation of anti-Americanism is *la francité* (Frenchness), an ideology that is grounded in the valorization and celebration of all things French. Since the turn of the twentieth century, *la francité* has been defined in opposition to "Americanism," a word that crystallizes the repertoire of French anti-American clichés[51] The most pervasive form of anti-Americanism is what Roger calls "cultural anti-Americanism." He suggests that this type of anti-Americanism is evident in the work of French intellectuals ranging from de Tocqueville to Sartre, and from Barthes and Foucault to Baudrillard.[52] Actually, in the early part of the twentieth century, while France extolled its cultural exceptionalism, it questioned whether the United States even had a culture or even an aptitude for culture. A common question of that period was, "*Y a-t-il une culture aux États-Unis*?" (Is there culture in the United States?).[53] The answer was almost always in the negative.

Philosophizing and re-inventing the Internet to Conform to the French Cultural Exception

It is in this cultural enviornment that the Internet diffused to France. The Internet diffused to France despite the fact that France had one of the earliest online systems, the Minitel, an interactive, online public videotex system. In the 1970s and 1980s videotex systems were innovative communication technologies that enabled telephone subscribers to have access to remote computers and databases through dial-up landline telephone networks and user-friendly terminals.[54] The Minitel was based on Transpac, a reengineered variant of networking (packet-switching) technology that was developed in the United States in the 1970s.[55] The Minitel was a product of French *dirigisme*, the system of centralized "state-capitalism" under which the government directs and shapes strategic sectors of the economy, industry, essential utilities and the telecommunications infrastructure for purposes of furthering governmental interests, and attaining certain collective social goal.[56] In the early 1990s, when the Internet began to change from an esoteric network for computer scientists and researchers to a global communication, commercial educational, cultural, social and entertainment platform, open to everyone, the French intelligentsia dismissed it as a nefarious American cultural tool that was incompatible with French Cartesian logic, a centralist mathematical and philosophical paradigm which is the foundation of French governmentality and intellectualism.[57] Additionally, the Internet was considered alien to French culture,[58] and tradition.[59]

The Internet and French Cultural Policy

The French government, which has sought, over the years, to protect French national identity, language and culture, through legislative action, saw the Internet as a conveyor belt for "Anglo-Saxon" culture and an instrument of American politico-cultural domination of the world.[60] The venerable French newspaper, *Le Monde,* reported that French government officials viewed the Internet as nothing but an American cultural "Trojan horse."[61] The French government clearly viewed the Internet as a threat to the country's "cultural sovereignty," to use the expression of Armand Mattelart.[62] This expression refers to the right of countries to control the instrumentalities of telecommunication as well as the messages they transmit within their national territories. In the 1990s, some French scholars claimed that information flows, including Internet content, were beginning to erode state sovereignty.[63] Leila Bouachera put the French cultural protectionist posture succinctly:

> mastery of information constitutes henceforth, a new attribute of sovereign power. . . . Information sovereignty includes the right to restrict or place certain conditions on information access and communication to certain countries. . . . A state can only have pretensions of sovereignty the moment it is in a position to control all informational activities that take place on its territory or outside its territorial limits, when the information concerns it.[64]

Additionally, the decentralized, non-hierarchical nature of the Internet was seen as a destabilizing force that went against French bureaucratic centralism and economic *dirigisme*. Mattelart suggested that American information and communication technologies, as well as U.S. governmental policies, imposed upon the world, a certain competitive liberalism that undermined state control of information and communication technologies and policies, thereby undermining national sovereignty and cultural specificity.[65] Mattelart further stated that the increasingly sophisticated electronic commerce of the 1990s—business transactions on the Internet—led to a clash of two freedoms: the freedom of expression of citizens versus the freedom of commercial expression.[66] In other words, Mattelart perceived the Internet as an instrument that granted companies unlimited commercial rights at the expense of human rights.

This philosophizing and negative logic towards the Internet perplexed some French observers. Eric Benhamou, a French computer scientist and entrepreneur based in the United States, lamented that as late as 1997, many French intellectuals saw the Internet as an "Anglo-Saxon phenomenon . . . failing to distinguish between the instrument and its content. They saw the Internet as one more sign of Yankee cultural expansionism."[67] As we saw earlier, the initial skepticism about the Internet was driven in part by the fact that France already had its home-grown online service, the Minitel, a sort of proto-Internet.[68] Schneider and his colleagues suggest that French Minitel policy was: "an element of a wider industrial policy strategy by which the American hegemony in information technology was to be challenged."[69]

However, France soon realized that it was being left behind in the new knowledge economy as the English-language dominated Internet diffused at exponential speeds around the world and ultimately supplanted the Minitel and rendered it obsolete.[70] The French government then decided to reluctantly enter what French Senator, Pierre Laffitte described as the "Anglo-Saxon online world . . . in order to impose multiculturalism and multilingualism . . . so that the whole world does not express itself in basic American English."[71] Thereafter, France embraced the new communication platform, with the intention of imposing its national cultural norms on the infrastructures and networks that existed in, or traversed France, as well as on the Internet content that was hosted or accessed on its national territory. As we see in chapter 2, France soon extended its jurisdiction to all Internet content that could be accessed by anyone in France. The practical result was that regulations governing freedom of expression in the traditional media were extended to the Internet.

Beginning in 1996, a number of governmental departments and agencies were created to co-regulate the Internet.[72] The 1978 Law on Information Technology, Databases and Freedoms, which was aimed at protecting the privacy of individual data in computer databases, was amended to require that all websites in existence in France be officially registered with a government agency, the *Commission Nationale de l'Informatique et des Libertés* (National Commission on Information Technology and Freedoms, CNIL).[73]

The 1986 Law on Freedom of Communication, *La Loi Léotard* (named after Minister of Culture, Claude Léotard) was amended and extended to networked communication and the Internet. The law enumerated the responsibilities of Internet Service Providers (ISPs) towards their clients.[74] These responsibilities include informing clients of the existence and availability of technical means (software) that could assist them in blocking access to racist, anti-Semitic and other types of hate speech criminalized under the French penal code.[75] Furthermore, under this law, web page owners are not allowed to post material anonymously on the Internet. As a result, Internet Service Providers and hosts are required to obtain personal identifying information like names and addresses from their clients in the event material posted by these clients on the Internet is declared objectionable by third parties or is found to be in violation of French laws. However, French Internet Service Providers (ISPs) are neither criminally nor civilly liable for the content that is saved on, or transits through their servers, if they exercise no editorial control over the material.[76]

The French Exception and Internet "Jurisdiction Without Borders"

As we noted above, the exponential diffusion of the Internet across the globe—and especially in France, took the French politico-cultural establishment by surprise. As we see in chapter 5, the power of the Internet was first felt in France through an act of judicial defiance. After the *Tribunal de Grande Instance de Paris* (High Court of Paris) banned a book about late French President, François Mitterrand, a French cybercafé owner scanned the prohibited volume and uploaded it on the Internet. Hundreds of thousands of French citizens logged on to the website containing the banned book and either read or downloaded the book free of charge. French authorities were powerless to enforce the ban in a new medium which they regarded with suspicion, and which was, up to this point, lawless, unregulated, and primarily American.[77]

Things changed abruptly in 1998 when, in an unprecedented ruling, the *Tribunal de Grande Instance de Paris* (High Court of Paris) applied French exceptionalist logic to the Internet. It ruled that French courts had "universal jurisdiction over the totality of content disseminated on the Internet."[78] This "jurisdiction without borders" ruling came out of the Holocaust denial Faurisson case discussed at the beginning of this chapter.[79]

The Minitel Versus the Internet

When the United States government made the Internet available for commercial, economic, social, cultural and educational uses, without regard to jurisdiction, the French government and the French intelligentsia were indifferent, even hostile to the new network of computer networks. The most important reason for French indifference towards the Internet was that France already had its own home grown, online digital communication system, the

Acquisition Numérique et Télévisualisation d'Images Organisées en Pages d'Ecriture (ANTIOPE), a videotex service that was launched in 1977, and came to be known by its trade name, Minitel. The word "Minitel" is a contraction of "mini" (small) and "tel" (terminal and telephone).[80] The Posts, Telegraph and Telecommunications Directorate of the governmental telecommunications company, France Telecom, managed the system. The Minitel was part of the French government's *télématique* initiative, which was aimed at harnessing the combined advantages of computer technology (digitization) and telecommunications for purposes of improving communication services, private financial transactions, document transmission, database consultation, and teleconferencing.[81] The Minitel was a system designed to distribute information to large publics at relatively low cost.[82] With its rudimentary graphics and slow display speeds, the Minitel was essentially a proto-Internet that had possibilities for interactive electronic publishing, financial services and a host of other applications. Subscribers could request, retrieve and display information from databases stored in mainframe computers, on to special terminals or TV sets equipped with decoders.[83]

The Minitel was a revolutionary, interactive digital data packaging system that delivered local news, sports, weather, stock prices, train and other transportation timetables, classified advertisements and lots of information of interest to users.[84] Customers could also carry out bank transactions, make theater and other performance seat bookings. They could also transmit and receive messages. The most common usage to which the Minitel system was put was the *Annuaire éléctronique*, a digital online electronic telephone directory. The Minitel was part of the French exception in the area of telecommunications. The French government developed the technology within the Framework of its centralized bureaucratic system.[85] The Minitel was also entirely in French. In order to popularize the system, the French telecommunications authorities arranged with the French computer company, Bull, to mass-produce a cheap "dumb" terminal that was initially made available free of charge, to certain regions of the country.

The advent of the Internet sounded the death knell of the statist Minitel, whose limitations included—lengthy delays in accessing requested information, the small size of the screen, low quality graphics (only still images could be transmitted), the aesthetics of the system, and the difficulty inherent in reading television rather than watching it.[86] The Internet was revolutionary and very different from the Minitel. Actually, the Internet was considered alien to French culture,[87] and tradition.[88] However, it was a global phenomenon, it had superior networks, nodes, interfaces, graphics, and data transmission protocols. France has since changed its posture towards the Internet. In order to create a French and Francophone presence and increase French language content on the Internet, the French government created the *Fonds francophone des inforoutes* (Francophone Fund for "Information highways").[89]

The French Exception and Intellectual Property Law

The French exception is woven into the fabric of the French intellectual property regime, which is grounded in the *Code de la propriété intellectualle* (the Code of Intellectual Property). To the French, the term "copyright" is a rather narrow, foreign concept that expresses only part of the two components of intellectual and property rights that accrue to authors under French law. The French equivalent of the word "copyright" is the expression, "*droit d'auteur,*" (right of the author). Under French law, intellectual property consists of two rights: 1) a patrimonial (economic) right, and 2) an intangible, inalienable *droit moral* (moral right), that exist independent of the French or any other legal system. According to Kamm, moral rights "exist by moral argument."[90] Moral right is a rather "romantic" right of personality that seeks to protect the unique expression and metaphysical cachet or "mental signature" of the author on his or her work. Under this regime, authors retain moral rights in their works even after economic rights in the work have been exercised and the rights have been transferred to third parties pursuant to contracts.[91] Furthermore, moral rights can be the subject of testamentary transfers to heirs and other parties.[92] In France, intellectual property is viewed as an important component of the French cultural exception because intellectual property is an instrument for the protection and promotion of French culture. French exceptionalism in intellectual property law is thus expressed in terms of a heightened recognition of the importance of cultural and knowledge production, as well as recognition and celebration of authors of *œuvres d'esprit* (works of the mind) as cultural institutions. France has historically conceptualized works of the mind as *lieux de mémoire culturel* (sites of cultural memory) as well as propagators of national cultural heritage.[93] The Declaration of the Rights of Man and of the Citizen of 1789, which is the preamble of the French Constitution, recognized intellectual property. The Declaration states that property is a sacred, inviolable right of which citizens cannot be divested except in situations of legally ascertained political necessity, and on condition that a just and prior compensation be paid to them.[94] The French *Conseil Constitutionnel* (Constitutional Council), the institution whose task is to review the constitutionality of all bills before they are enacted, has reaffirmed the idea that intellectual property rights are part of the sacred human rights enumerated in articles 2 and 17 of the Declaration of the Rights of Man and of the Citizen of 1789.[95]

Conclusion

In France, the Declaration of the Rights of Man and of the Citizen of 1789, and the law on Freedom of the Press of 1881 are positive charters of liberties, which empower the government to take affirmative steps to regulate freedom of speech and expression in the country. Freedom of expression on the Internet is grounded in an exceptionalist logic whose main feature is a governmentally created "marketplace for ideas," to use the expression of van Gerven.[96] In this marketplace, speech is regulated on the basis of its content, and organized interest groups are monitors and co-regulators, with the government, of Internet content. The French exception is an interventionist logic under whose framework the government actively intervenes in public discourse for purposes of eliminating speech and expression that are believed to adversely affect human rights and human dignity, invade the privacy of individuals, is detrimental to health and morality, and damages the reputation of public officials, public figures, and private citizens. Though the American and French communication law regimes have constitutional provisions protecting freedom of expression, in their different historical and political contexts, the different exceptionalist logics of both countries make the reality of freedom of expression different in both countries.

NOTES

1. Le Procureur de la République, l'Unadif, la Fndir, l'Undivg, la Fondation pour la Mémoire de la déportation et la ligue des droits de l'homme c/Robert Faurisson *(Prosecutor of the Republic et al., v. Robert Flaurison)* Tribunal de grande instance de Paris, 13 nov. 1998, http://www.vho.org/aaargh/fran/polpen/justice/1998/rf981113.html.
2. See Pierre Rosanvallon, Le Modèle Politique Français (The French Political Model) 109, 112 (2004).
3. See Pierre Legrand, *Reasons for the Current Upsurge in Memory*, Eurozine (2002) www.eurozine.com.
4. See Nick Hewett, France and Exceptionalism, in The French Exception, Emmanuel Godin and Tony Chafer (EDS.) 3 (2005).
5. See Thomas Carlyle, The French Revolution, A History 4 (1840).
6. See Bernard Spolsky, Language Policy 63 (2004).
7. Pierre Legrand, *The Same and the Different, in* Comparative Legal Studies: Traditions and transitions 240, 254 (Pierre Legrand & Roderick Munday eds. 2003).
8. Arts. 1 & 2 Constitution of France (1958).
9. Feldman AT 7.
10. See Nick Hewett, France and Exceptionalism, in The French Exception, Emmanuel Godin and Tony Chafer (EDS.). 7 (2005).
11. See Jacques Rigaud, L'exception Culturelle: Culture Et Pouvoir Sous La Ve République (The Cultural Exception: Culture And Power Under The Fifth Republic) 16 (1995).
12. See Jacques Rigaud, L'exception Culturelle: Culture Et Pouvoir Sous La Ve République (The Cultural Exception: Culture and Power under the Fifth Republic) 113, 127 (1994).
13. See Charles De Gaulle, Mémoires De Guerre, L'appel, 1940-1942 (War Memoires, The Call, 1940-1942) 1 (1954).
14. See Jean Baudrillard & Marc Guillaume, Radical Alterity (Ames Hodges trans., MIT Press 2008) (1992).

15. See Margaret Majumdar, Exceptionalism and Universalism: The Uneasy Alliance in the French-speaking World, In The French Exception 16-29 (Emmanuel Godin and Tony Chafer (eds., 2005).

16. See Law No. 94-88 of February 1, 1994 (La Loi Toubon), journal Officiel de la République Française [J.O.] [Official Gazette of France], February 2, 1994, arts. 2 & 12.

17. Commission générale de terminologie et de néologie [General Commission on Terminology and Neology], Vocabulaire du Courrier électronique [Vocabulary of Electronic Mail], journal Officiel de la République Française [J.O.] [Official Gazette of France], June 20, 2003, *available at* http://www.culture.gouv.fr/culture/dglf/cogeter/20-06-03-courriel.htm (presenting officially approved French equivalents for the original English terminology for e-mail and related communication technologies).

18. See *Le Francais: Cadre Legal.* French: Legal Framework. Available at: http://www.dglf.culture.gouv.fr/

19. See David Beriss, Culture as Race and Race-as-Culture, in Herrick Chapman and Laura Frader (eds.). Race In France 115 (Berghan Books 2004).

20. See Herrick Chapman and Laura Frader, Race in France, in Herrick Chapman And Laura Frader (EDS.). Race In France 1-2 (2004). See also Lyombe Eko, New Media, Old Regimes: The Historical and Ideological Foundations of French and American Regulation of Bias-Motivated Speech and Expression on the Internet, 28 Loyola International and Comparative Law Review 101-156 (2005), and also Jonathan Laurence and Justin Viasse, Integrating Islam: Political and Religious Challenges in Contemporary France XIII (2006) (Stating that the French political system recognizes only individuals, not groups).

21. See e.g. *René Descartes, Règles pour la Direction de L'Esprit* (Rules for the Direction of Our Native Intelligence), in Oeuvres Philosophiques (Philosophical Works) (Ferdinand Alquié Ed., 1963); See also Jeffrie Murphy And Jules Coleman, Philosophy Of Law: An Introduction To Jurisprudence 11 (1990) (Natural law theories hold that there is a connection between law and morality).

22. See generally, François Marie Arouet de Voltaire, Treatise on Tolerance (1673).

23. See generally, Jean-Jacques Rousseau, The Social Contract (1762).

24. See Denis Diderot and Jean D'alembert, Encyclopedia (Nelly s. Hoyt and Thomas Cassirer trans. The Library of Liberal Arts (1965) (1765) (The Encyclopedia was one of the main vehicles for the expression of Enlightenment ideas).

25. See Charles Louis de Secondat, Baron de la Brède et de la Montesquieu The Spirit of Laws 235-238 (Thomas Nugent, trans., Hafner Publishing Co. 1949) (1748) (Suggesting that all men are born equal and that slavery is unnatural). See also Jean-Jacques Rousseau The First And Second Discourses & Essay On The Origin Of Languages 83 (Victor Gourevitch, trans. Harper Torchbooks 1986) (1750) (Criticizing European notions of Africa as an immense, impenetrable continent whose people are "laden with vices").

26. See e.g. John Locke, Of Civil Government (1690) (government must be based on the consent of the governed); see also A. Fouillé, J. et al., Modern French Legal Philosophy 51-52 (trans. Franklin w. Scott & Joseph Chamberlain, Boston Book Company (1916).

27. See Jacques Derrida, Force De Loi (Force Of Law) 45 (1994).

28. Article XI (Declaration adopted August 26, 1789).

29. Id. (emphasis added).

30. Id. Articles 4&5.

31. See Francois Furet, Revolutionary France: 1770-1880, 537 (trans. Antonia Nevill, Blackwell Books (1992) (1987).

32. See Georges Vedel, Qu'est-Ce La Constitution? (What Is The Constitution?) (1998), available at http:://www.conseil-constitutionnel.fr/dossier/quarante/q01.htm (The French Constitutional court has held that the human rights and social principles expressed in the Declaration of the Rights of Man and of the Citizen of 1789 and the Preamble of the Constitution of 1946 respectively, are incorporated in the Constitution of 1958).

33. See Frederick Schauer, The Exceptional First Amendment, in Michael Ignatieff (Ed.) American Exceptionalism and Human Rights 46 (2005).

34. See David Strauss, Menace In The West, The Rise Of French Anti-Americanism In Modern Times 578 (1978).

35. See generally, Jacques Portes, Une Fascination Réticente: Les États-Unis Dans L'opinion Française, 1870-1914 (A Reticent Fascination: The United States In French Public Opinion, 1870-1914 (1990).

36. See Lyombe Eko, New Media, Old Regimes: The Historical and Ideological Foundations of French and American Regulation of Bias-Motivated Speech and Expression on the Internet, 28 Loyola International And Comparative Law Review 101-156 (2006).

37. See Jacques Portes, Une Fascination Réticente: Les États-Unis Dans L'opinion Française, 1870-1914 (A Reticent Fascination: The United States In French Public Opinion, 1870-1914, at 346) (1990).

38. See Guy Scarpetta, *L'Anti-Americanisme primaire* (Primary anti-Americanism). Le Monde, November 5, 1980, at 2.

39. See Jacques Portes, Une Fascination Réticente: Les États-Unis Dans L'opinion Française, 1870-1914 (A Reticent Fascination: The United States In French Public Opinion, 1870-1914, at 349-350) (1990).

40. See Bénédicte Fauvarque-Cosson, Comparative Law in France, in The Oxford Handbook Of Comparative Law 35 (Mathias Reimann & Reinhard Zimmermann (Eds., London, Oxford University Press 2007).

41. See Cheryl Hudson, in American Popular Culture and Anti-Americanism, in 1 Anti-Americanism: Causes And Sources 239, 248 (Brendon O'Connor, ed. 2007).

42. Richard Kuisel, Seducing The French: The Dilemma Of Americanization (1993).

43. See Angélique Durand, American Audiovisual Propaganda in France, 1948-1955, in France And Its Spaces Of War 263, 265 (Patricia M.E. Lorcin & Daniel Brewer, eds., 2009).

44. See Angélique Durand, American Audiovisual Propaganda in France, 1948-1955, in France And Its Spaces Of War 263, 272 (Patricia M.E. Lorcin & Daniel Brewer, eds., 2009).

45. See generally Jacques Portes, Une Fascination Réticente: Les États-Unis Dans L'opinion Française, 1870-1914 (A Reticent Fascination: The United States In French Public Opinion, 1870-1914) (1990).

46. See Dennis Alger, Identity, Insecurity And Image: France And Language 98 (Clevendon, UK: Multilingual Matters, 1999).

47. See David Strauss, Menace In The West, The Rise Of French Anti-Americanism In Modern Times 6, 453 (1978).

48. See Philippe Roger, *L'ennémi Americain*: Génélologie De L'antiamericanisme Français (The American Enemy: Genealogy Of French Anti-Americanism) 442, 499 (2002).

49. See Jacques Portes, *Une Fascination Réticente: Les États-Unis Dans L'opinion Française 1870-1914* (A Reticent Fascination: The United States In French Public Opinion,1870-1914) 345-346 (1990).

50. See Philippe Roger, *L'ennémi Americain*: Génélologie De L'antiamericanisme Français (The American Enemy: Genealogy Of French Anti-Americanism) 440-441 (2002). See also David Strauss, Menace In The West, The Rise Of French Anti-Americanism In Modern Times 6 (1978).

51. See Philippe Roger, *L'ennémi Americain*: Génélologie De L'antiamericanisme Français (The American Enemy: Genealogy Of French Anti-Americanism) 15 (2002).

52. See Philippe Roger, *L'ennémi Americain*: Génélologie De L'antiamericanisme Français (The American Enemy: Genealogy Of French Anti-Americanism) 14, 87, 566-568 (2002).

53. See Jacques Portes, *Une Fascination Réticente: Les États-Unis Dans L'opinion Française 1870-1914* (A Reticent Fascination: The United States In French Public Opinion, 1870-1914) 355-356 (1990).

54. See Volker Schneider, Jean-Marie Charon, Ian Miles, Graham Thomas and Thierry Vedel, The Dynamics of Videotex Development in Britain, France and Germany: A Cross-national Comparison, 6 European journal Of Communication, 187 (1991).

55. See Rémi Després, x.25 virtual circuits—Transpac in France—Pre-internet data networking, 48 IEEE Communications Magazine 43 (2010).

56. See Lyombe Eko, *New Media, Old Regimes: Case Studies in Comparative Communication Law and Policy* 209 (2012).

57. See Ferdinand Alquié (Ed.) Rene Descartes, Regles Pour La Direction De L'esprit (Rules For The Direction Of Our Native Intelligence) In, Oeuvres Philosophiques, Tome 1

(Philosophical Works, Tome 1) AT 99 (1963), original work published 1684. (France prides itself of its Cartesian logic which is based on mathematical order, method and hierarchy enunciated by philosopher, Rene Descartes. The extreme decentralization, 'disorder' and absence of hierarchy in cyberspace goes against the grain of French thinking).

58. See Bernard Sananès, Internet et partis: cyber-renouveau? (The Internet and Political Parties: Cyber-rebirth? Le Monde, January 11, 2001 at 14 (The Internet has rendered the organizational charts of French political parties useless, diminished hierarchical relationships, and minimized the sacred, intangible word of the party boss).

59. See Pierre Delaroche, Les Bons Calculs du Minitel (The Good business of the Minitel) L'Express, June 26, 1997 at 71 (France Télécom, the national telephone company, made so much profit from the 7 million subscribers to its home-grown online service, Minitel, that it chose it over the Internet).

60. See Michel Alberganti, La main américaine tisse la Toile d'Internet, (Americans want to weave the web of the Internet). Le Monde, July 11, 1997.

61. See Michel Alberganti, *La Main Américaine Tisse la Toile d'Internet*, [*The American Hand Weaves the Web of the Internet*], Le Monde, July 11, 1997, at I.

62. Armand Mattelart, La Mondialisation de la Communication [Globalization of Communication] 92 (3rd Ed., 2002). *See also* Armand Mattelart, *L'Information Contre L'Etat [Information Against the State],* Le Monde Diplomatique (Fr.), March 2001, at 28 (suggesting that American information technologies and governmental policies have instituted competitive liberalism that have undermined state tutelage, law and sovereignty).

63. See Leila Bouachera, *La Souveraineté informationelle entre utopie et projet* [Informational Sovereignty between Utopia and draft], Le Monde (Fr.), Feb. 1, 1996, at 15 (suggesting that the transnational flow of information poses certain challenges for state sovereignty).

64. Id.

65. Armand Mattelart, *L'Information contre l'Etat* (Information Against the State) *Le Monde Diplomatique*, March 2001, at 28.

66. See Armand Mattelart, La Mondialisation De La Communication (3rd Ed.) (Globalization Of Communication) 94-95 (2002).

67. See Christophe Agnus, L'Intelligentsia a rejeté Internet (The Intelligentsia has rejected the Internet) L'Express, June 26, 1997 at 72.

68. See Gail R. Chaddock, France Aims to Beat The Net by Curbing it, The Christian Science Monitor, April 5, 1996 at 20.

69. See Volker Schneider, Jean-Marie Charon, Ian Miles, Graham Thomas and Thierry Vedel, The Dynamics of Videotex Development in Britain, France and Germany: A Cross-national Comparison, 6 European journal Of Communication 187, 203-204 (1991).

70. See Lyombe Eko, New Media, Old Regimes: Case Studies in Comparative Communication Law and Policy 209 (2012).

71. See Christophe Agnus, Je Suis en Croisade (I am on a Crusade), L'Express, June 26, 1997 at 72.

72. See Annie Kahn, *Vers une tutelle pour l'Internet français* (Towards tutelage for France's Internet), Le Monde (Television, Radio, Multimedia) June 10, 1996 at 28. As early as 1996, the French Senate passed a law creating the Comité superieur del la télématique, CST (The Higher Committee for Telematics) to supervise the activities of Internet access providers. Government agencies empowered to "coregulate" the Internet include the Commission nationale de l'informatique (CNIL), the Agence de Regulation des télécommunications, ART (Agency for the Regulation of Telecommunications), and the Conseil supérieure de l'audiovisuel, CSA (Higher Audiovisual Council).

73. Articles 15 & 16 of Law No. 78-17 of January 6, 1978 on Information Technology, Databases and Freedoms (journal Officiel of January 7, 1978) have been applied to the Internet. Under its provisions, a "Declaration of Processing of Personal Information within the Framework of a Webpage" has to be made to the Commission nationale de l'informatique, CNIL (The National Commission on Informatics and Freedom).

74. See art. 43-7 & 43-8 (*Loi 86-1067 du 30 september 1986 Relative à la liberté de Communication "Loi Léotard") J.O. du 2 ao û t 2000* (Law 85-1067 of September 30, 1986 (as amended) On Freedom of communication "Loi Léotard") J.O. of August 2, 2002.

75. See e.g. Law No. 2000-719 of August 1, 2000 (journal Officiel No. 177 of August 2, 2000, page 11903), amending Law No. 86-1067 of September 30, 1986 on Freedom of Communication (Internet Service Providers required to inform subscribers of the availability of "technical means" of restricting access to, or blocking certain online content, and offering subscribers these services).

76. See art. 43-8 (Loi 86-1067 du 30 septembre 1986 Relative à la liberté de Communication "Loi Leotard" J.O. du 2 août 2000) (Provisions that made ISPs criminally and civilly liable for objectionable content on their servers if they failed to act promptly to block access to such content pursuant to a court order, were declared unconstitutional by the French Constitutional Court in 2000).

77. Daniel Schniedermann, Le juge et le "cafétier" (The judge and the Internet café keeper) LE MONDE TV, RADIO, MULTIMEDIA, January 28, 1996 at 39.

78. Le Procureur de la République, l'UNADIF, la FNDIR, l'UNDIVG, la Fondation pour la mémoire de la déportation et La ligue des droits de l'homme c/ Robert Faurisson (*Prosecutor of the Republic et al. v. Robert Flaurison*), Tribunal de Grande Instance de Paris, nov. 13, 1998 (High Court of Paris, Nov. 13, 1998).

79. Le Procureur de la République, l'UNADIF, la FNDIR, l'UNDIVG, la Fondation pour la mémoire de la déportation et la ligue des droits de l'homme c/Robert Faurisson (*Prosecutor of the Republic et al., v. Robert Flaurison*) Tribunal de grande instance de Paris, 13 nov. 1998, http://www.vho.org/aaargh/fran/polpen/justice/1998/rf981113.html

80. See Alain Rey & Josette Rey-Debove, Le Petit Robert 1205 (1992).

81. Michael Binder, Videotex And Teletext: New Online Resources For Libraries 49 (1985).

82. See Alan J. Mayne, The Videotex Revolution 1 (1982).

83. See Alan J. Mayne, The Videotex Revolution 2 (1982).

84. See Efrem Sigel, Joseph Roizen, Colin Mcintyre & Max Wilkinson, Videotext: The Coming Revolution In Home/Office Information Retrieval 115 (1980).

85. See Leonard Graziplene, Teletext:Its Promise And Demise 125 (2000).

86. See Leonard Graziplene, Teletext, Its Promise And Demise 118 (2000).

87. See Bernard Sananès, *Internet et partis: cyber-renouveau?* (The Internet and Political Parties: Cyber-rebirth? Le Monde, January 11, 2001 at 14 (The Internet has rendered the organizational charts of French political parties useless, diminished hierarchical relationships, and minimized the sacred, intangible word of the party boss).

88. See Pierre Delaroche, Les Bons Calculs du Minitel (The Good business of the Minitel) L'Express, June 26, 1997 at 71 (France Télécom, the national telephone company, made so much profit from the 7 million subscribers to its home-grown online service, Minitel, that it chose it over the Internet).

89. *Ministère de l'Économie, des Finances et de l'Industrie, Fonds francophone des inforoutes*, (Ministry of the Economy, Finance and Industry, Francophone Information Highway Fund) (2010) at: http://www.telecom.gouv.fr/rubriques-menu/soutiens-financements/fonds-francophonc-inforoutcs/fonds-francophonc-inforoutcs-314.html

90. See F.M. Kamm, Rights, in The Oxford Handbook Of Jurisprudence & Philosophy of Law 475, 477 (2002).

91. See *Claude M'Barali (MC Solaar) et autres v. Société Media Consulting et autres Claude M'Barali* (MC Solaar and others v. Société Media Consulting and others Tribunal de Grande Instance de Paris, 3ème chambre, 2ème section (High Court of Paris) Jugement du 7 novembre (Judgment of November 7, 2003). Available at http://www.legalis.net/jurisprudence-decision.php3?id_article=1032 Last visited September 28, 2008. (Holding that a media company which licensed a musician's compositions from a copyright clearing house for use as cell phone ring tones violated the musician's moral rights because the musician did not authorize modification of the quality of the music).

92. Art. L. 121-1 *Code de la propriété intellectuelle* (Intellectual Property Code), version consolidée au 22 décembre 2007. (Consolidated version). Available at LegiFrance, http://www.legifrance.gouv.fr/affichCode.do?cidTexte=LEGITEXT000006069414&dateTexte=2008030 (Last visited March 24, 2008).

93. See François Azouvi, Descartes in Pierre Nora (Ed.) Lieux De Mémoire (Tome 3) (Sites Of Memory) (Vol. III) 4475 (Paris: Quarto Gallimard (1997) (Stating that French Philosopher, Réné Descartes is a "site of memory").

94. See Art. 17, Declaration of the Rights of Man and of the Citizen (1789). Available at: http://www.legifrance.gouv.fr/html/constitution/const01.htm (The Declaration is the preamble to the French Constitution of 1958, the supreme law of France).

95. See *Décision n° 2006-540 DC du 27 juillet 2006-Loi relative au droit d'auteur et aux droits voisins dans la société de l'information*, journal Officiel du 3 août 2006, p. 11541 (Non conformité partielle).

96. See Walter Van Gerven, The European Union: A Polity Of States and Peoples 242 (2005).

Chapter Five

New Media, Same Old Sex Scandals

Comparative Exceptionalism, Freedom of Expression and Invasion of Privacy in France and the United States

Internet law and policy reflects the governmentality or logics of governance of specific nation-states. Furthermore, exceptionalist mentalities undergird media law in general, and Internet law in particular, in the United States and France. This is because the Internet is woven into the political, social, cultural, and economic fabric of American and French society. This has not always been the case. The Internet was developed as part of efforts to strengthen the command and control system of the United States during the Cold War. Its non-military parts were the domain of esoteric academic researchers and computer science enthusiasts.[1] When the American Congress passed the Scientific and Advanced Technology Act of 1992, in a bid to open up the Internet to science, technology and engineering, as well as educational, cultural, and commercial activities, the network of computer networks quickly became a virtual, interactive, global, multi-communication platform.[2] When the United States Congress opened the Internet to the world, so to speak, the nascent multi-communication platform quickly became a sphere of freedom of expression. It also became the domain of electronic commerce, as well as pornography. The fledgling Internet quickly made itself felt in the politico-cultural arenas of France and the United States.

The Mitterrand/Pingeot Affair and the Internet in France

The Internet crashed into the placid surface of the French politico-legal system in 1995, in a rather dramatic fashion. In effect, the Internet was literally introduced to France and the French judiciary for the first time in the context of the so-called "affair Gubler," a scandal involving President Francois Mitterrand, and his mistress, Anne Pingeot. In effect, shortly after former French President François Mitterrand died of prostate cancer in 1996, his former personal physician, Dr. Claude Gubler and journalist Michael Gonod, published a tell-all book titled *Le Grand Secret* (The Big Secret). In the book Dr. Gubler revealed that President Mitterrand, who had terminal prostate cancer while still in office, had ordered the physician to issue "doctored" medical reports about the true state of the president's health. Gubler revealed that François Mitterrand had been practically incapacitated during the last two years of his presidency.[3] The book also gave details about Mitterrand's long-running affair with his mistress, Anne Pingeot, and the daughter, Mazarine, born of that extra-marital affair. The book hit the French political scene like a tsunami. More than 40,000 copies were sold on the first day it was released. The "two Mitterrand families"—his wife Danielle, and his mistress Anne Pingeot, and their respective children—promptly sued Dr. Gubler for invasion of privacy and breach of medical confidentiality. The *Tribunal de grande instance de Paris* (High Court of Paris) issued a temporary injunction against distribution of the book just one day after its publication, and barely ten days after President Mitterrand's death. On appeal, the Paris Court of Appeals affirmed the injunction but went further. It issued a permanent injunction against *Le Grand Secret* and ordered all printed copies of the book seized. The appeals court judge ruled that the book was an abuse of the right of freedom of expression, a violation of doctor-patient confidentiality, and an "extremely serious intrusion into the intimacy of the private family life of [late] President François Mitterrand, his wife, and children."[4]

In an unprecedented *coup de théâtre*, the Internet became an important complicating factor in the Mitterrand/Gubler affair. In effect, an early phenomenon of the Internet age, the cybercafé—a public place where patrons could have coffee and surf the nascent medium—had diffused to France. Immediately after the "The Big Secret," was banned, Pascal Barbraud, a cybercafé owner in Besançon, Franche-Comté, scanned the book and uploaded it to the Internet. The sensational nature of the case made the book an international *cause célèbre* of international freedom of expression activists. The website was mirrored in several countries, and the book was translated into several languages by volunteers—without the knowledge or authorization of Dr. Gubler or *Éditions Plon*, the publisher. Hundreds of thousands of French citizens, and interested parties from around the world logged on to the Besançon website or mirror sites in other European countries and the United States where the banned book was hosted, and read or downloaded it free of any charge. The Mitterrand/Gubler affair became the subject of discussion on hundreds of bulletin boards.

Digitization and transference of the banned Mitterrand book from real space to cyberspace, without the consent of the author, the publisher or the court took the French authorities by surprise.[5] French judicial authorities were powerless to enforce the ban in this new American medium which they did not understand, and which was, up to this point, legally undefined, lawless, and unregulated.[6] The public prosecutor in Besançon, where Barbraud's server was located, declared that digitizing the banned book and putting it on the Internet broke French law, but he took no legal action against the cybercafé owner because neither the publisher nor the author of the illegal book had lodged a complaint of intellectual property violation against Barbraud.

However, a few days later, Pascal Barbraud, the owner of the Besançon cybercafé and website was arrested for desertion of his family and failure to pay alimony and child support. Later, the police seized the computers and server of the cybercafé for non-payment of his business loan, pursuant to a court order obtained by Barbaud's creditors. This effectively shut down the cybercafé. From his jail cell, Pascal Barbraud claimed that his arrest, the seizure of his computers, and the closure of his cybercafé were directly linked to his attempts to "defend freedom of expression in France" by uploading the banned Mitterrand book on the Internet.[7]

In reaction to the banning of "The Big Secret," Gubler's co-author, Michel Gonod, published another book, a prize-winning volume entitled, "*Le Secret du Docteur Gubler*" (Dr. Gubler's Secret),[8] in which he repeated the claims that Mitterrand had ordered Gubler to issue false medical reports. Gonod also gave more details about Dr. Gubler's diagnosis of the president's incapacity to lead the country because of his poor health. Gubler read Gonod's manuscript before it was published and attested to its accuracy. The marathon legal battles over Mitterrand's health and affair that started with the publication of *The Great Secret* in 1996, continued for nearly ten years and ended up before the European Court of Human Rights.

The Mitterrand/Gubler affair provided an opportunity to analyze the early encounter between freedom of expression and invasion of privacy on the Internet within the context of the French exception. Since France has a very strong individual privacy tradition, Dr. Gubler's book was considered an egregious invasion of privacy. It became a major scandal against Dr. Gubler and his publisher, and led the country to take steps to exercise jurisdiction over the Internet, and mold those parts of the network of computer networks that either existed on its national territory or were accessible from there, to fit the contours of the French exception. This scandal therefore provides us an opportunity to analyze the transfer of media law from real space to cyberspace, within the context of French exceptionalist logic.

The Clinton/Lewinsky Affair and the Internet in the United States

In the United States, the fledgling Internet became the focal point of American exceptionalism in matters of freedom of speech and expression. It also became the platform on which information that was not adequately verified, or was too sensitive to be published in the traditional media, was posted. Indeed, the first American political scandal of the Internet age involved a series of sexual "affairs" involving the president of the United States, William Jefferson Clinton. What is notable about the Clinton affair is that it was first made public on the Internet rather than by the traditional media. In effect, in June 1997, the *Drudge Report*, a news aggregation website—an Internet portal that links to news stories on other websites—reported that Ken Starr, a Special Prosecutor investigating the involvement of Bill and Hillary Clinton in a real estate scandal in Arkansas, had interviewed several women about Bill Clinton's extra-marital sexual relationships, within the context of a sexual harassment suit that had been filed against the president by one Paula Corbin Jones.[9] Six months later, on January 17, 1998, the *Drudge Report* website had this banner headline:

> World Exclusive: NEWSWEEK KILLS STORY ON WHITE HOUSE INTERN BLOCKBUSTER REPORT: TWENTY-THREE-YEAR-OLD FEMALE WHITE HOUSE INTERN SEX RELATIONSHIP WITH THE PRESIDENT.[10]

With this banner headline, the *Drudge Report* broke the news that *Newsweek* magazine had killed a story that would have revealed that President William Jefferson Clinton had had a sexual affair in the White House with a twenty-one-year-old intern.[11] By rushing to report these events that the traditional media wished to further investigate and verify, the *Drudge Report* had scooped the traditional media, and journalism would never be the same again. Millions of Americans tried to log on to the *Drudge Report* site to read the story. The next day, the *Drudge Report* informed the world that the intern at the center of the scandal was called Monica Lewinsky, and that she had been subpoenaed to give a deposition at Paula Jones' sexual harassment case against President Clinton.[12] It turns out that *Newsweek* reporter, Michael Isikoff, did indeed have enough information about the Clinton real estate scandal and the emerging story of the Clinton-Lewinsky sex scandal to publish an article on the subject, but the editors of the newsmagazine decided to postpone the story due to an excess of caution, in order to do additional reporting and verification of the claims against Clinton.[13] Newsweek ultimately published a story on the scandal on its website days after the *Drudge Report* scoop, and its print competitors had published their own stories of the scandal. The Internet quickly became the platform where the world turned to, for purposes of learning about the salacious details of the private sexual activities of the President of the United States. Millions of people around the world followed the unfolding scandal in the traditional media and on the Internet with amazement.[14]

In hindsight, the Clinton-Lewinsky scandal became a turning point for American journalism. The *Drudge Report* would go on to break other stories that traditional print journalism would not publish without verification, since traditional journalism is a fact-based, craft grounded in an ethic of verification. The Internet had introduced a twenty-four-hour news cycle that was alien to the type of deliberative, well-researched, well-sourced, and verificatory journalism that weekly news magazines like *Newsweek*, *Time*, and *U.S. News* and *World Report* had practiced for decades.

Aim of the Chapter

This chapter is concerned with how France and the United States dealt with a similar issue—presidential sex scandals and the associated political and privacy issues they gave rise to. Why did the Clinton/Lewinsky affair become a major historical and political scandal that deeply affected American society, provided a "shock to the [American] body politic," and led to the impeachment of President Clinton for perjury, and a historic Senate trial,[15] while the Mitterrand/*Pingeot* affair had very little or no political or legal ramification in France? The aim of this chapter is to study the clash between freedom of expression and the right of privacy in real space and cyberspace, using as a comparative case study, the Clinton/Lewinsky affair and the Mitterrand/Pingeot affair in the United States and France respectively. The study was carried out within the context of American exceptionalism and the French exception. Additionally, the unprecedented publication of stories and texts about both affairs on the Internet provided an opportunity to analyze conceptualization of the role and place of the fledgling network of computer networks within the exceptionalist freedom of expression regimes of the United States and France. In France, the Internet has been woven into the fabric of the country's exceptionalist privacy regime. Under this regime, the right of privacy of public officials takes precedence over freedom of expression. By way of contrast, in the United States, the exceptionist principles of the First Amendment, including the public's right "to know," have been woven into the sinews of the Internet, and trump the right of privacy of public officials. This chapter explores the tension between freedom of expression and the right of privacy of public officials in both countries.

The Mitterrand/Pingeot Affair and the Clinton/Lewinsky Affair: Legal Aspects

The handling of the Clinton/Lewinsky[16] affair by the American mass media—including the fledgling Internet—and the political establishment reflects the unique sociopolitical culture, the exceptionalism, of the United States. This uniqueness is evident when the scandal is compared and contrasted with the identical extra-marital relationship involving the former President of France, François Mitterrand.[17] What the French press called *l'affaire Paris- Match* or *l'affaire Gubler,* was actually two intertwined scandals involving 1) President Mitterrand's long-running extra-marital relationship, with Anne Pingeot (a daughter, Mazarine, was born of this relationship), and 2) the successful cover-up of the gravity of Mitterrand's terminal prostate cancer, through "doctored" medical reports issued by his personal physician, Dr. Claude Gubler. In view of the strikingly different outcomes of the Clinton and Mitterrand "affairs" which involved essentially the same issues—extra-marital sexual relationships and lying—it would be interesting to explore the legal, political, cultural, and media contexts that led to such contrasting reactions and outcomes.

The historic trial and acquittal of William Jefferson Clinton, President of the United States of America, by the United States Senate,[18] subsequent to his equally historic impeachment by the United States House of Representatives on charges of perjury and obstruction of justice in connection with a sexual harassment suit, and a sexual relationship he had with White House Intern, Monica Lewinsky,[19] was the first global sex scandal of the Internet age. This story was a global story due to a confluence of several historical, religious and cultural factors. The Internet, the mass media and the American political establishment transformed the Clinton/Lewinsky relationship into the biggest sex scandal in the history of the American presidency; a scandal which affected American law, politics, religion, the workplace, mass media, and culture.[20] Not only was the Lewinsky scandal the top story of 1998 in the United States, it was among the top ten media stories in most parts of the world.[21] Clinton's impeachment and trial were the culmination of legal actions,[22] partisan political maneuvers replete with religious overtones,[23] and sensational mass media revelations.[24]

The French Exception and American Exceptionalism

This comparative case study exemplifies "*l'exception française*" (the French exception), the declaration that there is a marked linguistic, political and cultural difference between France and the rest of the world.[25] The study also exemplifies American exceptionalism—the premise that the United States is a political and cultural outlier that is different from most of the rest of the world—in matters of freedom of speech, freedom of expression, and invasion of privacy.[26] This chapter shows how both of these exceptionalist regimes had to come to terms with the realities of the Internet and its associated multi-communication platforms, as soon as it became an open global phenomenon.

The first part of the chapter will survey the Mitterrand/Gubler affair within the framework of French invasion of privacy laws. The chapter shows that

Mitterrand's extra-marital affair and successful cover-up of his grave illness are rooted in a French political culture, which values individual privacy above freedom of the press and the right to know. The second section of this chapter will analyze the Clinton/Lewinsky scandal within the framework of the exceptional First Amendment law of privacy in the United States. The chapter shows that the French exception in matters relating to the privacy of public officials tends to be prejudicial to freedom of expression, as well as to the democratic principles of transparency and accountability. By way of contrast, the consensual sexual relationship between the President of the United States and Monica Lewinsky became a major political and media scandal because America's political and social culture—American exceptionalism—often balances the right to privacy with the public character of political leadership, and the right to know. The chapter concludes that from the perspective of freedom of speech and of the press, the American model of individual privacy is often the recipe for sensationalism and media excesses, while the French model of subordinating freedom of expression to the right to privacy, unduly restricts freedom of expression and the right to know. It also leads to conflict of interest involving journalists and politicians.

Sex, Lies, and Pictures: Mitterrand, the *Paris-Match* and Gubler affairs and the Right to Privacy in France

In November 1994, the front cover of *Paris-Match*, a French "celebrity journalism" magazine, published a picture, taken in a public place, of President François Mitterrand, who was married, with his illegitimate daughter by his long-time mistress, Anne Pingeot. The magazine reported that Mitterrand was very fond of the girl and that he had been seen in public with her on a number of occasions.[27] The edition of *Paris-Match* containing the revelations about Mitterrand's extra-conjugal relationship had hardly reached the newsstands when a chorus of denunciations erupted from across the French political spectrum and the media establishment. In effect, *Paris-Match* had broken a taboo, an unwritten code of the French exception, namely, the private lives of public figures are off limit to the press. Though the pictures of the president and his illegitimate daughter were taken in a public place, *Paris-Match* was vilified across the political spectrum for invading the privacy of the French president. Jean Miot, Managing Editor of *Le Figaro*, a conservative French newspaper, and President of the *Fédération national de la presse française* (National Federation of the French Press) said it was regrettable that under the false pretext of exposing hypocrisy, some French members of the journalistic profession were sinking into the gutter, and invading the privacy of public officials like "Anglo-Saxon" (read Anglo-American) journalists had the habit of doing.[28]

The First Secretary of the French Socialist Party (Mitterrand's party), Henri Emmanuelli said publication of the Mitterrand photographs represented "extraordinary mediocrity, if not extraordinary baseness."[29] Jacques Delors, former President of the European Commission, asked the press to "make a distinction between public and private life, just as a distinction must be made between religious convictions and political convictions."[30] Even the French Communist Party newspaper, *l'Humanité*, called the journalistic practices of *Paris-Match* "deplorable for readers and dangerous for democracy."[31]

The venerable French newspaper, *Le Monde*, said the mass media must create a strict separation between the public and private lives of public figures. The newspaper stated that the secrets of the private lives of politicians can be of interest to the public only if they reveal a practice of lying which contradicts the politicians' public declarations, and if these secrets influence their public functions.[32] *Le Monde* concluded that:

> Mitterrand is the father of a natural child [from his mistress]. He shares this good fortune with many other Frenchmen. It doesn't stop him from working. He has never defined, for electoral reasons, the socialist norms of bourgeois good morals. . . . He has a daughter, Mazarine. So What?[33]

Other newspapers proclaimed that the "last taboo" (publication of the private love affairs of public figures) had been broken by the publication of the Mitterrand pictures.[34] Members of the legal profession lamented the loss of respect for individual privacy. Jean-Denis Bredin, a lawyer and member of the *Académie française,* stated that the wind of invasion of privacy, which was blowing from America and affecting French society with its calls for transparency and truth was imposing "moralistic systems and comfortable despotisms" which were a threat to human dignity and democracy. He said the law of privacy protected all, including the president, and that the truth cannot be above the law.[35] The Editor-in-chief of *Paris-Match* defended his magazine by stating that François Mitterrand had explicitly consented to the publication of the photographs in order to lift the taboo himself. "This is a public figure who has flaunted his private life in public,"[36] the magazine wrote.

Never before had pictures of the private life of a French politician, let alone the president of the republic, been published in France. This was a scandal, and the scandal was not that Mitterrand had a daughter by his mistress, but that *Paris-Match* and other mass media outlets had revealed the affair. It was only after Mitterrand's death, two years later, that the true story behind the publication of the photographs came to light. As early as 1984, three years into his first term of office, Mitterrand was asked, off the record, during a breakfast with journalists at the *Elysée* (presidential) palace, whether he had a natural (illegitimate) daughter with his mistress, as was rumored. He is reported to have replied, "Yes, I have a natural (illegitimate) daughter called Mazarine. So what?"[37] That reply led to a ten-year, near-total media blackout on the story.[38] In the meantime, Mitterrand met with the girl, Mazarine, in public, including at the *Elysée* (presidential) palace. She was even one of the official guests during a state dinner offered in honor of the visiting Emperor of Japan.[39]

In 1994, when *Paris-Match* came into possession of photographs of Mitterrand and his daughter as they left a restaurant in Paris, the magazine informed Mitterrand, through his press office, that it was aware of the existence of his then twenty-year-old daughter from an "extra-marital" relationship, and that it had a beautiful photograph of the president and his daughter in a public place.[40] The magazine wanted to inform the president that it intended to publish the pictures. Mitterrand, through his Prime Minister, Roland Dumas, succeeded in convincing *Paris-Match* to postpone publication of the story and the picture for three weeks in order to give him time to prepare his wife Danielle, his mistress Anne Pingeot, and the daughter in question, Mazarine, for the impending revelations.[41] Mitterrand nevertheless complained to an aide, Georges-Marc Benamou, that the story amounted to an invasion of his privacy. Furthermore, he said the child was born when he was a member of parliament, before he became president of France. Nevertheless, when he became president, he had continued to see his mistress, sometimes taking vacations with her.

Interestingly, when *Paris-Match* informed Mitterrand of the existence of the pictures, Mitterrand seemed relieved that by admitting paternity, he had done his duty by the girl, Mazarine.[42] Ultimately, nothing came of the revelations. The studied indifference of virtually all French publications and media outlets with respect to the revelation,[43] as well as subsequent successful legal action taken by Mrs. Mitterrand, Anne Pingeot, and their respective children to protect Mitterrand's privacy and reputation even after his death, can be contrasted with the media frenzy and the political tumult that greeted every revelation of every intimate detail of the Clinton/Lewinsky affair in the United States.[44] The fledgling Internet drove the media frency over the Clinton-Lewinsky scandal.

Protecting Mitterrand's Right of Privacy After his Death

Publication of the Mitterrand pictures by *Paris-Match* in 1994 did not lead to legal action because Mitterrand implicitly and explicitly consented to their publication. As we saw above, when Mitterrand died of prostate cancer in 1996, his former personal physician, Dr. Claude Gubler, who nursed grievances about the unceremonious manner in which he had been abruptly dropped from Mitterrand's medical team, published a tell-all book, *Le Grand*

Secret (The Big Secret).[45] The book came out just nine days after Mitterrand's death. When President François Mitterrand died, newspaper reports claimed that he and his doctors had hidden his illness from the French people for eleven years. Some of the reports stated that the president had dismissed his medical doctor, Claude Gubler, and opted for "alternative" experimental medical treatment.

Dr. Claude Gubler, Mitterrand's personal physician for twelve of the fourteen years in which he had prostate cancer, considered that these press reports—which were subsequently denied by the National Order of French Physicians and by Mitterrand's family—called his reputation into question. Those are the circumstances under which he published *Le Grand Secret*, a book that had been written before Mitterrand's death. In the book, Dr. Gubler claimed that for fourteen years, President François Mitterrand had hidden from the French people, the fact that he suffered from prostate cancer and that the president had ordered his doctors to classify his illness as a state secret. Dr. Gubler further claimed that Mitterrand had instructed him to issue false and misleading medical reports about the president's health, which the doctor did.[46] Gubler also claimed that during Mitterrand's last two years in office, the president was practically incapacitated and unfit to serve as president. Additionally, Gubler claimed that François Mitterrand had a "second family" (made up of his mistress, Anne Pingeot, and his "natural" daughter, Mazarine), which he housed in an official government residence free of charge. Dr. Gubler stated that Mitterrand was a "national adulterer" whose mistress, Anne Pingeot, and her daughter, Mazarine, occupied a "preponderant" place in Mitterrand's life.[47]

The Mitterrand/Gubler Affair and Invasion of Privacy

Hell hath no fury like an exposed French first family. Dr. Claude Gubler soon received a ten-year lesson in the consequences of violation of French exceptionalism on matters touching on the private lives of French public figures. The Gubler case was the triumph of law over the right of freedom of expression. As we saw earlier, on the day *Le Grand Secret* (The Big Secret) was published, President Mitterrand's widow and children, lodged an urgent application with the *Tribunal de grande instance* de Paris (High Court of Paris) complaining that the book constituted a breach of medical confidentiality, an invasion of President Mitterrand's privacy, and a cause of injury to Mitterrand's relatives' feelings. The *tribunal de grande instance* de Paris issued a temporary injunction prohibiting Dr. Gubler, his co-author, Michel Gonod, and his publisher, Èditions Plon, from continuing to distribute the book, on penalty of 1,000 French francs ($200) per book distributed. The court instructed a bailiff "to procure all documents containing details of the print run and the number of copies in circulation."[48] The Paris Court of

Appeals upheld the injunction. Dr. Gubler was also censured by the *Conseil de l'Ordre des Médecins* (Council of the Order of Physicians) for violating the Hippocratic oath, the French code of medical ethics, and violation of medical confidentiality.

With the injunction in effect, the French government decided to criminally prosecute Dr. Gubler, his co-author, the journalist, Michel Gonod, and his publisher, Èditions Plon. The physician was charged with breaching medical confidentiality. He was convicted and given a four months' suspended sentence by the Paris Criminal Court. His co-defendants, Michel Gonod, and Olivier Orban, managing director of Éditions Plon, the publisher of the book, were found guilty of aiding and abetting the offence. All three were given heavy fines.[49]

While the criminal trial against Gubler, Gonod and Orban was going on, Mitterrand's two families—his wife Danielle, her two sons, and his natural daughter, Mazarine—stung by the revelations, jointly commenced civil proceedings against Dr. Gubler and Mr. Orban (in his personal capacity and as the statutory representative of the publishing company, Éditions Plon) in the *Tribunal de grande instance* de Paris (High Court of Paris) for invasion of privacy—revealing Mitterrand's extra-marital relationship with Anne Pingeot—and breach of doctor-patient confidentiality under the French Penal Code.[50] They sought "an order prohibiting resumption of the publication of *Le Grand Secret* or, in the alternative, deleting certain pages and paragraphs" from the book.[51] They also sought an award of damages. They claimed that the book "contained disclosures that breached medical confidentiality and invaded President Mitterrand's privacy in such a way as to interfere with the feelings and personal life of his widow and children." They further submitted that these revelations and "indiscretions amounted to direct personal attacks on their own sphere of intimacy."[52] Under French law, private relationships are out of bounds to the mass media. Information about such relationships can only be published with the consent of one of the persons involved in the relationship. The French Penal Code makes it a criminal offense to "print, record, or transmit voluntarily, without consent, the image of a person who is in a private place, or to preserve it or bring it or allow it to be brought to the knowledge of the public or to third parties.[53] In their defense, Dr. Gubler, Gonod, and Orban claimed that they had not violated Mitterrand's privacy because during the president's election campaign, he had promised to publish regular reports of the state of his health, unlike his predecessors like Georges Pompidou, who had hidden the gravity of his medical problems from the French people until the very end.

The issue before the court was whether by promising—at the time of his election—to publish regular reports on the state of his health, President François Mitterrand had effectively given Dr. Gubler consent to make his medical records public, such that the doctor could not be charged with violating doctor-patient confidentiality, and invading the privacy of the two Mitterrand families. The court held that Mitterrand's political promise did not constitute consent. The court found for Mitterrand's two families. The judge said the book was an abuse of freedom of expression, a violation of doctor-patient confidentiality and an "extremely serious intrusion into the intimacy of the private family life of president François Mitterrand, his wife and children."[54] The court ordered Dr. Gubler, and his co-accused, to pay damages to Mrs. Mitterrand and the other claimants, and maintained the ban on distribution of *Le Grand Secret.*

On appeal, the Paris Court of Appeals rejected the action brought by the Mitterrand family with respect to protection of the late President Mitterrand's private life. The court pointed out that only living persons could prohibit disclosures about their private affairs. However, the court affirmed the fines and maintained the ban on distribution of the book because it breached the duty of medical confidentiality.[55] The French Supreme Court (*Cour de cassation*) affirmed the violation of medical secrets charge against Gubler but did not rule on the invasion of privacy charge.[56]

In November 1999, a decree (executive order) issued by President Jacques Chirac, Mitterrand's successor, stripped Dr. Claude Gubler of the national Medal of Honor that had been conferred on him for exemplary services rendered to the state and to the medical profession.[57] The French Order of Physicians followed suit and struck Dr. Gubler off the list of medical practitioners. Gubler appealed his disbarment to the State Council. In 2000, the appeal was rejected and he was officially struck off the register of licensed physicians in France.[58]

The Mitterrand/Gubler affair at the European Court of Human Rights

The marathon legal battles over Mitterrand's "doctored" health reports and extra-marital affair that started with the publication of *The Big Secret* in 1996, continued for nearly ten years. The French courts re-presented the norms and values of the country with respect to the right of privacy and penalized Gubler, Gonod and their publisher, *Éditions Plon*. After exhausting all remedies available to it in France, *Éditions Plon,* the publisher of *The Big Secret*, lodged an appeal with the European Court of Human Rights in 2000. In its complaint to the ECtHR, *Éditions Plon* claimed that the permanent injunction issued by the Paris Court of Appeal in 1996 against publication and distribution of the book, and a court order requiring it to pay "exorbitant" damages to the family of late President François Mitterrand for invading their privacy through the content of the banned book, violated its right of freedom of expression guaranteed under Article 10 of the European Convention on Human Rights.[59]

The ECtHR took the opportunity to present anew, European conceptualization of freedom of expression under the Convention. The issues before the court was whether 1) the permanent injunction and fines imposed on Èditions Plon interfered with the publisher's right of freedom of expression, 2) whether the interference was justified (that is, prescribed by law), 3) whether it furthered a legitimate social function, and 4) whether it was necessary in a democratic society.[60] The court held that French courts had interfered with Plon's freedom of expression, and that the interference complained of was prescribed by law. The court concluded that the penalties imposed on Plon were:

> intended to protect the late President's honour, reputation and privacy, and the national [French] courts' assessment that these 'rights of others' were passed on to his family upon his death does not appear in any way unreasonable or arbitrary. . . . Accordingly, the interference at issue pursued at least one of the 'legitimate aims' set out in the second paragraph of Article 10 of the Convention.[61]

As to whether banning *The Great Secret* on a permanent basis was "necessary in a democratic society," the court held that Article 10 does not prohibit prior restraints on publications, it also does not prohibit banning of the distribution of books per se. However, the court said it had to determine whether the prior restraint in question—the permanent injunction against distribution of the book on Mitterrand—was "proportionate to the legitimate aim pursued," namely protection of the honor of the late president, as well as the privacy rights of his heirs.[62]

The court proceeded to split doctrinal hairs by holding that the interim injunction issued by the *Tribunal de grande instance de Paris* (Superior Court of Paris) in 1996 against distribution of the book, the day after its publication, and barely ten days after President Mitterrand's death, was "'necessary in a democratic society' for the protection of the rights of [late] President Mitterrand and his heirs" because the information contained in the book "constituted a *prima facie* breach of medical confidentiality that could only have intensified the grief of the President's heirs following his very recent and painful death."[63]

The court however held that even though the interim prior restraint was justified in the short term, "a general and absolute" permanent injunction—nine months later—against distributing the book, no longer served a "pressing social need."[64] Noting that 40,000 copies of the book had already been sold before the injunction and that an electronic version of the book had been made available on the Internet in several languages, and had been commented on by the media despite the injunction, the court concluded that a permanent injunction against distribution of *Le Grand Secret* under the circumstances was a violation of Article 10 of the European Convention.[65] The outcome of this verdict was that *Éditions du Rocher* republished *Le Grand Secret* in 2005, nine years after it had been banned in France. The ban had been enforced outside France by Mitterrand family lawyers through threats of legal action against non-French websites that had dared to host copies of the banned book. The practical effect of this ruling was that Mitterrand's two families: His wife, Danielle, and their children, and his mistress, Anne Pingeot, and Mazarine, the daughter she had with Mitterrand, could no longer continue to protect the late former president's privacy nine years after his death.

The European Court of Human Rights and the Disbarment of Dr. Gubler

The qualified free speech victory of *Èditions Plon*, and by extension, Dr. Claude Gubler, in the European Court of Human Rights, did not resolve the issue of Gubler's disbarment from the medical profession for issuing "deceptive and misleading" medical reports about Mitterrand's health, and for breach of medical confidentiality through revelations in *The Big Secret*. Gubler had appealed to the European Court of Human Rights, claiming that his disbarment by the National Council of Physicians was an unfair violation of his human rights because the organization had brought the complaint against him and the same organization's disciplinary section had disbarred him. The doctor claimed that President Mitterrand had authorized him to write a book about his illness, and that the false and misleading medical reports he had issued about Mitterrand's health for more than 10 years were issued on the express orders of the president who had stated that he wanted the state of his health treated as a state secret. Gubler said Mitterrand had further ordered that his medical reports should be sanitized or made "neutral" for *raisons d'état (*reasons of state).

The issue before the European Court of Human Rights was whether the National Council of Physicians was independent and impartial when it disbarred Gubler.[66] The court held that though the French system set up to discipline violators of medical confidentiality was "archaic," there was no evidence to support suggestions that it was not impartial. The court therefore held that the disciplinary procedures leading up to the disbarment of Dr. Gubler by the National Order of Physicians did not violate the European Convention on Human Rights.[67]

This being the end of the legal road, Dr. Gubler lost his medical license permanently. When the French State Council affirmed the decision of the Disciplinary Section of the National Order of Physicians to strike Dr. Gubler off its rolls, the French newspaper of record, *Le Monde* expressed the mood of the disappointed French media:

> *Ainsi est définitivement récompensé de sa sollicitude le médecin, certes complaisant, d'un président de la République qui ne le fut pas moins, mais qui ne sera jamais, lui, sanctionné, pour avoir abuser le peuple dit souverain.*[68]
>
> Thus is irrevocably rewarded for his solicitude, the doctor, complacent, to be sure, of a president of the Republic who was no less complacent, but who will never be sanctioned for deceiving the so-called sovereign people [of France].

In the *Mitterrand v. Plon* and *Mitterrand v. Gubler* cases, the French justice system was faced with major discontinuities—Globalization, Americanization, sensationalism, and the Internet—that threatened to undermine centuries' old French respect for, and deference towards imperial presidencies and republican monarchies; a system where strict medical confidentiality laws bred official deceptions about the health or lack thereof, of kings, emperors and presidents. This culture had also engendered strict journalistic reticence and careful avoidance of anything touching on the health or private lives of public figures. In the face of these challenges from the Internet, French courts used the Mitterrand/Gubler affair to present old values, principles and modus operandi anew to the parties concerned and to the rest of the world. However, the imposition of old-style prior restraint in the new global media environment was not very successful. Despite the nine-year injunction against its publication and distribution, *Le Grand Secret* was available on the Internet in several languages. The print version of the book became legal in France in 2004.

The *Mitterrand/Paris-Match/Gubler affairs*, French Exceptionalism, and the Law of Privacy

Now that we have discussed the Mitterrand/Paris Match/Gubler affairs and their outcomes, this section will explain the politico-cultural and legal context of these legal outcomes. I suggest that the chorus of condemnation that greeted the *Paris-Match* publication of the Mitterrand pictures, the total indifference with which the French political and media establishments greeted news that President Mitterrand's mistress and her daughter were being housed free of charge in a government residence, coupled with the disbarment of Dr. Claude Gubler, can be explained by the French exception in matters relating to the private lives of public figures. The personal moral or religious values or lack thereof, of French politicians, as well as their private activities and indiscretions are not of importance to the French people as long as these activities do not adversely affect the public functions of these politicians. The reasons for this are an historical artifact of the French exception.

The French Exception and Invasion of Privacy: Historical Antecedents

When pictures of President François Mitterrand and his daughter from his long-running extra-marital relationship were published, a Belgian newspaper, *Le Soir*, wrote that France was reviving its monarchical traditions where its Roman Catholic kings always had "favorites" or mistresses.[69] In effect, from the Middle Ages to the Revolution of 1789, French kings entered into political marriages with princesses from other European countries in order to maintain the international balance of power, while they had mistresses on the side. These relationships were part and parcel of royal tradition and culture for hundreds of years. King Henri IV (he had 33 mistresses and 16 children out of wedlock), King Louis XIV, and King Louis XV, are notorious for the number and influence of their mistresses. Some of these mistresses had enormous influence on the affairs of state. Louis XIV went as far as secretly marrying one of his mistresses, Madame de Maintenon.[70] An influential courtesan, Madame de Pompadour, the mistress of King Louis XV, is probably the most famous mistress in French history.[71] After the Revolution of 1789, the tradition of political leaders having mistresses continued. Emperor Napoleon Bonaparte had tens of mistresses, so did Napoleon II. This royal tradition is the basis for the stringent individual privacy regime of France.

The liberation of the French press from centuries of censorship after the Revolution of 1789 led to the publication of anonymous pamphlets and tracts, which raised concerns about invasion of privacy. This early concern is reflected in France's post-revolutionary jurisprudence, which has consistently sustained the theory that invasion of privacy is an abuse of the freedom of expression set forth in the Declaration of the Rights of Man and of the Citizen.[72] Stringent respect for individual privacy has continued to be one of the hallmarks of the French exception. Under this regime, respect for individual privacy trumps freedom of speech and expression regarding even truthful matters.

Contemporary France has one of the most stringent privacy law regimes in the world. This regime is bolstered by a battery of statutes against invasion of individual privacy on the part of the mass media. Under the law of privacy, the public and private lives of politicians are strictly compartmentalized. The principle is that revelation of information, even truthful information about the private lives of public officials or public figures constitutes invasion of privacy, if these facts do not have a message capable of affecting society. The French law of privacy is spelled out in Article 9 of the French Civil Code, which became applicable through the law of July 17, 1970.[73] This law states *inter alia*: "every one has a right to respect for his private and family life." [74] This includes privacy of one's body, health, death, and dead body, privacy of filiation, pregnancy and childbirth, privacy of one's sentimental or love life, privacy of love, residence, home and image.[75] This law also protects French public figures and celebrities. Even if the truthful information about the private life of the public official is intertwined with a matter of public concern, it may still be an invasion of privacy if the information is made public. For example, the fact that President François Mitterrand provided a government-owned Parisian residence for his mistress, Anne Pingeot and their "natural" daughter, Mazarine, free of charge, was not sufficient to make Dr. Gubler's revelations a matter of public concern. Under privacy law provisions, judges can impose penal sanctions and other measures against defendants to ensure that individual privacy is protected. Penalties may include ordering the sequestration and seizure of offending publications. The New Penal Code makes it an offense to "fix, record, or transmit voluntarily, and without consent, the image of a person who is in a private place, as well as to conserve these documents, bring them or allow them to be brought to the knowledge of the public or a third party."[76] Under this statute, it is illegal for a photographer to take pictures of a person, without that person's consent, in a private place or residence even if that person can be seen from the street, and even if that person has no expectation of privacy. The New Penal Code also states that journalists can take pictures of a person in private, on French soil, only with that person's consent. Even in public places, photographers generally need consent to take pictures of people.[77] Those who break the law risk criminal prosecution.

Additionally, France incorporates the individual privacy clause of the European Convention on Human Rights into its privacy law regime.[78] The first clause of article 9 of the French Civil Code is a verbatim *reprise* of article 8 of the European Convention on Human Rights. The Convention gives governments the authority to penalize the mass media if they encroach on individual privacy.[79] Unfortunately, the term "privacy" is not defined in either the French Civil Code or the European Convention on Human Rights. Under French law, the expressions, *la vie privée* (private life), and *l'intimité de la vie privée* (the intimacy of private life) are wide legal umbrellas which cover anything that is neither public nor of general interest.[80] Included in an individual's private life are: "family life, married life, and 'extra-marital' or sentimental life."[81] Thus, public officials of all capacities can sue for defamation and invasion of privacy, even though the offending material is true because the *exceptio veritatis* (defense of truth) is subordinate to higher governmental and societal interests.[82] Therefore, truth is not a defense in either the criminal or civil actions for invasion of privacy.[83] Furthermore, facts (even facts on the public record) about an individual's conduct are excluded from the defense of truth in criminal or civil proceedings, if these facts go back more than ten years.[84]

Lack of a clear definition notwithstanding, invasion of privacy is considered both a tort and a criminal offense. It can be committed through both pictures and words. It does not matter whether the victim is a public official, a public figure, or a private citizen.[85] However, consent is presumed if the photography, video or audio recording takes place within sight and with the knowledge of the participants in the course of a meeting. The law gives judges the power to seize publications and issue injunctions in order to prevent encroachment on the intimacy of private life.[86] Civil penalties for invasion of privacy include banning of offending publications, deleting offending passages from a book,[87] and the destruction of all the copies of an infringing publication at the publisher's warehouse.[88] *La Cour de Cassation* (Court of Cassation), the French court of last resort for civil and criminal matters, has held that banning an issue of a newspaper or a book does not infringe on freedom of the press when a court finds that the book or the issue of the newspaper in question contained information that constitutes invasion of privacy.[89] Historical legacies, legislative enactments, judicial interpretations and journalistic reporting on the issue of individual privacy clearly demonstrate that at the heart of the French right to privacy is a right to secrecy—for the powerful and well-connected—who advance their personal interests under the cloak of secrecy, as was clearly the case in the Mitterrand scandal. Many members of the French political establishment clearly use the law of privacy to hide their lack of transparency and accountability.

A statute protecting the privacy rights of French citizens with respect to computer databases and data processing adds to this formidable arsenal against invasion of privacy. This law, which states that computers and databases shall be at the service of every citizen, brings information and communication technologies within the ambit of the French exception in matters of invasion of privacy. The law expressly states that computerized databases may not be used to infringe an individual's right to privacy.[90] Individuals, companies or governmental entities which intend to place computerized directories and individual data on the Internet are required to seek special permission from the National Commission on Informatics and Individual Freedoms before the information is placed online.[91] The European Convention for the Protection of Individuals With Regard to Automatic Processing of Personal Data is also incorporated in French individual privacy law.[92] The United States and the European Union have clashed over this law, which forbids online transfer of personal information from European Union countries to countries whose individual privacy law regimes are not considered adequate by European standards. The European Union places the United States in this category.[93]

The Clinton/Lewinsky Scandal, and the Right to Privacy in the United States: Background

What came to be known around the world as the "Clinton/Lewinsky scandal" or the "Lewinsky affair" started in 1992 with a revelation in the *New York Times* that while he was governor of Arkansas, presidential candidate William Jefferson (Bill) Clinton, had been involved in an alleged conflict of interest. He and his wife were involved in a land development called Whitewater, together with a savings-and-loan operator whom his government regulated.[94] The Whitewater affair caught up with Bill Clinton after he was elected President of the United States. The savings-and-loan company, which had financed the Whitewater land deal collapsed, and was being investigated by federal regulators. In 1993, Vince Foster, the White House lawyer who had handled the Whitewater deal for the Clintons, was found dead in Fort Marcy Park, Virginia. Attorney General Janet Reno appointed a special prosecutor to look into the matter.

In 1994, a conservative magazine, *The American Spectator*, published an article alleging that while he was governor of Arkansas, Bill Clinton had used state troopers to procure women for extra-marital sexual relations. The same year, Paula Corbin Jones, a former employee of the state of Arkansas filed suit against President Clinton for sexual harassment that allegedly occurred in 1991, while Clinton was governor of Arkansas.[95] Clinton sought temporary immunity from the suit, claiming that the alleged sexual impropriety occurred years before he became president of the United States. A United States District Court granted the president temporary immunity from the suit until after he left office.[96] The United States Court of Appeals for the Eight Circuit reversed the immunity.[97] Clinton appealed to the Supreme Court of the United States which granted a writ of certiorari and held that the Constitution of the United States did not afford the president temporary immunity from civil litigation over matters that took place before he assumed office. The Court held that the doctrine of separation of powers did not require federal courts to stay all private actions against the president until after he left office.[98]

The Clinton/Lewinsky Affair and the Internet

We saw in chapter 3 that in *Reno v. ACLU,* the Supreme Court of the United States ruled for the first time that the Internet had full First Amendment protection.[99] The practical effect of that ruling was that it transferred American First Amendment exceptionalism from real space to cyberspace, and in the process, globalized First Amendment values. The fledgling medium wasted no time assuming a First Amendment checking function vis-à-vis the government and public figures. The relative anonymity accorded

Internet publishers, and the low costs associated with online publishing soon transformed the Internet into a gargantuan marketplace of ideas where all kinds of information, disinformation, and rumors were disseminated. Many Internet publishers assumed the role of watchdogs of the public interest.

While the Paula Jones sexual harassment case against President Clinton was at bar, Clinton got involved in a sexual relationship with Monica Lewinsky, a White House intern. Monica provided Linda Tripp, a disgruntled former White House worker, graphic descriptions of her sexual liaison with the president. Unbeknownst to Lewinsky, Tripp secretly recorded their conversations and handed the tapes to Paula Jones' lawyers and to Kenneth Starr, the Independent Counsel[100] who was investigating the Whitewater affair.[101] The aim of Tripp, Paula Jones' lawyers, and Kenneth Starr was to show that Clinton was an unreliable liar who sexually harassed women and took advantage of those who worked for him. Lewinsky filed an affidavit stating that she did not have sexual relations with the president. Clinton later made a video-taped deposition in the Jones case in which he denied having a sexual relationship with Lewinsky. Starr subsequently seized Monica Lewinsky's computer hard drive and emails from which he obtained further evidence of their sexual relationship. Lewinsky's affidavit and the president's deposition soon turned out to be less than truthful.[102]

Knowing that Lewinsky had filed an affidavit that contradicted what she had said on tape to Tripp, the Independent Counsel threatened Monica with prosecution for perjury if she did not cooperate with his office. She entered into an immunity deal with the Independent Counsel's office and revealed in great detail, the extent of her relationship with the president, including the existence of a semen-stained dress.[103] In the face of these revelations, Clinton reluctantly admitted having "an inappropriate intimate contact" with Monica Lewinsky.[104] As soon as the trial of Jones' sexual harassment case got underway, Jones stuck to the strategy. She sought to show the Federal District Court in Arkansas that Clinton had a habit of sexually harassing women.

In September 1998, Independent Counsel, Kenneth Starr, submitted a report of his investigation to a Republican-led House of Representatives. The report or referral recounted in minute detail, and with voyeuristic exactitude, specific sexual acts between Monica Lewinsky and the President of the United States.[105] In the referral, Starr concluded that the president should be impeached and removed from office on eleven grounds.[106] The House of Representatives subsequently impeached Clinton on two grounds: perjury (about his sexual relations with Monica Lewinsky) and obstruction of justice. William Jefferson Clinton thus became only the second President in American history to be impeached. In accordance with constitutional stipulations, the matter was sent to the United States Senate where Clinton was tried and subsequently acquitted of the charges of perjury and obstruction of justice.[107] Paula Jones' sexual harassment case was dismissed before trial and she appealed. Clinton subsequently settled the case with Jones for $850,000.

The Clinton/Lewinsky Scandal and American Exceptionalism: Historical Origins of the Law of Privacy in the United States

The historic impeachment of President William Jefferson Clinton was possible because of American exceptionalism in matters of freedom of expression. Furthermore, since openness is a fundamental characteristic of American democratic exceptionalism, the private sexual peccadilloes of public officials are considered matters of public concern. Under American exceptionalism, freedom of expression, transparency, and the people's right to know trump the privacy rights of public officials. The Clinton/Lewinsky scandal exemplifies the legal aphorism that justice must not only be done, it must be seen to be done.[108] When some traditional media outlets declined to report on the Clinton-Lewinsky scandal and its salacious details, the Internet proved to be a veritable global electronic scandal sheet, which disseminated the minutest details of the scandal to all corners of a perplexed, interconnected world.

To many observers around the world, this was a reincarnation of America's Puritanical ways. The French newspaper, *Le Monde*, which had staunchly defended Mitterrand's right of privacy in the Paris Match affair, likened the Clinton/Lewinsky affair to a New England puritanical witch trial, complete with an inquisitorial prosecutor, Kenneth Starr. According to the newspaper, "*l'affaire Kenneth Starr*" (the Kenneth Starr affair) was sheer totalitarianism with a religious face, an affair which gave the American media an opportunity to indulge in the public rape of Lewinsky and Clinton, under the guise of restoring morality.[109] By calling the Clinton/Lewinsky scandal, "*l'affaire Starr*" (The Starr affair), *Le Monde* and most of the rest of the French press left no doubt as to whose behavior was more scandalous, and who was on trial in the minds of the European intelligentsia.

Historically, *Le Monde* was on target when it linked the Clinton/Lewinsky affair to America's Puritan origins. The scandal was a modern-day exemplar of American exceptionalism. As we saw in chapter 3, America's contemporary political culture owes much to, and is consistent with, the exceptionalist ideology that was a major creed of the Puritans founders of New England. Character has always been a very important element in American politics because Puritans believed that man's natural condition was depravity.[110] Therefore, character was one of the most important attributes of Puritan leadership. When they first settled in New England, the leaders of the Puritan community saw themselves as God's soldiers whose responsibility was to protect God's people from the moral decay within. Church membership and good character were therefore a prerequisite for leadership.[111] The political leaders (magistrate) were viewed as God's vice-regents who were responsible for maintaining public morality (the purity of the church).[112] To the Puritans, the good ruler was the "God's vice-regent who brought justice to the world through special God-given talent.[113] The Puritan ideal of a good leader was a person who "maintained and encouraged the people's virtue" in order that corrupt moral practices would not undermine the commonwealth.[114] The private and public lives of individuals, particularly leaders, were therefore inseparable in the eyes of Puritans. All known evildoers in the church were to be expelled or excluded.[115] "Sexual love between husband and wife was a mirror of the ecstatic union between the soul and Christ, but adultery, fornication, homosexuality, bestiality, and the like, were perversions of God's gifts and sins to be severely punished."[116]

As we saw in chapter 3, Puritan ideals had a profound influence on the American Revolution.[117] American political, cultural and social ideals—the "American way of life" is grounded on Puritan values and principles.[118] In the political sphere, the Founding Fathers believed that character and personal responsibility were important in a chief executive or president.[119] Public scrutiny of the private lives of public officials is thus rooted in America exceptionalism. Furthermore, exceptionalist concepts like "the watchdog role of the press," "the people's right to know," "newsworthiness" and "fitness for office" made the Clinton/Lewinsky relationship a uniquely American affair. The concept of "fitness for office," also comes out of Puritan religious and political ideas, which held morality and good character as being essential ingredients of leadership.[120]

The Clinton/Lewinsky Affair and the Law of Privacy in the United States

The question generally asked in connection with the Clinton/Lewinsky scandal is whether by investigating the consensual sexual relationship between Clinton and Lewinsky, and publishing graphic details about the time, place and manner of these activities, Independent Counsel, Kenneth Starr had invaded their privacy. There are also questions whether the extensive Internet speculation and mass media coverage of the minutest titillating details of the sexual relationship amounted to an invasion of privacy. Under American exceptionalism, the activities of Starr and the media do not rise to the level of invasion of privacy. The right to privacy is a relatively recent but-well developed branch of tort law. The Supreme Court of the United States has defined the right to privacy as "the right to be left alone."[121] The general right of privacy has two main aspects, namely, privacy law which is part of tort law (this is generally a matter of state law) and the constitutional right of privacy against government invasion of the privacy of its citizens. This right is embodied in the Privacy Act of 1974.[122] In this act, the United States Congress recognized a constitutional right to privacy when it said: "The right to privacy is a personal and fundamental right protected by the Constitution of the United States."[123] Though it is not specifically mentioned in the Federal Constitution, the right of privacy has been recognized by the Supreme Court of the United States as a distinct constitutional right implicit in the Due Process Clause of the Fourteenth Amendment.[124] The Court has also held that the right of privacy also exists in the "penumbras" and "emanations" of the Federal Constitution, particularly the First Amendment guarantee of freedom of speech and of the press.[125] The law of privacy is thus part and parcel of American exceptionalism.

The law of privacy in the United States has four branches: intrusion on the physical solitude of a person,[126] appropriation or using another person's name or image for commercial or business purposes without that person's consent,[127] giving publicity to private facts,[128] and publication placing a person in a false light.[129] As developed in case law, the mass media are free to publish information, even of the most intimate and indelicate nature, if it involves a matter of public concern,[130] and if it is made available to the media by government officials.[131] This was the case with the referral of the Independent Counsel, Kenneth Starr, to the United States House of Representatives.[132]

Newsworthiness and the public/private dichotomy

Newsworthiness is an important First Amendment principle that almost always comes into play in legal actions for invasion of privacy through the disclosure of embarrassing but true private facts that may be "highly offensive to a reasonable person."[133] Newsworthiness has been defined as 'the public's right to know.' Public scrutiny of public officials in the United States is premised on the assumption that the actions of public officials are newsworthy and contain information of value to the public. Additionally, the Supreme Court of the United States had held that "One of the costs associated with participation in public affairs is an attendant loss of privacy."[134] This principle requires that the private and public activities of all public officials and candidates for public office be scrutinized in the public interest. Today, the definition of "public interest" has become very broad. The concept includes "anything that might touch on an official's fitness for office."[135]

The principle of "fitness for office" is well established in American jurisprudence. As early as 1908, a court held that "a candidate for office must surrender to public scrutiny and discussion so much of his private character as affects his fitness for office."[136] The Supreme Court of the United States has also held that society's interest in public officials is not limited to the formal discharge of their official duties. The Court said that the public's interest in a public official extends to "anything which might touch on that official's fitness for office. . . . [F]ew personal attributes are more germane to fitness for office than dishonesty, malfeasance, or improper motivation, even though these characteristics may also affect the official's private character."[137]

Thus, under American law, religious heritage, and political culture, there is a connection between the public and private lives of public officials and public figures. This is traceable to the Puritans, who made no distinction between "public and private, sacred and secular."[138] It was their view that behavior was a sign of character—a person's outward life is a gauge of his/her inner life.[139] William Bennett echoed Puritan ideals when he wrote that the private lives of public officials are relevant in discussions of their fitness for public office. He argued that in Clinton's case, the distinction between the public and private life of the president had collapsed because the president had used his public office to cover up his private sexual activities.[140] Bennett also echoed the views of many conservatives when he wrote that "[private] sexual indiscipline can be a threat to the stability of crucial [public] human affairs."[141] Therefore, Clinton's "private adultery" revealed a lot about his "character and judgment; his prudence and judiciousness; his honor and trustworthiness; his governing ability and stability."[142] Bennett concluded that "[S]exual indiscipline is a threat to the stability of crucial human affairs."[143]

For his part, Alan Dershowitz observed that the difference between the United States and Europe on the issue of the privacy of presidents and presidential candidates boils down to the way presidents are elected. One of the hallmarks of American exceptionalism is that in the United States, candidates participate in political beauty contests, which showcase their charm, charisma, personal lives, religious and family values. In Dershowitz's view, the American political system makes the personal, private lives of public officials public.[144] This is not the case in Europe. Though European elections are becoming more and more "Americanized," in appearance—they now have highly publicized campaign pseudo events and high profile television debates—the political culture of the separation of the public and private lives of public officials is still largely intact in most European countries.

In the United States, the private lives of public figures are not immune from public scrutiny because their private actions illuminate their public character and give indications about their fitness for office. On this score, the lives of public officials are supposed to be open books for all to read. Furthermore, under the exceptional First Amendment, if their actions are determined to be newsworthy—and this determination is increasingly being made by Internet news aggregators, blogs, social media, and traditional media outlets driven by ratings rather than the public interest—they cannot seek refuge in their right to privacy.

Consequently, under this well-settled principle, despite its explicit sexual subject matter, the Clinton/Lewinsky scandal was newsworthy and the Starr referral was a document of public concern. Even though some people lamented Internet and traditional media sensationalism and round-the-clock coverage of the Clinton/Lewinsky scandal, most pundits agree that the intimate details of the Clinton/Lewinsky sexual relationship were newsworthy.[145] William Bennett also argued that Americans would have been ill-served if the Clinton/Lewinsky sexual affair, which had been "*forced* in our face, on the front page, by the president's own irresponsible, self-indulgent conduct" had been ignored or kept in the closet.[146] Internet and other media fixation on the scandal was the natural reflex of the American press whose traditional role is to serve as the watchdog of the public interest. This involves denouncing not only government excesses but also human predation and exploitation of other human beings.[147] One can argue that President Bill Clinton used his position of power to sexually exploit an intern young enough to be his daughter, in contravention of elementary ethics of sexual harassment.

Comparative Analysis and Discussion

The French exception and American exceptionalism are functionally equivalent worldviews that explain the privacy law regimes of both countries. These ideologies explain how the different politico-cultural political systems of France and the United States deal with the clash between freedom of expression and individual privacy in real space and cyberspace. The peculiarities of the French exception and American exceptionalism explain why the extra-marital sexual indiscretions of presidents Mitterrand and Clinton had different legal and political outcomes. In France, the Mitterrand/Pingeot and Mitterrand/Gubler affairs were viewed as gross and tasteless invasions of Mitterrand's privacy, and a breach of doctor-patient confidentiality respectively, while Clinton's extra-marital relationship with Monica Lewinsky led to his historic impeachment by the United States House of Representatives and his trial by the Senate. Indeed, the Mitterrand and Clinton "affairs" are comparative exemplars of the fact that in matters of invasion of privacy, the French exceptionalist worldview, under which the privacy of public officials takes precedence over truth, transparency, newsworthiness, and sometimes even the public interest, stands in contradistinction to the American exceptionalist system where freedom of expression, fitness for office, newsworthiness, and "the right to know" take precedence over the right of privacy. Both "affairs" provided an opportunity to compare and contrast how the Internet and the traditional media, the courts, and the political establishments of both countries, conceptualize and manage the private sexual indiscretions of their highest public officials. The contrasting reactions of the French and American political and media establishments to the Mitterrand and Clinton scandals exemplify the fundamental differences between the United States and France in terms of the their characterization of the individual's right to privacy as well as issues of "character" and leadership.

The Mitterrand/Anne Pingeot and Mitterrand/Gubler "affairs" did not have serious political repercussions in France because under French jurisprudence—and under the French exception—strict respect for individual privacy is one of the foundations of human dignity, liberty, and democracy. Finally, France does not have the sexual reticence and Puritan religious heritage of the United States. Historically, the royal mistress was a recognized institution in the *ancien regime*, and during the post-revolutionary Napoleonic Empire. As a result, the extra-marital affairs of presidents and public officials did not have the stigma that the same relations had in the United States. Furthermore, the official "religion" of France is "secular republicanism," the political creed, which emphasizes the separation of church and state. Under this exceptionalist regime, the purely material and cultural aspects of religion—cathedrals, church buildings, cemeteries and the like—are protected as part of the *patrimonie culturel* (cultural heritage) of the country. The doctrinal or normative aspects of Roman Catholicism have been de-emphasized and ignored in France for centuries. Under this exceptional French "compartmentality," French politicians conceptualize their religious beliefs as being separate from their political beliefs.

For its part, the French press, which is an active partner in the enforcement of the French exceptionalist policies of freedom of expression and individual privacy, promotes a system that unduly restricts freedom of the press and protects the right to individual secrecy rather the right to individual privacy. Privacy and secrecy have been eroded by globalization of information and communication technologies. The death in 1997, of Princess Diana, her companion, Dodi Al-Fayed, and their bodyguard in a car accident in Paris, as their driver tried to escape from sniffing paparazzi, shows that even the draconian French invasion of privacy laws can not protect public officials and public figures from the glare of media publicity. The Mitterrand/Anne Pingeot/Gubler affairs was the first major episode in the Americanization of sections of the French press. The story of President François Mitterrand, his mistress, and his natural daughter, as well as Dr. Gubler's book about the president's concealment of his illness, broke the taboo against publication of the private foibles of public officials and public figures in France. The result is that invasion of privacy has never been the same in France.

Indeed, the very fact that President François Hollande, who was elected in 2012, was caught, early in his tenure in a indelicate position between his former mistress and former presidential candidate, Segolène Royal, and his current mistress, Paris Match journalist, Valérie Trierweiler, is a case in point. The French and international media have written about Hollande's "love triangle," between these two powerful ladies. However, this *affaire* has had no negative political repercussions on the presidency of Mr. Hollande. Though Dr. Gubler scored only a partial victory at the European Court of Human Rights—the court held that the permanent injunction against distributing *Le Grand Secret* violated his freedom of expression as well as that of his publisher—there is no doubt that this decision is one more building block in the court's expansion, standardization and homogenization of freedom of expression values in Europe. The Mitterrand/Gubler affair gave the French judiciary a crash course on the Internet and its ability to make a mockery of national legal sovereignty. The lessons learned from this controversy would lead France to give all its judges and magistrates crash courses on new media technologies and the Internet.

The Clinton/Lewinsky scandal had a major impact on the American political system, and on American society in general. This is because the United States has a culture of sexual "modesty" which frowns on all violations of sexual morality by public officials and public figures. The scandal represented a failure on the part of President William Jefferson Clinton to live up to the tenets of the exceptionalist Puritan heritage of the United States, which puts a premium on the moral character of political leaders. It can be argued that under American political culture and tradition, Clinton failed to be a "visible saint"; a role model—in the Puritan mold—whose private and public lives were supposed to be beyond reproach. His perceived failure to live up to this expectation led to his investigation, impeachment by the House of Representatives, and trial by the Senate.

In the final analysis, both affairs were historic events, which revealed the differing exceptionalist standards to which politicians are held in France and the United States. From a free speech and free press perspective, the American political model, which puts a premium on the moral character of public officials and public figures, lends itself to undue, even voyeuristic invasions of individual privacy. The Supreme Court of the United States expressed American exceptionalism in matters of freedom of expression when it held that "[e]xposure of the self to others in varying degrees is a concomitant of life in a civilized community. The risk of this exposure is an essential incident of life in a society which places a primary value on freedom of speech and of press." Therefore, even information that is obtained illegally is protected by the First Amendment if it involves a matter of public concern.[148]

As enforcers of the high moral expectations of society, the media often indulge in unbridled sensationalism for the sake of ratings and Internet page views. In this age of globalization and instantaneous interconnection of nations and peoples, journalists who are schooled in the American system of watchdog journalism—with its emphasis on the public's right to know, fitness for office, and denunciation of the political hypocrisy—must be aware that these values are not universal, and may even lead to prosecutions for invasion of privacy in many countries.

NOTES

1. See National Technical Information Service, United States Department Of Commerce, Militarily Critical Technologies List 1-6 (1984) (Computer network technology was critical to the United States military). See also Defense Advanced Projects Agency, Technology Transition 19 (1997) (DARPA'S packet-switching technology has become the dominant network technology in the world).

2. See Scientific and Advanced Technology Act of 1992, 42 U.S.C. 1862 (a) (1992).

3. See Résutats Normaux (Normal Results) 15 992 *Le Figaro* (January 1996) at 11.

4. See *Le Monde*, January 20, 1996 at 1, 6, 14.

5. See Lyombe Eko, *The Law of Privacy in the United States and France: One President's Impeachable Offense is Another's Invasion of Privacy*, 22 Comm. & L. 1, 15-18 (Dec. 2000).

6. Daniel Schniedermann, Le juge et le "cafétier" (The judge and the Internet café keeper) LE MONDE TV, RADIO, MULTIMEDIA, January 28, 1996 at 39.

7. Daniel Schniedermann, Le juge et le "cafétier" (The judge and the Internet café keeper) LE MONDE TV, RADIO, MULTIMEDIA, January 28, 1996 at 39.

8. See Michel Gonod, Le Secret Du Docteur Gubler (Dr. Gubler's Secret) (Éditiions du Rocher, 1997).

9. See the Drudge Report Flash, June 25, 1997. At: http://www.drudgereportarchives.com/dsp/specialReports_pc_carden_detail.htm?reportID={13695BF9-81E4-406C-BF67-F17F8007547B}

10. Drudge Report, Newsweek Kills story on White House Intern, January 17, 1998 Available at: http://www.drudgereportarchives.com/data/2002/01/17/20020117_175502_ml.htm

11. See the Drudge Report, January 17, 1998, at http://www.drudgereportarchives.com/data/2003/06/04/20030604_135223_ml.htm

12. See the Drudge Report, January 17, 1998, at http://www.drudgereportarchives.com/data/2003/06/04/20030604_135223_ml.htm

13. See Michael Isikoff, Monica Lewinsky: The Inside Story of an Epic Newsweek Scoop, The Daily Beast, December 24, 2012. Available at:http://www.thedailybeast.com/newsweek/2012/12/23/monica-lewinsky-backstage-at-the-ultimate-washington-drama.html(Ironically, *Newsweek* filed for bankruptcy, and ceased publishing as a print magazine on December 31, 2012. Meanwhile, the *Drudge Report* recorded more than 11 billion page views in 2012).

14. See Kenneth Starr: The Starr Report (Pocket Books, 1998).

15. See Pat Wingert, Daniel Klaidman and John McCormick, The Fallout, *Newsweek,* February 8, 1999.

16. The scandal that came out of the sexual relationship between President Clinton and Monica Lewinsky has been variously called the "Lewinsky scandal," the "Lewinsky affair," the "Clinton/Lewinsky affair" or the "Starr affair." In this paper, it will be referred to as the Clinton/Lewinsky affair or scandal.

17. The word "affair" is used in two ways in this paper. When it refers to Clinton's relationship to Monica Lewinsky, it means "scandal." When it describes the Mitterrand/Pingeot/Gubler story, it is used interchangeably with the words "scandal, events, stories, or cases in court." In the "affaire Paris-Match" the "scandal" was the media revelation of Mitterrand's second family, not the fact that he had one.

18. See 145 Congressional Record S1458 -S1459 (Feb. 12, 1999).

19. See H. R. Res. 611, 105th Cong. (1998), *See also* 144 Congressional Record H11975 (1998).

20. See Pat Wingert et al. *The Fallout*, Time, Feb. 8, 1999 at 28-33.

21. See *World Press Review,* March 1999 at 12.

22. See *Clinton v. Jones*, 520 U.S. 681 (1997).

23. See Victor S. Navasky, *Starrism*, The Nation, October 19, 1998 at 5. (The Independent Counsel Starr Investigation and subsequent report was "sexual McCarthyism"). See also Lisa Jardine, *Object of Oppression*, The New Statesman, April 2, 1999 at 46-47. (The impeachment proceedings against Clinton are similar to the seventeenth-century Salem witch trials) And also Thomas Fields-Meyer, *The Inquisitor: dogged in his pursuit of the president, special prosecutor Kenneth Starr just keeps going . . . and going . . . and going*, People Weekly, February 16, 1998 at 182-187 (1998).

24. See Bruce E. Gronbeck, Character, Celebrity, And Sexual Innuendo In The Mass-Mediated Presidency, In James Lull & Stephen Hinerman (Eds) Media Scandals (1997) AT 123-142.

25. See Nick Hewett, France and Exceptionalism, in The French Exception, Emmanuel Godin And Tony Chafer (Eds.). 3 (2005).

26. See Frederick Schauer, The Exceptional First Amendment, in Michael Ignatieff (Ed.) American Exceptionalism And Human Rights 29, 30, 42 (2005).

27. See *Paris-Match*, November 3, 1994 at 1.

28. See *Plusieurs responsables politiques appellent les journalistes à respecter la vie privée des hommes publics.* (Several political leaders call on journalists to respect the privacy of public figures). *Le Monde*, November 5, 1994 at 21.

29. Id.

30. Id.

31. Id.

32. See Jean-Yves Lhomeau, Et alors *Le Monde*, November 4, 1994 at 11.

33. Id.

34. See *The Independent,* November 4, 1994 at 12. See also, International Press Institute Reports, January-February 1995 at 31.

35. See Jean-Denis Bredin, Intimité et transparence (Intimacy and transparence) Le Monde, November 24, 1994 at 2.

36. See note 71 supra

37. See Jean-Yves Lhomeau, Et alors? *Le Monde*, November 4, 1994 at 11 (The Elysée palace denied reports that Mitterrand had taken Mazarine with him to South Africa on his last visit to that country as president of France).

38. Id. (Only an extreme right wing weekly publication, published an extract of abook about it).

39. See Mitterrand était oppose à la publication des photos de sa fille, *Le Monde*, November 6, 1994 at 18.

40. See *Paris-Match,* January 25, 1996 at 2, 36, 44, 100.

41. See Georges-Marc Benamou, Le Dernier Mitterrand (The Last Days Of Mitterrand) (1996) serialized in *Paris-Match*, December 1996, at 84

42. Id.

43. See for example, *Vie Publique, vie privée* (Public life, private life) *Le Monde*, November 19, 1994 at 2. (The newspaper did not publish the revelations. It only responded to readers' questions on the issue. Its rational was that its professional curiosity and media responsibility had limits in matters related to the private lives of politicians--unless there was an abusive interference of the politician's private life on his public functions or vice versa. It said this was one of the particularities of French media savoir-vivre).

44. See Joan Konner, Of Clinton, the Constitution and the Press, *Columbia Journalism Review*, March/April 1999 at 6.

45. See Claude Gubler & Michel Gonod, Le Grand Secret (The Big Secret) (Plon, 1996).

46. See Résultats Normaux (Normal Results) *Le Figaro*, (January 17, 1996) at 11.

47. See Colette Porlier, *Le Docteur Gubler sans interdits* (Uncensored Dr. Gubler) *Paris-Match* Archives, December 1998 http://www.parismatch.com/archives/news (visited June 2009).

48. See *Éditions Plon v. France,* no 58148/00, ECtHR (CEDH) 2004IV), para. 30 (2004).

49. See *Éditions Plon v. France,* no 58148/00, ECtHR (CEDH) 2004IV), para. 12 (2004).

50. See Nouveau Code Pénal, article 226-13 (divulgation of professional secrets carries a penalty of one year's imprisonment and a fine of 100,000 French francs ($17,000)).

51. See *Éditions Plon v. France,* no 58148/00, ECtHR (CEDH) 2004IV), para. 12 (2004).

52. See *Éditions Plon v. France,* no 58148/00, ECtHR (CEDH) 2004IV), para. 14 (2004).

53. See Nouveau Code Pénal, Articles 226-1 & 226-2 (This offense carries a maximum penalty of one year's imprisonment and a fine of 300,000 French francs ($50,000)).

54. See *Le Monde*, January 20, 1996 at 1, 6, 14.

55. See *Éditions Plon v. France,* no 58148/00, ECtHR (CEDH) 2004IV), para. 15 (2004).

56. See *Plon v. Mitterrand*, Arrêt No. 1402. Rejet. La Cour de Cassation, Chambre civile, 16 juillet 1997 (Lexis Nexis).

57. J.O. No. 267 of November 18, 1999 at 17110.

58. Détail d'une jurisprudence administrative N° 211240 (Detail of Administrative Jurisprudence) Recueil Lebon of December 29, 2000. Available at: http://www.legifrance.gouv.fr/affichJuriAdmin.do?oldAction=rechJuriAdmin&idTexte=CETATEXT000008144050&fastReqId=983332432&fastPos=3#

59. See *Éditions Plon v. France,* no 58148/00, ECtHR (CEDH) 2004IV).

60. See *Éditions Plon v. France,* no 58148/00, ECtHR (CEDH) 2004IV), paras. 22-35 (2004).

61. See *Éditions Plon v. France,* no 58148/00, ECtHR (CEDH) 2004IV), para. 34 (2004).

62. See *Éditions Plon v. France,* no 58148/00, ECtHR (CEDH) 2004IV), para. 42 (2004).

63. See *Éditions Plon v. France,* no 58148/00, ECtHR (CEDH) 2004IV), para. 47-48 (2004).

64. See *Éditions Plon v. France,* no 58148/00, ECtHR (CEDH) 2004IV), para. 51-52 (2004).

65. See *Éditions Plon v. France,* no 58148/00, ECtHR (CEDH) 2004IV), para. 55 (2004).

66. *Gubler v. France*, no 69742/01 para 27 (2006).

67. *Gubler v. France*, no 69742/01 para 30 (2006).

68. See Jean-Yves Nau, Le Monde, December 17/18, 2000, at 10.

69. See LE SOIR, cited in, Le Monde, November 5, 1994 at 21.

70. Veronica Buckley, The Secret Wife Of Louis Xiv: Françoise D'aubigne, Madame De Maintenon (2009).

71. See Margaret Crosland, Madame De Pompadour: Sex, Culture And The Power Game (2001).

72. See Michel Winock, *La Naissance du Quatrieme Pouvoir* (The Birth of the Fourth Estate) *Le Monde*, August 19, 1998 at 2.

73. See Art. 22, J.O. July 19, 1970, Juris Classeur Périodique, 1970.1.2377.

74. Article 9, French Civil Code. Law No. 70-643 of July 17, 1970; Art. 22, J.O. of July 1970, 6751

75. See Jean-Denis Bredin, *Intimité et transparence* (Intimacy and Transparency), Le Monde, Nov. 24, 1994, at 2.

76. See Nouveau Code Pénal (New Penal Code), art. 226-1 AND 226-2 (1970).

77. Id. (The offense carries a maximum penalty of one year's imprisonment and a fine of 300,000 French Francs ($50,000).

78. European Convention on Human Rights and Fundamental Freedoms, art. 8 (1) (1950).

79. European Convention on Human Rights and Fundamental Freedoms, art. 10 (2) (1950).

80. See Joelle Hannelais, *Defamation in France,* in The International Libel Handbook 133 (Nick Braithwaite and Clifford Chance, eds. 1995).

81. Claude Bellanger, Jacques Godéchot, Pierre Guiral & Fernand Terrou, Histoire Générale De La Presse En France (General History Of The French Press 136 (1976).

82. See *Éditions Plon v. France,* no 58148/00, ECtHR (CEDH) 2004IV), para. 47-48 (2004).

83. See Joelle Hannelais, *Defamation in France,* in, The International Libel Handbook 133 (Nick Braithwaite and Clifford Chance, eds. 1995).

84. Id. at 134.

85. See Daniel Amson, Morale républicaine et vie privée (Republican morality and individual privacy. Le Monde, January 27, 1996 at 13 (French law generally frowns on disclosure of information about the health of public officials, public figures and private individuals).

86. Id.

87. Trib.grande instance du Seine, ref. 8 juillet 1965, cons. Rotschild, Juris Classeur Périodique., 1965.II.114.
88. Trib. Paris. 8 Juillet 1970, Epoux Rosso et éditions Julliard.
89. Cass. 12 juillet 1966, Bull., 1966, II No. 778, p. 545.
90. Law # 78-17 of January 6, 1978 On Computer Data Processing, Databases and Individual Freedoms.
91. Id.
92. Convention for the Protection of Individuals With Regard to Automatic Processing of Personal Data (1981) (visited November 2007) at http://www.europa.eu.int/comm/dg15.
93. See Peter Swire And Robert Litan, None Of Your Business: World Data Flows, Electronic Commerce, And The European Privacy Directive 3 (1998) (The European Union is trying to impose its privacy policies in an extraterritorial fashion).
94. See Jeff Gerth, Clintons joined S&L Operator in Ozark Real-Estate Venture, New York Times, March 8, 1992 AT A1.
95. *Jones v. Clinton*, 869 F. Supp. 690 (E.D.Ark.1994).
96. See Id.
97. See *Jones v. Clinton*, 72 F.3d 1354 (C.A. 8 1996).
98. See *Clinton v. Jones,* 520 U.S. 691, 1650 (1997) .
99. *Reno v. ACLU* 521 U.S. 844 (1997).
100. The investigation, which was eventually expanded to include alleged efforts by the president and his friend, Vernon Jordan to obstruct justice in the Paula Jones case, included several related scandals not relevant to this paper. See The Starr Report: The Independent Counsel's Complete Report To Congress On The Investigation Of President Clinton (Pocket Books, 1998) at 24-25.
101. See Phil Kuntz, Introduction, in The Starr Report: The Independent Counsel's Complete Report To Congress On The Investigation Of President Clinton At Xi-Xv (Pocket Books, 1998).
102. See The Starr Report: The Independent Counsel's Complete Report to Congress on the Investigation of President Clinton (Pocket Books, 1998) at 51-56.
103. Id. at 46-47.
104. Id. at 52.
105. Id. at 306-324.
106. See Referral to the United States House of Representatives Pursuant to Title 28, USC, Section 595 (c). House Doc 105-316 (1998).
107. The Senate could not muster the 60 votes needed to convict the President on either of the counts. The vote was 55 to 45 against the perjury charge, and the vote was 50-50 on the obstruction of justice charge.
108. See *Richmond Newsaper v. Virginia,* 448 U.S. 555 (1980) (Holding that there is a presumption of openness in criminal trials).
109. See Francis Martens, Vers un totalitarisme moral (Toward moral totalitarianism). *Le Monde,* September 20, 1998 at 1.
110. See Gail Sheehy, Character: America's Search For Leadership 12 (1988).
111. See T.H. Breen, The Character Of The Good Ruler, Puritan Political Ideals In New England 1630-1730, 78 (1970).
112. See Id. at 39.
113. See Id. at 77.
114. See Id. at 164.
115. See Edmund S. Morgan, Visible Saints, The History Of A Puritan Idea 29-31(1963).
116. See Id. at 50.
117. See Ralph Barton Perry, Puritanism And Democracy 33, 192 (1944).
118. See William J. Bennett, The Death Of Outrage 34 (1998).
119. See Alexander Hamilton Federalist No. 70 (1788).
120. See T.H. Breen, The Character Of The Good Ruler (1970) (Ideal ruler had to display piety, wisdom, wealth, justice, and moderation).

121. See *Katz v. U.S.* 389 U.S. 347, 350 (1967). See also *FCC v. Pacifica Foundation*, 438 U.S. 726, 728 (1978) (individuals have a legitimate right to be left alone in the privacy of the home).

122. 5 U.S.C.A. § 552 (a) (4).

123. Id.

124. See *Roe v. Wade*, 410 U.S. 113 (1973), reh. denied 410 U.S. 959 (While the Constitution does not specifically mention any right of privacy, a certain right of privacy does exist under the Constitution. The roots of privacy can be traced to the First Amendment, the Fourth Amendment, the Fifth Amendment, and the penumbra of the Bill Of Rights). See also *Cohen v. California*, 403 U.S. 15 (1971) (The government may prohibit unwelcome views and ideas from intruding into the privacy of the home even though such ideas cannot be totally banned from the public dialogue).

125. See *Griswold v. Connecticut*, 381 U.S. 479 (1965).

126. See *Galella v. Onnassis*, 487 F.2d 986 (2d Cir 1973). See also Dietemann v. Time, Inc, 449 F. 2d 245 (1971) (The First Amendment is not a license to trespass or intrude on the physical solitude of others).

127. See *Zacchini v. Scripps-Howard Broadcsting Co.*, 433 U.S. 562 (1974).

128. *Cox Broadcasting v. Cohn,* 420 U.S. 469 (1975). See also *Florida Star v. B.J.F.* 491 U.S. 524 (1989).

129. See *Time Inc v. Hill*, 385 U.S. 374 (1967). See also *Cantrell v. Forest City Publishing Co.*, 419 U.S. 245 (1974). See also Restatement (Second) of Torts §§ 652A-E (1977).

130. *Bartnicki v. Vopper*, 532 U.S. 514 (2001) (The media may broadcast material illegally obtained via a third party's invasion of privacy). See also *Cinel v. Connick*, 15 F.3d 1338 (1994) (Broadcast of sensational, home-made child pornography videos belonging to a Roman Catholic priest was not invasion of privacy because it was a matter of public concern).

131. *Cox Broadcasting v. Cohn*, 420 U.S. 469 (1975) (The media broadcast the name of a rape and murder victim is legal because the name was obtained from public court documents).

132. See e.g. *Florida Star v. B.J.F.*, 491 U.S. 524 (1989).

133. See Restatement (Second) of Torts § 652A, 652B, 652C, 652D, 652E (1977).

134. See *Bartnicki v. Vopper*, 532 U.S. 514 (2001).

135. See *Monitor Patriot Co. v. Roy,* 401 U.S. 265 (1971).

136. *Coleman v. MacLean* 78 Kan 711 (1908).

137. *Garrison v. Louisiana*, 379 U.S. 74, 77 (1964). See also *Ocala star-Banner co. v. Damron*, 401 U.S. 295 (1971).

138. See Francis Bremer, Shaping New Englands: Puritan Clergymen In Seventeenth-Century England And New England 75 (1994) .

139. See Francis Bremer, Shaping New Englands: Puritan Clergymen In Seventeenth-Century England And New England 49 (1994).

140. See Id. at 25.

141. See William J. Bennett, The Death Of Outrage 19 (1998).

142. See Id. at 24.

143. See William J. Bennett, The Death Of Outrage 19 (1998).

144. See Alan M. Dershowitz, Sexual Mccarthyism 49, 50 (1998).

145. *Of Clinton, the Constitution and the Press, Columbia Journalism Review*, March/April 1999 at 6.

146. See William J. Bennett, The Death Of Outrage 22 (1998).

147. See Melvin Defleur And Everette Dennis, Understanding Mass Communication 65 (1998).

148. *Bartnicki v. Vopper*. 532 U.S. 514 (2001).

Chapter Six

Intellectual Property Law and the Transfer of Collective Journalistic Works from Real Space to Cyberspace

The Case of the United States and France

The information and communication technology revolution of the late twentieth century, whose innovative vortex is the network of computer networks that came to be known innocuously as the Internet, changed the media, and the world in several ways. The Internet interconnected nations and cultures around the globe, and led to the convergence of the previously discrete media industries—music, books, newspapers, magazines, film, radio, television, video games, and computers—and created multiple networked digital platforms for the development, storage, and delivery of digitized media content in real space and cyberspace. The practical effect of these unprecedented developments was the emergence of a global information society characterized by the fluid exchange of information and knowledge across frontiers. In other words, the powerful centrifugal forces unleashed by the Internet and its associated networked technologies, platforms and social media have shaken the traditional media industries, fragmented their audiences, and undermined their paid subscription and advertising economic model.

These forces have had unforeseen negative consequences on journalism. Information and communication technologies and the Internet have essentially diminished the role of journalism as the proverbial news "gatekeeper" and societal storyteller whose selection, processing and publication of "newsworthy" happenings and events in accordance with professional values and conventions, presented audiences daily slices of reality. Journalists are no longer the exclusive reporters of the news that serves as the rough sketch or template of the panorama of history."[1] We saw in chapter 5 that Internet news aggregators undermined the gatekeeping role of traditional print journalism whose professional culture of verification of facts through multiple-sourcing, was no match for the lower ethical standards and twenty-four-hour news cycles of Internet bulletin boards, listservs, blogs, and social media. Actually, the first phenomenon that raised serious issues about the value of journalistic work, and the journalistic craft itself was the digitization and transfer—virtualization—of previously published journalistic material from the old reference and storage media in real space—library card-catalogues, dusty discolored newspaper archives, microfiche, microfilm, slides, and the like—to the dematerialized world of cyberspace. Due to technological innovations the world of searchable electronic databases has itself evolved from disk-based systems like CD-ROMs to interconnected Internet servers, and so-called or "cloud" storage.

In this virtual environment, old journalistic products published in print as collective works, gained a new lease on life as valuable, computer interactive materials whose individual components—stories, contributions, and columns—became searchable as individual entities. Ironically, the transformation of archived news articles and other journalistic works from printed form to computer searchable, digital databases was pioneered in 1980 by Lexis-Nexis to give journalists a database of journalistic pieces that would help them make informed editorial decisions about news coverage.

As the demand for expensive searchable electronic databases grew in the academic, governmental and corporate world, newspapers, magazines and other publications began to license their archives wholesale to global, commercial database companies like LexisNexis for exorbitant sums of money. This was the genesis of the algorithmic search phenomenon that has since become the stock-in-trade of global information and communication technology behemoths like Google, Microsoft, Yahoo!, Apple Computer Inc., Netscape, and others. Indeed, the commercial electronic search phenomenon has transformed these global corporations into the gatekeeper of the information age whose secret, perpetually changing, proprietary, algorithmic formulae determine the kinds and hierarchies of knowledge and information available to users of different languages in different regions, countries, and jurisdictions around the world. This corporate algorithmicization (manipulation through systematic computer processing) and hierarchization (rank-ordering of search results) of information and knowledge in hundreds of languages around the world for purposes of obtaining maximum profit in the global economy, is what Kaplan calls "linguistic capitalism."[2] This ideologically-laden moniker refers to the commercialization and monetization of knowledge and information, through algorithmicization, the opaque, and highly dynamic computerized manipulation of language and digitized content.

Digitization, Space-shifting and Intellectual Property Law

The digitization and transfer of news articles and other journalistic works from print to searchable electronic form "hosted" in databases and the online editions of newspapers and magazines is an act of technological space-shifting. This is because changing the format of the journalistic content from print or analog to digital (electronic shape-shifting), and making it available to selected research and other publics, involves transferring or publishing that "re-mastered" material from real space to cyberspace. This technological transformation of journalistic and other content had several intellectual property implications for authors of collective works—newspaper and magazine companies—contributors to these collective works, and the database companies that "host" this de-materialized content. The fundamental problem confronting policy makers was how to apply intellectual property rules and regulations developed for tangible intellectual property assets that exist in real space—music, video programs, videogames, books, photographs, motion pictures, art works, computer software and the like—to digitized, intangible, de-materialized works that exist in cyberspace in searchable electronic databases. The basic idea of copyright is that it grants copyright holders exclusive physical and contractual control over their intellectual property. In continental European countries, authors also have moral rights which empower them to forbid modification of their works without their consent. This right includes controlling the digitalization and transfer of intellectual property works from real space to cyberspace.

The knowledge economy engendered by information and communication technologies changed that logic with respect to archives and databases. The aim of searchable electronic databases is to aggregate vast amounts of knowledge and information, and literally put it at the fingertips of as many paying customers as possible. The more users there are, the more valuable the networks and databases became. Therefore, before they could become the wellsprings of the fluid exchange of knowledge and information around the globe, commercial database companies had to overcome significant intellectual property obstacles. They had to obtain permission from copyright holders. In print journalism, both full-time and freelance journalist around the world had a stake in this transition from real space to cyberspace, given the vast sums of money paid by database companies to license and digitize news articles and other journalistic content.

The common problem that confronted intellectual property regimes around the world was how to apply culture-specific intellectual property rules and regulations designed for real space and real time to the de-materialized world of cyberspace, and especially to new communication technologies and networked phenomena like databases, servers and the so-called "cloud." Unlike physical, copyrighted works, digitized works are copied and distributed with lightening speed around the globe. The history of intellectual property law in the age of globalization and networked communication has been a history of attempts to bring the de-materialized, digital world of cyberspace within the ambit of intellectual property law at the national, supranational and international levels.

The transformation of print journalism products through shape-shifting (digitalization) and space-shifting (from real space to cyberspace) posed new challenges that had to be resolved by the exceptional intellectual property regimes of the United States and France. In the United States, freelance writers whose articles and other journalistic works produced under short-term contracts were being licensed to third party commercial document companies for digitization and storage in searchable electronic databases without their consent, took legal action that culminated in the landmark case, *New York Times v. Tasini*. In France, the transfer of past and current journalistic products from print newspapers and magazines in real space to the dematerialized world of searchable electronic databases, and the searchable online editions of traditional print newspapers, led to legal disputes that led to re-presentation of certain tenets of French intellectual property law. The first dispute involved examination of the nature of the online editions of traditional newspapers, while the second involved the place of the historic system of French journalistic unionization in the age of online journalism, blogs and social media. These disputes were of great importance for society and for the journalistic profession because newspapers and magazine archives are considered "the first rough draft of history."[3] They are the raw materials that historians, political scientists, communications scholars, and other researchers use to accomplish their scholarly tasks, which is to advance human knowledge.

Purpose of the Chapter

Despite the problems associated with making the leap from real space to cyberspace, the United States and France have brought the Internet within the ambit of their respective exceptionalist regulatory logics. Each country regulates intellectual property—that family of intangible rights conferred on authors and inventors under the law by different national and international regimes—within the framework of its particular exceptionalist ideology.[4] This aim of this chapter is describe and explain how the United States and France negotiated and resolved the clash between the privileges of authors of collective journalistic works and the rights of journalists and other contributors to their individual contributions in these works under the exceptional intellectual property regimes of both countries. The chapter therefore compares and contrasts the cultural constructions of intellectual property in the United States and France, using as a comparative case study, application of the intellectual property rules and regulations of both countries to the phenomenon of digitization and transfer of journalistic works from real space (library stacks, paper archives, repositories, microfilm, microfiche, and so on) to cyberspace (searchable commercial electronic databases, CD-ROMS, the Internet or the "cloud").

Specifically, I use American exceptionalism and *l'exception française* (the French exception) as theoretical frameworks for the analysis of how the United States and France used their respective intellectual property regimes and journalistic traditions to regulate the transfer of news articles and other journalistic works from real space to cyberspace. As a comparative case study this chapter contrasts the experiences of the *New York Times* and the venerable French newspaper, *Le Figaro* in the domain of digitization. The units of comparison are the U.S. Supreme Court decision in *New York Times v. Tasini*, and the decision of the *Cour d 'appel de Paris* (Paris Court of Appeals) *in the case, Le Figaro v. SNJ.* The focus of the chapter is on how the philosophically different intellectual property regimes of both countries apply intellectual property rules to the common problem of digitization and transfer of news articles and other journalistic works from real space to searchable electronic databases in the dynamic, technologically fluid, and amorphous domain of cyberspace.

The first part of this chapter will discuss the place of journalistic content under the American Copyright Act of 1976, with an emphasis on the privilege of publishers of collective journalistic works like newspapers and magazines, and the status of individual contributions to these collective journalistic works. The second part of the chapter will explore the status of collective journalistic works under the *Code de la propriété intellectuelle* (Intellectual Property Code), and the status of journalists as intellectual workers under the French system of journalistic unionization. The third section will discuss the politico-cultural context of the regulation of the transfer of journalistic works from paper where they were originally published, to searchable electronic databases. This section will also discuss the exceptional French regime of journalistic trade unionism. The fourth section will analyze two landmark intellectual property cases that resolved the tension between newspaper publishers' interest in licensing their archives for digitization and storage in searchable electronic databases, and protection of the intellectual property rights of journalists who contribute to collective works in the United States and France.

Traditionally, in Continental Europe, intellectual property protection resided in "literary and artistic works" that were the embodiment or physical forms of the intellectual expression of authors.[5] In the United States, copyright was available to "original works of authorship fixed in any tangible medium of expression."[6] In both jurisdictions, emphasis was therefore placed on the physicality of the copyrighted material. The presumption was that the copyright holder had physical or contractual control over copying and distribution of the tangible work. The common problem that confronted these different regimes was how to how apply intellectual property rules and regulations designed for real space and real time to the de-materialized world of cyberspace, and especially to new communication technologies and networked phenomena like searchable commercial electronic databases.

Periodicals (Collective Works) Under Study: The New York Times and Le Figaro

The New York Times

The *New York Times* is one of the most influential journalistic institutions in the United States. The *Encyclopedia Britannica* calls it the national "newspaper of record . . . one of the world's great newspapers. Its strength is in its editorial excellence."[7] The *New York Times* was one of the earliest newspapers that developed a broad, international footprint in its coverage. With more than twenty-five bureaus around the world, the newspaper has been a pioneer in the use of new technologies—from wireless transmission of news from a battle field in 1904, to satellite phones and social media in journalistic reporting. The *New York Times* has also expanded the scope of freedom of the press in the United States through the litigation in which it has been involved. The most famous cases in which the *New York Times* has been involved include *New York Times v. Sullivan*,[8] a case that revolutionized media law in American by bringing defamation law under the ambit of the exceptional First Amendment.

The *New York Times* was also involved in the famous Vietnam War-era case, *New York Times v. United States*.[9] This was the so-called "Pentagon Papers" case. In this case, the Supreme Court of the United States held as unconstitutional, attempts by the Nixon Administration to prevent the *New York Times*, the *Washington Post* and other newspapers from publishing material from a leaked secret government report detailing how the United States got involved in the Vietnam war. Though the *New York Times* has been involved in other litigation that further advanced freedom of speech and expression in the United States, its most significant case in the era of the Internet was the landmark case *New York Times v. Tasini*. This was an intellectual property case which tested the limits of the privileges enjoyed by publishers like the *New York Times*, who are classified as the "authors" of collective works (their newspapers) under the Copyright Act of 1976. The case also tested the contours of the rights enjoyed by freelance writers who contribute to collective works like newspapers, when their articles that are part of these collective works are transferred from the print media in which they were initially published, to searchable electronic databases, servers, and the "cloud" from which they can be retrieved as single, downloadable entities.

Le Figaro, French Literary journalism, and Collective Works

Transfer of the archives of the periodical press from the print format in which the newspaper or magazine was published to the dematerialized space of searchable electronic databases and servers posed special intellectual property problems for French journalists and freelancers because of the history and nature of the journalistic profession in France. The "singularity" of French journalism, to use the expression of Erik Neveu,[10] is that journalism, or newspaper and magazine columns were, for many ambitious intellectuals and literary figures, a way station, a stepping-stone to a literary, political, academic, or administrative career in government. Notable newspapers like *Le Monde, L'Express, Le Figaro, Le Nouvelle Observateur* and *l'Humanité*, opened their pages to intellectuals who shared their political and ideological views. These views often aligned with the ideological orientation of the specific newspaper. French newspapers and magazines thus became forums for intellectual speculation, philosophical exposés, political debates, trenchant polemics, literary criticism, sociological analyses, and film criticism.

In short, France developed a tradition of literary journalism rather than American-style narrative, fact-based journalism. French journalism considers itself a journalism of ideas, not a journalism of events. Indeed, some of the greatest French literary and philosophical icons have used the pages of newspapers to express their ideas, indulge in philosophical speculation, and advance specific political ideologies. French literary giants who graced the editorial pages of newspapers and magazines include: Raymond Aron, Alain Badiou, Honoré de Balzac, Pierre Bourdieu, Albert Camus, Georges Clemenceau, Michel Foucault, André Gide, Eugene Ionesco, François Mauriac, Marcel Mauss, Jean-Paul Sartre, and so on. The result of this close relationship between the French intellectual class and the periodical press is that newspapers and magazines became the first outlets for the writings of famous French intellectuals, philosophers and academicians. These intellectuals often wrote without compensation. Their main aim was to get their ideas out into the public sphere. Protecting the intellectual property rights of these famous contributors, and tens of journalists and freelancer was an absolute necessity.

Le Figaro as Collective Work

Le Figaro has the distinction of being the oldest daily newspaper in Paris, having been founded as a satirical sheet in 1854. The newspaper was successful because it abandoned "the sad and doctrinal tone" of traditional

French journalism.[11] As the most famous newspaper of the French "right," *Le Figaro* maintained a close relationship with the French conservative intelligentsia, as well as the *Academie Française*, the venerable institution which has set the standards for French language and culture since 1635. As a result, *Le Figaro* was the forum of choice for a long list of distinguished French conservative intellectuals. No other French newspaper or magazine has published the writings of more French intellectuals who later became members of the prestigious French Academy than *Le Figaro*.[12] Despite the fact that France is constitutionally a socialist country that is dominated by Marxist thought, *Le Figaro* has, over the years, been consistently anti-Communist, pro-business, pro-free-market economy, pro-NATO and pro-American.[13] The newspaper has consistently argued in its editorials that the capitalist system, with its imperfections, ensures the best standard of living for, and does the least injustice to all citizens.[14] With *Le Figaro's* heavy menu of contributions from the French intelligentsia, the unauthorized transfer of the work of these larger-than-life contributors from newspapers or microfilm in real space, to searchable electronic databases in cyberspace was problematic from an intellectual property perspective. Things were especially contentious because these works were accessible and downloadable as single editorial columns or articles isolated from the context of the collective works in which they were originally published.

American Copyright Law and Collective Works

The Anglo-American concept of copyright or the right to reproduce previously published work has evolved from a novel instrument "for the encouragement of learning," conceptualized in the Statute of Anne of 1710, to an instrument for the furtherance of creativity and innovation in the United States.[15] The Statute of Anne was a British copyright act whose stated rationale, in addition to the encouragement of learning, was to compensate "the authors or proprietors" of books. The rationale for the law was that printers, booksellers and "other persons" were reproducing published books:

> without the consent of the authors and proprietors for such books and writings, to their very great detriment, and to often to the ruin of the and their families: [the statute was] For preventing therefore such practices for the future and for the encouragement of learned men to compose and write useful books...[16]

Though the rationale for the Statute of Anne was solicitude for the material welfare of authors and publishers, the act effectively served as an instrument of information control. Since it was the first copyright at in the world, the Statute of Anne served as the model for copyright acts in the Anglo-American countries (former British colonies and overseas territories). However, American copyright jurisprudence has an exceptionalist underpinning that is reflected in a unique incentive philosophy set forth in the Constitution. It also has an inextricable linkage to the exceptional First Amendment freedom of speech regime.[17] The American Constitution gives Congress the power:

> To promote the progress of science and useful arts, by securing for limited times to authors and inventors the exclusive right to their respective writings and discoveries.[18]

The aim of copyright is the betterment of society, not philosophical or moral solicitude for the economic welfare of authors.

The Copyright Act of 1976 grants copyright protection to "original works of authorship fixed in any tangible medium of expression, now known or later developed, from which they can be perceived, reproduced, or otherwise communicated, either directly or with the aid of a machine or device."[19] This definition is relevant because it includes fixation of material onto specific media of communication, anticipates technologies, search functions, and reproducibility. The Copyright Act specifically grants copyright protection to individual contributions to collective works. The Copyright Act defines the term "collective work" as: "a work, such as a periodical issue, anthology, or encyclopedia, in which a number of contributions, constituting separate and independent works in themselves, are assembled into a collective whole."[20]

The act then sets forth the privilege of the "author" who owns the copyright to the collective work as well as the rights of the individual contributors to the collective work:

> Copyright in each separate contribution to a collective work is distinct from copyright in the collective work as a whole, and vests initially in the author of the contribution. In the absence of an express transfer of the copyright or of any rights under it, the owner of copyright in the collective work is presumed to have acquired only the privilege of reproducing and distributing the contribution as part of that particular collective work, any revision of that collective work, and any later collective work in the same series.[21]

This provision was put to the test when the *New York Times* Company, *Newsday*, *Time* Inc., and other periodicals, licensed archives of their collective works—including the contributions of Tasini and other freelance writers—to commercial document companies, Lexis/Nexis, and University Microfilms, for digitization and storage in searchable electronic databases that are licensed to libraries around the world. Library clients in these libraries are able to retrieve the contributions of each writer as a discrete entity pursuant to author, keyword, or subject searches. These search results can be consulted, downloaded, or printed. The search and retrieval functions of academic databases essentially disassemble periodical issues (the collective works) of newspapers and magazines.

The French Intellectual Property Law Regime and Collective Works

The French exception is woven into the fabric of the French intellectual property regime, which is grounded in the *Code de la propriété intellectualle* (the Code of Intellectual Property). To the French, the term "copyright" is a rather narrow, foreign concept that expresses only part of the two-fold intellectual and property right that accrues to authors. The French equivalent of the word "copyright" is the expression, "*droit d'auteur*," (right of the author). Under French law, intellectual property consists of two rights: a patrimonial (economic) right and an intangible, inalienable moral right. Moral right is a rather "romantic" right of personality that seeks to protect the unique expression and metaphysical cachet or "mental signature" of the author on his or her work. Thus, authors retain moral rights in their works even after economic rights in the work have been exercised and the rights have been transferred to third parties pursuant to contracts.[22] Additionally, moral rights can be the subject of testamentary transfers to heirs and other parties.[23] In France, intellectual property is viewed as an important component of the French cultural exception because intellectual property is an instrument for the protection and promotion of French culture. French exceptionalism in intellectual property law is thus expressed in terms of a heightened recognition of the importance of cultural and knowledge production, as well as recognition and celebration of authors of *œuvres d'esprit* (works of the mind) as cultural institutions. France has historically conceptualized works of the mind as *lieux de mémoire culturel* (sites of cultural memory) as well as propagators of national cultural heritage.[24]

French intellectual property law is governed by the *Code de la propriété intellectuelle* (Intellectual Property Code), which stipulates that authors of original "works of the spirit" have incorporeal intellectual, moral and patrimonial or property rights to their creations.[25] As we have seen before, a fundamental characteristic of French intellectual property law is the doctrine of *droit moral* (moral rights). This legal provision confers on authors, the personal, "perpetual, inalienable and imprescriptible" right to have their names, quality and work recognized.[26] Moral rights continue to exist even after patrimonial or economic rights—the rights of representation and reproduction—have been contractually accorded to other parties.[27]

Clearly, under French intellectual property law, the focus is on the rights of the individual author rather than on the social benefits of conferring copyright monopolies on authors or on the nature of copyrighted works, as is the case with copyright law in the United States.[28] The *Code de la propriété intellectuelle* stipulates that intellectual property protection extends to "authors of translations, adaptations, transformations or arrangements of works of the spirit without prejudice to the author of the original work."[29] Despite the fact that intellectual property law in France traditionally has at its center, a human author, a physical person who is a cultural icon and a site of memory, the law also recognizes the intellectual property rights and privileges of "authors" of collective works. These authors may be "moral persons." That is, corporate entities that are associations of physical persons. As such, these moral persons have speech and press rights. They can own and dispose of intellectual property rights. It is in this context that the Intellectual Property Code recognizes collective works:

> *L'oeuvre collective est, sauf preuve contraire, la propriété de la personne physique ou morale sous le nom de laquelle elle est divulguée.*
> *Cette personne est investie des droits de l'auteur.*[30]
>
> The collective work is, unless there is proof to the contrary, the property of the physical [human] or moral [corporate] person in whose name the work was published. This person is invested with author's rights.

The emergence of the Minitel, the Internet and electronic databases set up a conflict between the privileges to which the author of a collective work is entitled under the Intellectual Property Code, and the intellectual property rights that accrue to individual journalists, freelancers, and intellectuals who contribute to these collective works.

Under the French system of bureaucratic trade unionism and labor classification, French journalists are granted a certain social status as news and knowledge workers. They are literally "press card-carrying workers" in a government-approved system in which the intellectual property rights of full-time journalists and freelancers are granted identical protections. This chapter explores how France negotiated and legislatively resolved the tensions that arose when newspapers began to transfer collective works (their archives) that had been published in print, to electronic databases in the face of strident opposition and legal challenges raised by journalists, freelancers, and other contributors.

The *Problem* of Searchable Electronic Databases

Before we analyze the landmark case that set the intellectual property standard for the transfer of journalistic and other material from print newspapers and magazines in real space to electronic databases and servers in cyberspace, we need to discuss the conceptualization of databases under French law. One of the realities of French history is that databases are very controversial. This is because databases are sites of negative collective memory due to their misuse, and infamous reputation as facilitators of the tragic human rights violations of the World War II era in France. In effect, because of a well-documented, historic, anti-Judaic tradition, France kept an intricate database of all its Jewish citizens, the so-called *fichier juif* (Jewish Files).[31] The *Fichier Juif was a* database created by the French government for bureaucratic and administrative control reasons. The Jewish database was the concrete manifestation of the perceived spiritual otherness, separation and non-assimilability of French Jews into the mainstream Gallic, Latin, and Roman Catholic culture of France.[32] When Hitler attacked and conquered France in 1940, the *fichier juif* facilitated the collaborationist Vichy government's arrest, internment, and deportation of French Jews to concentration camps even before the Nazi German occupiers asked the war time Vichy government to be part of the "final solution" to the "Jewish problem."[33] Since World War II, successive French governments have sought to make amends for the sins of the past. They tightly regulate databases and their content under human rights and invasion of privacy principles. The French government does not collect data on the race, ethnicity or religion of its citizens—even during the French national census.

In 1978 the French government passed "The Law on Informatics, Databases, and Freedoms," which was aimed at protecting the privacy of individual information in computerized databases. This law, which states that computers and databases shall be at the service of every citizen, brought information and communication technologies within the ambit of the French exception. The law expressly states that computerized databases may not be used to infringe on an individual's right to privacy.[34] Individuals, companies, or governmental entities, which have the intention of placing computerized directories and individual data in databases, in the "cloud," or on the Internet, are required to obtain special permission from the National Commission on Informatics and Individual Freedoms before directories are placed online.[35] Furthermore, the European Convention for the Protection of Individuals With Regard to Automatic Processing of Personal Data is also incorporated in French individual privacy law.[36]

Politico-cultural Context: The Exceptional Regime of Journalistic Trade Unionism in France

One of the characteristics of the French exception is the country's peculiar regime of assigning each profession a bureaucratic "status" and classifying it in the *Code de travail* (Labour Code). The journalistic profession, which emerged on the scene as a "Fourth Estate," during the meeting of the *Etats Généraux* (Estates General) that sparked the Revolution of 1789, is part of this system. In effect, when King Louis XVI summoned the three estates (classes) that comprised French society—the aristocracy, the clergy, and the third estate (commoners)—to address the financial crisis of the French state brought in part by French military support for the American Revolution, pamphleteers and other members of the "press," who did not belong to any of the three estates, essentially became a "fourth estate."[37] However, it took close to a century for journalism to be recognized as a "codified" profession in France. In effect, in its fiery zeal to break with the monarchical past and its labyrinthine professional monopolies, the Revolutionary Constituent Assembly promulgated a number of laws that would ultimately be prejudicial to freedom of assembly, and expressive conduct like labor strikes. In order to liberalize trade, and reinforce freedom of entrepreneurship, the Constituent Assembly passed the *Loi Allarde* (Allarde's law) in March 1791. This law essentially eliminated "corporations;" that is, monopolistic medieval guilds and professional associations. In June of the same year, the Constituent Assembly enacted the *Loi Chapelet (Chapelet's law)*, a decree that banned all "coalitions;" that is, the assembling of individuals for purposes of undertaking group action. This ban included professional groupings, labor unions, and strikes. It also banned peasant assemblies. The logic and effect of these two laws is that they instituted a universal individualism expressed in terms of universal "individual interests" and imposed a statist "general interest," not the corporate interest of professional groupings. Statist "general" interest quickly became the *raison d'Etat* (reason of state) of France.[38] The prohibitions against professional associations and labor unions lasted until 1884, and affected the unionization of journalism and allied media professions in France.

Journalism in France has a strong tradition of *syndicalisme* (trade unionism) and activism. When freedom of the press was officially recognized by the "Law of July 27, 1881 on Freedom of the Press," journalists who had borne the brunt of authoritarian oppression for decades under successive regimes, formed an association to defend their rights. One of the exceptional characteristics of contemporary France is that journalism is a highly bureaucratized profession in which journalists are regulated through a system of "professionalization" that involves governmental classification and codification of the profession in the *Code du travail* (Labor Code), and registration of journalists through the issuance of official press passes. The *Code du travail* (Labor Code) requires all professional journalists to carry professional identity cards "press cards" issued by the government, within the framework of the highly unionized and bureaucratized nature of media professions in France.[39] The first Official Journalists' union, the *Syndicat national des journalistes* (National Union of journalists, popularly known by its acronym, SNJ) was created in 1918. In 1937, the SNJ became affiliated with the French umbrella labor organization, *La Confédération générale du travail* (General Confederation of Labor, popularly known by its acronym CTG) and became known as SNJ-CTG. The journalists' union essentially became part of the *Front populaire,* (Popular Front), a coalition of leftist and radical parties that included the Radical-socialist party, the French Communist Party, the French Section of the Workers' International, and a host of other shady political groups. Membership of the French Union of journalists in the labor confederation, CGT, led to the radicalization of French journalists.[40]

The French Press Card System

The unionization and radicalization of French journalism was made possible by the law of March 29, 1935, which created *La Commission de la Carte d'Identité des journalistes Professionnels* (The Commission for the Issuance of Identity Cards to Professional journalists, CCIJP). The law of 1935 recognized journalism as a profession on the same footing as doctors, lawyers and teachers. This was crucial in a country where all professions and professional affiliations are recognized and validated by law, and are given a bureaucratic status under the *Nouveau Code du travail* (New Labor Code).[41] The aim of the law was to give journalists professional status, in a country where the government recognizes, and puts its bureaucratic imprimatur on, and meticulously codifies every profession. This "press card" commission is made up of the "*collège des employeurs*" (consortium of media employers), representatives of public and private sector media employers (including governmental news agencies and public broadcasters), as well as elected professional journalists from the public and private sectors. To be recognized as such, journalists in France have to be members of one of the half dozen officially recognized journalists' unions. Members of the press card commission, CCIJP are officially "appointed" by an executive order of the Minister of Culture and Communication to serve for three-year periods on the commission.[42] The task of this commission is to issue professional identification cards (press cards) to professional journalists and "*postulants*" (applicants) who meet certain criteria. Though the law grants the Commission for the Issuance of Press Cards (CCIJP) the task of issuing the cards, the *Conseil d'Etat* (State Council) determines the conditions under which the press card can be issued, the duration of validity of the card, as well as the conditions and means by which the card can be invalidated.[43] Additionally, in 1976, media corporations and journalists' unions signed the *Convention collective nationale de travail des journalistes* (the journalists' National Collective Labor Agreement, popularly known by its acronym, CCNTJ). The CCNTJ is a national collective framework agreement that governs all aspects of collective bargaining between members of the journalistic professions—including freelance journalists—and media *patrons* (employers). The CCNTJ, which is renewed every two years by the French government, applies to the 37,000 press card-holders in France, whether they be members of a union or not.[44] Incidentally, advertising and public relations officers are not considered journalists because they have a separate status under the Labor Code. Additionally, public service (government) media workers cannot be granted the status of journalists.[45] As we see below, this system of bureaucratic trade unionism was used to champion the cause of journalists and freelancers whose work was transferred from real space to cyberspace—searchable electronic databases, servers, archives, and web pages—without authorization or compensation.

Space-Shifting and Intellectual Property Law: New York Times v. Tasini

Preservation of past issues of newspapers and magazines has always been a challenge given the flimsy nature of the medium on which news and other journalistic works are printed. The invention of microfilm and microfiche, film-based technologies that reproduced miniature copies of entire editions of newspapers and magazines, made these materials accessible and retrievable with specialized, bulky readers and unwieldy equipment. This development ensured the security, safety and accessibility of newspaper and magazine archives for decades. However, the invention of computer databases and digital technologies enabled commercial document storage companies and libraries to scan and transform their paper and film-based newspaper, magazine and other journalistic archives into searchable CD-ROMs. Ultimately the dematerialized digital or electronic copies were saved in burgeoning online databases.

The transfer of copyrighted newspapers and magazines from real space to searchable databases stored on networked servers, and ultimately to the "cloud," raised important intellectual property problems in jurisdictions around the world. These issues included the status of databases under the law, the rights of newspaper and magazine publishers in the collective works they produced on a daily basis, and the rights of individual authors—specifically freelance writers—in the works they contribute to collective journalistic works. In the United States, the digitalization and transfer of collective journalistic works from paper, microfilm, or microfiche into searchable digital databases from which individual articles could be accessed and downloaded pursuant to a computerized subject, author or keyword search raised several intellectual property issues that were ultimately resolved by the courts just as the Internet was opened up to educational, commercial, cultural, and political content.

The landmark case that set the standard of intellectual property law in the issue area of digitalization and storage of newspaper and magazine archives into searchable electronic databases was *New York Times v. Tasini*,[46] a case that was decided 2001, a year after an identical case was decided by the French courts. These cases demonstrate the respective exceptional intellectual property regimes of the United States and France. In *Tasini*, the Supreme

Court of the United States handed down a ruling on the intellectual property rights of freelancers, the privileges of newspaper and magazine publishers, as well as the place of database owners in the system.

Though the digitization of print media archives and storing them in searchable databases promised to provide a financial windfall for newspaper companies, it raised questions about the intellectual property rights of journalists and freelance writers who had written articles for collective editions of periodicals that were being transferred to digital databases, searched, read, downloaded or printed as single entries. That was the bone of contention in *New York Times v. Tasini.* In effect, freelance writers, Tasini, Mifflin, and Blakely, wrote articles for the *New York Times*, *Newsday*, *Sports Illustrated*, and *Time* Inc., under works-made-for-hire contracts. Under these contracts, the freelancers who actually wrote the articles were not the "authors" of the articles because they wrote the articles as independent contractors, on behalf of the publishers, in exchange for monetary compensation. The *New York Times* Co. licensed Lexis/Nexis, and University Microfilms, Inc. to transfer the texts of articles in its archives, including the articles of Tasini and others freelance writers, into searchable electronic databases for purposes of licensing them to libraries and other third parties. These searchable databases enable users to search discrete articles using certain search terms, titles, author names, subjects, keywords, and the like.

In 1993, Tasini and his freelance author colleagues filed a civil suit in the United States District Court for the Southern District of New York, alleging that by licensing their articles that were published as part of collective works—specific newspaper and magazine editions—to Lexis/Nexis for archiving in databases from which they could be retrieved as discrete articles outside the context of the original collective publication, the *New York Times*, Lexis/Nexis and University Microfilm had violated their copyrights protected under §201 of the Copyright Act. This section of the Copyright Act sets forth the privileges of the "author" and the rights of contributing freelance writers in collective works.

The plaintiffs said that when the *New York Times* paid for their freelance work, it acquired only the privilege of reproducing and distributing their articles as part of specific "collective works," (editions of newspapers and magazines), not the privilege to digitize and transfer the news articles to searchable electronic databases from which they could be retrieved as individual articles.

In its defense, the *New York Times*, stated that the reproduction and distribution privilege accorded owners of collective works under section §201 of the Copyright Act gave it the authority to digitize the collective work and transfer it into searchable electronic databases. The district court held that the *New York Times* had the privilege to transfer the collective work to electronic form and publish it in another platform under authority granted to it by §201 of the Copyright Act The court therefore found for the *New York Times* and granted it summary judgment. Tasini and his freelancer colleagues appealed to the United States Court of Appeals for the Second circuit, which reversed and granted summary judgment to the freelance writers, stating that electronic databases were not part of the "collective works" protected by §201 of the Copyright Act. The *New York Times* appealed to the Supreme Court of the United States, which granted a writ of certiorari.

The issue before the Court was whether transferring the freelance writers' articles from print to searchable electronic databases without their consent was privileged and permissible under §201 of the Copyright Act.[47] In other words, did the *New York Times* and Lexis/Nexis violate the copyright of the freelance journalists when, without written consent, they included these freelancers' articles in a searchable electronic database from which the articles could be retrieved as discrete items? The Court answered in the affirmative. It held that the author's privilege that is set forth in §201:

> . . . does not override the [freelance] Authors' copyrights, for the Databases do not reproduce and distribute the Articles as part of a collective work privileged by §201(c).[48]

The court held that both the *New York Times* and the database companies (Lexis/Nexis and University Microfilm) had violated the copyrights of the freelance writers. The court reiterated the fact that under American copyright law:

> Copyright in *each separate contribution to a collective work* is distinct from copyright in *the collective work as a whole* . . . unlike the conversion of newsprint to microfilm, the transfer of articles to the Databases does not represent a mere conversion of intact periodicals (or revisions of periodicals) from one medium to another. The Databases offer users individual articles, not intact periodicals. . . . The crucial fact is that the Databases . . . store and retrieve articles separately within a vast domain of diverse texts. Such a storage and retrieval system effectively overrides the [freelance] Authors' exclusive right to control the individual reproduction and distribution of each article.[49]

In the light of the above findings, the Supreme Court of the United States concluded that Lexis/Nexis and University Microfilm, which it described as "Electronic Publishers" had infringed on the freelance writers' copyrights by reproducing and distributing their articles without their written consent. The court also concluded that the *New York Times* and the other newspaper defendants, had infringed on the free lance writers' copyrights by authorizing Lexis/Nexis and University Microfilm to digitize and place the news articles in question, in the databases and by aiding Lexis/Nexis and University

Microfilm to transfer the news articles from real space (print) to cyberspace (electronic databases and online archives).[50]

Some scholars suggest that under American jurisprudence, there is an inequality of arms between authors, publishers and distributors of copyrighted works.[51] Tarleton Gillespie suggests that the balance of power is tilted against authors: "[H]istorically, copyright has privileged not the authors of cultural work but its distributors."[52] In the case of collective works, the scales were clearly tilted in favor of the authors, not the freelance journalists. In *New York Times v. Tasini*, the Supreme Court of the United States created a certain equilibrium, in keeping with Congressional intent, when it rose to the defense of freelance journalists who ran the risk of losing the intellectual property rights in their individual news articles that were being licensed to commercial document companies for hefty fees, digitized and transferred from real space to the dematerialized world of searchable electronic databases. The Court's ruling reminded the *New York Times* that freelancers had licensed their articles for publication as part of collective works in print form. Removing these articles from their original print context violated the copyright of the contributors. Therefore, transforming (digitizing) these periodical pieces into individually searchable stories isolated from their collective context and storing them in searchable electronic databases without explicit permission or compensation constituted an infringement of the copyright of the freelance writers. As a result of this decision, the freelance writers won a compensation pool of eighteen million dollars. Tasini served as a precedent for two subsequent photojournalism cases. In *Faulkner v. National Geographic Enterprises, Inc.*,[53] the United States Court of Appeals for the Second Circuit held that *National Geographic* magazine had not violated the copyright of a group of writers and photographers when it reproduced entire editions of its magazines in the form of CD-ROMs, for sale to the general public. In *Greenberg v. National Geographic*, the United States Court of Appeals for the Eleventh Circuit held that: *The Complete National Geographic*, a thirty-disk CD-ROM containing complete editions of all issues of the magazine published since 1888, did not violate the copyright of a photojournalist because the CD-ROMs "faithfully preserve the original context of *National Geographic*'s print issues."[54]

Space-Shifting of Journalistic Products in France: *Le Syndicat national des journalistes v. Figaro*

In France, the intellectual property disputes between journalists and their publishes began when the Internet diffused to France in the late 1990s. We have seen in chapter 4 that France had a successful but technologically, linguistically, and geographically limited online *telematic* system, the Minitel.[55] As the Internet diffused in France and began to supplant the Minitel,

French newspapers and magazines began to create a web presence, and transfer their archives and content to the network of computer networks, which provided them the kind of global reach and audiences that the Minitel could not provide. *Le Figaro*, a venerable French newspaper, created a hybrid online edition that offered its readers access to its searchable archives on the Minitel, as well as the possibility of obtaining copies of specific articles through fax machines or an e-mail address listed on its Internet website.

Alarmed that this development infringed on the rights of journalists, the *Syndicat national des journalistes* (National Society of journalist, herein after, SNJ) and eight journalists sued *Le Figaro* at the *Tribunal de grande instance de Paris* (High Court of Paris), seeking an injunction barring *Le Figaro* from operating its objectionable website, and asking the court to designate an expert to calculate how much money *Le Figaro* owed journalists for this infringement of their author's rights in work that had been published as part of collective editions of the newspaper, on these new distribution platforms—the Minitel and the Internet.[56] In 1999, the court issued an injunction barring *Le Figaro* from distributing the articles of the plaintiffs without their express written authorization on its Minitel site or Internet website, failing which the newspaper would be required to pay a penalty of 10,000 French Francs (about $2,000) per day. The court appointed an expert to determine the sums of money due to the journalists as a result of the "counterfeit" use of their work on the Minitel. The Internet was still a novelty at that point.

Le Figaro appealed to the *Cour d'Appel de Paris* (Appeals Court of Paris) claiming that under article L-113-5 of the Intellectual Property Code, it was the "author" of the collective work (newspaper editions) in which these articles were published in print form. As a result, it had the right to publish an online edition of the collective work in which these articles were originally published. *Le Figaro* further argued that the rights the individual journalists who contributed to the collective work granted the newspaper was not limited to a single print publication. On the contrary, the rights granted by the journalists include the possibility of using their work in several editions of the newspaper, including an *édition télématique* (online edition), without prejudice to the right to distribute individual articles as distinct entities to third parties outside the newspaper.

For their part, the plaintiffs claimed that *Le Figaro* had only the right of first publication of the articles in the collective work. As such, it was an infringer of the copyright of the journalists and freelance writers who contributed to its collective work. The journalists therefore asked the court to ban distribution of the work of *Le Figaro*'s journalists and freelancers on the Minitel and on the Internet. The plaintiffs asked the court to order *Le Figaro* to pay the plaintiffs and other journalists and freelancers not before the court, damages for infringing distribution, infringement of the right of reproduction, the right of publication, and moral rights.

The issue before the court was whether *Le Figaro* had infringed the intellectual property rights of its journalists and freelance writers when it created the Minitel and Internet websites containing searchable archives of the newspaper and made their individual contributions available to the public without the express written consent of the reporters. The Paris Court of Appeals answered in the affirmative. It said that neither the individual contracts of the journalists nor the collective contract between *Le Figaro* and the *Syndicat national de journalistes* (National Union of journalists) had provisions for online distribution of works produced by the journalists. It therefore did not matter whether the articles in question were part of a collective work. The Paris Court of Appeals said that an online edition of *Le Figaro* on the Minitel and the Internet, as well as a searchable electronic version of *Le Figaro* archived on a server were completely different from the paper edition of the newspaper and thus required the written authorization of the journalists. The court further said the Minitel and the Internet were new technologies that were not provided for in the contracts of the journalists, that *Le Figaro* was charging online readers for searching its electronic archives, and that search results did not produce the entire newspaper (the collective work) just the individual contributions of specific journalists to the collective work. The court affirmed the injunction against the distribution of *Le Figaro* on the Minitel and extended it to the Internet:

> *cette interdiction doit être étendue, à toute forme d'exploitation desdits articles sur internet, s'agissant, là encore, d'un mode d'exploitation non prévu lors de la conclusion des contrats*

> this prohibition must be extended to all forms of distribution of the said articles on the Internet, since that also is a new means of distribution not provided for in the contracts [of the journalists].

The Appeals Court of Paris therefore barred *Le Figaro* from distributing the articles written by its own journalists and freelancers on the Internet without the express written consent of the authors of the articles published in the print version of the newspaper. It gave *Le Figaro* one month to take down the articles in question or pay a fine of 10,000 French Francs per day ($2,000) for every day the articles stayed on the Minitel or the Internet. Finally, *Le Figaro* was ordered to pay its journalists and freelance writers 20,000 French Francs ($4,000) plus costs of the two-year long litigation.

SNJ v. Figaro, was a landmark case for the French press because it set the parameters within which French newspapers could transfer articles written by their full-time and freelance reporters from their print editions to searchable archives on the Minitel and the Internet. This decision must be understood within the exceptional intellectual property regime of France, as well as the country's system of journalistic trade unionism. The SNJ was granted standing to act as a party in the suit against *Le Figaro* because of its important role in journalistic trade unionism. When the French government came to terms with the idea that the Internet had virtually supplanted the Minitel, it decided to phase out the venerable online system.[57] In 2009, it enacted a law regulating the production and dissemination of French and French-language content on the Internet. The "Law of June 12, 2009 on Furthering the Dissemination and Protection of Production on the Internet," inserted certain provisions in the Intellectual Property Code to regulate the dissemination of journalistic products, and their transfer from real space to cyberspace. The Law of June 12, 2009 stipulates that the journalistic works of full-time and freelance journalists may be disseminated on several platforms in real space and cyberspace for limited periods stipulated in the journalists' contracts. After that limited contractual period, freelance and full-time journalists are to be remunerated for use of their work (in searchable electronic databases, archives and websites).[58] This is a compromise solution that takes newspapers' need for a presence in multiple platforms into consideration but gives journalists and freelance writers a stake in newspaper archives that appreciate over time, and are licensed and transferred to commercial document companies for placement in searchable electronic databases, archives and servers. Therefore, while French intellectual property law still protects the intellectual property of newspaper and magazine publishers in the collective works they publish in real space and cyberspace, those rights have temporal limitations. In order for newspaper and magazine companies to transfer news articles and other journalistic works to searchable commercial databases or online archives after contractually relevant dates, they are required to remunerate the authors at rates agreed to in union agreements.

Conclusion and Comparative Analysis

Transferring journalistic and other content from real space to cyberspace raised all kinds of professional and intellectual property issues. Traditionally, in Continental Europe, intellectual property protection resides in "literary and artistic works" that are the embodiment or physical forms of the intellectual expression of authors.[59] In the United States, copyright is available to "original works of authorship fixed in any tangible medium of expression."[60] In both jurisdictions, emphasis was traditionally placed on the physicality of the copyrighted material. The presumption was that the copyright holder had physical or contractual control over copying and distribution of the tangible work. In effect, intellectual property rules and regulations "had traditionally been regarded primarily as a means to exclude or limit others from using certain protected subject matter, through litigation if necessary."[61] The emergence of searchable electronic databases changed that logic. This chapter was a comparative analysis of how the exceptional intellectual property law regimes of the United States and France managed the transfer of intellectual property law governing collective journalistic works (newspapers and magazines), from real space (print) to cyberspace (digital electronic databases, servers, the Internet and the "cloud"). These policy transfers were necessitated by the emergence of innovative technologies that made it possible to transfer journalistic archives from card catalogues, library stacks, microfiche and microfilm, to searchable digital electronic databases, DVD-ROMs, and the Internet. Both countries approached the task within the framework of their respective, exceptional intellectual property law regimes. In the United States, courts refused to transfer wholesale, the law of collective works that is applicable to the print media in real space, to the dematerialized realities of searchable databases in cyberspace. The Supreme Court of the United States held that unauthorized digitization of newspaper and magazine articles that were originally published in print, and transferring them to searchable electronic databases from which they could be retrieved and downloaded as single entities, made them "electronic publications" that violated the copyrights of the freelance journalists who had originally written the articles. This decision extended intellectual property protection to works produced by freelance writers for collective works in print, if these works are digitized and placed in searchable commercial databases from which they could be accessed as single entities. In the United States, journalists' unions played no formal part in the litigation because they do not have the kind of status, standing, and power that French journalists' unions have under labor and intellectual property law. The Union to which Tasini and the other freelance writers belonged, the National Writers' Union (NWU), did not have standing under American law to sue the *New York Times* for copyright violation.

The *Tasini* case shows that the *New York Times* and newspapers and magazines in the United States and other parts of the world, did not have a vision or well-thought out plan for transitioning both their archives and their current journalistic output from real space to cyberspace. In their quest for short-term monetary gain, they were willing to license their archives to commercial database companies like Lexis/Nexis for digitization and transfer to searchable electronic databases without a coherent strategy that took into consideration the interests of their full-time reporters and their freelance writers. This lack of solicitude for the writers who produced the work that made newspapers attractive to advertisers, led to a devaluation of journalism. Virtually all newspapers transitioned to the Internet and gave away their products free of any charge without thinking through the implications. Advertisers did not reward the print media for giving away its products for free. The results have been devastating for the print media industry.

In France, the situation was more complex. When the Internet became a global, interconnected, multi-communication platform, each major French newspaper and magazine sought to create a "web presence" on the Internet in addition to its presence on the Minitel, the pioneering French online service that was eventually supplanted by the Internet. While the outcome of the decision of the Appeals Court of Paris in *SNJ v. Le Figaro* was that unauthorized digitization and publication amounted to a violation of the rights of the journalists and freelancers who had written the articles, and the politico-cultural context of both decisions were different. We saw above how the SNJ, the National Union of journalists used its century-long tradition of rallying journalists and even radicalizing them, to fight against the unauthorized transfer of journalistic content from real space to cyberspace. Due to this long history, the SNJ was granted standing to sue *Le Figaro*. This case confirmed what the French Constitutional court (*Conseil d'État*) had said about regulation of the Internet: "There is no Internet law, only the law applied to the Internet."[62]

The outcomes of the cases *New York Times v. Tasini* and *SNJ v. Figaro*, heard by American and French courts, respectively, were identical. Courts in both countries ruled that unauthorized digitizing and transferring of journalistic pieces contained in collective works from real space (print newspapers and magazines) to cyberspace (searchable electronic databases, servers and the "cloud,") from which articles could be retrieved and downloaded as discrete entities violated the intellectual property of the contributors. While these controversies show that legal provisions governing the privileges of authors and the rights of individual contributors to collective works are functionally equivalent in the United States and France, the contexts, and the philosophical rationale for the decisions are different in both countries. The American case involved only freelance journalists while the French case involved both freelance contributors and full-time journalists. Additionally, the differences in the amount of money awarded the victorious freelancers in the United States and France is telling. In the United States, the plaintiffs were ultimately awarded $18 million, while in France, the victorious union and the eight plaintiffs were awarded a symbolic sum of 20,000 French Francs ($4,000) plus costs. The symbolic act of protecting the moral rights of the plaintiffs without unduly restricting public access to the work of reporters and intellectuals who had graced the pages of *Le Figaro* over the years, might explain the rather lenient monetary compensation.

NOTES

1. See generally, Todd Andrlik, *Reporting the Revolutionary War: Before it was History, it was News* (2012).

2. See Frédéric Kaplan, *Nos langues à l'heure du capitalisme linguistique* (Our languages in the age of linguistic capitalism) (2012). Available at: http://www.internetactu.net/2012/04/06/nos-langues-a-lheure-du-capitalisme-linguistique/

3. See generally Todd Andrlik, *Reporting the Revolutionary War: Before it was History, it was News* (2012).

4. See David L. Lange And H. Jefferson Powell, No Law: Intellectual Property in the Image of an Absolute First Amendment 171 (Stanford Univ. Press 2009).

5. Art. II, Berne Convention for the Protection of Literary and Artistic Works (Paris Text, 1971).

6. Copyright Act of 1976 (as amended), 17 U.S.C. §102 (1976).

7. See the New York Times *Encyclopædia Britannica Online*. Retrieved from: http://www.britannica.com/EBchecked/topic/412546/The-New-York-Times.

8. 376 U.S. 254, (1964).

9. 403 U.S. 713 (1971).

10. Erik Neveu, *Sociologie du journalisme* (2004).

11. Claude Bellanger, Godechot, J., Guiral P., & Terrou, F.,(Eds.). 120 (1969). *Histoire générale de la presse française* (tomes 1-2). [General history of the French Press (vols.1-2)].

12. See Christian Delporte, *Le Figaro*, in *Dictionnaire des intellectuels français (Dictionary of French Intellectuals)* 489-490 (1996).

13. A. Piettre, A. Les illusions du socialisme (The illusions of Socialism). *Le Figaro,* September 21, 1972 at 1.

14. Emmanuel Derieux & Jean Textier, *La presse quotidienne française* (The French Periodical Press) 150 (1974).

15. See Statute of Anne, 8 Anne c. 19 (1710) available at: http://www.copyrighthistory.com/anne.html

16. See Statute of Anne, 8 Anne c. 19 (1710) available at: http://www.copyrighthistory.com/anne.html

17. See Frederick Schauer, The Exceptional First Amendment, in American Exceptionalism And Human Rights 29, 56 (Michael Ignatieff, Ed. 2005).

18. U.S. Constitution, Art. 1 §8, cl.8.

19. 17 U.S.C. §102(a) (1976).

20. 17 U.S.C. § 101 (1976).

21. 17 U.S.C. § 201(c) (1976).

22. See *Claude M'Barali (MC Solaar) et autres v. Société Media Consulting et autres. Claude M'Barali (MC Solaar) and others v. Société Media Consulting and others*. Tribunal de Grande Instance de Paris, 3ème chambre, 2ème section (High Court of Paris) Jugement du 7 novembre (Judgment of November 7, 2003). Available athttp://www.legalis.net/jurisprudence-decision.php3?id_article=1032Last visited September 28, 2008. (Holding that a media company which licensed a musician's compositions from a copyright clearing house for use as cell phone ring tones violated the musician's moral rights because the musician did not authorize modification of the quality of the music).

23. Art. L.121-1 *Code de la propriété intellectuelle* (Intellectual Property Code), version consolidée au 22 décembre 2007. (Consolidated version). Available at LegiFrance, http://www.legifrance.gouv.fr/affichCode.do?cidTexte=LEGITEXT000006069414&dateTexte=2008030.

24. See François Azouvi, Descartes in Pierre Nora (Ed.) Lieux De Mémoire (Tome 3) (Sites Of Memory) (Vol. 3) 4475 (Paris: Quarto Gallimard (1997) (Stating that French Philosopher, Réné Descartes is a "site of memory").

25. Art. L. 111-1 *Code de la propriété intellectuelle* (Intellectual Property Code), version consolidée au 22 décembre 2007. (Consolidated version). Available at LegiFrance, http://www.legifrance.gouv.fr/affichCode.do?cidTexte=LEGITEXT000006069414&dateTexte=2008030 (Last visited March 24, 2008).

26. Art. L. 121-1 *Code de la propriété intellectuelle* (Intellectual Property Code), version consolidée au 22 décembre 2007. (Consolidated version). Available at LegiFrance, http://www.legifrance.gouv.fr/affichCode.do?cidTexte=LEGITEXT000006069414&dateTexte=2008030 (Last visited March 24, 2008).

27. See *Claude M'Barali (MC Solaar) et autres v. Société Media Consulting et autres. Claude M'Barali (MC Solaar) and others v. Société Media Consulting and others.* Tribunal de Grande Instance de Paris, 3ème chambre, 2ème section (High Court of Paris) Jugement du 7 novembre (Judgment of November 7, 2003). Available at: http://www.legalis.net/jurisprudence-decision.php3?id_article=1032Last visited August 28, 2008. (Holding that a media company which licensed a musician's compositions from a copyright clearing house for use as cell phone ring tones violated the musician's moral rights because the musician did not authorize modification of the quality of the music).

28. See Art. I, §8, Constitution Of The United States (1787) (stating that the aim of conferring copyright monopolies to authors for limited periods of time is to "promote the progress of science and the useful arts"); See also Copyright Act of 1976, 17 U.S.C §102 et seq.

29. Art. L.112-3, Art. L. 112-2, *Code de la propriété intellectuelle* (Intellectual Property Code), version consolidée au 22 décembre 2007. (Consolidated version). Available at Legi-France, http://www.legifrance.gouv.fr/affichCode.do?cidTexte=LEGITEXT000006069414&dateTexte=2008030

30. Article L.113-5, Code de la propriété intellectuelle, *Loi 92-597 1992-07-01 annexe JORF 3 juillet 1992 (Article L.113-5, Intellectual Property Code, Law 92-597 1992-07-01 annex, J.O. July 3, 1992).*

31. See Le Centre Historique des Archives Nationales [Historical Center of the National Archives], *Fiche d'orientation: Les sources conservées aux Archives nationals relatives à la spoliation des Juifs de France* [*Guide to National Archives Holdings on the Despoiling of French Jews*] (1998), *available at* http://www.archivesnationales.culture. gouv.fr/chan/chan/notices/aj38f9.htm. (Archives of the Vichy regime's *Commissariat aux questions juives* (Commission on Jewish Questions) whose policy of "Aryanization" was aimed at eliminating Jewish influence from the French economy through the seizure and sale of their businesses, companies and private properties to French "Aryans" These archives contain very detailed personal information on all Jewish adults and children).

32. See Henri Amouroux, Pour en Finir Avec Vichy: Les Oublis de la MÉmoire [Coming to Terms with Vichy: The Oversights of Memory] 444 (1997) (suggesting that Vichy France and Nazi Germany were parallel genocidal "Jew crushing machines," and that the French anti-Semitic machine was the first to go into gear as early as 1938).

33. See Stuart Eizenstat, Imperfect Justice, Looted Assets, Slave Labor, and the Unfinished Business of World War II, at 248, 252 (2003) (suggesting that the Jewish Question is political abuse that arises out of antagonistic attitudes produced in non-Jews by Jews and that the Nazis considered Jews nonassimilable because they could not be "driven into uncritical acceptance of dogma"); *see also* Jay R. Berkovitz, Rites of Passages: The Beginnings of Modern Jewish Culture in France, 1650-1860, at 16 (Univ. of Penn. Press 2004).

34. Law # 78-17 of January 6, 1978 On Computer Data Processing, Databases, and Individual Freedoms.

35. Id.

36. Convention for the Protection of Individuals with Regard to Automatic Processing of Personal Data (1981) (visited November 2007) at http://www.europa.eu.int/comm/dg15.

37. See Michel Winock, *La naissance du quatrième pouvoir* (The birth of the Fourth Estate). *Le Monde,* August 18, 1988 at 2.

38. *La Confédération général du travial* (General Confederation of Labor, Cgt), *110e anniversaire du congrès Constitutif de la Cgt* (110th Anniversary of the Founding Congress of the CGT) (2005). Available at: http://www.cgt.fr/110e-anniversaire-du-congres.html

39. See Article L7111-6, *Code de travail* (Labor Code). Available at: http://www.legifrance.gouv.fr/affichCode.do?cidTexte=LEGITEXT000006072050&dateTexte=20111127M

40. See CGT, *Le Syndicat: Histoire du SNJ-CGT* (The Union, History of the SNJ-CGT) (2005). Available at: http://www.snj.cgt.fr/index1bis.html

41. See article L7111-1–L7114-1, *Nouveau code du travail, Partie Legislative* (Labor Code, Legislative Section) (2008).

42. See *Nouveau code de travail*, articles R 7111-18 et seq. (New Labor Code R. 7111-18 and following).

43. See article L7111-6, *Nouveau code du travail, Partie Legislative* (Labor Code, Legislative Section) (2008).

44. *La convention collective nationale de travail des journalists, The National Collective Bargaining Agreement for journalists* (2010). Available at: http://www.snj.cgt.fr/spip/spip.php?article31

45. *La Commission de la Carte d'Identité des journalistes Professionnels* (CCIJP) (The Commission for the Issuance of Identity Cards to Professional journalists), Conditions for Issuing Professional Identity Cards [to journalists]. Available at: http://www.ccijp.net/article-10-conditions-d-attribution-de-la-carte-professionnelle.html

46. 533 U.S. 483 (2001).

47. 17 U.S.C §201(c).

48. 533 U.S. 483 (2001).

49. 533 U.S. 483 (2001).

50. 533 U.S. 483 (2001).

51. See e.g. *New York Times v. Tasini*, 533 U.S. 483 (2001) (Holding that publishers who, without consent, included articles of freelance writers in databases from which licensed users could reproduce or distribute discrete copies, violated the copyright of the freelance authors).

52. See Tarleton Gillespie, Wired Shut, Copyright And The Shape Of The Digital Culture 10 (Cambridge, MIT Press 2007).

53. 405 F.3d 26 (2nd Cir., 2005).

54. 488 F.3d 1331 (11th Cir. 2007).

55. See Lyombe Eko, New technologies, Old Mentalities: The Internet, The Minitel, and Exceptionalist Information and Communication technology Policy, in *New Media, Old Regimes: Case Studies in Comparative Communication Law and Policy* 209 (2012).

56. Le Figaro c/ Le syndicat national des journalistes (S.N.J.), *Cour d'Appel de Paris, 1ère chambre A, Arrêt du 10 mai 2000.* (Appeals Court of Paris, 1st Chamber, Decision of May 10, 2000).

57. See Lyombe Eko, New Media, Old Regimes: Case Studies in Comparative Communication Law and Policy 209 (2012).

58. *LOI n° 2009-669 du 12 juin 2009 favorisant la diffusion et la protection de la création sur internet* (1) (Law No. 2009-669 of June 12, 2009, Furthering the Dissemination and Protection of Production on the Internet), J.O. No. 0135 of June 13, 2009 (p. 9666).

59. Art. II, Berne Convention for the Protection of Literary and Artistic Works (Paris Text, 1971).

60. Copyright Act of 1976 (as amended), 17 U.S.C. §102 (1976).

61. World Intellectual Property Organization (Wipo), Development Of Wipo's Dispute Resolution Services, *World Intellectual Property Organization, 1992-2007*, Part III, pp. 93-104 (2008) (Available at: http://www.wipo.int/amc/en/history/

62. Jean-François Thery and Isabelle Falque Pierrotin, *Conseil d'État* (Council of State) Internet et les Réseaux Numériques (Internet and Digital Networks) (1998).

Chapter Seven

New Media, Old Interest Groups

Civil Society and Internet Regulation in the United States and France

In October 2004, the Union of French Jewish Students (UEJF), an interest group dedicated to the eradication of all kinds of racist and anti-Semitic speech and expression from French society, launched a multi-media, anti-racist "sensitization campaign."[1] The core of the campaign was a parody of a national, multi-media, road safety campaign entitled, "Road safety, It's Everyone's Business." UEJF intended to drive home the message that anti-Semitism was still rampant in France and that all French citizens had a part to play in ensuring that it was eradicated from the country. To this end, it used huge posters and roadside billboards of iconic images of Jesus Christ and the Virgin Mary to make its point. However, each of these iconic images was defaced with a gangster-style graffiti tag: "Dirty Jew." The bottom of each image also had this statement: "Anti-Semitism, what if it were everyone's business?"[2] The campaign also had an online component. UEJF said that the aim of its campaign was to launch a public debate on anti-Semitism in France. The organization stated that though the French government and the political establishment had become conscious of the problem of anti-Semitism in France, the general public was indifferent to it. UEJF added that it wanted the French people to know that anti-Semitism was, like road safety, "everyone's business."[3]

The UEJF's "sensitization" campaign was too sensitive for many French citizens. The campaign quickly backfired on the UEJF. The Roman Catholic Church called the parody "anti-Christian," while local government officials said it was too provocative.[4] UEJF's partner in arms, *La Ligue International Contre Le Racisme et l'antisémitisme* (The International League Against

Racism and Anti-Semitism, LICRA), urged UEJF to cancel or modify the campaign because the defaced images of Jesus Christ and the Virgin Mary could shock the French people and exacerbate religious tensions within France, a nation that was historically and culturally Catholic.[5] The uproar was so great that on the day the "sensitization campaign" against anti-Semitism was to officially begin, UEJF decided to remove the controversial images of Jesus Christ and the Virgin Mary in its literature and billboard messages in real space and cyberspace.[6] UEJF did not want to endanger the financial support it received from the political establishment.

Defaced images of Jesus and Mary, whether online or in an offline campaign against anti-Semitism were objectionable in France, a country that has been aptly described as having a "*Catho-laique*" (Catho-secular) culture.[7] In effect, contemporary French society still experiences the tension between France's foundational Roman Catholic culture—the founding event of the French nation was the conversion and baptism into Roman Catholicism of Clovis, King of the Franks, together with 3000 of his soldiers on Christmas day, in 496 AD—and its post-Revolutionary Constitutional secularism. In effect, the mass baptism of 496 AD had transformed the nascent nation that was to be called "France" after its Frankish founders, *La fille aineé de l'Église* (the Eldest daughter of the [Roman Catholic] Church).[8] After the Revolution of 1789 and the subsequent disestablishment of the Roman Catholic Church and the de-Christianization of the state, France developed a reputation as a bastion of secular republicanism.[9] "Catho-secularism" is one of the hallmarks of the French exception. In this chapter, we will explore the relationship between the government and interest groups under French law, as a characteristic of that French specificity that we call the French exception. We will also explore the roll of American organized interest groups within the exceptionalist First Amendment regime of the United States.

Interest Groups and Free Speech in the United States

Interest groups have also been a crucial part of the politico-cultural and legal landscape of the United States since the founding of the Republic. The wide range of interest groups that exist in the United States have been on both extremes of the freedom of expression continuum. While a good number have, like the French interest groups campaigned in the political and social arena to restrict speech and speakers that they found objectionable on a number of grounds, an equal or even larger group of libertarian free speech advocates have campaigned to extend the contours of permissible speech within the Framework of the exceptional First Amendment. The most ferocious and emotional battles have involved the free speech rights of disreputable groups like the Ku Klux Klan (KKK), the National Socialist (Nazi) Party of America, and the Aryan Nations. In 1998, Barry Black led a Ku Klux Klan rally on private property in Carroll County, Virginia, with the permission of the property owner, who was in attendance. Members of the Klan uttered hateful and threatening statements against African Americans and "Mexicans." They then proceeded to burn a cross, Historically, the KKK has used cross burning a symbol of hate, a tool of intimidation, and a threat of impending violence against African Americans and even whites who did not fit their ideology. The County Sheriff arrested Black for violating a Virginia law that made it a crime to burn a cross with the intent to intimidate a person or a group of persons. The law further stated that the act of burning a cross was *prima facie* evidence of intent to intimidate. Black, the organizer of the rally, was charged with violating a Virginia statute against cross burning. He was convicted despite protestations that his actions were protected by the First Amendment. The case wound its way to the Supreme Court of the United States, which had to decide whether Virginia's statute banning cross burning with "an intent to intimidate a person or group of persons," violates the First Amendment.

The Court said it did, and ruled that "while a State, consistent with the First Amendment, may ban cross burning carried out with the intent to intimidate, the provision in the Virginia statute treating any cross burning as *prima facie* evidence of intent to intimidate renders the statute unconstitutional." The Supreme Court of the United States essentially ruled that burning a cross—an act which communicated a message of hate and violence—absent an intent to intimidate, was protected speech under the First Amendment. This is because cross-burning is symbolic speech that also communicates a message of identity and shared ideology.[10]

What is interesting about this case is that a prominent American libertarian group, the ACLU provided defense lawyers for the KKK, including an African-American lawyer, David P. Baugh. The second ACLU connection in this case came in the person of Justice Ruth Bader Ginsburg, the former General Counsel of the ACLU. Not surprisingly, Justice Ginsburg concurred with the opinion that the Virginia statute that banned cross-burning was unconstitutional. Incidentally, the ACLU had also provided a lawyer to defend the Nazi Party of America, which successfully sought to march in a predominantly Jewish neighborhood of Chicago.[11]

Clearly, while the UEJF and other French interest groups focused on eradicating racist and anti-Semitic speech from the French public sphere, American interest groups led by the American Civil Liberties Union (ACLU), focused on eradicating laws that they felt eroded civil liberties in the United States in areas as diverse as freedom of speech and of the press, separation of church and state, the free exercise of religion, equal protection under the law, reproductive freedom, and individual privacy. The ACLU has consistently resorted to the remedies of the law—legal proceedings against the government and other alleged offenders—since litigation is a powerful instrument of political advocacy and social reform in the United States.[12]

The aim of this chapter is to analyze the role and impact of organized interest groups on Internet regulation in the United States and France, using as a comparative case study, the contrasting roles played by interest groups fighting racism and anti-Semitism in France, and libertarian groups in the United States that were involved in free speech controversies and disputes that have had a lasting impact on Internet law and policy in the country. The study focused on the two anti-racist groups—UEJF and LICRA—that are quasi-institutional partners of the French government in matters of objectionable Internet content, on the one hand, and the ACLU, on the other hand. The ACLU and other American civil libertarian groups have successfully challenged congressional attempts to restrict "objectionable speech" on the Internet. While other interest groups like the Electronic Frontier Foundation (EFF) and Green Peace France have been instrumental in exposing warrantless governmental surveillance of the Internet,[13] and furthering freedom of expression in cyberspace through freedom of information litigation and trademark parody respectively, the main interest group actors that have affected Internet law and content are the American Civil Liberties Union (ACLU) and the French anti-racist groups, UEJF and *La Ligue Internationale Contre le Racisme et l'Anti-sémitisme* (The International League Against Racism and Anti-Semitism, LICRA). These groups helped shape the nascent Internet law regime in the United States and France, respectively.

The controversial content that was the subject of the intervention of these American and French civil society groups included: 1) Legislation restricting online material of a sexual or scatological nature in the United States, and 2) Internet-based bias-motivated Holocaust denial, as well as the display of Nazi memorabilia and the hosting of hate speech—vitriolic expressions of hatred directed at individuals or groups on the basis of their race, ethnicity, religion, national origin, or sexual orientation in France.[14] The different national and cultural interpretations of bias-motivated or hate speech stems from the fact that freedom of speech does not have a universally accepted definition.[15] As we saw in chapters 3 and 4, France and the United States have historically had different legal, political, and cultural approaches to freedom of expression.[16] The United States has a marketplace **of** ideas in which the rights of the speaker outweigh by far, the feelings of the listener, while France has a marketplace **for** ideas[17] in which the government's interest in human dignity, civility, solidarity, fraternity, equality, protection of the reputations of individuals, and protection of the right to privacy, often take precedence over freedom of expression.[18] When the United States and France first transferred their respective legal doctrines developed for traditional speech and the media in real space, to the virtual world of cyberspace, civil society interest groups in both countries were instrumental in shaping the communication law regimes in general, and the Internet regulatory regimes in particular, of these countries.

Contrasting Conceptualization of Freedom of Expression by the ACLU, UEJF & LICRA

While several American interest groups have influenced Internet law and regulation in the United States, no other group has impacted the American free speech regime in real space and cyberspace like the ACLU. The American Civil Liberties Union (ACLU) is a civil libertarian interest group organized in 1920 to defend the rights of conscientious objectors who were being prosecuted for failing to enlist during World War I. The organization subsequently defended political dissidents in the inter-war years. Since World War II, the ACLU has stridently and vigorously—its critics would say stubbornly and coercively—defended what it considers the constitutional rights of mostly eccentric and outlier groups and individuals of all political persuasions. The main weapons in the organization's arsenal are litigation and lobbying in support of its avowed civil libertarian goals.[19] The ACLU was selected for this study because through its legal actions, it has had a profound impact on American First Amendment law in general, and Internet law and policy in particular, in real space and cyberspace. The ACLU has been at the forefront of organized interest groups fighting for freedom of expression on the Internet. The ACLU was also selected for this study because it came face to face with French groups fighting racism and anti-Semitism on the Internet. In effect, this encounter, which was essentially a clash of American and French freedom of expression values, occurred over the famous Yahoo! Nazi memorabilia cases decided in French,[20] and American courts from 2000 to 2005.[21]

French Anti-Racist Groups and Groups fighting Anti-Semitism

In France, UEJF and LICRA play a role that contrasts sharply with that of the ACLU—they support and promote governmentally-sanctioned or "official" versions of history. They also take affirmative steps to monitor, denounce and eliminate the following content from the public sphere: Hate speech and symbolic expression, specifically, speech that they believe amounts to expressions of racism, anti-Semitism, and Holocaust denial. They seek out and denounce speech or symbolic expression that ridicules or demonizes individuals or groups of individuals on the basis of their religion, ethnicity, sexual orientation, resistance to Nazi German occupation during World War II, and so on. These happen to be categories of speech that are criminalizes as antisocial under the French Criminal Code. Though this type of speech usually originates from extremist and outlier groups, speech by many mainstream individuals, organizations, and companies has been caught in the malleable, content-based dragnet of French interest groups.

Since 1972, self-described anti-racist interest groups have been granted standing to serve as watchdogs—and civil complainants who trigger criminal prosecutions—against alleged purveyors of bias-motivated speech and other objectionable content under French law. When the fledgling Internet became a global, trans-media, multi-communication and commercial platform in the 1990s, these French interest groups went on the offensive against what they considered illegal and objectionable bias-motivated or hate speech hosted mostly on servers based in the United States. The UEJF and LICRA were chosen for this study because through their legal actions, they jointly and severally succeeded in "cleansing" France of objectionable speech in real space and cyberspace.

The ACLU's "defensive" legal actions against Internet censorship, and UEJF and LICRA's "offensive" prosecutions of hate speech ultimately resulted in protracted legal battles in French and American courts. The global interconnectedness of the Internet ultimately led the American and French groups to appear on opposite sides of a major transnational Internet law controversy, the so-called Yahoo! affair that is the subject of this chapter. Legal proceedings and court decisions emanating from the diametrically opposed legal actions of the ACLU and the French anti-racist interest groups led to a clash of the free speech cultures of the United States and France, and to a conflict of laws situation between the two countries. As courts in both countries sought to resolve the disputes raised by these interest groups over Internet content, these courts re-presented or presented anew, the role and place of organized interest groups within the context of their respective exceptionalist political and communication law regimes.

Significance of this Comparative Analysis

The significance of this study lies in the fact that it exemplifies the differential conceptualizations, roles and impact of French and American public interest groups on Internet content regulation. Since the Internet is a global, interconnected, multi-platform phenomenon, the outcomes of the legal actions undertaken by American and French interest groups, and the decisions of American and French courts impacted global Internet law and policy, and directly affected the type of Internet content available to the rest of the world. Therefore, legal actions undertaken by interest groups in specific countries to transfer national, politico-cultural, legal and ideological norms, as well as value systems from real space to cyberspace is essentially global "rule-making." When it comes to Internet governance, every regulation or court decision in every country has the potential of affecting the content of the Internet around the globe. The role and influence of interest groups on Internet content can best be understood within a comparative framework. While each country has the sovereign right to regulate Internet infrastructure and content within its jurisdiction under its specific legal framework, communicational sovereignty becomes problematic when national legislative and judicial actions become extra-territorial effects.

Summary of the Chapter

Since comparative research requires some criterion or yardstick against which the objects of comparison—in this case, French and American interest groups that have influenced free speech on the Internet—can be measured,[22] this study will focus on the legal contexts or regimes within which the interest groups under study operate, as well as the actions they undertook to restrict or expand the scope of freedom of expression on the Internet. The first part of this chapter sets forth the theoretical perspective that guided this comparative case study—the exceptional political sociology of interest groups in the political regimes of the United States and France—and applies it to the interest groups under study. The second part surveys the role of the organized interest groups under study—the ACLU, UEJF and LICRA—in matters of freedom of expression and civil rights. The focus is on how these interest groups—and the courts—re-presented American and French national norms and values, and used the law to advance social and political interests related to freedom of expression. In the United States, the ACLU uses the law to advance its ideology of civil liberties in general, and free speech in particular in the traditional media and on the Internet, while the UEJF & LICRA, with France as their base, use the law and the courts to eliminate bias-motivated or racist speech in real space and cyberspace. The third part of this chapter focuses on the impact of the interest groups on Internet content regulation in the United States and France, while the fourth part focuses on how these interest groups' roles in the Yahoo! affair, a series of cases heard in French and American courts, led to a conflict between the free speech laws the United States and France. The last section discusses resolution of the conflict. It compares, contrasts, and analyzes the different roles and the impact of the interest groups on Internet law and policy in both countries.

The Political Sociology of Organized Interest Groups

The terms "interest groups," "special interest groups," or "organized interest groups,"[23] refer to private sector voluntary political or social groupings whose *raison d'être* is to influence public policy through influencing elected or appointed public officials.[24] Organized interest groups (hereinafter, interest groups) are part of democratic civil society.[25] They have been fixtures of

American politics since the early days of the republic.[26] Interest groups have also been part of the French political system since the Revolution of 1789.

The comparative approach to the study of the role of public interest groups in the political process is an old one. The pioneer of this approach was Alexis de Tocqueville.[27] In the 19th century, de Tocqueville compared and contrasted the roles of civil society groups in the United States and Europe. He stated that in the United States, the freedom of civil society groups to challenge authority plays an important salutary role in the democratic process: "extreme liberty corrects the abuses of liberty . . . extreme democracy obviates the dangers of democracy."[28] By way of contrast, in Europe, he wrote, civil society groups act differently from American civil society groups: "European associations consider themselves, in some degree, as the legislative and executive council of the people, who are unable to speak for themselves; moved by this belief, they act and they command. In America . . . they argue and petition."[29] This study seeks to determine if the two French anti-racist groups and the American Civil Liberties Union adhere to the model advanced by de Tocqueville in the nineteenth century.

The Role of Organized Interest Groups in the U.S. & France

This section compares and contrasts the role of specialized interest groups in the political and social systems of the United States and France within the framework of political sociology. Political sociologists have advanced several perspectives that help to explain interest group networks and activities in specific political dispensations. That is, interest groups operate within the context of specific *"governmentalities"* to borrow the neologism of Michel Foucault.[30] These are the conceptualizations, institutional logics, procedures, strategies of control, rationalizations and practices of "rulership"; in short, the exercise of power. If we apply this concept to interest groups, governmentality would be the differential "arts of [political] governance,"[31] the posture of governments with respect to organized interest groups.

The most common categorization employed in interest group studies is a four-part typology made up of the pluralist, Marxist, elitist, and corporatist perspectives that explain the role of interest groups in policy making, as well as the relationships between interest groups and nation-states.[32] From a pluralist perspective, interest groups play a central role in the liberal democratic political process. As part of civil society, they put pressure on politicians and political institutions such that policy decisions result from complex interactions and bazaar-style bargaining and compromises among, and within different competing sets of interest groups and political actors, each seeking to promote its interests and policy goals.[33] Additionally, in pluralist countries, the government arbitrates between competing interest groups, without necessarily favoring any particular groups, or ignoring civil society groups altogether, and trying to impose its own solutions on society.[34]

For its part, the Marxist perspective of the role of interest groups in society emphasizes class struggles, state intervention in, and policy bias towards certain social classes, at the detriment of other interest groups.[35] The elitist perspective holds that elite interest groups—often interested in intangible issues of freedom and rights rather than bread and butter issues—are politically active while the majority of the citizenry is passive or indifferent to such issues.[36]

The corporatist perspective attempts to explain interest group activities in democratic regimes, particularly those in Europe. Indeed, the European conceptualization of the role of interest groups in the political system is markedly different from that of the United States. Under many European regimes, interest groups are virtual co-powers who partner with the state to advance governmental social and political interests in specific issue areas.[37] As such, many European interest groups are essentially co-regulators with the government. Schulz and Held argue that in the fields of telecommunication and the mass media, globalization, deregulation and privatization have transformed the erstwhile European sovereign state into a "corporate bargaining state."[38] One of the hallmarks of the corporate bargaining stats is that it outsources some of its erstwhile responsibilities in the media and telecommunications fields to highly regulated private-sector entities whose intervention further substantial governmental social and political interests under a system of "regulated self-regulation."[39]

Granados and Knobe state that the fundamental feature of the European-style corporatist regimes is the leading role of the government "in orchestrating interest group participation in policy processes . . . characterized by explicit, officially recognized, and regular cooperation and reciprocity between these groups and the state, aimed at achieving harmony among special interests and participant obligations to promote the collective good and social solidarity."[40] Thus, under the corporatist system, interest groups are essentially adjuncts of the state; co-powers that are granted "monopolistic representation" of civil society interests in specific issue areas in order that they can speak for their constituents and assist the government in implementing public policy decisions that ensure social peace and stability.[41]

If we apply this typology to the United States and France, the pluralist, and elitist perspectives of the interest group typology apply to the United States while the corporatist model corresponds to the French system. Since the bulk of the legal disputes initiated by the ACLU, the Electronic Frontier Foundation (EFF), UEJF, LICRA, and other interest groups almost always involve content issues—matters touching on race, ethnicity, and bias-motivated online speech—this case study was also informed by the sociopolitical conceptualization of race and state advanced by David James and Kent Redding.[42] Under this framework, racial identity is presumed to be not only the source, but also the effect of state-enforced racial policies. James and Redding contrast the racial state, which sponsors race-conscious policies, and liberal democratic states, which enforce equal citizenship rights for all irrespective of membership in specific racial, ethnic or other status groups.[43] In their comparative analysis of organized interest groups, James and Redding distinguish France, which they call "a republican democracy," from the United States, which they describe as a "liberal democracy."[44] The main premise of this chapter is that the Internet content regulatory regimes of the United States and France are a result of the exceptional governmentality of each country, as it responds to the exercise of power and pressure by interest groups, acting within the context of each country's sociopolitical, cultural, and legal framework.

Interest Groups and the Regulation of Freedom of Expression in the United States and France

Researchers have found that the public policy postures of liberal democratic countries are the result of political conflicts in which specific aspects of national political, social and cultural ideology are invoked and written into law.[45] In these countries, state institutions, structures, and processes act as gatekeepers for political ideas that enter into the national mix.[46] Though the United States and France are Western democratic countries, their political and legal regimes can be distinguished by their respective politico-cultural philosophies and ideologies.[47] Civil society groups are important political and social actors in both countries. However, the different historical and political contexts of both countries have bequeathed different roles to organized interest groups in both regimes. This is especially true in the issue area of freedom of speech and expression. As a general rule, one can say that while the ACLU and other organized interest groups in the United States struggle—mostly against federal, state and local governments—to protect and promote freedom of expression and other expressive civil rights, the UEJF, LICRA and other organized interest groups in France struggle to restrict and circumscribe the right of extremist and other outlier groups to indulge in uncivil, extreme speech and expression.

Interest Groups in the American Political Regime

In the United States, bills that are enacted into law are the outcomes of ongoing struggles among interest groups and classes for political and economic advantage and power.[48] While the dominant groups tend to have their interests enshrined in law, they often make compromises with the minority groups on whom they may rely to pass legislation. Robert Lieberman put it succinctly when he said that "these struggles take place within historical and institutional contexts that define the allocation and exercise of political power and so shape policymaking, especially by constraining political behavior through the operation of rules, norms and organizational settings."[49]

The exceptional Free speech regime of the United States is the result of compromises made by the "Founding Fathers" of the American republic at the infancy of the fledgling federation. The Constitution that was adopted at the Constitutional Convention of 1787 was the crowning achievement of the American Revolution. However, the constitutional order that emerged was not accepted unanimously by the 13 colonies. The absence of a Bill of Rights was a stumbling block that needed to be overcome. The final contours of the regime were set in place through political pragmatism and compromise. The idea of a Bill of Rights, which guaranteed freedom of the press, was at best a contested proposition. Alexander Hamilton and the Federalists, who campaigned for ratification of the Constitution, saw no need for a Bill of Rights because in their view, the Constitution itself was the Bill of Rights.[50] Indeed, Hamilton saw Bills of Rights as primitive documents that had no place in modern constitutions. In his view, freedom of the press was a function of public opinion and governmental action, not constitutional declarations.[51] The Anti-Federalists, who opposed ratification of the Constitution, used the absence of a Bill of Rights as a wedge issue to tear asunder support for the document. Ultimately, pragmatism and compromise carried the day. In exchange for ratification of the Constitution by the thirteen original states, the Federalists agreed that Congress would, as the first order of business, pass a number of amendments (the Bill of Rights) that would be added to the document.[52] The Bill of Rights is thus the result of a compromise by the Federalists, the Anti-Federalists, and other factions. The exceptional American free speech regime is thus the product of compromises reached during the writing and ratification of the American Constitution and the Bill of Rights. The First Amendment (ratified in 1791) guarantees freedom of speech and the press.

First Amendment jurisprudence has evolved into a unique, exceptional, free speech regime whose major characteristic is the theory that the United States is a marketplace of ideas.[53] The freedom of speech tradition of the U.S. gives the benefit of the doubt to the speaker rather than the government and, in the words of Matthew Bunker, "leads us to exercise great caution before silencing viewpoints with which we disagree."[54] Jeffrie Murphy and Jules Coleman state that under the First Amendment, American citizens can bring "claims against certain kinds of interferences"[55] with their rights of freedom of speech. Of course the First Amendment does not demand that the government take affirmative steps to promote acceptable speech; it merely forbids the government from injecting itself into the public speech arena and unduly interfering with content that it finds politically or socially objectionable.[56] The result is that intolerant speech is tolerated even if by its very nature, it forecloses other types of speech. The uniqueness of the regime is that even in speech controversies not involving the government, the expressive rights of the speaker take precedence over the feelings of the listener.[57]

Furthermore, under the American system, the government is required to maintain a non-discriminatory, content-neutral policy in terms of regulations appertaining to speech and expression—including symbolic speech and expressive conduct—especially if the intent of the regulation is to suppress objectionable speech or expressive conduct.[58] Indeed, the Supreme Court of the United States has held that all governmental content-based regulations[59] have a higher hurdle to scale than content-neutral regulations.[60] That is to say, content-based regulations must pass the exacting "strict scrutiny" test, which means that in order to justify content-based regulations, states must show that "the regulation is necessary to serve a compelling state interest and is narrowly drawn to achieve that end."[61]

America's constitutional framework and decentralized federal structure is the seedbed on which large numbers of organized interest groups sprout.[62] Alexis de Tocqueville, one of the most perceptive commentators on interest groups and associations in the United States, wrote that interest groups in the United States are unique because Americans are traditionally wary of, and mistrust authority. As a result, they form interest groups that act as instruments of moral resistance against authorities and against legal enactments that are perceived as constraining freedom. The role of American interest groups is thus to fight against the tyranny of the majority and against the abuse of power.[63] These interest groups consequently help to make political institutions more responsive and accountable to the public.[64]

The United States is classified as a pluralist state where interest groups play an important role in the political process. In the United States, political power is perceived to be "fragmented and widely dispersed among competing interest groups, with policy decisions resulting from complex interactions and bargaining within different sets of groups defined by specific matter or kind of personal traits."[65] Though the United States has a system of checks and balances between the executive, the legislative and the judicial branches of government, it is not a system of discrete branches of government that make policy in isolation. Indeed, in the United States, the traditional, "textbook," separation of powers doctrine, whereby the federal executive or presidential power is exercised by the president,[66] the legislative power is vested in the Congress,[67] and the judicial power rests in a judiciary which has the power of judicial review,[68] is now extremely blurred by what Robert Kagan calls "adversarial legalism."[69] This is the unique, American-style policy-making, implementation, and dispute resolution process marked by "legal contestation and political revision."[70] In this system, organized advocacy groups take legal action, file appeals, and pressure judges to act as policy-makers—which they sometimes do—and if these groups do not succeed in court, they pressure legislators to overrule courts (which they also sometimes do).[71]

Miller and Barnes suggest that the American regime is a very open system whose dynamic policy-making process allows inputs from all branches of federal, state and local governmental entities, as well as from a wide array of nongovernmental actors and interest groups.[72] Indeed, governance in the United States is, in the words of Miller and Barnes, "dialogue . . . an ongoing colloquy among roughly co-equal actors in various branches and levels of government who seek to promote a mix of strategic, institutional and policy goals."[73] The researchers use the term "adversarial legalism" to describe the exceptional governance regime of the United States, and claim that the colloquies in which the various political interests indulge are driven in part by the distinct political culture of the United States, which "distrusts centralized authority . . . it occurs because of the distinctive evolution of adversarial legalism, which has given public interest groups tools to participate in—and second-guess—administrative decision-making and momentary concentrations of power in a given policy area."[74] The essence of American adversarial legalism is a "decentralized, rights-based administrative state, which often places courts at the center of complex—and contested—regulatory disputes."[75] This is an expansion of the Constitutional doctrine of judicial review, a system whereby politicians and legislatures defer to the courts, thereby making the judiciary the final arbiter on legal and constitutional matters.[76]

The ACLU as a Counter-Power in the United States

The ACLU is a uniquely American libertarian organization whose vocation has been to promote its idea of individual and group civil liberties under the Bill of Rights (the first ten amendments to the Constitution of the United States). Since it was founded in 1920, the ACLU has made it its vocation to promote America's culture of individual liberty under the Constitution.[77] From its early fight for conscientious objectors and free speech during World War I, the ACLU has promoted and defended—sometimes to the point of intimidating private corporate entities—its ideology of civil liberties in the United States in areas as diverse as freedom of speech and of the press, separation of church and state, the free exercise of religion, equal protection under the law, reproductive freedom, and individual privacy. The ACLU has particularly used its very broad interpretation of the First Amendment to push for a widening of the scope of freedom of speech and expression in the country.

In the United States, litigation is a powerful instrument of political advocacy and social reform.[78] Many interest groups have taken advantage of this reality to advance their political, ideological, and social goals. The American

Civil Liberties Union (ACLU) is at the forefront of these groups. As a result, it has influenced Internet law and policy in the United States more than any other group. Indeed, it has had a profound impact on American law, culture, and values.[79] The ACLU has used its very broad interpretation of First Amendment guarantees of Freedom of Speech and of the press to transform itself into a crusader—some would say enforcer—for civil liberties at the Federal, state, and local levels. The ACLU has therefore been at the forefront of America's "rights revolution" and identity politics to the point of legal intimidation of those who disagree with its views.[80] As noted above, the ACLU has defended the free speech rights of groups as diverse as the Nazi Party of America,[81] the Ku Klux Klan, and terrorism suspects in the post-911 era.[82]

While the ACLU has petitioned American courts, Congress and the White House to put civil liberties at the top of the political agenda. In keeping with its interpretation of the Bill of Rights, the organization's campaign of freedom of speech and expression on the Internet has enabled it to globalize its civil libertarian values.[83] Indeed, some researchers claim that the United States Supreme Court's decision[84] to grant full (American) constitutional protection to the Internet after legal action by the ACLU, essentially made the First Amendment the law of an unwitting and often an unwilling planetary village.[85] Some politicians and activists also claim that the American-made and controlled Internet architecture and transmission protocols create *a de facto lex Americana, a* global reign of American legal values and ideals on the Internet.[86] This is because in the age of information technology and the Internet, "code is law,"[87] to use Lawrence Lessig's formulation, and "control of code is power," as William Mitchell suggests.[88] The United States government, under pressure from the ACLU—a virtual counter-power—has written laws, regulations, policies, and freedoms—into computer code. The strident and sometimes extreme libertarian activism of the ACLU has opened it up to criticism as being anti-American, anti-traditional family, anti-religion, anti-Christmas, anti-children, and so on.[89] However, it is in its crusade for freedom of expression that the ACLU has made its greatest mark on American society. In that sense, the ACLU can be called the keeper of the First Amendment temple.

Anti-Racist Interest Groups, Freedom of Expression, and Group Defamation in France

France is a highly centralized administrative state whose motto is the revolutionary slogan: *Liberté, Égalité, Fraternité* (Liberty, Equality, Fraternity). However, in France, equality is more important than liberty.[90] The French free speech regime is a legacy of the conflicts, contestations and compromises of the tumultuous Revolution of 1789 and the numerous regimes that succeeded each other in the next century. Under French law, freedom of speech and expression is rooted in the Declaration of the Rights of Man and of the Citizen of 1789,[91] which, together with the preamble to the Constitution of 1946, are incorporated by reference in the Constitution of 1958, the supreme law in France.[92] Article XI of the Declaration of the Rights of Man and of the Citizen of 1789 states that "the free communication of thoughts and opinions is one of the most precious rights of man."[93] However, this clause is qualified by a *provisio,* which states that people are free to speak, write, and print freely, *on condition that they answer for any abuse of this freedom.*[94] Additionally, the Declaration states that, "the exercise of the natural rights of each person has no bounds but those which assure to other members of the society, the enjoyment of these same rights."[95]

These exceptions are the basis for prohibition of bias-motivated speech and expression. French philosopher, Paul Ricœur put it aptly when he said that under French secular republican ideology, "only the intolerant is intolerable."[96] In theory, then, all expressions that are not perceived as intolerant are tolerable. However, intolerance of expressions that are classified as intolerant can mask intolerance of different ideas and viewpoints. The French regime's dogmatic intolerance of a class of vague and undefined speech that is classified as "intolerance," gives activists who have axes to grind, the power to have the last word on what is intolerable intolerance in a wide domain of speech and expression. Under French jurisprudence, newspapers, editors and journalists may be liable for criminal and civil penalties if they violate certain laws in the course of newsgathering or as a result of publication of the material gathered.

Additionally, in France, the right to individual privacy is paramount in both the old and the new media. Therefore, all Internet sites are required to abide by the Charter of Laws on Information Technology, Data Processing and Individual Freedoms (CNIL) of 1978, which restricts the collection, storage and transfer of personal information in databases. The law requires that Internet users be given the right to access, correct, and suppress all data concerning them in any website if they so desire. The only thing aggrieved citizens need to do is send an e-mail to the owner or host of the site containing the objectionable information. Additionally, individual data cannot be processed without the consent of the individual concerned except in specific medical emergencies defined by law.[97] The French law of freedom of expression has a moral philosophical rationale. The law seeks to balance the freedom of expression of writers and publishers—in the traditional media and on the Internet—against protection of individuals or groups who can be harmed by certain kinds of activities and speech—particularly hate speech—that is considered a misuse or abuse of freedom of expression.[98]

Freedom of Expression and Group Defamation

While the ACLU and other American libertarian groups are pre-occupied with civil liberties in general, and freedom of expression in particular, the French organized interest groups under study are preoccupied with the representation of race and ethnicity in the media and in public discourse. This is paradoxical and ironical given that France does not officially classify its citizens by race, ethnicity, national origin, society, or religion.

Nevertheless, France has never been a color-blind society. It has a long tradition of race-based interest groups whose mission was precisely to eradicate the problem of racism that did not officially exist. In 1788, Jacques Pierre Brissot de Warville founded one of the first human rights interest groups in the world, *La Société des Amis de Noirs* (Society of Friends of Blacks), which advocated liberty and equality for black people and campaigned for the abolition of slavery in French colonies, as well as in the United States.[99] From a political sociology perspective, contemporary France is an exemplar of a state where interest groups operate in a corporatist environment. Sammy Smooha classified democracies in terms of the extent to which they restrict individual rights in order to protect minority and other group rights. He described France as a "republican democracy" which enforces policies of cultural homogenization, uniformization, and assimilation.[100]

France has a secular, republican ideology that is rooted in the Revolution of 1789. Though France has been described as a "*catho–laïque*," (Catho-secular) nation because of its historic Catholic culture,[101] the country exists—in theory at least—as a secular nation of culturally homogeneous people whose distinct ethnicity and religion is insignificant as long as they play by the secular rules of the unitary state.[102] Thus, all persons in France are to be assimilated into the French Republic as *individuals*, with one culture—the French culture—not as members of specific ethnic or religious communities.[103] Indeed, David Beriss argues that hegemonic, neo-republican notions of France as a culturally unified nation make French culture, rather than race the central tenet of French identity.[104] Therefore, the official policy is to assimilate all immigrants and minorities, organize or accredit, and finance their interest groups, and inoculate them with enough "Frenchness" (broad immersion into French language and culture) to enable them to "relate vertically to an ideal image of the French nation. The aim of this policy is to enable these newcomers' interest groups to find common ground with other immigrants who have embarked on this process of "Frenchization" or "becoming-French"[105] This means all immigrants are expected to embrace secular republicanism and the state-directed Frenchness that rejects multiculturalism and renounces overt, non-French, ethnic, religious and other affiliations and symbols like the Islamic headscarf or burqua. Thus, in France, immigrants are expected to jettison their racial identity or ethnic group membership at the border in order to become good French citizens.[106]

This is the exceptionalist philosophical and cultural underpinning of French criminalization of racist and anti-Semitic speech and expressions. The role of interest groups in the regulation of hate speech can be traced to the post-World War II era. Anti-Semitism and other racial ideologies that had diffused from Nazi Germany to France on the eve of World War II reached fever pitch in sections of the French press. This led to the passage, in 1939, of the "*décret-Loi Marchandeau,*" a statute which criminalized defamation committed by organs of the press against a group of persons on account of their race or religion. With passage of that law, the term "race" officially became a part of French legal lexicon. Though the "*décret-loi Marchandeau,*" was abolished by the Vichy regime after the fall of France in 1940, the historical irony of its passage is that it put an end to French denial of the existence of race and racial discrimination. By criminalizing racial discrimination and religious intolerance, the French government was explicitly admitting the existence of races in France. In effect, there can be no racial and ethnic discrimination without races or ethnicities.

The racial atrocities of the Nazis and their French collaborators, the Vichy regime (1940-1944) have been officially recognized by the French state.[107] Though France had a 1,400-year-old tradition of anti-Semitism and racism the Holocaust showed that despite the humanitarian pronouncements of the Declaration of the Rights of Man and of the Citizen of 1789, racial and religious animus lay just under the surface of French society, waiting for a spark to ignite it. The horrors of the Second World War led to post-war legislative attempts by the French Communist Party and its allied interest group, MRAP,[108] to ban all racist and anti-Semitic speech in France.[109] The consequence is that France has very strict laws against hate speech and group defamation.

Article 24 of the Law of July 29, 1881 on Freedom of the Press (as amended) criminalizes the public or mass mediated display of writings, printed matter, drawings, engravings, paintings, emblems, images and other audiovisual material that justifies war crimes, crimes against humanity, or collaboration with the enemy. Furthermore, the law stipulates that it is a criminal offense to use any media outlet to incite discrimination, hatred or violence toward a person or a group of persons because of the origin, and membership or non-membership of these persons in an ethnic group, a nation, race, or specific religion.[110] The law states that those who use media outlets to deny the existence of one or several crimes against humanity—the Jewish Holocaust and the Armenian genocide are notable examples—committed by an organization declared criminal under the provisions of international law, face criminal prosecution and civil penalties.[111] Under the provisions of this law, Holocaust denial by neo-Nazi and racist groups on the Internet is a criminal offense.

Additionally, the French parliament passed the Anti-racism Law of July 1, 1972,[112] which abrogated the pre-World War II *Décret-loi Marchandeau*. The 1972 law, which was an amendment to the 1881 Law on Freedom of the Press, officially criminalized racist speech and granted all officially registered associations whose mission was to fight racism, standing to bring legal actions as "civil parties" in cases of discrimination, hatred or violence towards a person on account of that person's "origin, membership or non-membership in an ethnic group, nation, race or religion."[113] Additionally, the law gives all organizations or associations whose mission is to defend "the memory of slaves and the honor of their descendants, to fight racism and to assist the victims of discrimination based on national, ethnic, racial, or religious origin," the right to take legal action on behalf of individuals or groups that are the victims of hate speech and expressive conduct.[114] In short, these interest groups are empowered to represent victims of racial discrimination or to take legal action on their behalf. The hate speech provisions of the Law on Freedom of the Press of 1881 has since been amended and expanded to include civil society groups and associations whose objective is to "defend the moral interest and honor of the resistance or of [Holocaust] deportees. Furthermore, these interest groups can be plaintiffs in matters concerning apologies for war crimes and crimes against humanity."[115] This provision of the law automatically confers legal standing on anti-racist groups and effectively transforms them into quasi-governmental racial and ethnic victims' rights advocates who are accredited to work with the government in order to achieve regulatory objectives. Statutory recognition of the role of anti-racist interest groups in a country that does not officially recognize race is a paradox. Race is not an official demographic category in France.[116] Relationships between French anti-racist interest groups and the French government are, to borrow the expression of Michel Foucault part of the "strategic apparatus of power relations"

> Political power has deeper roots than is suspected. It is diffuse and operates through invisible, little-known centers and fulcrums. Even institutions that seem to be neutral and independent are instruments of political power. However, power is not only oppressive, it is also productive. It produces knowledge and discourse that constructs the reality of the world to the exclusion of other realities.[117]

Actually, recognition of anti-racist groups as influential *parties civiles* (civil plaintiffs) in legal proceedings against persons accused of racism, racial violence, and hate speech, under the Anti-racist Law of 1972, was an attempt to "placate and co-opt potentially active organizations" and canalize their militant fervor within the confines of the ideology of French republican citizenship, which emphasizes individual rather than group membership and equality before the law over communitarian interests.[118] Thus, anti-racist and interest groups and groups fighting anti-Semitism are not defined by race. They are expected to be non-racial, and to eschew ethnic political activism. These groups clearly serve to disseminate governmental immigration policies, not to challenge the orthodoxy of French secular republicanism, namely, that France is a nation of culturally homogeneous people without ethnic specificities.[119] As a result of this situation, minority ethnic and religious interest groups have not succeeded in becoming effective advocates for their communities.[120]

Furthermore, French government recognition and funding of anti-racist groups essentially transformed them into forces of mediation and conflict management on behalf of the government. French anti-racist groups are, in the words of Fysh and Wolfreys, "transmission belts" for the government's initiatives.[121] As such, they preach "moralistic anti-racism," under the country's assimilationist ideology of universal republicanism.[122]

As such, these interest groups are empowered to act as social watchdogs that promote governmental interests in the abolition of racism and anti-Semitism, and in the promotion of cultural assimilation and homogeneity.

In pursuance of this policy, the French government has granted official recognition and funding to certain anti-racist interest groups that further the government's assimilationist interest in matters touching on race and ethnicity. Even though, race is not institutionalized in France, that is to say, it is not recognized in official census tabulations and other social and economic indicators, under the provisions of the anti-racist law, la *Loi Gayssot*, social groups or associations formed to fight racism and anti-Semitism may exercise a right of reply (*droit de réponse*) in the media, to objectionable media content if the groups act on behalf of consenting individuals or groups of persons "who are the object of imputations touching on their honor or reputation by reason of their origin or their membership or non membership in a specific ethnic group, nation, race or religion."[123]

Indeed, the *raison d'être* of anti-racist, anti-Semitic, and other ethnic-based groups is to keep the memory of slavery, genocide, and crimes against humanity alive in French society,[124] and to work with the government in suppressing attempts to minimize the gravity of these historical wrongs through presentation of non-official versions of historical facts.[125] As a result, the government not only officially recognizes thc specificities of the claims of victimhood of each of these interest groups,[126] it arrogates onto itself, the role of final arbiter of the truth concerning the real and imagined historical injustices suffered by members of these groups.[127] This background information explains the role of French interest groups in the eradication of objectionable Internet content.

Interest Groups and Internet Content Regulation in the United States and France

The United States and France have distinct conceptualizations of the nature, role, and regulation of the Internet. The United States has a neo-mercantilist model of Internet regulation rooted in American exceptionalism. This model combines several libertarian principles designed for activities in real space—intellectual property protection, the market place of ideas, *laissez-faire* economics, free trade, and the free flow of information, goods, and services—and transfers them to the global, networked virtual world of the Internet, thereby making them global concepts.[128] Additionally, these principles ensured that the Internet came under the ambit of the exceptional First Amendment.[129]

France is a culturist country where the national ideology is that all persons in France are to be assimilated into the French Republic as *individuals*, with one culture—the French culture—not as members of given religious, racial or ethno-linguistic cultural communities.[130] In short, there are no hyphenated French citizens. While the ACLU was fighting in the United States to eliminate regulations designed to eliminate uncivil and indecent speech on the Internet, UEJF and LICRA were fighting vigorously in France to enforce regulations against bias-motivated speech and expression (uncivil speech) from the traditional media and the Internet. Since the ACLU's libertarian ideology is diametrically opposed to the types of restrictions on speech championed by the French anti-racist interest groups and organizations, the two opposing speech camps would ultimately come face to face in the now famous Yahoo! Nazi and Third Reich Memorabilia "affair" that was heard and decided by courts in the United States and France.

The ACLU and Internet Content Regulation

The American Civil Liberties Union and other civil libertarian groups in the United States have historically struggled to expand the scope of civil liberties in general, and freedom of expression, in particular. They have done this through a vigorous campaign of litigation against governmental attempts to restrict free speech. It is immaterial to the ACLU that its defense and promotion of civil rights has led to the protection and toleration of uncivil speech and expression. When the Internet was transformed into a global, interconnected, multi-communication platform in the 1990s, the ACLU sought to bring this new medium within the ambit of the First Amendment by challenging governmental attempts to restrict certain types of online content.

The ACLU has a long track record of successfully defending the free speech rights of racist, anti-Semitic and other hate groups. Actually, the ACLU of Illinois provided a lawyer, David Goldberger, who ironically happened to be Jewish, to defend the National Socialist (Nazi) Party of America's right to due process of the law, as well as its right to be free from government imposed prior restraints on a provocative, anti-Semitic march it was organizing in a Jewish neighborhood.[131] The result of this ACLU intervention is that displaying the swastika was ruled to be legal expressive conduct in the United States.[132] As we saw earlier, the ACLU also provided a lawyer, David Baugh, who also ironically happened to be African American, to defend the Ku Klux Klan in a Virginia cross burning case, in which the Supreme Court of the United States held that burning a cross absent an intent to intimidate, was protected speech under the First Amendment.[133] Ultimately, the ACLU and other civil libertarian groups persuasively argued before the Supreme Court of the United States that content-based regulation of the Internet was unconstitutional. The legal actions of the French and American organized interest groups under study had two results: *Reno v. ACLU* and other American cases essentially globalized American online free speech culture. *UEJF and LICRA v. Yahoo!* introduced French-style content-based regulations on the Internet and inevitably led to a long and expensive Franco-American legal conflict over Internet content regulation. The two sides were on a collision course. In the Yahoo! cases heard in American courts, UEJF and LICRA squared off against the ACLU, which wrote a friend-of-the-court brief on behalf of Yahoo!

In 1996, the American Congress passed the Communications Decency Act (CDA)[134] as part of the Telecommunications Act of 1996.[135] Two provisions of the CDA sought to protect minors from harmful material on the Internet.[136] Several interest groups, led by the ACLU, filed suit[137] challenging the constitutionality of the two provisions which criminalized 1) "the knowing transmission of obscene and indecent material to minors under eighteen years of age, and 2) the knowing transmission of material that describes in patently offensive terms, sexual or excretory activities or organs." A U.S. District Court entered an injunction against enforcement of both provisions of the act stating that they violated the First Amendment by reason of their vagueness and over-breadth.[138] The Government appealed to the Supreme Court of the United States and certiorari was granted.

The issue before the Court was whether the two contested provisions of the Communications Decency Act violated the freedom of speech guaranteed by the First and 14th Amendments. The Court held that they did. The judges decided that the two provisions in question were an imprecise, content-based, blanket restriction on speech that had the potential of censoring speech that adults have a constitutional right to receive and impart.[139] The main outcome of this case was that the Supreme Court of the United States ruled for the first time, that the regulatory regime of the Internet is identical to that of the print media. Therefore, the Internet had full First Amendment protection unlike radio and television whose First Amendment rights are circumscribed by their technical limitations and invasive nature.[140] The ACLU considered its victory in *Reno v. ACLU*, one of the finest in its history.[141]

In the mean time, Congress passed the Protection of Children from Sexual Predators Act of 1998,[142] and tried to rectify the constitutional defects of the CDA through the Child Online Protection Act (COPA).[143] Several civil libertarian groups, again led by the American Civil Liberties Union, also challenged COPA. The United States Court of Appeals for the Third Circuit found that COPA was not narrowly tailored to serve the government's stated interest in protecting minors from harmful material on the Internet.[144] The court further held that undifferentiated, non-specific definition of the term "minors" in COPA was too vague and overbroad to meet First Amendment strict scrutiny and "narrow tailoring" standards.[145] The Government appealed the case to the Supreme Court of the United States, which invalidated COPA on the grounds that content-filtering and other technological solutions were preferable to governmental control of Internet content. The Court held that filtering imposed selective restrictions on web speech at the level of the receiver, and does not impose blanket restrictions on the senders of messages.[146] The Court has also held that a blanket ban on computer-generated images of children indulging in sexual activities is unconstitutional.[147] As a general rule, then, censorship of non-obscene material on the Internet is unconstitutional under American jurisprudence. In matters of Internet law, the ACLU has successfully acted as a counter-power that has challenged media content regulation in the United States and broadened the scope of the freedom of expression in real space and cyberspace. The ACLU is clearly the guardian of American First Amendment orthodoxy.

French Interest Groups and Regulation of Online Content

We saw at the beginning of this chapter that the Union of Jewish Students of France (UEJF) launched a controversial publicity campaign against anti-Semitism, in which gangster-style graffiti: "Dirty Jew" was scrawled on billboard images of Jesus Christ and his mother, Mary. This was one in a series of initiatives launched by UEJF, LICRA and other French anti-racist interest groups bent on suppressing certain kinds of bias-motivated speech and expression that were declared illegal under French law.[148] The activities of the two organizations are rooted in the anti-Judaic and racist catastrophes of 20th Century Europe. *La Ligue International Contre le Racisme et l'Antisémitisme* (The International League Against Racism and Anti-Semitism, LICRA) was founded in 1927 as *La Ligue Contre les Pogroms* (The League Against Pogroms). Its most influential members were physicist, Albert Einstein, and Russian novelist and dramatist, Maxime Gorki. The group's name was changed to *La Ligue International Contre l'Antisémitisme* (International League Against Anti-Semitism, LICA). In the run-up to the

Second World War, LICA denounced racism, racial crimes, racial discrimination, and the spread of racial theories in Germany and other parts of Europe. Its most influential members included psychoanalyst, Sigmund Freud, and writer, George Bernard Shaw. When Hitler defeated France in 1940, the Vichy regime of Marshall Pétain banned LICA. Many LICA members joined several French resistance organizations that fought against the Nazi occupation forces. This gave the organization a lot of credibility and influence in French political circles after the war. In 1979, the organization changed its name to its current one, LICRA. Its mission is to fight anti-Semitism, racism, xenophobia, intolerance, and discrimination.[149]

UEJF was founded in 1944 by a group of French Jewish students who were part of the French resistance to Nazi Germany. The purpose of the organization was to help young Jews who had survived Hitler's concentration camps to be reintegrated into society and regain their rights as students. The UEJF, which currently has members in all French universities, considers itself the depository of the memory of the Jewish Holocaust. The UEJF represents Jewish student interests in French government circles and works closely with the Ministry of Youth and Sports, and the Ministry of National Education.[150]

Empowered by French law and public policy, and financed by the French government, these and other organized anti-racist interest groups have become virtual auxiliaries or co-powers that work hand in hand with the French authorities in furtherance of the governmental interest in eliminating all illegal and objectionable bias-motivated or hate-related speech and symbolic expression from the Internet.[151] In effect the UEJF, which is dedicated to fighting racism, anti-Semitism and Holocaust denial, turned its attention to the Internet when the network of computer networks became the medium of choice of hate groups. One of the goals of the UEJF was to bring the Internet—the multi-communication platform that was beginning to make a mockery of France's anti-racist, anti-Semitic and hate speech laws—within the ambit of French law.[152] They have succeeded in transferring hate speech regulation from real space to cyberspace. In effect, under provisions of the French penal code, web pages dedicated to racist, neo-Nazi, anti-Semitic and Holocaust denial content are illegal. websites containing Adolf Hitler's vitriolic book, *Mein Kampf*, or the virulent Russian anti-Semitic publication, *Chronicles of the Elders of Zion,* are banned in France.[153]

The arrival of the Internet caught France unawares. Since the country had an early online system, the Minitel, it did not take the Internet too seriously. As we saw earlier, France and French intellectuals initially dismissed the Internet as an Anglo-American cultural Trojan horse.[154] French policy changed radically when the Internet became a global multi-communication platform, and French individuals and groups started leasing space on American servers to host their content. Some of the content of these web pages ran afoul of the French content-based media law regime, since they used the Internet to circumvent censorious laws and court orders.[155]

France soon realized that it could not ignore the Internet. As the country struggled, from 1996 onwards, to extend its penal code to those parts of the Internet accessible to French citizens, its institutional partners, LICRA and UEJF were active participants in the endeavor. Indeed, UEJF was at the forefront of those who scoffed at the cyber utopians who believed that the Internet was a lawless "cyber Wild West."[156] UEJF, *LICRA*, and a third anti-racist interest group, *Le Mouvement Contre Le Racisme et Pour L'Amitie entre les Peuple*s, (Movement Against Racism and For Friendship Among Peoples, MRAP) aggressively took legal action against individuals, online hate groups, Internet Service Providers (ISPs), and Internet hosts whose web pages, servers, and Web portals, contained objectionable content or speech and symbolic expression considered illegal under French law. As we saw earlier, under the French law of July 29, 1881 on Freedom of the Press,[157] anti-racist groups have standing to bring legal action on behalf of aggrieved ethnic, racial, religious and anti-Nazi resistance groups against all parties who allegedly possess or disseminate racist and anti-Semitic material online and offline. This UEJF and LICRA campaigns culminated in the so-called *affaire Yahoo!,* the series of Yahoo! cases heard in French[158] and American courts,[159] over the display of Nazi and Third Reich memorabilia on Yahoo! Auctions. These cases, which are discussed below, essentially extended France's highly elastic, content-based, hate-speech regulatory regime to the Internet, with the passive acquiescence of American courts.

Conflict of Laws: French Anti-racist Interest Groups v. American Information Technology Companies

The most visible manifestation of American exceptionalism and the French exception in the issue area of Internet regulation has been the legal tussles between French interest groups and "America Internet Inc.," (American global information and communication technology companies). The Internet, globalization and the interconnection of cultures, and legal jurisdictions around the world essentially gave French anti-racist and anti-Semitic groups a global platform on which to carry out their campaign to rid the world of hate speech. Since French law confers legal standing on anti-racist interest groups and effectively transforms them into racial and ethnic victims' rights advocates,[160] these interest groups enlarged the scope of their activities to include the Internet, and from their base in France went after American Internet Service Providers (ISPs) and American information technology companies. The result is that French courts have heard and decided tens of law suits involving the major American information technologies companies:

Microsoft, Google, IBM, AOL, Yahoo!, Network Associates, e-Bay, Facebook, Twitter, and so on.

The first salvo in the battle to banish bias-motivated speech from the Internet was fired in 1996 when *l'Union des étudiants juifs de France* (The Union of French Jewish Students, UEJF) sued nine French Internet service providers—including the French subsidiary of an American company, Compuserv—for hosting, disseminating or granting Internet access privileges to racist and anti-Semitic content, contrary to French laws against the display or publication of such material.[161] The UEJF claimed that the service providers and hosts should be held criminally and civilly liable for making the objectionable Internet sites available to French citizens, and failing to block the sites when the UEJF complained about their hateful content. In a bid to avoid criminal and civil liability, the nine Internet access providers agreed to cease and desist hosting or providing access to French websites containing racist, Nazi, neo-Nazi, Third Reich, anti-Semitic and other memorabilia that contravened French Penal Code provisions against hate speech and hate symbols.[162] A French Superior Court judge ruled that since it was technically impossible to block or filter foreign-based Internet sites at that time, the nine ISPs could not be held criminally or civilly liable for the objectionable United States-based content they had enabled French citizens to access.[163] The objectionable sites, except for that of provocative musician, Jean-Louis Coste were taken down shortly thereafter.[164]

However, that was not the end of the story. In 1997, UEJF found racist statements and lyrics on the website of Jean-Louis Coste, a provocative, race-baiting French musician and poet. In accordance with the provisions of French law, UEJF reported the matter to the authorities who carried out an investigation and discovered the objectionable statements online. UEJF sued Coste for disseminating hate speech on the Internet. When the case came to trial in 1998, Coste claimed that the lyrics in his music were a parody. He said he had uploaded them as far back as 1996 and that they had been online since the first UEJF legal action against him. He said that as a result, the three-month statute of limitation prescribed by the Law of July 29, 1881 on Freedom of the Press for plaintiffs to file defamation complaints against the media had expired. A judge disagreed and found Coste guilty of issuing public racial insults, public racial defamation, incitement to violence, and incitement to racial violence, in violation of the Law of July 29, 1881 on Freedom of the Press.

However, in 1999, an appeals court dismissed the case on grounds that the French government had failed to bring charges against Coste before expiry of the three-month statute of limitation prescribed by the Law of 1881 for plaintiffs to file defamation complaints against media defendants. The public prosecutor, UEJF and its sister organizations, LICRA, *la Ligue française pour la défense des droits des l'homme et du citoyen* (French

League for the Defense of Human and Citizens' Rights, LFDH), and *Le Movement contre le racisme et pour l'amitié entre les peuples (The Movement Against Racism and For Friendship Among Peoples,* MRAP) appealed. The issue before the court was whether the three-month statute of limitations prescribed by the Law of July 29, 1881 on Freedom of the Press was applicable to the Internet such that the case against Coste should be dismissed. The appeals court said it did not. The court held that Coste's website was a "continuous publication," that could be uploaded and taken down at will, and that changing the address of a website was tantamount to creating "a new publication" for purposes of the statute of limitation.[165] The ruling essentially made the three-month statue of limitations that was designed for the media in real space inapplicable to cyberspace. The stunning decision shook the French legal and media establishments. The Appeals of Paris upheld its own order in 2000.[166] The practical effect of this ruling is that French courts refused to transfer to the Internet, the statutory limitations that had been designed to shield the traditional media from the excesses of defamation law. The Internet therefore had, at the outset, less protection than the traditional media in the issue area of defamation.

After this resounding victory, the UEJF continued its self-styled campaign of "extreme vigilance" against online racist, anti-Semitic and Holocaust denial material on the Internet.[167] Buoyed by the idea of the State Council that the Internet was to be a space of "global civility," the organization and its allies decided that the Internet was not going to be a safe haven for hate speech. Less than a year later, it again took legal action in the Superior Court of Paris against an anarchistic musician's website and its Internet access provider, for publishing racist lyrics offensive to Blacks, Arabs, Jews and Japanese.[168] The UEJF claimed that publishing the material was a violation of French laws against the publication of racist material, making an apology for a racist crime, and refusing to change the content of the website despite multiple warnings from activists. The UEJF asked the court to shut down the objectionable websites. The French Internet service provider, Valentin Lacambre, claimed that the server which hosted the objectionable website was actually based in the United States and that he was merely renting hosting space from the U.S. in order to make the Internet accessible to French citizens.[169] He said he had no editorial control over the content of the websites. The court agreed with UEJF that the content of the website could be characterized as an exhortation to racial hatred and violence. This kind of material violated group defamation laws, as well as laws against speech directed at people on the basis of their membership or non-membership in a racial, religious, national, or ethnic group.[170] However, the court dismissed the case on the grounds that the plaintiffs, UEJF, had not specified the exact provision of the law under which it had brought the action.[171] A request for a rehearing was denied. The UEJF lost this case on a pure technicality despite the fact that the court agreed with the submissions of the group.

This minor reversal did not deter UEJF from its Internet surveillance activities, and its unrelenting campaign against anti-Semitism and racism on the Internet. In 2000, the organization found a website dedicated to Nazi ideology and asked the hosting company, Multimania, to shut the site down and reveal the identity of its owner. The website was immediately taken down but Multimania refused to divulge information about the website's owner, citing Internet privacy laws. The UEJF sued Multimania, charging that by not taking all necessary measures to ascertain the identity of the publisher of the illegal neo-Nazi website it had hosted, Multimania was criminally and civilly liable for the illegal content of the website. Furthermore, UEJF claimed that Multimania had not taken all necessary steps to ensure that the objectionable website could not be launched again at a later date. A judge ruled that as an Internet host, Multimania, could not be held liable for not detecting and removing the Neo-Nazi website. Furthermore, the court ruled that the Internet host had no legal obligation to ascertain the identity of the web page editor at the time the web hosting account was opened.[172] French law later granted Internet Service Providers immunity for hosting objectionable third-party content on the Internet just like American law had done years earlier.

The Yahoo! Neo-Nazi and Third Reich Memorabilia Cases

The aggressive legal maneuvers of LICRA and UEJF aimed at transforming the Internet from a "cyber Wild West" to a tame network created in the legal image of France, put French law on a collision course with American jurisprudence. Things came to a head in the famous "Yahoo! Nazi Memorabilia"cases that were heard in French and American courts from 2000 to 2006. In effect, in April 2000, two French organizations set up to fight racism and anti-Semitism—*la Ligue Internationale Contre Le Racisme* (The International League Against Racism) (LICRA), and UEJF—jointly sent a "cease and desist" letter to Yahoo!'s Santa Clara, California headquarters, informing the global information technology company that display of Nazi and Third Reich memorabilia on its Yahoo! Auctions portal, and Nazi-related discussions on its websites, violated French law. A third group, *le Mouvement contre le racisme et pour l'amitié entre les peuples* (The Movement Against Racism and For Friendship Among Peoples) (MRAP) soon joined the suit. The groups demanded that the offensive material be removed forthwith.[173] When Yahoo! Refused to remove the material from its servers, legal action promptly followed in French courts.

In its complaint, LICRA asked the *Tribunal de grande instance de Paris* (Superior Court of Paris) to order Yahoo! Inc., "to take all necessary measures to prevent the display and sale, on Yahoo.com, of Nazi objects on French territory."[174] On the same day, UEJF sued Yahoo! in the same court, on the same issue of Nazi paraphernalia on Yahoo!.com.[175] The UEJF asked the court to go one step further and order Yahoo! Inc. to:

> *[D]étruire toute donnée informatique stockée directement ou indirectement sur son serveur et cesser corrélativement tout hébergement et toute mise à disposition sur le territoire de la République à partir du site Yahoo!.com*[176]

> Destroy all computerized [anti-Semitic] material stored directly or indirectly on its server and to *correlatively* cease hosting and making available [anti-Semitic literature] on the territory of the [French] Republic from the Yahoo!.com website.[177]

The two cases were consolidated after oral arguments. Judge Jean-Jacques Gomez ruled that his court had jurisdiction because Yahoo! had a French subsidiary, Yahoo! France. In the face of this challenge to its lucrative auctions service, Yahoo! advanced a First Amendment defense, stating that as an American corporate citizen, the First Amendment protected the content of its Sunnyvale, California-based servers and websites. The *Tribunal de grande instance de Paris* found Yahoo!'s American Constitutional protestations unpersuasive. After lecturing Yahoo! on the moral and ethical necessity of civil speech in democratic societies, the French court dabbled in American First Amendment hermeneutics. In the preamble to its judgment, the court said that Yahoo! Inc. was at liberty to restrict Nazi material on its servers—as demanded by UEJF and LICRA—without prejudice to its First Amendment rights:

> *Attendu qu'en tout état de cause la société Yahoo! refuse d'ores et déjà sur son service enchères les ventes d'organes humains, de drogue, d'ouvrage ou d'objets en rapport avec la pédophilie, de cigarettes, ou d'animaux vivants, toutes ventes qu'elle exclut d'office et à juste titre du bénéfice du premier amendement de la constitution américaine garantissant la liberté d'opinion et d'expression;*[178]

> Whereas, in any case, Yahoo! already forbids the sale of human organs, drugs, materials and objects linked to pedophilia, cigarettes, or live animals on its auctions portal; sales of which it automatically excludes, and rightly so, under privileges it enjoys under the First Amendment of the American Constitution, which guarantees freedom of opinion and expression;

> *Attendu qu'il lui en coûterait très certainement fort peu d'étendre ses interdits aux symboles du nazisme et une telle initiative aurait la mérite de satisfaire à une exigence éthique et morale que partagent toutes les sociétés démocratiques.*[179]

> Whereas, it would certainly cost it (Yahoo!) very little to extend its prohibitions to symbols of Nazism; [and] such an initiative would have the merit of satisfying an ethical and moral exigency shared by all democratic societies.

The judge held that the Nazi Memorabilia and Third Reich content on Yahoo! Auctions offended the "collective memory of the country [France]"; as such, the Yahoo! websites constituted a "disturbance of public order" in France.[180] The court therefore ordered Yahoo! to do exactly what both LICRA and UEJF had asked for:

> *[P]rendre toutes les mesures de nature à dissuader et à rendre impossible toute consultation sur Yahoo.com du service de ventes aux enchères d'objets nazis et de tout autre site ou service qui constitue une apologie du nazisme ou une contestation des crimes Nazis;*[181]

> Take all steps necessary to dissuade and render impossible, all visits to Yahoo.com (Auctions) where Nazi memorabilia is available, as well as to any other site or service which makes apology for Nazism, or denies Nazi crimes;

Yahoo! was also ordered to remove all hyperlinks which directly or indirectly connected and treated the words "Holocaust" and "Holocaust denial" as equivalent. Failing which, Yahoo! was to pay the sum of ($13,000) per day of delay in removing the materials and/or $13,000 per kilobyte of information (images) maintained online in violation of the court order, until such a time that the order was fully complied with, among other penalties.[182]

Finally, the judge ordered Yahoo! to seek a "declaration of citizenship" from each and every visitor to the objectionable websites for the purpose of preventing French citizens (including presumably, the hundreds of thousands living outside France) from having access to the illegal sites. Yahoo! was essentially ordered to screen out all French citizens from its auction sites.[183] The Superior Court of Paris affirmed its own decision six months later, after hearing expert testimony to the effect that Yahoo! could identify the country of origin of its users in certain cases. The panel of experts included Vinton Cerf of the Internet Assigned Numbers Authority (IANA), which coordinated the central workings of the Internet. In one fell swoop, the French courts transferred national hate speech laws designed for real space, to the global, dematerialized sphere of cyberspace.

Though Yahoo! claimed that the French court order violated the First Amendment of the Constitution of the United States, it was forced, as a result of the ruling, and pressure from the anti-racist "anti-defamation" organizations in the United States and France, to modify its online auction policy. Its new rules prohibited placement of items that promote, glorify or are associated with Nazism or the Ku Klux Klan.[184] The French anti-defamation activists, who had waged a campaign since the mid 1990s, to eliminate racist, anti-Semitic and other objectionable material from the Internet, saw this move as a major victory for their cause. The ban on the display or purchase of Nazi and Third Reich memorabilia on Yahoo! Auctions and e-Bay, however, increased the value—and the prices—of the memorabilia and upset a number of American collectors of such memorabilia.[185]

ACLU, LICRA and UEJF before American Courts

While LICRA and UEJF savored their victory in the French High Court, questions began to arise whether the judgment against Yahoo! satisfied American First Amendment and due process standards such that the judgment could be enforced in the United States. Due process is the fundamental fairness to which all Americans are entitled under the 14th Amendment. Under international law, in order for the French court order to be enforced in the United States, a court in the United States would have to validate the judgment of the French High Court by declaring that the orders were judicially valid, applicable, and enforceable under American law.[186] In other words, an American court cannot enforce a foreign judgment that limits the personal freedoms of Americans because such an order would be repugnant or inimical to American public policy.[187] The fact is that American public policy requires that foreign laws that are at variance with First Amendment principles cannot be enforced in the United States.[188]

Yahoo! was persuaded that the judgment of the French court flew in the face of the First Amendment. Yahoo! co-founder Jerry Yang, told a French newspaper that the French justice system was naive to think that it could shield French citizens from governmentally-declared objectionable or illegal content on the Internet. In order to avoid further evisceration of its First Amendment rights, Yahoo! sought relief from the United States District Court for the Northern District of California, San Jose Division. Yahoo! asked the court to issue a declaratory judgment to the effect that the French High Court's orders were neither cognizable nor enforceable under the laws of the United States.[189]

The ACLU promptly joined a group of industry, professional, civil libertarian and public interest organizations in writing an *amicus curiae* (friend of the court) brief in support of Yahoo!'s request for a declaratory judgment. The ACLU was essentially opposing LICRA and UEJF's Internet cleansing activities. In an act of legal courtesy, the ACLU requested both Yahoo! and the two French groups for consent to file the friend of the court brief. Counsel for Yahoo! gave consent to ACLU and the other entities to file the brief, while counsel for UEJF and LICRA opposed ACLU's filing of the friend of the court brief. The reasons were obvious. The ACLU and its allies saw the French court decisions ordering Yahoo! to remove the neo-Nazi and Third Reich memorabilia from its servers in California as censorious, extraterritorial, and repugnant to First Amendment values of freedom of speech and expression. The friend of the court brief written by the ACLU and its allies stated in part:

> The French Judgment before this court represents a direct attempt by a foreign nation to apply its law extraterritorially to restrict the freedom of expression of U.S.-based online speakers who are protected by the First Amendment. . . . Granting recognition to the French court's judgment would have practical and legal ramifications that extend far beyond one nation's law or a single court order. It would establish a legal framework wherein **all** websites on the global Internet are subject to the laws of **all** other nations, regardless of the extent to which such a legal requirement conflicts with the law of the place where the speakers are located . . . the critical issues in this case is that all nations do **not** agree that there is "an ethical and moral imperative" to censor disfavored speech.[190]

The issue before the court was whether it was consistent with the Constitution of the United States for France to regulate speech by a United States corporate citizen, within the United States—that is, material hosted in Yahoo!'s Sunnyvale, California servers—on the grounds that such speech was illegal in France and that it could be accessed by French Internet users.[191] The court held that it was not. While the court expressed its deep respect for the historical motivations of the French government in enacting the laws Yahoo! was found to have fallen foul of, the court held that no American court could enforce the French court orders without violating the First Amendment. The reasoning of the court was that inasmuch as the French Court orders forbade the sale or distribution of certain items on Yahoo! Auctions on the basis of their association with a particular political organization, and banned the display of websites based on the authors' viewpoints with respect to the Holocaust and anti-Semitism, such an order was facially unconstitutional in the United States where the First Amendment bars the government from regulating speech based on its content or viewpoint.[192]

The U.S. district court stated that the blanket, content-based French court order could chill and even censor protected speech.[193] Writing for the Court, Judge Jeremy Vogel concluded that: "Although France has a sovereign right to regulate what speech is permissible in France, this Court may not enforce a foreign order that violates the protections of the United States Constitution by chilling protected speech that occurs simultaneously within our borders."[194] LICRA and UEJF appealed to the United States Court of Appeals for the 9th Circuit, on the grounds that the United States District Court for the Northern District of California did not have personal jurisdiction over them. The issue before the Court was whether the U.S. District Court had personal jurisdiction over the French interest groups. The ACLU did not succeed in convincing the court to appreciate the First Amendment issues at stake. In a surprise decision, the 9th Circuit held that the District court did not have jurisdiction, and reversed the court's decision.[195] The 9th Circuit held that imposition of penalties in France required further legal proceedings, which LICRA and UEJF had not undertaken, and that review of the French High Court's judgment against Yahoo! may not be undertaken by any American court. The United States Court of Appeals for the 9th Circuit essentially held that the case was not ripe for adjudication because American courts may only obtain jurisdiction over LICRA and UEJF when the French defendants availed themselves of an American forum by requesting a U.S. district court to enforce the French High Court judgment.[196]

The ruling of the 9th Circuit Court of Appeals in Yahoo!I was essentially procedural and addressed neither of the substantive issues, namely, Yahoo!'s First Amendment claims, nor concerns about the extraterritorial reach of French hate speech laws. It was assumed that Yahoo!'s First Amendment rights would be vindicated when or if LICRA and UEJF attempted to enforce the French High Court judgment in an American court. However, the French interest groups did not avail themselves of American courts to enforce the French court orders; they just reserved the right to do so.

The problem with the 9th Circuit's decision is that it was a mechanical application of legal precedent developed for the traditional media, to the new medium of the Internet. The French groups did not have to avail themselves of American courts to enforce the French court orders. Yahoo! had already been forced by French judicial and extrajudicial pressure to comply with part of the French court orders anyway. The French groups had declared victory. UEJF stated that its successful legal action against Yahoo! had forced the "American giant to restrict French Internet users from having access to Nazi auctions on its site. It [Yahoo!] finally decided to remove a large part of the incriminated material [from its auctions site]."[197] In the face of this de facto victory, the French defendants seemed content to have the French court judgment hang like a sword of Damocles over Yahoo!'s head. The Internet giant did not want to operate with that legal uncertainty for much longer so it sought and was granted a rehearing *en banc*.[198] The full court of the 9th Circuit heard the case *de novo*.

In a *per curiam* opinion, a fragmented court refused to address the substantive issues, confining itself to the niceties of procedural law, and essentially turning a deaf ear to Yahoo!'s First Amendment pleas.[199] The court held that though the Federal District Court properly exercised personal jurisdiction over LICRA and UEJF, the case was not ripe for adjudication because Yahoo! had taken no affirmative steps to "obtain an indication from the French court whether it believes that Yahoo! is in compliance, in 'large measure' or otherwise, with the terms of its interim orders" for there to be a justiciable First Amendment issue.[200] The court essentially sent Yahoo! back to France to get a court order certifying that the company had complied with the censorious court orders of 2000.

The practical outcome of the case is that the 9th Circuit put its imprimatur on France's politically-motivated, content-based regulation of the Internet. Nevertheless, the court indicated that if the French court's orders required Yahoo! to block access to anti-Semitic material by American users—which it clearly did—such an order would be unconstitutional in the United States.[201] In 2006, Yahoo! applied to the Supreme Court of the United States for a writ of certiorari to review the case. That request was denied.[202] The practical result of that decision is that it gave the final word on the Yahoo! cases—and on Internet content regulation—to French courts, and put French anti-racist interest groups in a position to decide when, where or how to enforce a clearly censorious court order against Yahoo! The prior restraints officially sought by these French interest groups are now firmly in place. Yahoo! no longer accepts Nazi, Third Reich or KKK material on its auctions portal. The outcome has clearly been a resounding victory for, and globalization of the exceptional, elastic, content-based, free speech regime of France over America's content-neutral regime and values—at least on matters related to bias-motivated speech on the Internet.

Comparative Analysis and Discussion.

The long-running Yahoo! affair exemplified the differential conceptualizations and regulation of freedom of speech in general, and Internet content in particular, under French and American law. The transnational Yahoo! controversy illustrated the point made by Alexis de Tocqueville in the 19th century when he compared civil society groups in the United States and Europe. He said that in the United States, civil society groups correct abuses of liberty and that in order to influence policy, they "argue and petition." That is the tactic the ACLU has consistently followed with respect to Internet regulation. In the United States, litigation is a powerful tool of political, social and judicial advocacy.[203] Laws have effectively been used as instruments of social and political intimidation and reform.[204] The emerging American Internet law regime is the result of legal challenges raised by interest groups and activists, led by the ACLU.[205] These groups petition and put political pressure on local, state, and federal authorities and courts to heed the lessons of history and cease and desist from interfering with freedom of speech and expression on the Internet. As a result, the ACLU has become a de facto counter-power that has consistently challenged legislative enactments that it views as limiting civil liberties at the local, state and federal levels. Its counter-discourses and legal successes have effectively succeeded in transforming the Internet into a free multi-communication space.

De Tocqueville also said that in Europe, civil society groups claim to act on behalf of the people, and that they "act and command" in pursuit of their aims. This is characteristic of French anti-racist groups, which have been empowered by the French government to monitor the Internet for objectionable racist and anti-Semitic content, on behalf of affected racial and ethnic minorities. For UEJF and LICRA, victories in the Superior Court of Paris and at the United States Court of Appeals for the 9th Circuit,[206] was the culmination of a long campaign to eradicate cyber Nazism, racism, anti-Semitism, and other bias-motivated content from the nascent Internet. Clearly, the French appellate court's order and the activities of the interest groups have had the intended chilling effect on Yahoo! and other Internet companies. Clearly, the characteristics of civil society groups in the United States and France have not changed over the years. American interest groups act against legislation and other governmental regulatory initiatives while French interest groups act against objectionable Internet speech and speakers. The actions of interest groups in both countries reflect the exceptional philosophical postures of the political regimes in both countries, with respect to freedom of expression. As we saw in chapter 4, in France, the government intervenes in the marketplace of ideas to root out objectionable content while in the United States, the First Amendment bars the government from intervening in the marketplace of ideas and regulating speech on the basis of its content. The result is a yet unresolved international conflict of French and American Internet content regulation.

Interest groups have succeeded in modifying Internet content in France and to a lesser extent in the United States. Ironically, the globalization of French hate speech values on the Internet carries the imprimatur of the 9th Circuit Court of Appeals. Thus, the free rein the Supreme Court of the United States gave the Internet in *Reno v. ACLU*,[207] has been countered—at least in matters of bias-motivated speech—by the *Tribunal de Grande Instance de Paris,* and heavily circumscribed by the 9th Circuit Court of Appeals in *Yahoo! II* and *Yahoo III.*[208]

The Yahoo! cases show that American courts can offer Yahoo! and other American companies First Amendment protection only if foreign groups attempt to enforce foreign court orders against American companies in the United States. That posture is an outdated, old media posture, which conceptualizes the world as a compartmentalized geographical entity made of discrete legal jurisdictions. The fact is that in the interconnected world of the Internet, content regulations of the kind the French court imposed on Yahoo! have an immediate global chilling effect that violates the First Amendment. *LICRA and UEJF v. Yahoo!* was a great victory for France in its war against perceived Anglo-Saxon domination of the Internet.

The main conclusion of this case study is that even in this age of globalization, the nation state still matters. The contrasting legal actions undertaken by interest groups in the United States and France to influence the Internet regulatory regimes of their respective countries have pulled Internet content regulation in diametrically opposite directions. Though the final outcome of the Yahoo! cases—a resounding victory for the French anti-racist groups over Yahoo! in both French and American courts—might suggest, at first glance that French and American courts essentially see eye-to-eye on matters of bias-motivated speech and symbolic expression on the Internet, such a conclusion would be inaccurate. The 9th Circuit clearly indicated that if the French court's orders required Yahoo! to block access to anti-Semitic material by American users—which it indirectly does—such an order would be unconstitutional in the United States.[209] The Yahoo! affair was an exemplar of the fact that when it comes to Internet law and policy, geography is not history; exceptionalist ideology, culture, and national jurisdictions still matter.

NOTES

1. See Laurence Girard and Henri Tincq, *L'UEJF lance dans la presse une campaigne choc contre l'antisémitisme* (The UEJF launches a shock campaign against anti-Semitism). Le Monde, October 23, 2004 at 30.
2. Id. This slogan was a take-off of a French national road safety campaign: "*La securité routière est l'affaire de tous*" (Road safety is everyone's business)."
3. Id.
4. Id.
5. See L'UEJF modifies a campagne contre l'antisémitisme (UEJF modifies its campaign against anti-Semitism." Le Monde, October 26, 2004 at 32.
6. See L'UEJF modifies a campagne contre l'antisémitisme (UEJF modifies its campaign against anti-Semitism." Le Monde, October 26, 2004 at 32.
7. See Edgar Morin, *Le trou noir de la laicité* (The black hole of secularism). 58 *Le Débat* 38 (1990).
8. See Gregory Of Tours, The History Of The Franks 144 (Lewis Thorpe. trans. Penguin Books (1974) (1512). See also Renée Mussot-Goulard, Le Bapteme Qui A Fait La France (The Baptism That Created France 131, 164 (1996). (Stating that the conversion and Baptism of King Clovis and 3000 of his soldiers, was the "founding event" of Roman Catholic France). and also Phillippe Delorme And Luc De Goustine, Clovis 496-1996:Research On His XVth Centenary. 172 (1996). (The Frankish Kingdom of the baptized, became known as the eldest daughter of the Roman Catholic Church).
9. In 1996, the French government officially recognized the baptism of King Clovis as the founding event of the nation. *See* François Furet, Revolutionary France: 1770-1880, at 537 (Antonia Nevill trans., Blackwell Books 1992) (1988). See also Herrick Chapman, & Lauren Frader, (Eds.), Race In France (2004).
10. *Virginia v. Black*, 538 U.S. 343 (2003).
11. *Village of Skokie v. National Socialist Party* 432 U.S. 43 (1977). The ACLU also wrote a friend of the court brief supporting the right to burn crosses in another case, *R.A.V v. City of St. Paul*, 505 U.S. 377 (1992).
12. See Gregg Ivers, American Constitutional Law: Power And Politics 13 (2002).
13. See Lyombe Eko, New Media, Old Regimes: Case Studies in Comparative Communication Law and Policy 251 (2012).
14. Black's Law Dictionary 1407 (7th Ed. 1999). *See also* Doe v. Univ. of Mich., 721 F. Supp. 852, 852, 856 (E.D. Mich. 1989); UWM Post v. Bd. of Regents Univ. of Wis. Sys., 774

F. Supp. 1163, 1163, 1165-67 (E.D. Wis. 1991); Dambrot v. Cent. Mich. Univ., 839 F. Supp. 477, 481-82, 484 (E.D. Mich. 1993). (Universities propagated the concept of hate speech and set its parameters. Courts have generally declared hate speech codes unconstitutionally vague and overbroad.) *But cf.* Jon B. Gould, *The Precedent that Wasn't: College Hate Speech Codes and the Two Faces of Legal Compliance*, 35 Law & Soc'y Rev. 345 (2001) (suggesting that many colleges and universities retained or created hate speech policies which contradicted national court cases).

15. See Douglas W. Vick, *Exporting the First Amendment to Cyberspace: The Internet and State Sovereignty, in* Media and Globalization: Why the State Matters 3 (Nancy Morris & Silvio Waisbord Ed., 2001) (suggesting that the concept of freedom of speech is culture-specific). *See also* William W. Van Alstyne, First Amendment: Cases and Materials 5 (2nd Ed., Foundation Press, Inc. 1995) (stating constitutional provisions for freedom of speech are different in most constitutions of the world).

16. See Alexis De Tocqueville, Democracy in America 121 (Henry Reeve trans., Oxford University Press 1955) (1835) (suggesting that America has no centralized control of information and that compared to France, American laws facilitate expansion of the press). *See also* Lyombe Eko, *The Law of Privacy in the United States and France: One President's Impeachable Offense is Another's Invasion of Privacy*, 22 Comm. & L. 1, 15-18 (Dec. 2000) (suggesting that in France, unlike in the United States, the private lives of politicians take precedence over freedom of the press).

17. See Walter Van Gerven, The European Union: A Polity Of States And Peoples 242 (2005).

18. See Frederick Schauer, The Exceptional First Amendment, in American Exceptionalism and Human Rights 45 (Michael Ignatieff Ed., 2005).

19. *In re Primus*, 436 U.S. 412 (1978).

20. The so-called "*affaire Yahoo*!" was heard and adjudicated by the Superior Court of Paris on three different occasions. LICRA & UEJF v. Yahoo! Inc. & Yahoo! France, No. 00/05308, Tribunal de grande instance [T.G.I.] [Superior Court], Paris, May 22, 2000, The Clerk of the Chief Justice Christine Bensoam Jean-Jacques Gomez, (Fr.), available at: http://www.juriscom.net/txt/jurisfr/cti/yauctions20000522.htm (Richard Salis, trans.); UEJF & LICRA v. Yahoo! Inc. & Yahoo! France, No. 00/05308, Tribunal de grande instance [T.G.I.] [Superior Court], Paris, Aug. 11, 2000, M. Jean-Jaques Gomez, (Fr.), *available at* http://www.legalis.net/jurisprudence-decision.php3?id_article=219; LICRA & UEJF v. Yahoo! Inc. & Yahoo! France, No. 00/05308, Tribunal de grande instance [T.G.I.] [Superior Court], Paris, Nov. 20, 2000, M. Jean-Jaques Gomez, (Fr.), available at: http://www.juriscom.net/.

21. See *Yahoo!, Inc. v. La Ligue Contre Le Racisme et L'Antisemitisme* (LICRA), 169 F. Supp. 2d 1181 (N.D. Cal. 2001) [hereinafter *Yahoo! I*], *rev'd*, 379 F.3d 1120 (9th Cir. 2004) [hereinafter *Yahoo! II*], *vacated and reh'g granted*, 399 F.3d 1010 (9th Cir. 2005) [hereinafter *Yahoo! III*], *rev'd*, 433 F.3d 1199 (9th Cir. 2006) (remanding and ordering dismissal of Yahoo!'s suit).

22. See Neil Nevitte & Roger Gibbins, New Elites In Old States: Ideologies In The Anglo-American Democracies 29 (1990).

23. See Francisco Granados and David Knoke, *Organized Interest Groups and Policy Networks*, in Thomas Janoski, Robert Alford, Alexander Hicks, And Mildred Schwartz, The Handbook Of Political Sociology 287-309 (2005).

24. Id. at 287-288.

25. See Marcella Riddlen Ray, The Changing and Unchanging Face of U.S. Civil Society 2 (2002).

26. See The Federalist No. 10 (James Madison).

27. See Alexis De Tocqueville, Democracy In America 191-195 (Henry Reeve, trans.Alfred A. Knopf (1980) (1835, 1840).

28. Id. at 198.

29. Id.

30. See Michel Foucault, Dits Et Écrits 1954-1988, Tome 3. (Sayings And Writings Of Michel Foucault, 1954-1988) Vol. III. 655, 720-721, 820 (1994): See also Michel Foucault,

The Hermaneutics Of The Subject, Lectures At The Collége De France, 1981-1982 252 (2005). (Arnold Davidson, Ed., Graham Burchell, trans. Palgrave, 2005) (2001).

31. See Michel Foucault, 1954-1988, Tome 3. (Sayings And Writings Of Michel Foucault, 1954-1988) Vol. III .655, 720-721 (1994).

32. See Fancisco Granados and David Knoke, *Organized Interest Groups and Policy Networks*, in Thomas Janoski, Robert Alford, Alexander Hicks, And Mildred Schwartz, The Handbook Of Political Sociology 289 (2005).

33. See Francisco J. Ganados and David Knobe, Organized Interest Groups and Policy Networks, in Thomas Janoski, Robert Alford, Alexander Hicks, And Mildred Schwartz, The Handbook Of Political Sociology 287-309 (2005).

34. Francisco J. Ganados and David Knobe, Organized Interest Groups and Policy Networks, in Thomas Janoski, Robert Alford, Alexander Hicks, And Mildred Schwartz, The Handbook Of Political Sociology 287-289 (2005).

35. See Francisco J. Ganados and David Knobe, Organized Interest Groups and Policy Networks, in Thomas Janoski, Robert Alford, Alexander Hicks, And Mildred Schwartz, The Handbook Of Political Sociology 287-309 (2005). 291.

36. See Francisco J. Ganados and David Knobe, Organized Interest Groups and Policy Networks, in Thomas Janoski, Robert Alford, Alexander Hicks, And Mildred Schwartz, The Handbook Of Political Sociology 287, 292 (2005).

37. See David Beriss, Culture as Race and Race-as-Culture, in Herrick Chapman And Laura Frader (Eds.). Race In France (2004).

38. Wolfgang Schulz And Thorsten Held, Regulated Self-Regulation 4 (2004).

39. Wolfgang Schulz And Thorsten Held, Regulated Self-Regulation 4 (2004).

40. See Francisco J. Ganados and David Knobe, Organized Interest Groups and Policy Networks, in Thomas Janoski, Robert Alford, Alexander Hicks, And Mildred Schwartz, The Handbook Of Political Sociology 287, 293 (2005).

41. See Francisco J. Ganados and David Knobe, Organized Interest Groups and Policy Networks, in Thomas Janoski, Robert Alford, Alexander Hicks, And Mildred Schwartz, The Handbook Of Political Sociology 287, 294 (2005).

42. See David James and Kent Redding, Theories of Race and State, in Thomas Janoski, Robert Alford, Alexander Hicks, And Mildred Schwartz, The Handbook Of Political Sociology 187-198 (2005).

43. Id. at 187.

44. See David James and Kent Redding, Theories of Race and State, in Thomas Janoski, Robert Alford, Alexander Hicks, And Mildred Schwartz, The Handbook Of Political Sociology 187-198 (2005).

45. See Robert Lieberman, A Tale of Two Countries: The Politics of Color-Blindness in France and the United States, in Herrick Chapman and Laura Frader (eds.). Race in France: Interdisciplinary Perspectives on the Politics of Difference, 181-216 (2004).

46. Id.

47. See Konrad Zweigert & H. Kötz, An Introduction To Comparative Law 69-75 (Tony Weir trans., Clarendon Paperbacks 3rd Ed. 1998) (1984).

48. See Robert A. Kagan, *American Courts and the Policy Dialogue, in* Making Policy, Making Law 32, Mark C. Miller and Jeb Barnes (Eds., 2004).

49. Id. at 191.

50. See The Federalist NO. 84 at 558 (Modern Library College Edition, 1937) (Alexander Hamilton argued that Bills of Rights were primitive documents that had no place in modern constitutions).

51. Id. at 558 ["what ever fine declarations may be inserted in any constitution respecting it [freedom of the press] must altogether depend on public opinion, and on the general spirit of the people and of the government].

52. *New York Times v. United States*, 403 U.S. 713, 715 (1971) (per curiam) (Black, J & Douglas, J. concurring).

53. See *Abrams v. United States*, 250 U.S. 616, 630 (1919) (Holmes, J., dissenting). *See also* Matthew D. Bunker, Critiquing Free Speech: First Amendment Theory and the Challenge of

Interdisciplinarity 2, 7-8 (2001) (discussing theories of the First Amendment including Marketplace Theory).

54. See Matthew D. Bunker, Critiquing Free Speech: First Amendment Theory and the Challenge of Interdisciplinarity 8 (2001).

55. See Jeffrie G. Murphy & Jules L. Coleman, *Philosophy of Law: An Introduction to Jurisprudence* 86 (rev. Ed., Westview Press 1990).

56. R.A.V. v. City of St. Paul, 505 U.S. 377, 382 (1992) ("[The] First Amendment generally prevents government from proscribing speech . . . because of disapproval of the ideas expressed.") (citation omitted).

57. *Hustler v. Falwell*, 485 U.S. 46 (1988); see also, *Snyder v. Phelps*, 562 U.S.(2011).

58. See *United States v. O'Brien*, 391 U.S. 367, 377 (1968).

59. Content-based regulations are regulations that approve of certain kinds of speech and frown on others based on the ideas, opinions or viewpoints expressed by the speakers. ((*Turner Broadcasting System v. the FCC*, 512 U.S. 622 (1994).

60. These are regulations that are applicable to all speakers irrespective of their point of view (See *Police Department of Chicago v. Mosley, 408 U.S. 92* (1972) (statute banning all picketing, except labor picketing was ruled unconstitutional).

61. See *Simon and Schuster, Inc. v. Members of the New York State Crime Victims Board*, 502 U.S. 105 (1991) (quoting *Arkansas Writers' Project Inc. v. Ragland*, 481 U.S. 221 (1987).

62. See Allan Cigler and Burdett Loomis, Introduction: The Changing Nature of Interest Group Politics, in Allan Cigler and Burdett Loomis (Eds.) Interest Group Politics (4th Ed.) 1, 5-6 (1995).

63. See Alexis De Tocqueville, Democracy In America 191-195 Henry Reeve, trans.Alfred A. Knopf (1980) (1835, 1840).

64. Id.

65. Francisco J. Ganados and David Knobe, Organized Interest Groups and Policy Networks, in Thomas Janoski, Robert Alford, Alexander Hicks, And Mildred Schwartz, The Handbook Of Political Sociology 287-289 (2005).

66. Art I, See Robert A. Kagan, American Courts And The Policy Dialogue, In Mark C. Miller And Jeb Barnes (Eds.). Making Policy, Making Law 13, 14 (2004).§I, Constitution Of The United States.

67. Art. I, §I, Constitution Of The United States (1787) ("All legislative powers herein granted shall be vested in a Congress of the United States").

68. *Marbury v. Madison*, 5 U.S. 137 (1803).

69. See Robert A. Kagan, Adversarial Legalism: The Rise Of Judicial Policy Making And The Separation Of Powers Doctrine, In Mark C. Miller And Jeb Barnes (Eds.). Making Policy, Making Law 13, 14 (2004).

70. See Robert A. Kagan, American Courts And The Policy Dialogue: The Role Of Adversarial Legalism, In Mark C. Miller And Jeb Barnes (Eds.). Making Policy, Making Law 13, 14 (2004).

71. Id.

72. See Mark C. Miller And Jeb Barnes (Eds.). Making Policy, Making Law 204-205 (2004).

73. Id.

74. Id.

75. See Jeb Barnes, Adversarial Legalism, The Rise of Judicial Policymaking and the Separation-Of-Powers Doctrine, In Mark C. Miller And Jeb Barnes (Ed.) Making Policy, Making Law 35, 36 (2004).

76. Art Iii, §2, Constitution of the United States.

77. See Samuel Walker, In Defense Of American Liberties: A History Of The ACLU 5 (1999).

78. See Gregg Ivers, American Constitutional Law: Power And Politics 13 (2002).

79. See Samuel Walker, In Defense Of American Liberties: A History Of The ACLU 3 (1999).

80. See generally, Alan Sears and Craig Osten, *The ACLU vs. America* (2005).

81. *Village of Skokie v. National Socialist Party*, 432 U.S. 43 (1977) (The Court held that a state appellate court which denied a petition for a stay of an injunction against the National Socialist Party of America, and also denied leave for expedited appeal of that stay, violated the due process of the National Socialist Party of America. The court was ordered to provide immediate appellate review or stay the injunction. An ACLU lawyer appeared for the Nazi Party of America before the Supreme Court of the United States).

82. *Virginia v. Black,* 538 U.S. 343 (2003). Holding that a state may not criminalize cross-burning unless it was intended to intimidate. The ACLU defended Barry Black, the KKK leader in this case).

83. See Douglas W. Vick, Exporting The First Amendment To Cyberspace: The Internet And State Sovereignty, In Nancy Morris And Silvio Waisbord, The Media And Globalization 3 (2001) (Suggesting that the First Amendment and its application to the Internet in Reno v. ACLU, was an impediment to international negotiation on Internet regulation).

84. See *Reno v. ACLU*, 521 U.S. 844 (1997).

85. See Douglas W. Vick, Exporting The First Amendment To Cyberspace: The Internet And State Sovereignty, In Nancy Morris And Silvio Waisbord, The Media And Globalization 3 (2001) (Suggesting that the First Amendment and its application to the Internet in Reno v. ACLU, was an impediment to international negotiation on Internet regulation).

86. See Michel Alberganti, *La main américaine tisse la toile d'Internet*, (Americans want to weave the web of the Internet). Le Monde, July 11, at (1997).

87. Lawrence Lessig, Code And Other Laws Of Cyberspace 6 (1999).

88. See William Mitchell, Softcities, in David Crowley and Paul Heyer (eds.). Communication in History 316 (1999).

89. See generally, Alan Sears and Craig Osten, *The ACLU vs. America* (2005).

90. See Bernard Spolsky, Language Policy 65 (2004) (Suggesting that under the Jacobin government, equality was more important than liberty).

91. Article XI, Declaration of the Rights of Man and of the Citizen (1789).

92. See Georges Vedel, Qu'est-Ce La Constitution? (What Is The Constitution?) (1998), available at http:://www.conseil-constitutionnel.fr/dossier/quarante/q01.htm.(The French Constitutional court has held that the human rights and social principles expressed in the Declaration of the Rights of Man and of the Citizen of 1789 and the Preamble of the Constitution of 1946 respectively, are incorporated in the Constitution of 1958).

93. Article XI (Declaration adopted August 26, 1789).

94. Id. (emphasis added).

95. Id. Articles 4&5.

96. See Paul Ricoeur, Lectures 1: Autours De La Politique (Readings 1: On Politics 1) 311 (1991).

97. See Law No. 78-17 of January 6, 1978 On Data Processing, Data Files and Individual Liberties (as amended) J.O. of August 7, 2004.

98. See Lyombe Eko, New Media, Old Regimes: The Historical and Ideological Foundations of French and American Regulation of Bias-Motivated Speech and Expression on the Internet, 28 Loyola International And Comparative Law Review 101-156 (2006).

99. See generally E. Ellery, Brissot De Warville: A Study In The History Of The French Revolution (1915).

100. See Sammy Smooha, Types of Democracy and Modes of Conflict management in Ethnically Divided Societies, 8 Nations And Nationalism 423-431 (2002).

101. See Edgar Morin, *Le trou noir de la laicité* (The black hole of secularism). 58 Le Debat 38 (1990) (Suggesting that France is a "*Catho-laique*" (Catho-secular) country that hides its religious culture and identity under the ideology of secularism).

102. See David Beriss, Culture as Race and Race-as-Culture, in Herrick Chapman And Laura Frader (Ed.) Race In France (2004).

103. See Herrick Chapman and Laura Frader, Race in France, in Herrick Chapman And Laura Frader (Ed.) Race In France 1-2 (2004). See also Lyombe Eko, New Media, Old Regimes: The Historical and Ideological Foundations of French and American Regulation of Bias-Motivated Speech and Expression on the Internet, 28 Loyola International and Comparative Law Review 101-156 (2006), And Also Jonathan Laurence And Justin Viasse, Integrating

Islam: Political And Religious Challenges In Contemporary France XIII (2006) (Stating that the French political system recognizes only individuals, not groups).

104. See David Beriss, Culture as Race and Race-as-Culture, in Herrick Chapman And Laura Frader (Eds.). Race In France 115 (2004).

105. See Françoise Lionnet and Shuh-mei Shih, Introduction, In Minor Transnationalism, Francoise Lionnet and Shuh-Mei Shih (Ed.) 1 (2006).

106. See Jonathan Laurence And Justin Viasse, Integrating Islam: Political And Religious Challenges In Contemporary France 54 (2006).

107. See *Loi No. 2000-644 du 10 juillet 2000 instaurant une Journée nationale à la mémoire des victims des crimes racists et antisémites de l'Etat français et homage aux "justes" de France* (Law No. 2000-644 of July 10, 2000 Establishing a National Day in Memory of the Victims of the Racist and Anti-Semitic Crimes of the French State and Homage to the "Righteous" People of France) J.O. of July 11, 2000 at 10483. See also *Loi No. 2001-434 du 21 mai 2001 tendant à la reconnaissance de la traite et de l'esclavage en tant que crime contre l'humanité* (Law no 2001-434 of May 21, 2001, Recognizing the Slave Trade and Slavery as Crimes Against Humanity) J.O. of May 23, 2001 at 8175.

108. MRAP later changed its name to Movement Contre le Racisme et pour l'Amitie entre les Peuples (Movement Against Racism and For Friendship among Peoples).

109. See Erik Bleich, Anti-racism Without Races: Politics and Policy in a Color-blind State, in Herick Chapman and Laurel Frader (Ed.) Race In France 162, 172 (2004).

110. Law of July 29, 1881 (as amended) Law on Freedom of the Press (1881). Art. 24.

111. Id. Art. 24.

112. J.O. of July 2, 1972 at 6803.

113. Art. 5 (II), Law No. 72-546 of July 1, 1972, J.O. of July 2, 1972 at 6803.

114. Law of July 29, 1881 (as amended) Law on Freedom of the Press (1881). Arts. 48-1 & 48-2

115. See Article 48-1 & 48-2, *Loi sur la liberté de la presse* (Law on Freedom of the Press) (1881) (as amended by Law No. 90-615 of July 13, 1990, On Suppressing Racist, Anti-Semitic and Xenophobic Acts (Loi Gayssot), J.O. of July 14, 1990 at 8333 and Law No. 2001-1066 of November 16, 2001,On the Fight Against Discrimination, J.O. No. 267 of November 17, 2001). (Associations set up for the purpose of defending the memory of slaves and the honor of their descendants, fighting racism or assisting victims of discrimination, where the discrimination was based on their national, ethnic, racial or religious origin, can be plaintiffs in cases of genocide, denial of such crimes, war crimes, crimes against humanity, and collaboration with the enemy. Furthermore, associations formed to "defend the moral interests and honor of the Resistance [to Nazi German occupation of France] or of deportees, can be plaintiffs in matters concerning apologies for war crimes and crimes against humanity").

116. See Erik Bleich, Anti-racism with out Races, in France, in Herrick Chapman and Laura Frader (eds). Race in France 162-166, 173. (2004) (Collecting race-based data or statistics is banned in France).

117. See Michel Foucault, Dits Et Ecrits (Sayings And Writings) Vol. II, 465 (1994).

118. See Erik Bleich, Anti-racism with out Races, in Herrick Chapman and Laura Frader (eds). Race in France 162-166-167. (2004).

119. See David Beriss, Culture-as Race or Culture-as-Culture, in Herrick Chapman and Laura Frader (eds). Race In France 111,114-121, 131 (2004).

120. Id.

121. See Peter Fysh And Jim Wolfreys, The Politics Of Racism In France (2nd Ed.) 173, 176 (2003) (Stating that the anti-racist group, SOS-Racisme was funded by the government and promoted by the French Socialist Party. In return, the group publicly endorsed President Francçois Mitterrand's campaign for re-election).

122. See Peter Fysh And Jim Wolfreys, The Politics Of Racism In France (2nd Ed.) 176 (2003).

123. Loi No. 90-615 of July 13, 1990 Aimed at Suppressing Racist, Anti-Semitic and Xenophobic Acts, (Loi Gayssot) J.O. of July 14, 1990, art. 13-1.

124. In 2001, France officially recognized slavery as a crime against humanity for the first time. See Law No. 2001-434 of May 21, 2001, Journal Officiel de la République Française [J.O.] [Official Gazette of France], May 23, 2001 at 8175.

125. See Lyombe Eko, New Media, Old Regimes: The Historical and Ideological Foundations of French and American Regulation of Bias-Motivated Speech and Expression on the Internet, 28 Loyola International And Comparative Law Review 101-156 (2006).

126. See e.g. Loi 2001-70 du 29 Janvier 2001, *Loi relative à la reconnaissance du génocide arménien de 1915* (Law Recognizing the Armenian Genocide of 1915), journal Officiel du 30 Janvier 2001.

127. *See* Madelaine Rebérioux, *Contre la Loi Gayssot sur le racisme* (*Against Gayssot's Law on Racism*), Le Monde (Fr.), May 21, 1996, at 1 (suggesting that the French government was restricting academic freedom by prescribing and putting the weight of law behind an "official version" of historical truth, to the exclusion—and criminalization—of contrary views).

128. Lyombe Eko, Many Spiders, One World Wide Web: Towards a Typology of Internet Regulation, 6 COMM. L. & POL'Y 448 (2001) (Suggesting that the Internet is regulated world—wide according to a five-part typology: Internationalist, neo-Merchantilist, Culturalist, Gateway & Developmentalist).

129. See *Reno v. ACLU*, 521 U.S. 844 (1997).

130. See Herrick Chapman and Laura Frader, Race in France, in Herrick Chapman and Laura Frader (Ed.) Race In France 1, 2 (2004).

131. See *National Socialist Party of America v. Skokie*, 432 U.S. 43 (1977) (A state appellate court which denied a petition for a stay of an injunction against the National Socialist Party of America, and also denied leave for expedited appeal of that stay, violated the due process of the plaintiff. The court must either provide immediate appellate review or stay the injunction).

132. See *Village of Skokie v. National Socialist Party,* 373 N.E.2d 21 (1978) (A court injunction prohibiting the National Socialist Party of America members from marching, walking or parading in the uniform of the party and displaying the swastika on or off their person, or distributing "hate" literature is an unconstitutional violation of the First Amendment); See also *R.A.V. v. City of St. Paul*, 505 U.S. 377 (1992) (Ordinance banning the display of swastika and other "hate" symbols ruled unconstitutional content-based regulation).

133. *Virginia v. Black,* 538 U.S. 343 (2003) (holding that a State, consistent with the First Amendment, may ban cross burning carried out with intent to intimidate). See also *Capitol Square Review and Advisory Board v. Pinette*, 515 U.S. 753 (1995).

134. 47 U.S.C. §223 et seq. (1996).

135. Pub.L. 104-104, 110 Stat.56 (1996).

136. 47 U.S.C § 223 (a) (1) (B) (ii) and 223 (d).

137. *American Civil Liberties Union v. Reno,* 929 F. Supp. 824 (Ed. Pa. 1996).

138. Id.

139. See *Reno v. ACLU*, 521 U.S. 844 (1997).

140. *FCC v. Pacifica Foundation*, 438 U.S. 726 (1978) (Holding that the government can regulate the content of over-the-air broadcasting because of the technical limitations of broadcasting).

141. See Samuel Walker, In Defense Of American Liberties: A History Of The ACLU (2nd Ed.) vii 1999.

142. Public Law 105--314 (H.R. 3494 (1998) (Under this act, enticing minors on the Internet to engage in sexual activity is illegal. The Internet is classified as an instrument of "interstate or foreign commerce)."

143. 47 U.S.C. § 231 (a) (1).

144. *American Civil Liberties Union v. Ashcroft*, 322 F. 3d 240 (3d Cir. 2003).

145. Id.

146. See *Ashcroft v. ACLU*, 542 U.S. 656 (2004).

147. *Ashcroft v. Free Speech Coalition*, 535 U.S. 234 (2002).

148. See Lyombe Eko, Many Spiders, One World Wide Web: Towards a Typology of Internet Regulation, 6 COMM. L. & POL'Y 448 (2001) (Discussion of UEJF and LICRA's legal action against Yahoo! for displaying Third Reich and other Nazi Memorabilia on Yahoo! Auctions).

149. See La LICRA Depuis 1927 (LICRA since 1927). Available at: http://www.licra.org/index.php?old_navigator=true&section=detail&id=2257. Last visited on June 14, 2007.

150. See "*Qui Sommes Nous?*" (Who are We?) Available at http://www.uejf.org/uejf_quisommesnous.php?sid= last visited June 14, 2007.

151. The 9th Circuit Court of Appeals called these groups "institutional partners" of the French government. See *Yahoo! Inc v. LICRA*, 433 F3d 1199, 1226 (9th Cir. 2006) (Ferguson, J.; O'Scannlain, J. and Tashima, J. concurring).

152. See Yves Eudes and Annie Kahn, Union des étudiants juifs de France, UEJF (Union of French Jewish Students), Le Monde (TV, Radio Multimédia supplement) June 9, 1996 at IV. See also Yves Eudes, L'UEJF repart en guerre contre le racisme sur le Web (The UEJF back on the war path against racism on the Web), Le Monde, May 25, 1997 at 34.

153. See Article R645-1 Code Pénal (Partie Réglementaire (Penal Code, Regulatory Section). (The display of flags, emblems, symbols and other indicia of groups found guilty of genocide and crimes against humanity is a criminal offense outside of a movie or a theatrical performance is illegal).

154. See Lyombe Eko, *Many Spiders, One Worldwide Web: Towards a Typology of Internet Regulation*, 6 Comm. L. & Pol'y 448, 469 (2001).

155. See Lyombe Eko, *The Law of Privacy in the United States and France: One President's Impeachable Offense is Another's Invasion of Privacy*, 22 Comm. & L. 1 (Dec. 2000) (Suggesting that the French government was caught unawares when a book about the extra-marital affair of President François Mitterrand that had been banned by a French court was scanned and placed on the Internet).

156. See Yves Eudes, L'UEJF repart en guerre contre le racisme sur le Web (The UEJF back on the war path against racism on the Web), Le Monde, May 25, 1997 at 34.

157. See Article 48-1 & 48-2, *Loi sur la liberté de la presse* (Law on Freedom of the Press) (1881) (as amended). (Associations set up for the purpose of defending the memory of slaves and the honor of their descendants, fighting racism or assisting victims of discrimination, where the discrimination was based on their national, ethnic, racial or religious origin, can be plaintiffs in cases of genocide, denial of such crimes, war crimes, crimes against humanity, and collaboration with the enemy. Furthermore, associations formed to "defend the moral interests and honor of the Resistance [to Nazi German occupation of France] or of deportees, can be plaintiffs in matters concerning apologies for war crimes and crimes against humanity").

158. The so-called "*affaire Yahoo*!" was heard and adjudicated by the *Tribunal de Grande Instance de Paris* (Superior Court of Paris) on three different occasions. *LICRA and UEJF v. Yahoo Inc and Yahoo! France*, No. 00/05308, Tribunal de Grande Instance de Paris (Superior Court of Paris), May 22, 2000. Available at http://www.juriscom.net/ *last visited September 2005; UEJF and LICRA v. Yahoo! Inc and Yahoo! France, No. 00/05308, Tribunal de Grande Instance de Paris (Superior Court of Paris) August 11, 2000 available at* http://www.legalis.net/cgi-iddn/french/afiche-jnet.cgi?droite=decisions/responsabilite/ord_tgi-paris_110800.htm *last visited September 2005; LICRA and UEJF v. Yahoo Inc. and Yahoo! France*, No. 00/05308, Tribunal de Grande Instance de Paris (Superior Court of Paris), November 20, 2000. Available at http://www.juriscom.net last visited June 2007.

159. *See Yahoo!, Inc. v. La Ligue Contre Le Racisme et L'Antisemitisme* (LICRA), 169 F. Supp. 2d 1181 (N.D. Cal. 2001) [hereinafter *Yahoo! I*], *rev'd*, 379 F.3d 1120 (9th Cir. 2004) [hereinafter *Yahoo! II*], *vacated and reh'g granted*, 399 F.3d 1010 (9th Cir. 2005) [hereinafter *Yahoo! III*], *rev'd*, 433 F.3d 1199 (9th Cir. 2006) (remanding and ordering dismissal of Yahoo!'s suit).

160. See Article 48-1 & 48-2, *Loi sur la liberté de la presse* (Law on Freedom of the Press) (1881) (as amended). (Associations set up for the purpose of defending the memory of slaves and the honor of their descendants, fighting racism or assisting victims of discrimination, where the discrimination was based on their national, ethnic, racial or religious origin, can be plaintiffs in cases of genocide, denial of such crimes, war crimes, crimes against humanity, and collaboration with the enemy. Furthermore, associations formed to "defend the moral interests and honor of the Resistance [to Nazi German occupation of France] or of deportees, can be plaintiffs in matters concerning apologies for war crimes and crimes against humanity").

161. See Yves Etudes & Annie Kahn, *Vers une tutelle pour l'Internet français* [*Towards French Tutelage of the Internet*], Le Monde (Fr.), June 9-10, 1996, at 28 (reporting UEJF actions against French ISPS and hosts).

162. See Noveau code penál [N.C. pén], art. R. 645-1 (2003) (Fr.) (criminalizing the display of flags, emblems, symbols and other indicia of groups found guilty of genocide and crimes against humanity).

163. See Michel Alberganti, *La justice reconnait l'impossibilité de bloquer des sites d'Internet* [*Court Recognizes Impossibility of Blocking Internet Sites*], Le Monde (Fr.), June 14, 1996, at 20.

164. This was the first of a number of cases against French or American ISPs who either provided French citizens access to objectionable sites, or hosted the sites in the United States destined for French citizens. See also *UEJF contre Costes, Altern-B et AUI [UEJF v. Costes, Altern-B & AUI]*, Tribunal de grande instance [T.G.I.] [Superior Court] Paris, Jul. 10, 1997 (Fr.), *available at* http://www.canevet.com/jurisp/970710.htm (holding that sites containing racist and anti-Semitic speech that were hosted in the United States did indeed violate French law; however, the case was dismissed on other grounds, and the sites were removed from the Internet shortly thereafter).

165. See Coste /Ministère public, LICRA, LFDH, MRAP et UEJF, Cour d'Appel de Paris, 11ème Chambre correctionnelle, section A Arrêt du 15 décembre 1999 (Coste v. Public Prosecutor, LICRA, LFDH, MRAP and UEJF, Court of Appeals of Paris, Criminal Division A, Decision of December 15, 1999. Available at http://www.legalis.net/breves-article.php3?id_article=180).

166. See Coste /Ministère public, LICRA, LFDH, MRAP et UEJF, Cour d'Appel de Paris, 11ème Chambre correctionnelle, section A Arrêt du 21 mars 2000 (Coste v. Public Prosecutor, LICRA, LFDH, MRAP and UEJF, Court of Appeals of Paris, Criminal Division A, Decision of March 21, 2000. Available at http://www.legalis.net/breves-article.php3?id_article=177).

167. See Michel Alberganti, *La justice reconnait l'impossibilité de bloquer des sites d'Internet* [*Court Recognizes Impossibility of Blocking Internet Sites*], Le Monde (Fr.), June 14, 1996, at 20. (reporting court verdict that Internet Service Providers were not criminally and civilly liable for internet content to which they had no control).

168. See UEJF contre Costes, Altern-B et AUI (UEJF v. Costes, Altern-B and AUI) (1997). http://www.aui.fr/Communiques/verdict-UEJF (Last visited October 2008.

169. See Yves Etudes, *L'UEJF repart en guerre contre le racisme sur le Web* (The UEJF goes back to war against racism on the Web) *Le Monde*, May 25–26, 1997 AT 34.

170. See Articles 24 (6) and 33 (3), Loi du 29 juillet 1881 (Loi sur la liberté de la presse) (Law of July 29, 1881, Law on Freedom of the Press as amended).

171. See UEJF contre Costes, Altern-B et AUI (UEJF v. Costes, Altern-B and AUI), Tribunal de Grande Instance de Paris (Superior Court of Paris) http://www.aui.fr/communiques/verdict-uejf-costes (last visited October 2008).

172. See Alain Hazan, Hébergement de sites: l'UEJF déboutée (Web hosting: UEJF case dismissed) *Le Monde* June 7, 2000 at IV.

173. *Yahoo! I,* 169 F. Supp. 2d at 1184.

174. See *UEJF & LICRA v. Yahoo! Inc and Yahoo! France*; LICRA & UEJF v. Yahoo! Inc. & Yahoo! France, No. 00/05308, Tribunal de grande instance [T.G.I.] [Superior Court] of Paris, May 22, 2000, *available at* http://www.juriscom.net/txt/jurisfr/cti/yauctions20000522.htm (Richard Salis, trans.). UEJF & LICRA v. Yahoo! Inc. & Yahoo! France, No. 00/05308, Tribunal de grande instance [T.G.I.] [Superior Court], Paris, Aug. 11, 2000, available at http://www.legalis.net/jurisprudence-decision.php3?id_article=219.

175. No. 00/05309, Tribunal de Grande Instance de Paris (Superior Court of Paris, April 10, 2000).

176. See *UEJF & LICRA v. Yahoo! Inc and Yahoo! France,* No. 00/05308, Tribunal de grande instance [T.G.I.] [Superior Court] of Paris, May 22, 2000, *available at* http://www.juriscom.net/txt/jurisfr/cti/yauctions20000522.htm (Richard Salis, trans.), (all translations by the author).

177. All translations by the author.

178. *LICRA and UEJF v. Yahoo!*, No. 00/05308, Order of November 20, 2000

179. Id.

180. LICRA & UEJF v. Yahoo! Inc. & Yahoo! France, No. 00/05308, Tribunal de grande instance [T.G.I.] [Superior Court], Paris, May 22, 2000, *available at* http://www.juriscom.net/txt/jurisfr/cti/yauctions20000522.htm (Richard Salis, trans.). See also Acacio Pereira, *Yahoo!: droit national contre réseau mondial (Yahoo!: National law versus global network)* Le Monde, August 14, 2000, at 1, 5.

181. LICRA & UEJF v. Yahoo! Inc. & Yahoo! France, No. 00/05308, Tribunal de grande instance [T.G.I.] [Superior Court], Paris, May 22, 2000, The Clerk of the Chief Justice Christine Bensoam Jean-Jacques Gomez, (Fr.), *available at* http://www.juriscom.net/txt/jurisfr/cti/yauctions20000522.htm (Richard Salis, trans.); UEJF & LICRA v. Yahoo! Inc. & Yahoo! France, No. 00/05308, Tribunal de grande instance [T.G.I.] [Superior Court], Paris, Aug. 11, 2000, M. Jean-Jaques Gomez, (Fr.), *available at* http://www.legalis.net/jurisprudence-decision.php3?id_article=219;

182. See Id. (One euro was worth about 95 US cents at the time of the court order).

183. See Acacio Pereira, *Yahoo! condamné à emp ê cher l'accès des internautes français aux sites illégaux (Yahoo! ordered to block French Internet users from illegal sites)*, Le Monde, November 22, 2000, at 12 (Yahoo! was also ordered not to deliver any Nazi memorabilia purchased from the site to any French address. The judge's decision was based on a report by three Internet experts who testified that it was possible to identify the geographic origin of 70 percent of Internet users).

184. *Yahoo! Inc. v. La ligue contre Le Racisme et l'anti-Sémitisme*, 169 F. Supp.2d 1181 (N.D.Cal. 2001).

185. See Lisa Guernsey, Ban on Nazi Items Upsets Collectors, The New York Times, May 10, 2001 at G11 (reporting that collectors of Nazi, Third Reich and other World War II memorabilia were upset by the ban on online auctions of such material, because sales were being pushed underground where prices were higher and values of the memorabilia inflated).

186. See Eugene Scoles, Peter Hay & Symeon Symeonides, Conflict Of Laws (3rd Ed.) 1148 (2000). See also Black's Law Dictionary (7th Ed.) 574 (1999).

187. See *Ackermann v. Levine,* 788 F.2d 830, 837 (2nd. Cir, 1986).

188. See *Matusevitch v. Telnikoff* 877 F.Supp. 1 (D.D.C. 1995) aff'd on other grounds, 159 F.3rd 636 (D.C. Cir. 1998).

189. See *Yahoo!, Inc., v. La Ligue Contre l'Anti-Sémitisme*, 169 F.Supp.2d 1181 (N.D. Cal. (2001).

190. See Brief of Amici Curiae, *Yahoo ! Inc. v. La Ligue contre le Racisme et l'antisémitisme* 169 F.Supp. 2nd 1181 (N.D. Cal. 2001). Brief available at: http://www.aclunc.org/cases/landmark_cases/yahoo_v._la_ligue_contre_le_racisme_et_l'antisemitisme.shtml. Last visited June 1, 2008.

191. *Yahoo!, Inc. v. La Ligue Contre Le Racisme*, 169 F.Supp.2d 1181, 1186 (2001).

192. Id. at 13.

193. Id. at 14.

194. Id. at 19 (citations omitted).

195. *Yahoo! Inc., v. LICRA & UEJF*, 379 F.3d 1120 (9th Cir. 2004) (hereinafter, *Yahoo! II*), *vacated and reh'g granted*, 399 F.3d 1010 (9th Cir. 2005).

196. *Yahoo! Inc., v. LICRA & UEJF*, 379 F.3d 1120 (9th Cir. 2004) (*Yahoo! II*).

197. See *UEJF Historique* (History of UEJF). Available at http://www.uejf.org/uejf_quisommesnous.php?histo=1&sid=. Last visited June 14, 2008.

198. . *Yahoo! Inc. v. LICRA* 399 F.3d 1010 (*vacating and granting reh'g en banc*, 379 F.3d 1120 (2004).

199. Yahoo! Inc v. LICRA. 433 F.3d 1199 (9th Cir. 2006) (hereinafter, Yahoo! III).

200. Yahoo! Inc v. LICRA, 433 F.3d 1199, 1216 (9th Cir. 2006).

201. Yahoo! Inc v. LICRA, 433 F.3d 1199, 1216, 1222 (9th Cir. 2006) (Yahoo! III).

202. See *LICRA v. Yahoo! Inc.*, (No. 05-1302) 547 U.S. (2006).

203. See *NAACP v. Button*, 371 U.S. 415 (1963).

204. See Gregg Ivers, American Constitutional Law: Power And Politics (Vol. II) 13 (2002).

205. 521 U.S. 844 (1997).

206. Yahoo! Inc, v. LICRA, 379 F.3d 1120 (9th Cir. 2004) *Yahoo! II*], *vacated and reh'g granted*, 399 F.3d 1010 (9th Cir. 2005) [*Yahoo! III*], *rev'd*, 433 F.3d 1199 (9th Cir. 2006) (remanding and ordering dismissal of Yahoo!'s suit).

207. ACLU v. Reno, 929 F. Supp. 824, 827 n.2 (E.D. Pa. 1996), *aff'd* 521 U.S. 844 (1997).

208. See *Yahoo!, Inc. v. La Ligue Contre Le Racisme et L'Antisémitisme* (LICRA), 169 F. Supp. 2d 1181 (N.D. Cal. 2001) [hereinafter *Yahoo! I*], *rev'd*, 379 F.3d 1120 (9th Cir. 2004) [*Yahoo! II*], *vacated and reh'g granted*, 399 F.3d 1010 (9th Cir. 2005) [*Yahoo! III*], *rev'd*, 433 F.3d 1199 (9th Cir. 2006) (remanding and ordering dismissal of Yahoo!'s suit).

209. Yahoo! Inc v. LICRA, 433 F.3d 1199, 1216, 1222 (9th Cir. 2006) (Yahoo! III).

Chapter Eight

Google Books, "Linguistic Capitalism," and the Exceptional Intellectual Property Law Regimes of the United States and France

"In the beginning was the Word."[1] This Biblical passage expresses the timelessness of God's word; it also expresses the timelessness of language, the immortality of the Word. There is a war of words, or rather, a war against words—English words to be precise—going on in France. In June 2011, the *Conseil Superieur de l'Audiovisuel* (Superior Council for the Audiovisual Media, CSA), the governmental agency that regulates the electronic media in France, sent a note to all French radio and television stations warning them that inviting their listeners and viewers to visit their "Facebook" and "Twitter," sites was a violation of French law. In effect, the CSA, whose mission includes the obligation to "ensure the defense and illustration of the French language and French culture in the French media," monitors the French media and publishes a monthly news letter in which it calls the attention of French broadcasters to the "incorrections" (read English words and expressions) that they may have used in their broadcasts in the past month. In its June 2011 news letter, the CSA ruled that French broadcasters who invited their audience members to visit their Facebook and Twitter pages were breaking a law against clandestine advertising, because they were essentially advertising these two American social media sites.[2]

The decision to ban the words "Facebook" and "Twitter" from French radio and television newscasts is the latest salvo in a historic "defensive" cultural "war of words" launched by the French authorities to protect the French language and culture from perceived external threats. In effect as early as 1635, Cardinal Richelieu, Chief Minister of King Louis XIII, created the *Académie française* (French Academy) to standardize and protect the French language. The French Academy continues to play an active role in the preservation and development of the French language through the publication of French language dictionaries (the Academy published its first French dictionary in 1694); organization of prestigious prizes for books published in French, and "enrichment" of the French language through the creation of new terminologies and neologisms to replace English words that emerge from the dynamic information and communication technologies as well as science and business.

The language policies of the French government demonstrate that France has been involved in "linguistic culturalism," the conceptualization and protection of language as the gateway to culture, for centuries. That is because language is inextricably linked to culture. This realization has inspired religious and governmental authorities who have control over language and its usage, to indulge in language manipulation and politicization.[3] The fact that English has become the *lingua franca* of the age of globalization, the language of networked information and communication technology and business has forced the French government to work overtime to protect the French language.

French "Encyclopedism" and The Challenge of Linguistic Capitalism

The French penchant to systematically accumulate knowledge in diverse branches of learning, what they call, *l'encyclopédisme* (encyclopedism), is evident in the country's great centers of knowledge and culture. These include national libraries, specialized academies, institutes, and museums. One of the greatest of these centers of "knowledge" is *la Bibliothèque nationale de France (National Library of France),* an institution founded by King Louis IV (1461-1483), and given a mission that has evolved from glorifying the king to preserving *le patrimoine national* (the national cultural heritage) of France. The French National Library was later given the ambitious mission of preserving "all the world's memory"—from a French perspective.[4] This mission is identical to that of the ancient Library of Alexandria, whose mission was to "gather all the knowledge of the world."

Knowledge acquisition and cataloging—the idea of collecting, systematically organizing, and preserving the cumulative, written knowledge of mankind in tangible media of communication, for purposes of easy retrieval—is a political, cultural and social practice whose origins have been traced to the oldest civilizations. From library card catalogues to *catalogues raisonnées*, exhaustive enumerations of institutional collections of *oeuvres d'esprit* (works of the mind), France has striven to create storehouses of information, knowledge, learning and culture. In the eighteenth century, French philosophers sought to create the *Encyclopédie*, a "balance sheet of knowledge" that would unite all the "disparate strands" of eighteenth-century thought.[5]

The Impact of New Information and Communication Technologies

The centuries' long French edifice of language protectionism and linguistic "culturalism," has been severely undermined by media convergence (the merging of once discrete media technologies), the interconnection of nations, peoples and cultures through networked communications, as well as the Internet and its associated social media, whose global *lingua franca* is ironically, English. For the first time in French history, media content from the networked information and communication technologies, and the innovative gadgets they have spawned easily bypass French governmental cultural gatekeepers and reach French consumers directly. Increasingly accurate Internet search engines, and the "search" industry they spawned, threaten to transform the French linguistic protection edifice into a linguistic *ligne Maginot* (Maginot Line), a strategically ineffective and ultimately useless defensive cultural fortification.

The Challenge of Search Engines and the Search Industry

The French culture of *encyclopédisme*, the systematic acquisition and retrieval of knowledge in real space has been frontally challenged in cyberspace by "upstart," American information technology companies like Google, Youtube, Apple Computer Inc., Microsoft, eBay, Facebook, Twitter, and others. The most brutal challenge to French encyclopedism has come from the Internet and Internet Search. Internet search engines are assemblages of computer and server software designed to systematically search and rank publicly available information on the World Wide Web, open databases, and open directories. Search engines have spawned the very profitable advertiser-driven search industry dominated by Google and Microsoft. Advertisers pay Google and other search companies to list their websites high on their search results. Google and other search companies make money when Internet users click on the web pages of advertisers or advertisements that accompany search results.[6] The Search industry is controversial because it has been accused of manipulating and misusing search results. Google the dominant search company, has been sued under the anti-trust law for using its market power and PageRank, its algorithmically generated, hierarchical search system to manipulate search results and rank them not on the basis of relevance but on the basis of paid advertising. Google has also been sued for manipulating search results about its main competitors by relegating their search results to the lower echelons of its search hierarchy. However, federal courts have dismissed these suits.[7]

The success of the burgeoning, multi-billion dollar Internet "search" industry, whose stock-in-trade is words, expressions, trademarks, service marks, business names, geographic locations, and other key words, has given rise to critiques, mostly from academia, about global corporate domination, monopolization, mathematization, commercialization and monetization of something as human as the search for knowledge and information. Indeed, European scholars, with their penchant for philosophizing communication phenomena over which they have very little or no control, have described search algorithms, as American commercialization of the word. French scholar Fréderick Kaplan has dubbed this new form of global monetization of language, which goes far beyond the traditional monetization of language in encyclopedias, dictionaries, thesauruses, and books, as *le capitalisme linguistique* (linguistic capitalism).[8] For his part, Swiss scholar, Yann Moulier Boutang, calls the search phenomenon "cognitive capitalism."[9] Outside the purely commercial arena, Google, Bing (Microsoft), and other search engines have essentially become the gatekeepers of online information because their page ranking determines which information appears at the top of Internet search results. In short, they create a hierarchization of knowledge and information based on commercial and economic considerations.

The Google Books "Affair" in France and the U.S.

As we saw above, Google become a global information and communication technology behemoth by performing a crucial function in the information society and the interconnected knowledge economy. The business model of Google and other search industry giants is to organize and rank the chaotic data of the Internet in response to key word searches. The Internet "search" model, algorithmically generated quantification, hierarchical classification, and arrangement of Internet searches is an unprecedented monetization of human language. Since we live in a global, interconnected world, the Internet search model diffused to France. Before too long, Google challenged the French exception in the domain of knowledge acquisition and retrieval. Google, whose stated mission is to "organize the world's information and make it universally accessible and useful,"[10] created a subsidiary, Google Books (later changed to Google Book Search) to digitize all published works in all the languages of the world for purposes of creating a universal digital meta library made up all printed books from every culture. The search giant subsequently created a French subsidiary, *Google Livres.* The next logical step was expansion of the Google Books phenomenon to all written languages of the world. In short, Google sought to do in cyberspace, what France, through its culture of encyclopedism, had endeavored to do in real space for centuries. In effect, Google Inc. took the ancient idea of creating a universal repository of the published knowledge of mankind from real space to cyberspace when it amalgamated that idea with its global search business paradigm. Google faced challenges in France, the United States, and elsewhere when it embarked on the digitization and the transfer of archival material from real space on library shelves and archives to searchable electronic databases in cyberspace, the so-called "cloud," where search engines can scour them for all kinds of information through key words. The conversion of millions of analogue books to digital books created a database that helped improve Google's PageRank proprietory search algorithm, which is at the heart of its business model. That commercial link was problematic for France.

The fundamental problem with the digitization and transfer of books from real space to cyberspace is that books are intellectual property and intellectual property laws, cultures and practices are not uniform around the world. The creation of a universal digital library also raised issues of power and control of these works, which collectively made up the heritage of mankind but had national cultural claims and individual copyright holders. The result was the so-called "Google Books affair"—a series of court cases, protocol, and digitization agreements between Google, and its French subsidiary, *Google Livres*, on the one hand, and copyright holders on the other hand, in the United States and France. The Google Books affair brought to the fore the contrasting intellectual property philosophies of the United States and France, and shaped the nature of digital libraries and commercial ebooks in both countries. The Internet, with its seemingly unlimited capacity to store and regurgitate digitized knowledge and information on demand, forced the American intellectual property regime to come to terms with its realities, and essentially compelled the French politico-cultural establishment to re-examine the exceptional French cultural model of knowledge creation, classification and storage; activities that are as old as the French state. The challenge for France was that if American companies digitized the ancient archives of the *Bibliothèque nationale de France*, these companies would control the electronic databases in which these materials would be stored. Furthermore, these databases would be stored on servers in the United States. That prospect was unthinkable.

Purpose of the Chapter

The Supreme Court of the United States has ruled that the law of copyright was developed in response to significant changes in technology, because technological developments often render copyright laws ambiguous.[11] The objective of this chapter is to describe and explain the application of intellectual property laws designed for real space to the dematerialized, virtual realities of cyberspace, using as a comparative case study, the legal obstacles faced by Google Books in the United States and *Google Livres*, Google's French subsidiary, in France. The inquiry focused on what happened when the idea of a universal, digital, online library created and controlled by Google Inc., a global information and communication technology "search" company based in the United States, is confronted by the highly proprietary, exceptional copyright regime of the United States, and the equally exceptional, bureaucratized, culturalist, intellectual property regime of France. The chapter explores cultural constructions of intellectual property in the United States and France within the context of the Google Books initiative. The chapter describes and explains application of intellectual property laws designed for real space to the dematerialized, virtual realities of cyberspace.

To address these issues, I carried out a comparative analysis of the legal challenges faced by Google Books in the United States, as well as the politico-cultural and legal obstacles faced by Google's French subsidiary, *Google Livres*, in France, as they sought to digitize and store millions of copyrighted books in online databases. This chapter also explores the postures of the intellectual property industry, the governments, and courts in the United States and France towards the Google Book Search phenomenon. I deploy American exceptionalism and *l'exception française* (the French exception) as functionally equivalent units of analysis that inform the application of intellectual property law designed for real space, to the reality of cyberspace in the issue area of the digitization, storage and retrieval of copyrighted works within the framework of the Google Books phenomenon in the United States and France.

This chapter proceeds in three parts. Part I will survey the imprint of American exceptionalism and the French exception on the respective intellectual property logics of both countries. I explain how each country's intellectual property regime reflects its specific national politico-cultural mentality, and how each regime is designed to promote certain governmental interests. Part II analyzes application of American intellectual property laws designed for real space to the dematerialized world of the Internet, and specifically to the Google Books phenomenon. This section will analyze judicial decisions regarding the Amended Settlement Agreement between Google Inc. and its adversaries. Part III analyzes the application of French intellectual property laws designed for real space to the dematerialized world of the Internet, and specifically to the Google Book Search phenomenon.

I argue that the pragmatic, utilitarian, Constitutional, "incentive" function of American copyright law guided governmental intervention and judicial decision-making in the Google Books affair in the United States, while in France governmental intervention and judicial decisions in the *Google Livres* (Google Books) affair were grounded in the cultural *Weltanschauung* of France, a cultural state, in which the government has historically been the national cultural engineer, and the main protector of a national "cultural memory," on which it has put its imprimatur. The government is also the "curator" of a universal, "all the world's memory" as collected, processed, catalogued, and displayed within the framework of the French exception.

Digitization, Space-shifting, and Intellectual Property Challenges

Digitization of books and other published material and storing them in online databases (essentially transferring them from real space to cyberspace) is a process of "space-shifting." The concept of "space-shifting" was first used to describe the transfer of media products from real space to cyberspace in the context of the landmark litigation that followed the emergence of peer-to-peer file-sharing networks in the 1990s. In effect, when the American recording industry, led by A & M Records, sued Napster, Inc. the pioneer peer-to-peer file-sharing network, for contributory and vicarious infringement of the copyright of record companies, Napster argued that peer-to-peer file-sharing was merely "space-shifting." Napster essentially argued that the unauthorized, dematerialization or conversion of music from analog to digital formats, and transferring the resulting digital files to databases, servers and online networks for purposes of peer-to-peer exchanges, was protected by the fair use provisions of the Copyright Act of 1976. Napster claimed that time-shifting (recording television programs on video tape recorders for later home viewing) and space-shifting (transfer of material from real space to cyberspace for purposes of P2P file-sharing) were analogous for purposes of fair use analysis. The United States District Court for the Northern District of California rejected this argument.[12]

The Google Digital Library "space-shifting" initiative also opened a can of intellectual property worms. Before the arrival of computers and the Internet, in Continental Europe, intellectual property protection has traditionally resided in "literary and artistic works" that were the embodiment or physical forms of the intellectual expression of authors.[13] In the United States, copyright has historically been available to "original works of authorship fixed in any tangible medium of expression."[14] In both jurisdictions, emphasis was generally placed on the physicality of the copyrighted material. The presumption was that the copyright holder had physical or contractual control over copying and distribution of the tangible work. With the advent of the digital media and the Internet, the common problem that confronted these different regimes was how to apply intellectual property rules and regulations designed for real space and real time to the de-materialized world of cyberspace, networked communication technologies, and especially phenomena like digital books. These are physical books digitized and stored in databases for purposes of retrieval on demand. Unlike physical, copyrighted works, digitized works are de-materialized data that can be searched, copied, downloaded and distributed with lightening speed to all parts of the globe. The history of intellectual property law in the age of globalization and networked communication is thus a history of attempts to bring the de-materialized, digital world of cyberspace within the ambit of intellectual property law at the national, supranational and international levels. The Supreme Court of the United States has ruled that the law of copyright developed in response to significant changes in technology, because technological developments often render copyright laws ambiguous.[15] This chapter deals with how American and French law designed to regulate intellectual property in real space was transferred to the reality of cyberspace in the context of the fluid, dematerialized phenomenon of Google digital books.

American Exceptionalism, *L'Exception Française* (The French Exception), and the Google Books Affair

As we saw in chapter 2, exceptionalism is "a theory that a nation, region, or political system is exceptional and does not conform to the [political or cultural] norm."[16] The United States and France are self-described "exceptionalist" countries. Since exeptionalism is a declaration of specificity, it is by nature, oppositional. It comes into play when a self-described exceptional civilization, culture or country sets itself apart from—and in opposition to—the rest of the world.[17]

The Google Books controversy brought to the fore, the differing conceptualizations of intellectual property and culture in the United States and France. This is because communication law is ensconced in specific national, supranational and international "contextual matrixes," to borrow the expression of Pierre Legrand. These matrices affect legal mentalities and influence the outcomes of legal disputes.[18] Exceptionalism is a contextual and conceptual matrix, a political and cultural *logic* that is the result of historical, political and cultural processes and strategies.[19] As we saw earlier, the United States and France have brought the Internet within the ambit of their respective exceptionalist regulatory logics. Each country regulates intellectual property—that family of intangible rights conferred on authors and inventors under the law by different national and international regimes—within the framework of its particular exceptionalist ideology.[20]

American Exceptionalism and Application of Intellectual Property Law to Cyberspace

The Internet is a relatively new, unprecedented—in the literal and legal sense of the term—frontier that the law is still struggling to come to terms with.[21] The digitization, storage, and on demand retrieval of copyrighted works hosted on servers and databases raised intellectual property issues. Intellectual property law and policy took on greater significance, as intellectual property became the life-blood of the knowledge economy and the information society. The challenge was thus to make intellectual property rules and regulations that had been drafted for real space content and real space media, relevant and applicable to cyberspace. This required a change of mentalities, different conceptualizations of the nature of the Internet, and different expectations regarding its role in society. In effect, the Internet engendered a number of intellectual property issues that policy makers in the United States and around the world had to address.

Copyright and Fair Use

American copyright law has a pronounced, exceptionalist or First Amendment component. Exceptionalism in copyright law is expressed in terms of certain First Amendment free speech protections that are built-into the copyright regime and safeguard expressive interests and concerns.[22] The Supreme Court of the United States had held that the First Amendment and copyright are inextricably linked because First Amendment protections are "embodied in the Copyright Act's distinction between copyrightable expression facts and ideas that are not copyrightable, and the latitude for scholarship and comment traditionally afforded by fair use."[23] This fundamental principle is set forth in the fair use provision of the Copyright Act, which states that:

> [T]he fair use of a copyrighted work, including such use by reproduction in copies or phono records or by any other means . . . for purposes such as criticism, comment, news reporting, teaching (including multiple copies for classroom use), scholarship, or research, is not an infringement of copyright. In determining whether the use made of a work in any particular case is a fair use the factors to be considered shall include—
> (1) The purpose and character of the use, including whether such use is of a commercial nature or is for nonprofit educational purposes;
> (2) The nature of the copyrighted work;
> (3) The amount and substantiality of the portion used in relation to the copyrighted work as a whole; and
> (4) The effect of the use upon the potential market for or value of the copyrighted work.[24]

Fair use is also an affirmative defense in circumstances where existing works are appropriated for purposes of creating new, transformative, critical works. Parody is a notable category of transformative works protected by the First Amendment. Parody serves as a vehicle for politico-social criticism.[25] However, fair use is only an affirmative defense available to the fair use claimant who is accused of infringing on exclusive intellectual property rights.[26] Fair use is thus an important limitation on the copyright monopoly. Put otherwise, copyright law has substantial free speech dimensions that are expressed in terms of fair use. Fair use is thus an exception to copyright that has expanded the scope of freedom of expression in the United States in areas ranging from journalistic reporting and satire to teaching. As we shall see later, fair use was one of the bones of contention in the dispute between Google and its adversaries in the litigation that followed in the wake of the digitization and transfer of books from real space to cyberspace within the framework of the Google Books initiative.

L'Exception Française (The French exception)

If American exceptionalism is the proclamation that the United States is a singular nation whose superior democratic system and unparalleled libertarian values set it apart from other nation-states, the French exception is a declaration of Gallic linguistic and cultural specificity. The French exception is therefore the ancient ideological posture through which France emphasizes the uniqueness and specificity of its language, culture, and civilization, in opposition to other languages and cultures. [27] French intellectuals have traditionally set France, a country that has been described as having a "Catho-secular," Latin culture, [28] as the foil of the United States, a country with Puritan, Protestant roots, and a libertarian culture. The French exception and its corollary, *l'exception culturelle française* (the French cultural exception) are synonymous cultural defensive mechanisms erected against perceived cultural threats from America's mass entertainment, "fast culture," free enterprise religion, and excessive linguistic knowledge and cultural capitalism.[29]

The French Exception, Intellectual Property, and Cultural Protectionism

French intellectual property law is exceptional in that it is *sui generis*. It is a system that is inseparable from Gallic *savoir-faire* and *savoir-vivre* because it covers everything from high fashion to the highly complex culture of gastronomic nomenclature: the *appellations d'origine controlées* (protected designations of origin). French exceptionalism in intellectual property law is expressed in terms of a heightened recognition of the importance of cultural and knowledge production, as well as a celebration of authors of *œuvres d'esprit* (works of the mind). The French government and the cultural class view works of the mind as *lieux de mémoire culturel* (sites of cultural memory) as well as propagators of national cultural heritage.[30] Since France views itself as a cultural state, it regulates the Internet within the framework of its exceptionalist ideology, *l'exception française* (the French exception). Under this national ideology the Internet is conceptualized as an instrument for the protection and promotion of French language and culture. As a result, the

French government has over the years viewed the technologies and business models of global information and communication technology companies like Google with disdain, and sought to restrain their perceived commercial excesses.

As we saw earlier, the French exception is woven into the fabric of the French intellectual property regime, which is grounded in the *Code de la propriété intellectualle* (the Code of Intellectual Property). To the French, the term "copyright" is a rather narrow, foreign concept that expresses only part of the two-fold intellectual and property right that accrues to authors. The French equivalent of the word "copyright" is the expression, "*droit d'auteur,*" (right of the author). Under French law, intellectual property consists of two rights: a patrimonial (economic) right and an intangible, inalienable moral right. Moral right is a rather "romantic" right of personality that seeks to protect the unique expression and metaphysical cachet or "mental signature" of the author on his or her work. Thus, authors retain moral rights in their works even after economic rights in the work have been exercised and the rights have been transferred to third parties pursuant to contracts.[31] Additionally, moral rights can be the subject of testamentary transfers to heirs and other parties.[32] In France, intellectual property is viewed as an important component of the French cultural exception because intellectual property is an instrument for the protection and promotion of French culture. Under French law, the term *le droit d'auteur* expresses a two-fold package of intellectual and literary rights that accrue to authors of "works of the intellect": 1) a patrimonial (economic) right, which represents the "pecuniary benefits resulting from the exploitation of an author's right of literary property,"[33] and 2) an intangible "moral right." Though most of Continental Europe recognizes the metaphysical, moral rights component of intellectual property, the doctrine has best been expressed, developed and practiced in France.[34] The *Code de la propriété intellectuelle* (Intellectual Property Code) sets forth the two dimensions of intellectual property:

> *L'auteur d'une oeuvre de l'esprit jouit sur cette oeuvre, du seul fait de sa création, d'un droit de propriété incorporelle exclusif et opposable à tous.*
> *Ce droit comporte des attributs d'ordre intellectuel et moral ainsi que des attributs d'ordre patrimonial. . . . L'existence ou la conclusion d'un contrat de louage d'ouvrage ou de service par l'auteur d'une oeuvre de l'esprit n'emporte pas dérogation à la jouissance du droit reconnu par le premier alinéa.*[35]

> The author of a work of the mind enjoys over this work, by reason of its creation, an exclusive incorporeal property right enforceable against all. This right includes intellectual and moral attributes as well as patrimonial attributes. . . . The existence or the conclusion of a works made for hire or a service

> contract signed by the author of a work of the mind does not mean derogation from enjoyment of the right recognized above.

In France, the "author" is therefore the object and focal point of intellectual property protection. His or her moral rights are so important that they trump "works made for hire" contracts.

Additionally, French intellectual property law is premised on an asymmetrical, adversarial relationship between authors and publishers, journalists and newspaper publishers, as well as artists and art dealers. Therefore, an exceptionalist function of French intellectual property law is to create equality of arms between authors and publishers. Under provisions of the French Intellectual Property Code, authors enjoy "personal, perpetual, inalienable and indefeasible" *droits moraux* (moral rights) that include the right of name recognition, respect for their status as artists, and respect for their work. Moral right is a right of personality that seeks to protect the unique expression and metaphysical "cachet" or "mental signature" of an author on his or her work. Thus, authors retain moral rights in their works even after economic rights in the work have been exercised and the work has been transferred to third parties pursuant to contracts.[36] French intellectual property law clearly tilts the balance of forces in the knowledge production process in favor of the author, whose rights take precedence over the rights of all the other parties involved in the production and distribution of works of the mind.

The Google Books Library Project

The Google Books affair in the United States and France began in 2004 when Google, the universal Internet search company, announced the creation of a revolutionary business model, the *Google Books Library Project*, whose ultimate aim was "to work with publishers and libraries to create a comprehensive, searchable, virtual card catalog of all books in all languages that helps users discover new books and publishers discover new readers."[37] The idea of the Google Books Library project was simple: Google wanted to transfer the logic and procedures of the library catalogue that is now largely obsolete in real space, to the innovative technological realities of the dematerialized, virtual world of cyberspace. The Google Books project involved entering into agreements with libraries around the world for purposes of scanning (digitizing) entire books and book collections, storing these dematerialized files in Google's digital online database and making the books searchable, retrievable, downloadable, and readable in a number of digital formats: the Internet, Android, the iPad, Kindle Nook, and other electronic book (ebook) readers. The main source of books for the project was institutional libraries, and the Partner Program, a program that allowed individual authors and publishers to voluntarily give Google permission to include their works in the project. Before too long, some of the major libraries of the world, from Harvard University Library to the University of Mysore Library, Karnataka, India, had signed on as institutional partners of the project. The terms of the agreement with institutional libraries were generally confidential but it is understood that the university library partners received a Library Digital Copy (LDC) of each digitized book in their collection for use by their members, as well as full review of books in the public domain. Google also provided readers review snippets of books under copyright, unless authors notified Google that they did not want their works to feature in the Library project; in which case Google withdrew the works.

For Google the digital book search was yet another step in fulfilling its mission to "organize the world's information and make it universally accessible and useful."[38] Furthermore, all the search results of the "snippet" views of the in-copyright books, and full views of out-of copyright books generated advertising revenues similar to all other Google search services. Additionally, conversion of millions of digital books created a database that helped improve Google's propriety search algorithm, which is at the heart of its business model.

It seems that Google and the universities went ahead with the book-scanning project, with the understanding that they were acting within the standards set forth by the "fair use" provisions of the Copyright Act of 1976. As we saw above, the "fair use" provisions allow for reproduction of copies of in-copyright works for "criticism, comment, news reporting teaching (including multiple copies for classroom use), scholarship or research.[39]

Google seemed to be confident that its "search" activity with snippet views on the Internet would be deemed as not infringing on copyright as it would fall within the purview of "fair use." Moreover, the Copyright Act immunizes libraries that make copies to preserve and replace damaged books from copyright infringement suits. Additionally, it was assumed that if section 108 of the Copyright Act were read with the case law on the Eleventh Amendment, which immunizes states (and state universities) from suits for money damages without their consent, the public university participants in the Google Books project would be protected from liability. However, this was not a guarantee. In effect, unlike other search activities by Google that use the proprietary algorithm that crawls across the virtual sphere of the Internet seeking information that the copyright holders had already placed by on the Internet, the Google Books project had already digitized, and stored millions of books on its servers without the consent of the copyright holders.[40] This raised major intellectual property issues in the United States and France.

Digitization and Intellectual Property Law in the United States and France

Intellectual property is a family of intangible exclusive rights,[41] grounded in different theoretical formulations, and conferred on authors and inventors under the law by different national, supranational and international regimes. These rights range from copyright, patents and trademarks in the Anglo-American common law countries, to authors' rights (including moral rights), patents and trademarks (*marques deposées*, *appellations controlées*) granted authors in the European civil law countries, under European Union directives and international law. In this chapter, the term "intellectual property" refers to copyright, author's rights and moral rights in mass mediated content, information and communication technology. It also refers to protection for the software that enables digital production, storage, and dissemination from illegal access and duplication. The intellectual property law regimes of the United States and France have philosophical differences over a number of issue areas of intellectual property law: copyright/authors rights, and moral rights, as well as classification of audio-visual and other mass mediated products under the international trade regime.

Digitization and Cultural protection: French Governmental Policy

While early digitization of periodicals and books in the United States was undertaken mostly by the private sector, in France, the situation was different. As we noted earlier, France is a cultural state in which the government, through the powerful Ministry of Culture and Communication, is the "engineer" and prime mover of all things cultural. The digitization of books and periodicals and the advent of digital libraries in the United States caused concerns in France. Not to be outdone by the developments in the United States, the French government proposed the creation of a "*Bibliothèque numérique francophone* (French Language Digital Library). In 1997, the *Bibliothèque nationale de France* (BnF) (French National Library), which was created in the 16th century to serve as the location where "all the world's memory" would be housed, launched a French language digital library project called *Gallica.*[42] In 2010, the *Bibliothèque nationale de France* signed an agreement with Microsoft to index and simplify access to the Gallica collection. The French government realized that it would take decades to digitize the millions of books, manuscripts, and artifacts held by the National Library. It soon announced a call for partnership with the private sector in order to expand and accelerate the digitization, and valorization (read monetization) of the Gallica digital library.[43]

The Google Books Affair in the United States and France

When Google, the world's largest Internet search company announced in 2004 that it had launched Google Book Search and Google Print, a service that had the ability to search the text of complete books that Google had digitized and stored in its databases, the news was received with mixed reactions. Many libraries welcomed it, while many copyright holders feared that scanning copyrighted books without the consent of their authors or copyright holders was tantamount to intellectual property infringement. The service, which ultimately became known as Google Book Search, was aimed at digitizing all books ever published in every language in every country. The ultimate objective of this unprecedented feat was the creation of a universal online library, the largest single repository of the world's knowledge. The Google Book Search project was an innovation that made it possible for readers to browse and review snippets of copyright books as well as works by authors and publishers who had signed on to Google's Partner Program and voluntarily allowed their books to be scanned and added to the Google Book Search project. Additionally, readers could browse and download books in the public domain, as well as browse, borrow or buy and print books from Google Book Search. Google Book Search was attractive to some publishers and authors because publishers had a say as to the amount of their works they wanted Google to display online. Publishers could choose "limited review," which showed several pages with the search keywords but no more than 20 percent of the content of the work, or "snippet" review, which showed no more than three snippets, each containing several sentences that had the search keywords.[44] Publishers also had the option of withdrawing their books from Google's digital database at will, and share the revenues generated from the ads Google posted close to their books.[45]

The *Google Books Library Project* had the potential of radically transforming how human beings created, stored, retrieved, and utilized the mighty rivers of information and knowledge that had been accumulated since early humans began to paint on the walls of their caves. This would be the biggest evolution since the ancient Sumerians invented one of the earliest arts of written expression, cuneiform on clay tablets in the thirtieth century BC, and ancient Egyptians developed hieroglyphic writing on papyrus—the medium that gave us the word "paper." Additionally, the *Google Books Library Project* fundamentally transformed the concept of "the book" as a physical collection of information and knowledge on bound sheets of paper delimited by two covers. Digitization transformed this concept, which dates back to the codex, the immediate ancestor of the modern book, that had been popularized by the Papacy as the format for reproducing the Bible.

Needless to say, Google's ambitions raised a number of conflicts of intellectual property law. Copyright holders around the world challenged Google's right to digitize and archive their works without their permission. The most serious of these conflicts was moral rights, the mostly continental European right of personality that seeks to protect the unique expression and metaphysical "cachet" or "mental signature" of an author on his or her work even after economic rights in the work have been exercised and the work has been transferred to third parties pursuant to contracts.[46] Furthermore, the duration of copyright or intellectual property, and the status of unclaimed or "orphan works" and works in the public domain differ from country to country, and sometimes from one region to another. Furthermore, since the Internet is an interconnected network of computer networks that spans the globe, Google's proposed electronic card catalogue fell squarely in the domain of international intellectual property, a simple literary and legal sphere where everything is complicated. This chapter focuses on how the intellectual property challenges raised by intellectual property holders against Google Books were handled under the American copyright and the French *droit d'auteur* intellectual property regimes.

Google Book Search and Copyright Law in the United States: *The Authors' Guild v. Google Inc.*

Since millions of the books digitized by Google and stored in its databases were copyrighted works, the Google Books Digital Library business model raised the hackles of tens of authors and publishers around the world. It sorely tested the American copyright ethos, where the Constitution grants authors and copyright owners monopolies over their work for limited periods of time for the betterment of society.[47] In 2005, the Authors Guild Inc. (AGI) and the Association of American Publishers (AAP), groups that represent authors and publishers, challenged Google's unauthorized digitization of copyrighted books for purposes of constituting a searchable "universal library." The most controversial aspect of the Google Books project was its "space-shifting" aspect. The digitization and transfer of whole books from the real, physical geographic spaces of libraries and bookstores to cyberspace, where Internet searches would result in the display of snippets from these books as part of Google's commercial search business model. In fact the digitization of books without the consent of the copyright holders, flew in the face of the fundamental principles of intellectual property.[48] The Authors' Guild and the Association of American Publishers filed a class-action copyright infringement suit against Google, claiming that the company's unauthorized digitization of their books, and displaying snippets of these books within the framework of its commercial search business amounted to copyright infringement. The Authors' Guild sought both damages and injunctive relief while the publishers asked the court to issue an injunction against Google Books. In the face of this massive class action suit, Google raised a defense of "fair use" under the Copyright Act, claiming that its digitization was permitted under the provisions of the act. There was a slim possibility that if the case went to trial, courts would have been forced to define the notion of "search" activity on the Internet, an outcome that could have had unforeseen consequences for Google's entire business model. The complexity and unpredictability of any outcome in the *Authors' Guild v. Google Inc.* case persuaded Google to seek an out of court class action settlement with the Authors' Guild and the Association of American Publishers (AAP). The United States District Court for the Southern District of New York suggested that the plaintiffs would not have an easy case either: "Further litigation would be complex, expensive and time-consuming . . . the legal and factual issues are complex, there is a risk that if plaintiffs were to proceed to trial, they would be unable to establish liability or prove damages."[49] One of the main bones of contention in settlement talks was an "opt-out" provision, which put the onus on copyright holders to take affirmative steps to inform Google Books that they did not want their works to be included in Google's universal library. That provision essentially turned upside-down the long-standing common law tradition whereby a person seeking to make copies of a copyrighted work sought permission from the rights holder first. In other words, in copyright law, the tradition has been for copyright holders to "opt-in" rather than "opt-out." Despite a provision for setting up an "Unclaimed Works Fiduciary,"[50] the "opt-out" provision would essentially have given Google the power to create an exclusive and universal library of "orphan works" and works already in the public domain. Two of Google's most vociferous adversaries, Amazon.com and Microsoft Corporation claimed that the involuntary transfer of unclaimed or "orphan works" to Google would violate the Copyright Act because under the American Constitution, only Congress had the power to enact laws to that effect.[51]

The Settlement Agreement and the Amended Settlement Agreement

In 2006, Google and its adversaries entered into settlement negotiations and filed a proposed settlement agreement with a court in 2008. The settlement was submitted for legal appraisal because under of the Federal Rules of Civil Procedure (Rule 23(e)), for a settlement of a class action suit to become final and binding on the parties, it had to be approved by a court. For their part, courts can put their imprimatur on the agreement only if they make a determination that the settlement is "fair, adequate, and reasonable." The proposed settlement provoked hundreds of objections. This made the parties to go back to the drawing board for purposes of addressing the objections raised. One year later, the parties executed an Amended Settlement Agreement (ASA) and filed a motion with the court for its final approval. When the court gave its preliminary approval to the amended settlement agreement, hundreds of parties to the class action suit—and these included authors and publishers who had copyright interests in the works covered by the Amended Settle Agreement—filed further objections to it. This time, the United States Department of Justice filed a statement raising concerns about the ASA.[52] The ASA, which concerned mostly out-of-print, non-commercially available works, authorized Google to continue to digitize books and sell access to the database, market eBooks, and sell advertising on pages from the digitized books. In exchange, Google agreed to pay the rights holders 63 percent of all revenues earned from its digitization and marketing activities. The Rights holders had certain rights that included the right to ask Google not to digitize their books, or to remove their books from the Google Books database.[53]

Google's main competitors—including Amazon.com and Microsoft Corporation—also raised strident objections to the Amended Settlement Agreement. They claimed that the scope of the ASA was so overbroad that if the court approved the instrument, it would essentially put its imprimatur on Google's business model—digitizing entire out-of-print and "orphan works," whose ownership was unknown, and storing them in databases for commercial exploitation—a model that raised copyright, anti-trust, privacy and international law issues.[54] The question before the court was whether the $125 million amended class action settlement agreement between groups that represent authors and publishers and Google, Inc. was "fair, adequate, reasonable, and not a product of collusion."[55] The court held that it was not. The court found that while the "ASA was a product of arm's length negotiations" between the parties, with the assistance of the United States Department of Justice, the objections of some of the parties to the class action suit were significant. Furthermore, the court held that the provision of the settlement that would "transfer to Google certain rights in exchange for future and ongoing arrangements . . . exceeds what the Court may permit under Rule 23 . . . the establishment of a mechanism for exploiting unclaimed books is a matter more suited for Congress than this court."[56] Additionally, the court held that the ASA would give Google a de facto monopoly over unclaimed or orphan works. As a result, the court concluded that the ASA was not adequate and reasonable. The court suggested that many of the objections to the ASA would be addressed if the ASA were "converted from an 'opt-out' settlement to an 'opt-in' settlement." This would give members of the class action suit an opportunity to voluntarily participate in it, while excluding those who did not wish to participate in it.[57]

To complicate matters further for Google, in 2010, Associational Plaintiffs, acting on behalf of the members of the American Society of Media Photographers (ASMP), and other visual artists' associations, together with several individual ASMP members, filed a separate class action suit against Google at the U.S. District Court for the Southern District of New York, for copyright infringement.[58] The suit was filed on behalf of individual copyright holders in certain photographs, illustrations and other visual works that are published in the books that Google had digitized and transferred from real space to cyberspace within the framework of the Google Library Project. They sought damages, injunctive and declarative relief. Google raised a defense of fair use and moved to dismiss the copyright claims of the Authors Guild and that of the other author and visual artists' organizations for lack of standing. Additionally, Google claimed that the fair-use test required individualized inquiry and the participation of individual members of the associations. The court denied Google's motion, stating that it could accommodate Google's fair-use defense by grouping association members and their respective works into subgroups. In 2012, the court granted the ASMP plaintiffs' motion for class certification. The practical result is that the Google Books case is sure to drag on for some time to come.

Google Book Search, the French Exception, and Intellectual Property

Innovative, global information and communication technology corporations take advantage of the unprecedented opportunities created by the interconnection of nations and peoples to extend their reach to all parts of the world. Despite their global visions, their business models are often grounded in the political, social, economic and cultural values of their home countries. This is especially true of Google Inc., the global Internet search company whose business model is grounded in American First Amendment and intellectual property law values. This section deals with the conflict between American and French law in the issue area of intellectual property. This conflict was engendered by *Google Recherche de Livres*, the French subsidiary of Google Books, which set out to do business in France within the framework of American intellectual property rules, as well as the First Amendment "values" on which the Google search business model is based. The conflict of laws arose because certain aspects of the intellectual property law regime of France are at variance with the American intellectual property law regime. The result is that Google's reliance on American intellectual property laws to further its search business in France was problematic.

The conflict of American and French laws came to the fore in the case, *Editions du Seuil and Others v. Google Inc. and Google France.*[59] This case arose when Google digitized hundreds of French language books, written by French authors, without the authorization of the French copyright owners, and stored the digitized books in its servers in the United States. French users of *Google Livres* (later renamed *Google Recherche de Livres* or Google Book Search to signal that Google was not claiming copyright over the books it digitized) could log on to Google's French portal, Google.fr, and access the digitized reproductions of the covers and snippets of the books. Google's actions flew in the face of centuries of French intellectual property culture and led to legal action. This case turned out to be about the application of American intellectual property laws designed for real space, to the transnational reality of cyberspace. In other words, the case was about the applicability of the exceptional First Amendment intellectual property law doctrine of "fair use," that was designed to promote freedom of speech and expression in the context of intellectual property law, to the business activities of Google in France.

Editions du Seuil and Others v. Google Inc. and Google France, and Conflict of French and American Intellectual Property Law

The French government was not amused when *Google Recherche de Livres*, commenced digitizing French language books for the French market. As we saw earlier, France is a centralized cultural state in which the government and the cultural elite have, from time immemorial, set the cultural policy of the country. Under the French culturalist perspective, books written by French authors, in the French language, and published in France are considered part of the country's *patrimoine écrit* (written cultural heritage). The French state had, since the 16th century, created an institution, *la Bibliothèque Nationale de France*, (French National Library) whose mission was to gather "*toute la mémoire du monde*" (all the world's memory). This memory was viewed, selected, and classified within the framework of the country's national politico-cultural perspective, and archived under one French governmental cultural roof. Google's universal library project flew in the face of this giant edifice of memory and its political, cultural and ideological assumptions. Indeed, Google's universal library was a challenge to French governmentally-sanctioned "truth," national collective memory, and the French cultural exception. The result is that the French publishing industry, French authors' syndicates and the French cultural industry launched a series of legal actions against Google—and its French subsidiaries, Google France and Google Recherche de Livres—in French courts.

The fact that an American company, Google Inc., was poised to become the digitizer and custodian—in American databases—of French cultural memory caused alarm in France. The French publishing industry decided to take legal action against Google Books for intellectual property violation. In 2006, a number of French publishers sued Google Inc, and Google France at the High Court of Paris, claiming that Google's unauthorized digitization, storage (in the United States) and display (on *Google Recherche de Livres*) of the covers and snippets of their copyrighted books constituted violations of their intellectual property rights under French law. They claimed that this digitization was tantamount to counterfeiting, an egregious, criminal infringement of the author's right, trademark and service mark provisions of the *Code de la propriété intellectuelle* (Intellectual Property Code).[60] The plaintiffs asked the court to issue an injunction barring Google from digitizing their works without authorization and storing these works in a new medium: online databases. They also asked the court to order Google to pay $21 million in damages to repair the prejudice caused by its infringement.

In response to these charges, Google stated that French law was not applicable to the case because the digitization activities complained about were carried out entirely and legally in the United States. The search giant claimed that display of the digitized covers and extracts of copyrighted French books by its French subsidiary, *Google Recherche de Livres,* did not constitute acts of intellectual property counterfeiting because the digitization, storage and display of extracts of the books were activities protected under the "fair use" provisions of the American Copyright Act of 1976,[61] and the short citation exemption of the French Intellectual Property code. This provision authorizes authors to use short extracts of other works in their writings.[62] Furthermore, Google sought refuge in article 5.2 of the Berne Convention for the Protection of Literary and Artistic Works of 1886, which stipulates what kinds of protections authors are entitled to inside and outside their countries of origin. Google claimed that under this provision of the Berne Convention, in situations of complex conflict of laws, the applicable law should be the laws of the country in which the intellectual property violations are alleged to have been committed unless an especially close proximity with another country—in this case, France—could be established. Google claimed that since the digitization of the French books in question had taken place in the United States, American Copyright law and its fair use provisions should be the applicable law.

The Applicability of the American "Fair Use" Copyright Doctrine in France

Since the Internet has always posed jurisdictional questions in transnational litigations of this nature, the first issue before the court in *Editions du Seuil and Others v. Google Inc. and Google France* was a conflict of laws issue. The question before the High Court of Paris was whether American or French law should be applicable, given that Google's unauthorized digitization and storage of copyrighted French books took place in the United States even though the digitized books could be accessed any where in the world. This question was crucial because the American Copyright Act of 1967 has unique, First Amendment "fair use" provisions that allow transformative works and protect the digitization and online display of the front covers and extracts of copyrighted books. By way of contrast, the French Intellectual Property Code has no comparable fair use provisions.[63] The High Court of

Paris ruled that only French law was applicable in this case. It held that the applicable law in situations of complex extra-contractual offenses is the law of the country in which the damageable act occurred. The court said that in this case, the location of the prejudicial act [unauthorized digitization of French copyrighted books] is understood to include the state in which the damage originated [the United States], and the state in which the damage occurred [France]. In the case at bar, the court ruled that the books in question were written by French authors, and that Google had digitized the books in order to make them available to French Internet audiences residing within the French national territory. Additionally, the court said that Google France was headquartered in France, that its domain name: www.books.google.fr had the French country domain extension ".fr," and that the content of the website was in the French language. France was therefore the country with the closest ties to the case. The applicable law was therefore French law. This decision was consistent with French declaration of universal jurisdiction on the Internet. In effect, in an unprecedented 1998 ruling, this same *Tribunal de Grande Instance de Paris* (High Court of Paris) had held that French courts had "universal jurisdiction over the totality of content disseminated on the Internet."[64] The court essentially held that material published anywhere on the Internet fell within the jurisdiction of French courts if the material could be accessed by search engines located on French territory.[65]

Having dispensed with the procedural conflict of laws issues, the court proceeded to address the substantive claims of the publishers. The first issue before the court was whether Google's unauthorized digitizing of the French publishers' books into its database, and displaying the covers and excerpts of the books on *Google Recherche de Livres* violated the publishers' intellectual property rights. The court answered in the affirmative, holding that Google had violated the rights of the publishers and infringed on their trademarks: "The digitization of a work, a technique which consists of scanning the totality of the work into a given digital format, constitutes a reproduction of the work which requires, if the work is protected, the prior authorization of the author or copyright holder."[66] The court held that by digitizing and communicating the entire covers of books to the public without authorization, and by choosing the snippets of the book displayed on its website haphazardly, Google's digitization project was ineligible for protection under the "short quotation exception" of the Intellectual Property Code. This exception allows the reproduction of brief extracts of copyrighted works.[67] Finally, the court held that by posting unauthorized extracts of digitized books haphazardly on the Internet, Google had violated the integrity of the copyrighted works whose extracts it had published.

The second question before the court was whether the unauthorized digitizing and storage of books in Google's database amounted to counterfeiting of the publishers' trade marks. The court answered in the negative. The court then issued an injunction prohibiting Google from digitizing and storing the books of the French complainants in its databases. The court ordered Google Books to stop scanning French books and making them available to French readers on the *Google Recherche de Livres* website with immediate effect or pay a fine of $15,000 per day. The court also ordered Google to pay the plaintiffs close to $700,000 in damages, plus costs. Google had hoped that its pending class action settlement in the United States would serve as a model for dealing with French intellectual property holders. That expectation seemed to be wishful thinking.

Google Recherche de Livres and Digitization Agreements with French Publishers

Just when things looked bleak for Google in France, a break-through occurred. In a *coup de théâtre* worthy of the best French dramatists, Google and Hachette Livre, one of the largest publishers and copyright holders in France, announced that they had signed a protocol agreement, a quasi-diplomatic document, that would allow *Google Recherche de Livres France* to digitize out-of-print French language works whose copyright is owned by Hachette Livre, one of the parties to the law suit against Google. *Google Recherche de Livres* and Hachette Livre ultimately signed a final agreement on digitization of thousands of out-of-print French books whose copyright Hachette controls, and which are not commercially available. Under the terms of the agreement, Hachette Livre would determine the books *Google Recherche de Livres* could digitize, the books that would appear in the form of ebooks sold via Google eBooks, and books that could be printed on demand. In order to get the French government's approval of the deal, the Google–Hachette Livre agreement stated that "Hachette Livre had the intention of letting public institutions like the *Bibliothèque Nationale de France* to benefit from works that will be digitized in the framework of this agreement, thus putting out of print books in the public domain back within the ambit of [French] cultural heritage and at the disposal of readers."[68]

The inclusion of a provision on public institutions in the *Google Recherche de Livres*-Hachette Livre agreement essentially acknowledged the reality that France is a cultural state in which the government treats books and other kinds of intellectual property as part of the cultural heritage of the country. The government thus had to have a say in the agreement. In effect, as soon as the *Google Recherche de Livre*-Hachette Livre protocol on digitization of French language books was announced in November 2010, the then Minister of Culture and Communication, Frédéric Mitterrand, issued a statement to the effect that all agreements on digitization must take into consideration French government policy on the subject. The policy was that all questions related to the digitization of French language works must be addressed within the framework of a governmental policy that required the involvement of authors, publishers and the Ministry of Culture, within the framework of the government's information technology initiative called "Investments in the Future." The Minister indicated that the government wanted Google Inc. to collaborate with "great [French] national institutions like *La Bibliothéque Nationale de France*" (The French National Library) in its digitization activities.[69] The policy of the Ministry of Culture and Communication was that French *patrimoine écrit* (written cultural heritage) was too important to be left to an American global information and communication technology company, Google, to exploit as it saw fit, within the context of its purely commercial linguistic capitalist logic.

Google hoped that its agreement with Hachette would serve as a model of collaboration between its French subsidiary, *Google Recherche de Livres*, and the principal actors in the French intellectual property and culture industries. That turned out to be the case because a few months later, Google signed another agreement with French publisher, la Martinière, a company that holds extensive intellectual property rights in many out-of-print books. The Google Recherche de Livres-la Martinière agreement covered the digitization and marketing, in the form of eBooks, of out-of-print books whose copyright was held by la Martinière. The company also had the option of selling its works on Google eBooks. This agreement essentially ended legal actions that la Martinière had initiated against Google in 2006 for digitizing its books without consent.

In order to win over a skeptical French public, Google stated that its agreements with French publishers were aimed at giving a second life to out-of-print books and to make "the immense French cultural heritage" available to the French reading public for the benefit of authors, publishers and readers.[70] Nevertheless, Google's agreements with Hachette Livre and la Martinière did not end the American company's problems in France. Three other companies: Gallimard, Flammarion and Albin Michel sued Google France and Google, Inc. for intellectual property infringement through unauthorized digitization of thousands of books to which they held copyrights. If the two agreements are anything to go by, it looks like Google will ultimately settle with these three publishers.

Comparative Analysis and Conclusion

The United States and France have brought the Internet within the ambit of their respective exceptional regulatory logics. Each country regulates intellectual property—that family of intangible rights conferred on authors and inventors under the law by different national and international regimes—within the framework of its particular exceptionalist ideology.[71] Implementation of the Google digital Books initiative in the United State and France provided an opportunity to analyze how the intellectual property regimes of both countries handled the digitization and transfer of books from real space to cyberspace. In the United States, the federal government intervened to protect the public interest in the class action suit against Google by ensuring that the settlement complied with class action, copyright, and antitrust law.[72] When the Amended Settlement Agreement (ASA) was put before the United States District Court for the Southern District of New York, the DOJ filed a statement with the court to the effect that the ASA had class action, copyright, and antitrust issues.[73] This is one of the reasons why the court refused to certify the ASA. The United States government did not intervene in the name of the protection of national cultural interests. It did not insist that the Library of Congress be involved in the digitization deal with Google. It was mostly concerned with copyright, free market, and competition issues.

Things were different in France. The French government was not amused when Google Books created a French subsidiary, *Google Livres*, and commenced digitizing French language books for the French market. As we saw earlier, France is a centralized cultural state in which the government and the cultural elite have, from time immemorial, set the cultural policy of the country. The French state had, since the sixteenth century, created an institution, *la Bibliothèque Nationale de France* (the French National Library) whose mission was to gather "*toute la mémoire du monde*" (all the world's memory).

The French government, true to its "dirigistic" role as the driving force of all things cultural, clearly saw Google's proposed universal library as a threat to the culturalized global memory of the French national imaginary. Minister of Culture and Communication, Frédéric Mitterrand promptly set in motion a process of French governmental control of the digitization French written culture. Mitterrand initiated, and ensured that the *Syndicat national de l'édition* (National Publishers' Syndicate), the trade group of the French publishing industry, *la Société des gens de letters de France* (the Society of Men of Letters of France), the well-known writers' association, and *la Bibliothèque nationale de France* (the French National Library), would sign a framework agreement on the digitization of out-of-print [French] books. On the occasion of the signature of the agreement in February 2011, Frédéric Mitterrand stated that framework was the French response to Google's plan to digitize all the books in the world. He said French government involvement in the digitization of French written culture would ensure that French intellectual property values, including moral rights would be respected in the digital environment. Therefore, government-directed digitization was:

> . . . *une garantie pour la transmission d'un patrimoine et d'une mémoire commune. . . . Au regard de la stratégie de Google, cette initiative est une réponse, une voie française sur le terrain de la numérisation des oeuvres*

> *écrites. Le livre numérique est aujourd'hui la « nouvelle frontière » de l'édition ; il sera demain un horizon partagé et un outil culturel diffusé. l'ambition numérique est l'un des outils permettant à la diversité culturelle de s'exprimer pleinement. . . . la France se doit non seulement d'être présente, mais également d'être exemplaire sur les valeurs qu'elle veut promouvoir et sur lesquelles elle s'est engagée sur le plan international.*[74]
>
> . . . A guarantee of the transmission of a heritage and a common memory. . . . In view of the strategy of Google, this initiative is a response, a French pathway to the digitization of written works. The digital book is today the "new frontier" of publishing; tomorrow it will be a shared horizon and a diffused cultural tool. The digital ambition is one of the tools that ensure cultural diversity. . . . France must not only be present, but it must also be an example of the values which she wishes to promote and to which she is engaged at the international level.

In France governmentalization of digitization was driven by a desire to protect French written culture. Google convinced sections of the French publishing industry and the French government that its French subsidiary, *Google Recherche de Livres* (Google Book Search) could be the protector and preserver of French national cultural memory. Influential sections of the French intellectual property and governmental establishments agreed, for cultural exceptionalist reasons. While this was tantamount to sacrilege in the eyes of sections of the French elite, the decision was a pragmatic one. It still came as a surprise when two giants of the French publishing industry dropped their strident opposition to *Google* and its perceived encroachment on their intellectual property rights and cultural heritage, with the blessing of the French government. Ultimately, governmentalization of digitization in France did not become an insurmountable obstacle to Google's market-driven, advertiser-funded universal library. The French government and had apparently learned from past unsuccessful attempts to resist the Internet and its innovative technologies. The Minister of Culture opted to work with Google in order to have a modicum of control over the digitization process of French books. By allowing Google Recherche de Livres to collaborate with *la Bibliothèque nationale de France* (the French National Library) in digitizing French national cultural memory, France ensured that there would be a French language component in Google's proposed universal library.

Conclusion

This chapter was concerned with the legalization and bureaucratization of Google's Library Project initiative and Google Book Search in the United States and France. It addressed the question of what happens when the idea of a universal digital, online library created and controlled by Google Inc., a global, information and communication technology company based in the

United States, comes face to face with the highly proprietary, exceptional copyright regime of the United States and the equally exceptional, bureaucratized, intellectual property regime of France. It was found that Google's initiative to digitize and transfer all published books in existence from their moorings in the physical, geographic spaces of libraries and archives in real space to the dematerialized sphere of cyberspace, in line with its "search" business model, has the potential to fulfill the ancient human dream of collecting, systematically cataloguing and archiving all human knowledge under "one roof." However, the universal, dematerialized scope of the project meant that it flew in the face of entrenched, intellectual property regimes, cultures, and interests in several countries. The United States and France are the most prominent countries in which these conflicts have taken place. Confronted with the exceptionalist, utilitarian, incentive-driven copyright regime of the United States, Google Books first "harvested" the low-hanging "fruit" of works in the public domain. It subsequently cut deals with major public libraries in several parts of the world to digitize their collections. In response to the legal roadblocks erected by authors, publishers, copyright holders, and Google's American competitors over so-called unclaimed "orphan works" and other issues, Google decided to settle.

Though the United States District Court for the Southern District of New York ruled that the Amended Settlement Agreement between Google and its adversaries did not meet the class action standard of "fair, adequate, and reasonable" set forth in Rule 23(e) of the Federal Rules of Civil Procedure, the conflict could be settled through a combination of Congressional action on "orphan works"—the main bone of contention—and compromises on the part of the parties on the other issues. Thought Congress had addressed the Orphan Works problem through the Preservation of Orphan Works Act, by adding orphan works to the list of works exempt from limitations on uses by libraries and archives, this act does not cover mass commercial digitizing and space shifting of the type carried out by Google Books and its subsidiaries around the world.[75]

Google's idea of digitizing all published works in the world and creating a universal, searchable library based on its highly successful "search" business model, also crashed head on with the exceptional, author-centered French intellectual property regime whose objective is to create equality of arms between powerless authors and powerful publishers. Despite losing legal battles in French courts over digitization of French books, *Google Recherche de Livres*, the French subsidiary of Google Books signed protocol agreements with major French publishers, Hachette Livre and *La Martinière* that paved the way for the digitization of tens of thousands of French language books. The agreements were possible because of the French government's involvement in the digitization debate. In effect, as the policy maker and driver of French national culture, the Ministry of Information and Communication indicated that it wanted the *Bibliothèque nationale de France* (the National Library of France), the repository of French literary culture, to be involved in the digitization process. The French government realized that fighting against Google was tantamount to swimming against the tide of technological innovation. In effect, the French government and industry had, from the 1960s, lost battle after information technology battle against IBM, the Internet, Apple Computer and its gamut of innovations, Microsoft, and so on. By working with Google—and Microsoft—rather than against them, the French government has been able to retain a modicum of control over the digitization of its national literary culture.

The role of the French government in setting national book digitization policy, and getting Google and its French partners to include provisions in their agreements stipulating that they would work with the French National Library in the digitization process, can be contrasted with the role of the United States government in the class action suit, the *Authors' Guild v. Google*. Since this class action settlement was the most complex and most extensive settlement of its kind in the history of the United States, the federal government intervened to protect the public interest in the Settlement and Amended Settlement Agreement by ensuring that the settlement complied with class action, copyright, and antitrust law.[76] When the parties to the dispute came up with the Amended Settlement Agreement, the United States Department of Justice (DOJ) continued to play the role of facilitator. When the Amended Settlement Agreement (ASA) was put before the United States District Court for the Southern District of New York, the DOJ again filed a statement with the court to the effect that the ASA still had class action, copyright, and antitrust issues.[77] This is one of the reasons why the court refused to certify the ASA. The United States government did not intervene to protect national cultural interests or insist that the Library of Congress be involved in the digitization deal with Google. It was mostly concerned with copyright, free market, and competition issues. The approach of the United States government toward Google's Digital Books initiative focused mostly on the copyright and antitrust ramifications of the digitization initiative, while the French government was concerned with the intellectual property and cultural heritage implications of the digitization of French books. The postures of both countries were consonant with their respective exceptionalist intellectual property regimes.

This chapter demonstrates that despite its universal ambitions, Google has come to terms with the fact that even in the age of interconnected communication and cyberspace, geography is not history. The company has wisely concluded that in order to expand its search business model to books, and in the process create its market-based universal digital library, it must mold its business decision and aspirations to suit the exceptionalist intellectual property regimes of the United States and France.

The agreements between *Google Recherche de Livres*, *Hachette Livre*, and *La Martinière*, demonstrate that compromise is possible even in the most hostile cultural environments. Google concluded that in order to create its market-based universal digital library, it must mold its business decisions and aspirations to suit the intellectual property regimes of the countries where it does business.

NOTES

1. "In the beginning was the Word and the Word was with God and the Word was God." St. John 1.1 (King James Version) (1611).
2. See Les Réseaux Sociaux et la Loi (Social Media and the Law), La Lettre du Conseil Superieur de l'Audiovisuel (CSA) No. 250 (Letter No. 250 of the Superior Council on Audiovisual Affairs) 7 (June 2011). Available at: http://www.csa.fr/Etudes-et-publications/La-Lettre-du-CSA/La-Lettre-du-CSA-n-250 (Ironically, the CSA has Facebook and Twitter pages to which one can link through the logos of both social media but not their names).
3. France is not the only nation involved in a war of words. See Baradan Kuppusamy, Can Christians say 'Allah'? In Malaysia, Muslims say No. Time, January 8, 2010. Available at: http://www.time.com/time/world/article/0,8599,1952497,00.html (Reporting that in 2010, the Malaysian High Court ruled that the Malaysian government has violated the right of freedom of speech and expression of Christians when it banned them from using the Arabic word for God, Allah, in their Malay language Bible and other Christian literature).
4. See Harvard Film Archive, Alain Resnais and the Enigmatic Art of Memory (2010). Describing Resnais' 1956 documentary of the French National Library, (la Bibliothèque nationale), Toute la mémoire du monde (All the World's Memory) Available at: http://hcl.harvard.edu/hfa/films/2010janmar/resnais.html
5. See Denis Diderot, et al., The Encyclopedia vii (Nelly S. Hoyt and Thomas Cassirer) (Trans.) (1965) (1765). Though the Encyclopédie was a celebrated achievement in human knowledge acquisition, it was not the first modern encyclopedia. The Académie française (French Academy) had published a dictionary in 1694, while Heinrich Zedler had published a sixty-volume encyclopedia, Grosses vollstandiges universal Lexikon aller Wissenschaften und Künste (Complete Universal Lexicon of All Sciences and Arts, 1732-1750).
6. See Neil Hume, Google Wins Landmark Australian Legal Case, The Financial Times, February 6, 2013. Available at: http://www.ft.com/intl/cms/s/0/4e27fa9c-7030-11e2-ab31-00144feab49a.html#axzz2KRgbNBvm
7. See e.g. KinderStart.com LLC v. Google, Inc., C 06-2057 JF (N.D. Cal. March 16, 2007).
8. See Frédéric Kaplan, Nos langues à l'heure du capitalisme linguistique (Our languages in the age of linguistic capitalism) (2012). Available at: http://www.internetactu.net/2012/04/06/nos-langues-a-lheure-du-capitalisme-linguistique/
9. See Yann Moulier Boutang, Le capitalisme cognitif : La Nouvelle Grande Transformation (Cognitive capitalism: The New Transformation) (2008).
10. http://www.google.com/about/corporate/company/ (Last visited June 23, 2011).
11. Sony Corporation of America, Inc., v. Universal City Studios, Inc. 464 U.S.417, 430, 432. (1984) (quoting Twentieth Century Music Corp. v. Aiken, 422 U.S. 151, 156 (1975).
12. A&M Records, Inc. v. Napster, Inc., 114 F. Supp. 2d 896 (N.D. Cal. 2000).
13. Art. II, Berne Convention for the Protection of Literary and Artistic Works (Paris Text, 1971).
14. Copyright Act of 1976 (as amended), 17 U.S.C. §102 (1976).
15. Sony Corporation of America, Inc., v. Universal City Studios, Inc. 464 U.S. 417, 430, 432. (1984) quoting Twentieth Century Music Corp. v. Aiken, 422 U.S. 151, 156 (1975).
16. "Exceptionalism." Dictionary.com Unabridged (v 1.1). Random House, Inc. (2009). Dictionary.comhttp://dictionary.reference.com/browse/exceptionalism.

17. See generally, Michael Ignatieff, Introduction: American Exceptionalism and Human Rights. In American Exceptionalism And Human Rights, Michael Ignatieff (Ed.) 26 (2005). See also Jacques Rigaud, L'exception Culturelle: Culture Et Pouvoir Sous La Ve République (The Cultural Exception: Culture And Power Under The Fifth Republic) 26-27 (1994).

18. See Pierre Legrand, The Same and the Different, in Pierre Legrand & Roderick Munday (eds.) Comparative Legal Studies: Traditions And Transitions 240, 261 (2003).

19. See Bernard Miège, The Capitalization Of Cultural Production 136 (1989).

20. See David L. Lange And H. Jefferson Powell, No Law: Intellectual Property in the Image of an Absolute First Amendment 171 (Stanford Univ. Press 2009).

21. See Orin S. Kerr, Applying the Fourth Amendment to the Internet: A General Approach, 62 Stanford Law Review 1005 (2010).

22. See Eldred v. Ashcroft, 537 U.S. 186, 221 (2003).

23. *Harper & Row Publishers, Inc. v. Nation Enterprises, Inc.*, 471 U.S. 539, 560 (1985).

24. Copyright Act of 1976 (as amended) 17 U.S.C §107.

25. Campbell v. Acuff-Rose Music, 510 U.S. 569 (1994) (Holding that a commercially successful music parody was fair use); see also Warner Brothers, Inc. v. American Broadcasting Corporation, Inc., 720 F.2d 231, 242 (2d. Cir. 1983) (Holding that a TV show parodying Superman is protected); and also Elsmere Music, Inc. v. National broadcasting Company, Inc., 623 F.2d. 252, 253 (2d. Cir. 1980) (Holding that Saturday Night Life TV parody of the song, "I Love New York" was protected).

26. See David L. Lange And H. Jefferson Powell, No Law: Intellectual Property in the Image of an Absolute First Amendment 52 (Stanford Univ. Press 2009).

27. See Pierre Rosanvallon, Le Modèle Politique Français (The French Political Model) 109, 112 (2004).

28. See Edgar Morin, Le trou noir de la laicité (The black hole of secularism) 58 LE DÉBAT 38 (1990) (describing France as a "Catho-laique" (Catho-secular) country.

29. See Richard Kuissel, Seducing The French: The Dilemma Of Americanization 131 (1993).

30. See François Azouvi, Descartes in Pierre Nora (Ed.) Lieux De Mémoire (Tome 3) (Sites Of Memory) (Vol. III) 4475 (Paris: Quarto Gallimard (1997) (Stating that French Philosopher, Réné Descartes is a "site of memory").

31. See Claude M'Barali (MC Solaar) et autres v. Société Media Consulting et autres Claude M'Barali (MC Solaar and others v. Société Media Consulting and others) Tribunal de Grande Instance de Paris, 3ème chambre, 2ème section (High Court of Paris) Jugement du 7 novembre (Judgment of November 7, 2003). Available athttp://www.legalis.net/jurisprudence-decision.php3?id_article=1032Last visited September 28, 2008. (Holding that a media company which licensed a musician's compositions from a copyright clearing house for use as cell phone ring tones violated the musician's moral rights because the musician did not authorize modification of the quality of the music).

32. Art. L. 121-1 Code de la propriété intellectuelle (Intellectual Property Code), version consolidée au 22 décembre 2007. (Consolidated version). Available at LegiFrance,http://www.legifrance.gouv.fr/affichCode.do?cidTexte=LEGITEXT000006069414&dateTexte=2008030 (Last visited March 24, 2008).

33. See Le Petit Robert 1) Dictionnaire Alphabetique et Analogique de la Langue Francaise (Petit Robert, Alphabetic and Analogic Dictionary of the French Language) 133 (1992).

34. See William Roeder, The Doctrine of Moral Right: A Study in the Law of Artists, Authors and Creators, 53 Harv.L.Rev. 554, 555 (1940).

35. See Art. L111-1, Code de le propriété intellectuelle (Intellectual Property Code), as amended by Law n°2006-961 of August 1, 2006 - art. 31 J.O of 3rd August 2006. Available at:http://www.legifrance.gouv.fr/affichCode.do?cidTexte=LEGITEXT000006069414&date Texte=2009010(Translation by the author).

36. See Claude M'Barali (MC Solaar et autres v. Société Media Consulting et autres) Claude M'Barali (MC Solaar and others v. Société Media Consulting and others) Tribunal de Grande Instance de Paris, 3ème chambre, 2ème section (High Court of Paris) Jugement du novembre 7 (Judgment of November 7, 2003). Available at: http://www.legalis.net/jurisprudence-decision.php3?id_article=1032 (Holding that a media company which licensed a

musician's compositions from a copyright clearing house for use as cell phone ring tones violated the musician's moral rights because the musician did not authorize modification of the quality of the music).

37. See Google Inc., Google Books Library Project—An Enhanced Card Catalog of the World's Books. Available at: http://books.google.com/googlebooks/library.html

38. http://www.google.com/about/corporate/company/ (Last visited June 23, 2011).

39. 17 U.S.C. §107.

40. For further information on how crawler algorithm works see Mark Levene, An Introduction To Search Engines And Navigation 82-83 (2010).

41. See David L. Lange and H. Jefferson Powell, No Law: Intellectual Property In The Image Of An Absolute First Amendment 171 (2009).

42. See Marc Tessier, Rapport sur la numérisation du patrimoine écrit (Report on the digitization of Written [Cultural] Heritage) (2010). Available at: http://www.culture.gouv.fr/layout/set/frame/searchproxy/proxy

43. See Ministère de Culture et de la Communication (Ministry of Culture and Communication), Appel à partenariat pour la numérisation et la valorisation des collections de la Bibliothèque nationale de France (BnF) (Call for partnership in the digitization and valorization of the collections of the National Library of France (2011). Available at: http://www.culture.gouv.fr/mcc/Espace-Presse/Dossiers-de-presse.

44. Kathleen Kubis. Page by Page, Click by Click, Users Are Reading Away Privacy Rights. 13 Vand. J. Ent. & Tech. L. 217 (2010).

45. Anick Jesdanun. Google Book Project: Digital-Age Test of Copyright Law. USA TODAY, September 18, 2005 (Online), available at: http://www.usatoday.com/tech/products/services/2005-09-18-google-copyright_x.htm

46. See Claude M'Barali (MC Solaar et autres v. Société Media Consulting et autres) Claude M'Barali (MC Solaar and others v. Société Media Consulting and others) Tribunal de Grande Instance de Paris, 3ème chambre, 2ème section (High Court of Paris) Jugement du novembre 7 (Judgment of November 7, 2003). Available at: http://www.legalis.net/jurisprudence-decision.php3?id_article=1032(Holding that a media company which licensed a musician's compositions from a copyright clearing house for use as cell phone ring tones violated the musician's moral rights because the musician did not authorize modification of the quality of the music).

47. U.S. CONSTITUTION, Art. 1 §8, cl.8.

48. See Complaint filed against Google. The Authors Guild Inc. v. Google Inc., CV 8136 (S.D.N.Y. Sep. 20, 2005). The McGraw Hills Co. v. Google Inc. CV8881 (S.D.N.Y. Oct. 19, 2005). See the copy of the original class notice at http://www.googlebooksettlement.com/r/view_notice (Last visited June 11, 2011).

49. See the *Authors' Guild et al. v. Google, Inc.*, 05 Civ. 8136 (DC) (S.D.N.Y, 2011) at 46.

50. Amended Settlement Agreement, p. 32.

51. See the *Authors' Guild et al. v. Google, Inc.*, 05 Civ. 8136 (DC) (S.D.N.Y, 2011) at 12.

52. See the *Authors' Guild et al. v. Google, Inc.*, 05 Civ. 8136 (DC) (S.D.N.Y, 2011).

53. See the *Authors' Guild et al. v. Google, Inc.*, 05 Civ. 8136 (DC) (S.D.N.Y, 2011).

54. See the *Authors' Guild et al. v. Google, Inc.*, 05 Civ. 8136 (DC) (S.D.N.Y, 2011).

55. See Id. quoting at 14 (Joel A. v. Giuliani, 218 F. 3d 132, 138 (2d Cir. 2000)).

56. See the *Authors' Guild et al. v. Google, Inc.*, 05 Civ. 8136 (DC) (S.D.N.Y, 2011) at 21-22.

57. See the *Authors' Guild et al. v. Google, Inc.*, 05 Civ. 8136 (DC) (S.D.N.Y, 2011) (S.D.N.Y, 2011) at 46.

58. See the *Authors Guild et al. v. Google, Inc.*, 05 Civ. 8136, American Society of Media Photographers, No. 10 Civ. 2977(DC) (S.D.N.Y. May 31, 2012).

59. Editions du Seuil and Others v. Google Inc. and Google France, Tribunal de grande instance de Paris 3ème chambre, 2ème section Jugement du 18 décembre 2009, at: http://www.legalis.net/spip.php?page=jurisprudence-decision&id_article=2812

60. Code de la Propriété Intellectuelle (Intellectual Property Code), sections L 122-1, L 122-2, L 122-3, L 122-4, L 122-5 and L 713-2 [Fr.] at: http://www.legifrance.gouv.fr/affichCode.do?cidTexte=LEGITEXT000006069414

61. 17 U.S.C §107 (1976).

62. See Article L. 122-5-3 of the Code de la propriété intellectuelle (Intellectual Property Code) [Fr.] at: http://www.legifrance.gouv.fr/affichCode.do?cidTexte=LEGITEXT000006069414

63. See Code de la Propriété Intellectuelle [C. Pro. Intell.] (Fr.), at: http://www.legifrance.gouv.fr/html/codes_traduits/cpialtext.htm (demonstrating that France does not have a fair use doctrine).

64. Tribunal de grande instance [TGI] [ordinary court of original jurisdiction] Paris, Nov. 13, 1998, juris. obs. M. Montfaur (Fr.).

65. Id.

66. Editions du Seuil and Others v. Google Inc. and Google France, Tribunal de grande instance de Paris 3ème chambre, 2ème section Jugement du 18 décembre 2009 at: http://www.legalis.net/spip.php?page=jurisprudence-decision&id_article=2812

67. Article L 122-5(3), Intellectual Property Code.

68. See France 24, Le petit séisme produit par l'accord Google-Hachette Livre (The Little Earthquake Produced by the Google-Hachette Livre Agreement). November 22, 2010. Available at:http://www.france24.com/fr/20101122-seisme-protocole-accord-google-hachette-livre-sne-etats-unis-edition-bookeen-numerisation.

69. See Ministère de la Culture et de la Communication, Communiqué de presse, Protocole d'accord conclu entre Google et Hachette Livre (Ministry of Culture and Communication, Press Release, Protocol Agreement between Google and Hachette Livre). November 17, 2010. Available at: http://www.culture.gouv.fr./mcc/Espace-Presse/Communiques/Protocole-d-accord-conclu-entre-Google-et-Hachette-Livre

70. See Google France, at: Un nouveau chapitre pour Google et le monde de l'édition (A new chapter for Google and the Publishing Industry). August 25, 2011. Available at: http://googlefrance.blogspot.com/2011/08/un-nouveau-chapitre-pour-google-et-le.html#!/2011/08/un-nouveau-chapitre-pour-google-et-le.html

71. See David L. Lange And H. Jefferson Powell, No Law: Intellectual Property in the Image of an Absolute First Amendment 171 (Stanford Univ. Press 2009).

72. See United States Department of Justice, "Statement of Interest of the United States of America Regarding Proposed Class Settlement (2009)" Available at: www.justice.gov/atr/cases/f250100/250180.pdf

73. See United States Department of Justice, Justice Department Submits Views on Amended Google Book Search Settlement (2010) Available at: http://www.justice.gov/opa/pr/2010/February/10-opa-128.html

74. See Ministère de la Culture et de la Communication (Ministry of Culture and Communication), Discours de Frédéric Mitterrand, ministre de la Culture et de la Communication, prononcé à l'occasion de la signature de l'accordcadre sur la numérisation et l'exploitation des livres indisponibles du XXème siècle (Speech of Frédéric Mitterrand, Minister of Culture and Communication, on the occasion of the signature of the Framework agreement on the digitization and Management of out-of-print books of the twentieth century), February 1st, 2011. Available at: http://www.culture.gouv.fr/mcc/Espace-Presse/Discours/Discours-de-Frederic-Mitterrand-ministre-de-la-Culture-et-de-la-Communication-prononce-a-l-occasion-de-la-signature-de-l-accordcadre-sur-la-numerisation-et-l-exploitation-des-livres-indisponibles-du-XXeme-siecle

75. Title IV, Family Entertainment and Copyright Act of 2005, Pub. L. No. 109-9, 119 Stat. 218, 226 amending section 108(i), title 17, United States Code (April 27, 2005).

76. See United States Department of Justice, "Statement of Interest of the United States of America Regarding Proposed Class Settlement (2009)" Available at: www.justice.gov/atr/cases/f250100/250180.pdf.

77. See United States Department of Justice, Justice Department Submits Views on Amended Google Book Search Settlement (2010) Available at: http://www.justice.gov/opa/pr/2010/February/10-opa-128.html

Chapter Nine

Intellectual Property, Freedom of Expression, and the Internet "Gripe Sites" Phenomenon in the United States and France

Innovations in the field of information and communication technology have transformed the media into dynamic forces that seem to change at lightning speed, while the law, which is designed to ensure that these new technologies do not compromise or negate human rights and freedoms, seems to move at snail's pace. This means that the law is perpetually struggling to keep up with the latest technological developments and the communicative rights issues they spawn. Furthermore, as innovations have transformed the Internet into a virtual platform for global information, social, commercial, cultural, educational, and entertainment activities. The challenge has been how to transfer culture-specific logics of governance (governmentalities) that were designed for the old media in real space, to the new media in the dematerialized digital world of cyberspace. Most governments have transferred universal values and laws of freedom of expression designed for the traditional media in real space *mutatis mutandis* to the Internet. However, many others—and they range from North Korea to Saudi Arabia—have imposed draconian controls on the infrastructures, networks, and content of those portions of the Internet that exist within their national territories.

This dilemma has been especially acute in the field of intellectual property law and policy. One of the main challenges national governments, supranational and international organizations face is to how to apply intellectual property rules and regulations designed to protect tangible intellectual property assets in real space, to the dematerialized, digital domain of cyberspace.[1]

This is an especially acute problem given the tension between the exclusive right of reproduction conferred on authors and copyright holders under national and international intellectual property law, and the right of freedom of expression—the right to copy protected intellectual property works for purposes of criticism, parody, news reporting and the like—embodied in fair use exception woven into the fabric of copyright regimes. This problem is especially acute in the area of Internet domain names. In the computer networking contexts, domain names are numerical strings or addresses used to identify specific websites on the Internet.[2] They are usually memorable names or alphanumeric strings that are attached to numerically addressed Internet addresses or web pages. In the age of the commercial Internet, domain names are virtually mnemonic devices, memory shortcut for famous registered trademarks, service marks and personal names.

Aim of the Chapter

The Internet has complicated intellectual property law in the area of trademarks, and service marks. This is especially true in the United States and France, where there is a conflicting public interest in intellectual property protection as well as a robust culture of freedom of expression through parody. The aim of this chapter is to compare and contrast French and American application of intellectual property laws designed for real space, to the dematerialized world of cyberspace, using as a comparative case study, regulation of parody websites in the United States and France. The focus is on the conflict between protection of trademarks and service marks under intellectual property law, and the subversive appropriation of these trademarks or service marks by parody or "gripe" websites for purposes of criticism, within the framework of constitutional guarantees of freedom of expression in the United States and France. The chapter therefore explores how both countries resolve the tension between intellectual property law and freedom of expression in real space and cyberspace in the issue area of "gripe" websites.

Parody, "Gripe" Websites, Trademark Law, and Cyberspace

Trademark parody is the mocking imitation or mimicry of a registered trademark, service mark, or trade name for purposes of social or political criticism. It is a variant of "parody," the literary genre that originated from the Greek word *parodeia;* a term that means: "a burlesque song or poem that is sung beside, or in a mock relation to another."[3] In modern usage, a parody is a work of literary or visual communication that mimics and pokes fun at an existing, often well-known original work, for purposes of social or political criticism.[4] The Oxford English Dictionary defines parody as "[a] composition . . . in which the characteristic turns of thought and phrase in an author or class of authors are imitated in such a way as to make them appear ridiculous, especially by applying them to ludicrously inappropriate subjects."[5]

One of the main purposes of parody is "to ridicule sacred verities and prevailing mores."[6] In cyberspace, parody takes diverse forms. The most common form being the website parody or "gripe" website. This is a digital form of criticism that is the vehicle for the anonymous expression of dissatisfaction with individuals, corporate, institutional, and governmental entities, public officials, or public figures. Depending on the work, trademark, or corporate entity that is mimicked and ridiculed, parodies can be humorous, contentious or controversial. Parody is a literary device that has become a fundamental instrument of freedom of speech and expression in modern democratic societies. As we shall see later, both the United States and France recognize parody under their respective intellectual property law regimes. This chapter is concerned with application of parody to trademark and service marks on the Internet.

"Gripe" or "complaint" websites are Internet websites set up to critique, ridicule, or mock individuals, geographic locations, politicians, corporations or other entities, for one reason or another. These websites are often created by anonymous critics, parodists, political opponents of politicians or disgruntled persons or groups, and are used as platforms for posting uncomplimentary information and caustic criticism. These anonymous critics usually register Internet domain names containing a target institution or corporate entity's trademark, trade name or service mark, plus a pejorative epithet like "sucks."[7] The United States Court of Appeals for the 9th Circuit has stated that "gripe" websites involve noncommercial use of a trademark as the domain name of a website for purposes of "consumer commentary about the products and services represented by the mark."[8] "Gripe" websites have become the village green of the information age. Indeed, these sites are global electronic communication phenomena that have taken intellectual property law, and specifically, trademark law, to uncharted regulatory territory. "Gripe" websites have caused freedom of expression and intellectual property controversies in the United States and France.

This chapter analyzes how the exceptional intellectual property and freedom of expression regimes of the United States and France manage the tension between intellectual property and freedom of expression on the Internet, using as a comparative case study, application of intellectual property rules and regulations designed for the offline environment, to the phenomenon of trademark parody, complaint or "gripe" websites on the Internet. Specifically, the paper is concerned with how the intellectual property law regimes of the United States and France regulate the unauthorized appropriation, and registration as domain names, of well-known corporate trademarks, trade names or service marks for purposes of parody, satire, and social criticism. In short, this chapter is a comparative endeavor that attempts to show

how the United States and France reconcile freedom of expression and trademark law in cyberspace. The comparative study was carried out within the framework of American exceptionalism and *l'exception française* (the French exception) two functionally equivalent constructs that describe and explain American and French self-described specificity in matters of politics, culture, and intellectual property.

American Exceptionalism, Intellectual Property Law, and Freedom of Expression

The main premise of this volume is that the United States and France are self-described "exceptional" countries that stress the specificity of their political regimes and cultural systems. As a consequence, they define themselves in opposition to each other and to the rest of the world. We have seen that American exceptionalism and the French exception are functionally equivalent theoretical constructs that define the ideological postures of the United States and France on the international political stage.[9] These ideological logics infuse the intellectual law and policy regimes of both countries. Both the United States and France regulate intellectual property—that family of intangible rights conferred on authors and inventors under the law by different national and international regimes—within the framework of their specific exceptionalist ideologies.[10] Both countries also balance the competing public interest in intellectual property and freedom of expression within the framework of their respective exceptionalist ideologies.

In this chapter, I deploy American exceptionalism and *l'exception française* (the French exception) as functionally equivalent units of analysis for the study of the application of intellectual property law designed for real space, to the phenomenon of trademark parody and gripe or complaint websites on the Internet.[11] The main tenet of American exceptionalism is that American laws and democratic system are unique and unparalleled in human history.[12] American exceptionalism manifests itself in two forms in the field of intellectual property: 1) American copyright jurisprudence is grounded in a unique incentive philosophy set forth in the Constitution of the United States, and 2) the copyright regime is inextricably linked to the country's exceptional First Amendment freedom of speech regime.[13] This linkage is realized through a series of limitations on exclusive copyright monopolies. American exceptionalism in copyright is therefore expressed in utilitarian terms. The Constitution of the United States stipulates that the function of copyright is: "To promote the progress of science and useful arts, by securing for limited times to authors and inventors the exclusive right to their respective writings and discoveries."[14] Though American law recognizes authors as repositories of copyright,[15] the underlying principle of copyright law is not so much validation of the institution of the author, his or her rights, and his or her role in the cultural life of society—as is the case in France—but the benefits that ultimately accrue to society from granting copyright protection to creative persons.[16]

Lange and Powell suggest that by its very nature and subject matter, copyright touches on, and coexists rather harmoniously with expression protected by the First Amendment: "the stuff from which intellectual property interests are spun is also the stuff of First Amendment interests."[17] In order to underline the link between copyright and freedom of expression, the Supreme Court of the United States has held that the Framers of the Constitution intended for copyright to serve as "the engine of free expression."[18] Therefore, American copyright law has substantial exceptionalist free speech dimensions that are expressed in terms of fair use. This fundamental principle is set forth in the fair use provision of the Copyright Act, which states in part:

> the fair use of a copyrighted work, including such use by reproduction in copies or phono records or by any other means specified by that section, for purposes such as criticism, comment, news reporting, teaching (including multiple copies for classroom use), scholarship, or research, is not an infringement of copyright.[19]

Fair use is also an affirmative defense in circumstances where existing works are appropriated for purposes of creating new, transformative, critical works. Parody, which serves as a vehicle for politico-social criticism, is a notable category of transformative works protected by the First Amendment.[20] This is one domain in which freedom of speech clearly takes precedence over exclusive copyright. However, fair use is only an affirmative defense available to the fair use claimant who is accused of infringing on exclusive intellectual property rights.[21] Nevertheless, fair use is an important limitation on the copyright monopoly.[22] Federal courts have transposed this fair use test in a rather fluid manner to the online environment as they have settled the legal disputes that followed in the wake of the emergence of "gripe" websites and trademark parodies on the Internet.

The French Exception, Intellectual Property Law, and Positive Restrictions on Authors' Rights

We saw in chapter 4 that the French exception also refers to the declaration of linguistic, cultural, political, economic, social, intellectual, cinematic, artistic, fashion, and culinary difference between France and the rest of the world.[23] *L'exception culturelle* grants the French government a greater role and responsibility for the management, and promotion of all things cultural—from architecture, culinary and circus arts, to viticulture and *haute couture* (high fashion)—than in any other democratic country.[24] Thus, the

French cultural exception can be expressed as centralized governmental management of culture and the means of cultural production. Furthermore, under French law, intellectual property consists of two rights: a patrimonial (economic) right and an intangible, inalienable moral right. Moral right is a rather "romantic" right of personality that seeks to protect the unique expression and metaphysical cachet or "mental signature" of the author on his or her work. Thus, authors retain moral rights in their works even after economic rights in the work have been exercised and these rights have been transferred to third parties pursuant to contracts.[25] The law also protects the intangible imprint or "cachet" of specific French geographic regions on agricultural, dairy, and other products from these spaces.

In France, intellectual property is therefore viewed as an important component of the French cultural exception because intellectual property is an instrument for the protection and promotion of French culture. French exceptionalism in intellectual property law is thus expressed in terms of a heightened recognition of the importance of cultural and knowledge production—specific agricultural and artistic products—as well as recognition and celebration of authors of *œuvres d'esprit* (works of the mind) as cultural icons and institutions. France has historically conceptualized works of the mind as *lieux de mémoire culturel* (sites of cultural memory) as well as propagators of national cultural heritage.[26]

However, even in France, where culture is inseparable from politics, the author is king, but intellectual property protection is not absolute. The *Code de propriété intellectuelle* (Intellectual Property Code) contains a parody exception intended to promote freedom of expression. This exception stipulates that:

> *La parodie suppose l'intention d'amuser sans nuire.*[27]
>
> Parody supposes an intention to amuse without causing harm.

Intellectual property law grants protection to parodies that cause no harm. Though the word "harm" is vague and undefined, the presumption is that parody can cause moral, emotional and economic harms. As we shall see later, in suits involving trademark parody and "gripe" websites, the maliciousness and negative impact of each parody is a factor that is taken into consideration when courts determine whether a parody is legal or not. Furthermore, though France does not have the equivalent of the fair use doctrine of the United States, French law allows limited copying of protected works for private use, as well as for purposes of news reporting and commentary.

Applying Intellectual Property Law to Cyberspace: Domain Names and Cybersquatting in the United States and France

As the Internet diffused to all parts of the world in the 1990s, and the so-called dot.com bubble (irrational and speculative investment and touting of all things related to the Internet) began, web pages on the Internet increased exponentially. All kinds of businesses, educational institutions, and individuals rushed to stake a claim in a very valuable virtual real estate—a domain name on the network of computer networks. The trademarks or service marks of companies served as the alphanumeric strings of their domain names became their virtual shop front, the gateway to their goods and services. Domain names therefore have an inbuilt intellectual property element. Legitimate domain name registrants own the intellectual property rights in their domains since they merely transfer their trademarks or service marks from real space to cyberspace.

However, many domain name "brokers" saw cyberspace as a new El Dorado, the place to make money by registering domain names willy-nilly. They rushed to register most of the words in the English language, for purposes of reselling these words to businesses that were interested in transitioning to the brave new world of cyberspace. These brokers also registered online, without authorization, the trademarks and service marks that well-known corporate entities had registered in real space under trademark law. The aim of these unauthorized domain name registrations was to traffic in the names—offer to resell to the rightful owners of trademarks in real space, their very own trademarks that had been registered as domain names in cyberspace without authorization.

The practice of unauthorized registration of trademarks and service marks as domain names on the Internet for purposes of trafficking in them came to be known as cybersquatting. This practice became so widespread that in 1999, Congress passed the Anticybersquatting Consumer Protection Act (ACPA).[28] Congress essentially amended and expanded the reach of title 15 of the U.S. Code, which forbids false designations of the origins of goods, false descriptions of goods and services, and dilution of trademarks and service marks, to the Internet. The Anti-Cybersquatting Consumer Protection Act defines cybersquatting as the practice whereby an individual or business entity, acting in bad faith:

> registers, traffics in, or uses a domain name that . . . is identical or confusingly similar to [a] mark . . . or in the case of a famous mark that is famous at the time of registration of the domain name, is identical or confusingly similar to or dilutive of that mark.[29]

The ACPA prescribes civil liability for abusive registration of famous trademarks and famous personal names as domain names.[30] The intent of the

ACPA was to eradicate fraudulent practices that impaired electronic commerce on the fledgling Internet. The ACPA granted trademark and service mark holders a course of action against cyberpirates (domain name traffickers). These are persons or companies who, in bad faith, registered the domain names of corporate entities and individuals for purposes of offering the domain name for resale to the rightful owner of the trademark or service mark.

The ACPA enumerates indicators of bad faith, and exceptions for legitimate, unauthorized fair use of domain names. In other words, the ACPA has an exceptionalist First Amendment component, which includes the fair use of trademarks and service marks for purposes of parody.[31] The fair use provisions of trademark law are affirmative defenses available to defendants in trademark infringement and dilution cases in real space. The exceptions to the exclusivity of trademarks and service marks set forth in this provision of the law were especially relevant when a parodist registered a specific corporation's trademark, trade name, or service mark without permission for purposes of spoofing, parodying or criticizing that company. The fair use provisions of trademark law have been transferred to cyberspace, a domain that is rife with parody domain names. The parody domain name is often distinguished from the original trademark or service mark by a pejorative epithet—a prefix or a suffix such as "x Corporation sucks.com"—that is intended to critique the corporate subject of the parody and portray it in a negative light.

Intellectual Property Law and Cybersquatting in France

As the dot.com bubble diffused to the rest of the world, the problem of cybersquatting also diffused to France. Under French law, cybersquatting is regulated under a number of legal codes. Since France does not have a statute equivalent to the Anti-Cybersquatting Consumer Protection Act of 1999 that regulates illegal trafficking in domain names, French courts essentially throw the book at alleged cybersquatters. They transfer intellectual property, business, and other laws designed for real space, to the exigencies of cyberspace. A good example occurred in the case *SNCF v. Benoît* M., a case in which a former intern at the state-owned, *Société Nationale des Chemins de fer Français* (French National Railway Corporation, SNCF), registered the domain name Sncf-usa.com and proceeded to offer rail travel-related services. The French government sued *Benoît* M for trademark infringement through violation of the registered trademark of the state transport corporation.

The issue before the High Court of Paris was whether *Benoît* M's registration of Scnf-usa.com violated the registered trademark of state-owned transportation company, SNCF, and whether the domain name, Sncf-usa.com was confusingly similar to Scnf.com, the famous trademark of SNCF. The court ruled in the affirmative, stating that the domain name, Sncf-usa.com, violated provisions of the Intellectual Property Code, specifically, article L.

713-5, which prescribes civil penalties for infringement of famous trademarks. Additionally, the court ruled that *Benoît* M's domain name constituted dilution of a domain name in violation of article 1382 of the Civil Code. The court also ruled that registration of Scnf-usa.com also constituted a violation of the deceptive business practices provisions of the Consumption Code (articles L. 121-1 I 1 and 1112), which proscribe fraudulent business practices that cause a likelihood of confusion between trademarks, service marks or symbols.[32] Clearly the High Court of Paris used several legal provisions designed to regulate intellectual property and business activities in real space, to resolve this trademark dispute over cybersquatting.

The Problem of Parody or "Gripe" Websites

Legislators and courts in the United States and France had to resolve not only disputes involving the unauthorized, abusive registration and trafficking in domain names, they also had to resolve disputes involving trademark and service mark parodies. The reality is that as business entities moved online, so did their critics. A new type of challenge therefore confronted intellectual property regimes around the world: mimicry of registered, famous and not so famous trademarks, trade names and service marks for purposes of parody and criticism. These so-called gripe, complaint, or commentary websites generally have no direct or indirect commercial or economic motive or incentive. As noted above, one of the first hurdles national, supranational and international intellectual property regimes faced was applying trademark and service mark rules and regulations designed to address conflicts in real space to the unprecedented realities of cyberspace. Courts also had to settle the acute tension between intellectual property protection and the exercise of constitutionally protected freedom of expression exercised by the creators of these parody or "gripe" websites.[33] The courts had to distinguish between illegally registered domain names that violated the intellectual property rights of legitimate trademark and service mark holders, and domain names that were set up to criticize, parody, or "gripe" about the owners of the trade or service mark appropriated and subverted. How the judicial authorities of the United States and France distinguish legal parody or "gripe" websites that represent an exercise of the right of freedom of expression, from illegal cybersquatting sites is influenced by their respective exceptionalist conceptualizations of freedom of expression and intellectual property. This section analyzes the law of trademark parody and "gripe" websites in the United States and France to illustrate the differences between the two regimes.

Trademark Parody, "Gripe" Websites, and Freedom of Expression in the United States

In the United States, the phenomenon of trademark parody has traditionally involved the clash of two important societal interests—avoidance of a likelihood of consumer confusion between identical products, and the public interest in freedom of expression guaranteed under the First Amendment. Therefore, in order to walk this legal tight rope, "[a] parody must convey two simultaneous—and contradictory—messages: that it is the original, but also that it is not the original and is instead a parody."[34] With the advent of "gripe" websites, the problem became a clash between maintaining trademark integrity (for purposes of avoiding consumer/audience confusion) and the public interest in freedom of expression, including the freedom to criticize corporations. In effect, the First Amendment protects parody, satire, sarcasm, and other forms of critical communication in real space and cyberspace, while the Lanham Act (Trademark Act) protects trademarks. This is a collective term that includes trademarks, service marks, trade names, and trade dress—the look and feel of a product—that identify the sources of products and services, and distinguish them from other products and services.[35] The following cases illustrate how American courts have handled the clash between trademark integrity and freedom of expression in the form of trademark parody and gripe or complaint websites. These cases demonstrate that in the clash between trademark protection and trademark or domain name parodies on the Internet, First Amendment protection for domain name or parody websites (so-called "gripe sites") depends on 1) the use or non-use of pejorative epithets in the domain name, parody or "gripe" websites, and 2) the presence or absence of a commercial element in the domain name/trademark parody or "gripe" website.

The Contours of Trademark Parody on the Internet: PETA v. Doughney

People for the Ethical Treatment of Animals (PETA) is a militant, animal rights group that uses various forms of symbolic speech and expressive conduct to protest perceived animal abuse in entertainment and public spectacles ranging from bullfighting to dog shows. PETA also protests the use of animal products in consumer goods ranging from fur coats to hamburgers. PETA's militant activities—and their subsequent controversies—are often drenched in irony. In 1993, the California Milk Processor Board, a nonprofit dairy marketing board funded by California dairy processors, and administered by the California Department of Food and Agriculture, launched the phenomenally successful, mass-mediated, "Got Milk," advertising campaign that featured celebrities sporting "milk moustaches." The aim of the campaign was to promote the consumption of milk in California. The campaign soon went national. In 2000, PETA launched a "Got Beer?" counter-campaign that parodied the "Got Milk?" campaign, on college campuses. The counter-campaign suggesting that beer was healthier than milk. After protests by Mothers Against Drunk Driving (MADD), PETA dropped the "Got Beer?" campaign and opted for a new campaign, "Milk Sucks," that was aimed at discouraging the consumption of milk. The ad claimed that milk caused cancer, heart attacks and strokes.

PETA's militant actions and parodies of existing media content soon led to counter-parodies against PETA. In *PETA v. Doughney*.[36] The defendant, Doughney, registered the domain name peta.org and created a parody website called "People Eating Tasty Animals," a spoof of the acronym and name of People for the Ethical Treatment of Animals. The parody website claimed that it was set up for "those who enjoy eating meat, wearing fur and leather, hunting, and the fruits of scientific research."[37] Additionally, the website contained links to organizations that dealt in meat, fur, leather, hunting, and animal research. Doughney, who was also a domain name broker, offered to sell PETA the peta.org domain name. PETA sued Doughney for service mark infringement, unfair competition, service mark dilution, and cybersquatting under federal and state law. In his defense, Doughney claimed that the website was a parody of PETA that was protected by the First Amendment.

The issue before the court was whether Doughney's website was a parody that was protected under the First Amendment. The United States District Court for the Eastern District of Virginia rejected the parody defense and found Doughney liable for cybersquatting under the Anticybersquatting Consumer Protection Act ("ACPA"). The court ordered Doughney to relinquish the PETA domain name, and transfer its registration to PETA. It also granted PETA summary judgment.[38] Doughney appealed to the United States Court of Appeals for the Fourth Circuit. The issues before the court were whether PETA possessed the mark in question; whether Doughney used the mark; whether Doughney's use of the mark occurred "in commerce"; whether Doughney used the mark "in connection with the sale, offering for sale, distribution, or advertising" of goods or services; and whether Doughney used the mark in a manner likely to confuse consumers.[39] The Fourth Circuit answered all the questions in the affirmative, noting that Doughney's website provided links to more than thirty commercial operations offering goods and services. By providing links to these commercial operations and entities, Doughney's use of PETA's mark was "in connection with" the sale of goods or services. The court affirmed the lower court's ruling which had stated that Doughney's PETA website was not a parody in the legal sense of the term. As a result, the website amounted to illegal cybersquatting.[40]

Ironically, while this legal action was going on, PETA launched another "Got Milk?" parody campaign. In 2000, when New York Mayor, Rudolf Giuliani announced that he had been diagnosed with prostate cancer, PETA used the mayor's image in huge billboards that parodied the "Got Milk?" advertising campaign. In the billboards, an image of Mayor Giuliani sporting a milk moustache is presented above the question, "Got Prostate Cancer?" The ad made a direct causal connection between milk consumption and cancer. After a hue and cry from the dairy industry, and a threat of legal action by Giuliani, PETA withdrew the campaign and apologized to the mayor.[41] However, if Giuliani had sued for libel, his chances of winning the case would have been slim since parody is protected speech under the First Amendment. Furthermore, since he is a public figure, he would have had to prove the *New York Times* actual malice. Meaning that he would have had to show that at the time PETA erected the billboard, it knew the information on it was false or it exhibited a reckless disregard for whether the material was true of false.[42] That is a subjective standard that is virtually impossible for public officials and public figures to meet.

Planned Parenthood Federation of America v. Bucci

One of the first "gripe" website cases to be heard by an American court was *Planned Parenthood Federation of America v. Bucci*.[43] This controversy was sparked by Richard Bucci, host of "Catholic Radio," an active participant in the anti-abortion movement. Bucci targeted Planned Parenthood Federation of America, Inc., a women's health clinic and abortion services provider, for derision, strident and caustic criticism. On August 28, 1996, Bucci registered the domain name "plannedparenthood.com," and created a website whose address was "www.plannedparenthood.com," without the authorization of the trademark owner, Bucci's home page displayed a book entitled, "The Cost of Abortion," by an anti-abortion campaigner, Lawrence Roberge. In addition, Bucci used the plannedparenthood.com website to solicit funds to promote his anti-abortion activities. Bucci had essentially appropriated the trademark of Planned Parenthood Federation of America, Inc., registered it as a domain name, and created a website that disseminated messages that denounced the activities of the trademark holder.

Planned Parenthood Federation of America, Inc., filed suit in the U.S. District Court for the Southern District of New York, seeking a temporary injunction against Richard Bucci's use of the domain name "plannedparenthood.com," and against using the Internet address, "www.plannedparenthood.com." Bucci claimed that the Lanham Act was not applicable to his website because it was non-commercial. He argued that his use of Planned Parenthood's trademark was protected from injunction because it was a parody that was protected by the First Amendment.

The issues before the court were whether Bucci's unauthorized appropriation and use of the trademark of Planned Parenthood Federation of America was commercial; whether the use was protected by the First Amendment;

and whether there was a likelihood of confusion between Planned Parenthood's official website and Bucci's unauthorized website. The court held that Bucci's activities were commercial in nature. As such, they were subject to the Lanham Act, which regulates matters of intellectual property in trade names, trademark dilution through tarnishment, as well as the likelihood of confusion between famous trademarks and counterfeit trademarks. The court held that Bucci's First Amendment parody defense was not persuasive. The website did not meet the standard of a parody, the court ruled, since it was neither ironic nor sarcastic. The court held that: "plaintiff has not sought, in any way, to restrain defendant from speech that criticizes Planned Parenthood or its mission, or that discusses defendant's beliefs regarding reproduction, family, and religion. The sole purpose of the Court's inquiry has been to determine whether the use of the "Planned Parenthood" mark as defendant's domain name and home page address constitutes an infringement of plaintiff's trademark."[44]

The court held that under the First Amendment, Bucci could legitimately use the Planned Parenthood trademark only as part of a communicative message, not to identify the source of a product. Since Bucci's use of the term "Planned Parenthood," was not part of a communicative message, it amounted to an infringement of Planned Parenthood's trademark, and so was not protected by the First Amendment. The appropriation was therefore subject to the Lanham Act. The court held: "When another's trademark . . . is used without permission for the purpose of source identification, the trademark law generally prevails over the First Amendment."[45] The practical result of this case was that Bucci was held liable for infringing the trademark of Planned Parenthood, Inc., because the website he created with the Planned Parenthood trademark was not a true "gripe" website.

Archdiocese of St. Louis and Papal Visit 1999, St. Louis v. Internet Entertainment Group, Inc.

On the occasion of Pope John Paul II's visit to St. Louis, Missouri, in 1999, the Roman Catholic Archdiocese of St. Louis set up the following websites: "Papal Visit 1999," "Pastoral Visit," "1999 Papal Visit Official Commemorative Items," and "Papal Visit 1999, St. Louis." In order to capitalize on the visit, an adult pornography company, Internet Entertainment Group, registered the following Internet domain names: "papalvisit1999.com," and "papalvisit.com," and linked them to a sexually explicit Internet site such that persons who clicked on these fake "Papalvisit" websites ended up in the adult pornography sites. While these fake papal websites may have been implicit statements about the Catholic Church or the Vatican, the Archdiocese of St. Louis was not amused. The Archdiocese sued Internet Entertainment Group at the United States District Court for the Eastern District of

Missouri for trademark dilution by tarnishment under the Lanham Act and the Missouri anti-dilution statute.[46] The issue before the federal district court was whether Internet Entertainment Group, Inc. had diluted the trademark of the Archdiocese through tarnishment.[47] The court ruled in the affirmative, holding that the Archdiocese had demonstrated that it would succeed in proving that Internet Entertainment Group, Inc. had been diluting the distinctiveness of its marks by using the name "papal visit 1999" and its derivatives to identify a sexually explicit Internet site. The court concluded that:

> Internet Entertainment Group's use of the Archdiocese's common law trademarks and trade name as its Internet domain names tarnished the Archdiocese's family of marks by associating them with adult entertainment venues that are inconsistent with the positive and spiritually uplifting image plaintiffs have striven to create and maintain in connection with the Pope's upcoming visit to St. Louis.[48]

The court ordered Internet Entertainment Inc. to stop using the common law trademarks and trade name of the Archdiocese as its Internet domain names, as well as in connection with the advertising, operation or maintenance of any Internet website, including any sexually explicit material or other pornographic content. The court also ordered Internet Entertainment Inc. to request the Internet registry, Network Solutions, Inc., to deregister the infringing domain names: "papalvisit1999.com" and "papalvisit.com."[49] This was a clear case of misappropriation that did not even have a parody pretense.

Taubman Co. v. Webfeats & Mishkoff

Taubman v. WebFeats involved the unauthorized registration of a company's name as as a domain name and website. When Mishkoff, a web developer heard that the Taubman Company, was building a shopping mall called "The Shops at Willow Bend," in Plano, Texas, he registered the domain name, "shopsatwillowbend.com," and created an "unofficial," Internet "fan" website lauding the new shopping mall.[50] The mall developer, the Taubman Company, brought legal action against Mishkoff and his company, Webfeats, at the United States District Court for the Eastern District of Michigan, claiming that the domain name, shopsatwillowbend.com, infringed on its trademark, in violation of the Lanham (Trademark) Act.[51] Taubman asked the court for a preliminary injunction and a surrender of the domain name "shopsatwillowbend.com." In response, Mishkoff registered five "complaint" or "gripe" domain names: taubmansucks.com, shopsatwillowbendsucks.com, theshopsatwillowbendsucks.com, willowbendmallsucks.com, and willowbendsucks.com, to protest what he considered frivolous and vexatious harassment by Taubman and its lawyers. The district court granted the preliminary injunction against Mishkoff and ordered him to cease and desist from using the domain name shopsatwillowbend.com, as well as the five gripe domain names he had registered.

Mishkoff appealed to the United States Court of Appeals for the 6th Circuit. The issue before the court was whether Mishkoff's complaint domain names amounted to appropriation of Taubman's registered trademark for commercial purposes, thereby bringing the domain names in dispute within the ambit of the Lanham Act, and relegating them to the category of commercial speech deserving of less First Amendment protection than non-commercial speech. The court held that since Mishkoff's websites had no commercial links that could be described as being "in connection with the advertising" or sale of competing goods and services, the Lanham Act did not come into play. Furthermore, the court said that Mishkoff's websites did not lead to confusion between Taubman's official website and Mishkoff's unofficial websites. Mishkoff's gripe domains did not therefore violate the Lanham Act. The court concluded that:

> The rooftops of our past have evolved into the Internet domain names of our present. We find that Mishkoff's use of Taubman's mark in the domain name "taubmansucks.com" is purely an exhibition of Free Speech, and the Lanham Act is not invoked. And although economic damage might be an intended effect of Mishkoff's expression, the First Amendment protects critical commentary when there is no confusion as to source, even when it involves the criticism of a business . . . [t]he domain name is a type of public expression, no different in scope than a billboard or a pulpit, and Mishkoff has a First Amendment right to express his opinion about Taubman, and as long as his speech is not commercially misleading, the Lanham Act cannot be summoned to prevent it.[52]

In dissolving the preliminary injunctions that barred Mishkoff from using the domain name, "shopsatwillowbend.com," and the five gripe domain names he had registered, the United States Court of Appeals for the Sixth Circuit essentially held that enjoining the gripe domain names amounted to a prior restraint under the First Amendment since Mishkoff was not directly competing against Taubman in the commercial marketplace. In this case the Fourth Circuit Court of Appeals fluidly transferred free speech principles from real space to cyberspace when it analogized Internet domain names as the rooftops, bully pulpits, and soapboxes of the age of digital online communication.

Jews for Jesus v. Brodsky

Jews for Jesus, Inc., is an international religious organization whose mission is to: "make the messiahship of Jesus an unavoidable issue to our Jewish people worldwide."[53] This posture has earned the organization many enemies. In *Jews for Jesus v. Brodsky*,[54] a militant opponent of Jews for Jesus,

Steven Brodsky, registered the following "bogus" Jews for Jesus Internet website for purposes of "deceit and trickery:" "jewsforjesus.org." The aim of the registration was to deliberately divert Internet users from the official website of Jews for Jesus to the bogus Internet website created by Brodsky. Jews for Jesus sued Brodsky seeking a preliminary injunction forbidding Brodsky from diluting its registered trademark, unfairly competing with Jews for Jesus, and falsely designating, describing and representing the origin of the bogus Jews for Jesus website. Brodsky claimed that his criticism of Jews for Jesus was protected by the First Amendment. The issue before the court was whether Jews for Jesus was likely to succeed on its claims of trademark infringement, unfair competition and false designation of origin because the use of the federally-registered mark, "Jews for Jesus" in the domain name created by Brodsky was a false designation of the origin of the website that was likely to cause confusion.[55] The court answered in the affirmative and ruled that Brodsky used the registered trademark of Jews for Jesus to lure individuals to his Internet site where he made disparaging statements about the organization. His website then referred these individuals, to another Internet website that was also critical of Jews for Jesus. The court said Brodsky's Internet site was designed to be a false designation of the origin of his website. Relying on *Planned Parenthood v. Bucci,* the court ruled that "[s]uch conduct amounts to "blurring" and "tarnishment" of the mark and the name of the Plaintiff Organization."[56] The court granted a preliminary injunction after it determined that Jews for Jesus would likely succeed on the merits.

Statutory Developments: The Exceptional First Amendment Principles of the Trademark Dilution Revision Act of 2006 (TDRA)

The law of trademark parody has evolved since the 1990s as American courts have sought to keep abreast of rapidly evolving technologies and the unprecedented uses to which they are being put. As the cases analyzed above demonstrate, courts tended to almost reflexively frown on unauthorized, unorthodox uses and abuses of trademarks on the Internet. In 2006, Congress passed a number of statutes that defined the contours of intellectual property law on the Internet and added a modicum of predictability to Internet law. As we saw above, the Anticybersquatting Consumer Protection Act of 1999 (ACPA) clarified trademark law and allowed a parody exception in it for the first time. This brought trademark law within the ambit of the First Amendment. Henceforth, parody domain name and "gripe" website registrants run the risk of infringing registered trademarks only if they have a bad faith commercial intent.

The Trademark Dilution Revision Act of 2006 (TDRA) expanded the scope of First Amendment protections in the area of trademarks. The TDRA granted owners of famous trademarks the right to assert claims of infringement based on a likelihood of dilution by blurring (impairment of the distinctiveness of a famous mark through associating it with a similar mark that is prejudicial to its distinctiveness) or dilution by tarnishment (associating a famous mark or trade name with a similar but less reputable mark such that the association harms the reputation of the famous mark).[57] Another salient feature of the TDRA is that it clarified the intersection between the First Amendment and trademark law by enumerating and reinforcing the fair use exceptions in this crucial issue area of intellectual property law. The fair use provisions of the TDRA exclude from liability, the following categories of expression from dilution by blurring or dilution by tarnishment:

> (A) Any fair use, including a nominative or descriptive fair use, or facilitation of such fair use, of a famous mark by another person other than as a designation of source for the person's own goods or services, including use in connection with—
> (i) advertising or promotion that permits consumers to compare goods or services; or
> (ii) identifying and parodying, criticizing, or commenting upon the famous mark owner or the goods or services of the famous mark owner.
> (B) All forms of news reporting and news commentary.
> (C) Any noncommercial use of a mark.[58]

The TDRA's exceptions for fair use of famous trademarks expanded the exceptional First Amendment norms that Congress had inserted in trademark law. By so doing, it tilted the scales in favor of freedom of expression by providing an expansive breathing room not only to obvious media activities like news reporting and news commentary, but also to Internet domain name and trademark parodies. The law also affects non-commercial, complaint or "gripe" websites whose stock-in-trade is political and social commentary. The law also broadly allows for "any non-commercial use of a mark." This law has turned out to be a boon to bloggers, parody websites, Internet satirists, commentators, and content aggregators. It has also been a boon to Internet Service Providers, Internet Hosts like Youtube, and social network services providers like Facebook, Myspace, Twitter, Linkdin, Instagram, Tumbler, and so on.

Trademark Parody, Freedom of Expression, and "Gripe" Websites under French Intellectual Property Law

France has one of the most extensive, and most restrictive trademark regime in the world. This is because the French cultural exception is woven into the very fabric of the French intellectual property regime. The French *Conseil Constitutionnel* (Constitutional Council), the institution whose task is to review the constitutionality of all bills before they are enacted into law, has reaffirmed the idea that intellectual property rights are part of the sacred human rights enumerated in articles 2 and 17 of the Declaration of the Rights of Man and of the Citizen of 1789.[59] This historic French political and cultural intellectual property logic is reflected in the nation's culture of gastronomic nomenclature under which product names and marks have national cultural significance, and cultural products have intellectual property qualities that make them sites of national and regional cultural memory.

The centralized, state-driven, French intellectual property law regime covers a wide swathe of economic and cultural activity ranging from the products of the seasonal *industrie de haute couture* (high fashion industry),[60] to the highly complex regime of *appellations d'origine controlées* (protected designations of origin) under which the French government grants certification to French geographical indications (trade names and trademarks associated with wines and food products identified with specific French regions). The highly complex French regime of gastronomic nomenclature—the *appellations d'origine controlées*—which originated in the sixteenth century, grants proprietary rights to geographical nomenclature for wines, ciders, cheeses, butters, meats, vegetables, honey, and other agricultural product names, and protects them from misuse, imitation, and dilution.[61] Indeed, wines and their *appellations d'origine controlées* are so much a part of French culture that they have a quasi-religious function. French historian, Philippe Roger suggests that in France, "wine is communion and civilization."[62] Additionally, under the French intellectual property regime, the government certifies *obtentions végétales* (new plant varieties).[63]

Protected Designations of Origin (*Appellations d'origine controlées*) in Cyberspace

A question that arises is how this highly restrictive, centralized, sixteenth-century bureaucratized regime of gastronomic nomenclature and protected designations of origin squares with the realities of modern global business practices, as well as freedom of expression in real space, and especially in cyberspace. This section looks at how French courts have applied intellectual property provisions designed to regulate parody in real space have been applied to the new reality of cyberspace. The transformation of the Internet into an interconnected, global multi-communication platform that did not have a specific "geometric" center of control posed serious challenges to several domains of the French politico-cultural and legal regime.[64] While these challenges have been mostly in the issue area of media content regulation and freedom of expression in real space, the French intellectual property regime has also had to deal with challenges posed by the Internet. As early as 1997, a French court applied the real space law of counterfeiting to an Internet company, Eurovirtuel, that had registered the domain name, www.saint-tropez.com. The name "Saint Tropez" was the protected geographical nomenclature of the famous resort commune of Saint Tropez, on the French Riviera. The court held that by registering the protected geographical nomenclature, "Saint-Tropez," without the authorization of the commune, Eurovirtuel was liable for violating the proprietary rights of the commune through counterfeiting (defined in the intellectual property code as the identical or quasi-identical reproduction of another's mark through a fraudulent imitation that is close enough to the original mark to cause confusion).[65] Eurovirtuel's argument that there was no likelihood of confusion between the top-level domain names that it had registered: *saint-tropez.com, saint tropez.org,* and the national domain *saint-tropez.fr,* that was the registered intellectual property of the commune, was unpersuasive. This case demonstrated that in the field of intellectual property, French courts made no distinction between real space and cyberspace.

One of the challenges French courts have had to face is how to balance freedom of expression and intellectual property on the Internet. Though the French *Code de propriété intellectuelle* (Intellectual Property Code) does not have American-style "fair use" *per se*, a number of provisions in the code, taken together, provide functionally equivalent fair use exceptions that promote freedom of expression in the content-based regulatory context of French media law. Exceptions to intellectual property monopolies include reproductions for purposes of criticism, polemics, pedagogy, news reporting, academic research, political, administrative, judicial and academic pronouncements, teaching, parody, pastiches and caricature.[66] Nevertheless, the parody or pastiche exception is rather narrow:

> *La parodie suppose l'intention d'amuser sans nuire.*[67]
>
> Parody supposes an intention to amuse without causing harm.

Though the word *nuire* (harm) is vague and undefined, the law presumes that parody can cause moral, emotional and economic harm. In trademark law, *marques de fabrique* (trademarks or service marks) include patronymic names, pseudonyms, and geographic names. There are no fair use exceptions in French trademark law.[68] A number of French court decisions have applied trademark and parody law designed for real space, to the reality of online parodies of trademarks or service marks. The following decisions are illustrative.

RATP v. Laurent M. & Valentin Lacambre

We saw in *Commune de Saint-Tropez v. Eurovirtuel* that French courts started applying intellectual property law designed for real space to the realities of the Internet in a rather mechanical fashion. Trademark parody cases posed legal challenges that required a more subtle approach because these cases represented a clash between intellectual property and freedom of expression, in a country that has a long history and tradition of caricature and satire. The first trademark parody challenge the French legal system faced involved the public transport company, *la Régie autonome des transports parisiens,* RATP (The Autonomous Public Transport Corporation of Paris).[69] RATP registered a stylized, semi-figurative version of its logo as its trademark. The public transportation company created a Website, *Ratp.fr*, based on the French country domain, *.fr*, to promote its services. A critic of the public transporter, Laurent M. created a complaint website, *ratp.org,* which reproduced and parodied RATP's registered trademarks, and criticized what the author described as the "dysfunctional services" of the state company. The website contained an image and text which suggested that RATP employees consumed alcoholic beverages while on the job.

RATP sued Laurent M., the creator of the "gripe" website at the *Tribunal de grande instance de Paris* (the High Court of Paris), for trademark counterfeiting and blamable product disparagement or trade libel under provisions of the intellectual property code. The public transporter asked the court to ban the critical website and fine its owner. Laurent M., the gripe site creator, claimed that his website was set up to parody the "dysfunctional services" provided Parisians by the public transporter. He said he had no intention of harming the company. As such, he claimed, his website fell within the scope of the parody exception set forth in the intellectual property code. He suggested that his website was not a counterfeit site because it had no commercial purpose, and that his criticisms of the company were permissible noncommercial satirical expressions.

The issue before the court was whether Laurent M's web page, *ratp.org,* amounted to trademark counterfeiting that resulted in a *dénigrement fautif* (blamable disparagement) of RATP. The court answered in the affirmative. The judge ruled that Laurent M's website fell foul of the intellectual property code, which forbids: "the reproduction, use or apposition [addition of a word or phrase next to a trademark, service mark or trade name for purposes of modifying its meaning] of a trademark even with the words 'formula, way, system, imitation, genre, method' as well as usage of a reproduced trademark for products and services that are identical to those designated in the trademark registration."[70] The court proceeded to distinguish author's right law from trademark law. It said that the parody exception recognized in author's rights law (the French equivalent of copyright) was not a valid defense in trademark law because author's rights law was different from trademark law. The court held that trademarks are essentially designed to accompany a product or service with "an intrinsic commercial value capable of being harmed by illicit use." The court concluded that though the information on the "gripe" website was mostly satirical, the statements about the alcohol consumption of the RATP personnel and the deformation of the company's trademark constituted blamable denigration or disparagement. The court ordered Laurent M. to cease and desist from his illegal activities and imposed a substantial fine and costs.[71] This was the first case in which a French court directly applied intellectual property law to a cyberspace parody case. It is noteworthy that the court found the defendant responsible for adding text to the logo of the company. Interestingly, the court distinguished author's rights law, where parody was recognized, from trademark law, where it is not recognized.

One.Tel v. Nicolas M. and Trademark Parody

A notorious French case that dealt with trademark parody on the Internet was *One.Tel v. Nicolas M.*[72] In 2000, One.Tel, an Australian telecommunications company which had a French subsidiary, Sarl *One.Tel,* sued Nicolas M., for publishing a complaint website, "OneTelFuck," that criticized One.Tel and its website, "onetel.fr." Nicolas M. stated in the welcome page of "OneTelFuck" that the website was a parody website dedicated to criticizing One.Tel. In its legal action, One.Tel claimed that the website violated its registered trademark, in contravention of article L713-2 of the French Intellectual Property Code. This section of the Code criminalizes, the unauthorized "reproduction, use, or apposition [addition of a word or phrase next to a trademark, service mark or trade name for purposes of modifying its meaning] . . . the suppression or modification of a regularly affixed mark."[73] This provision of the law thus forbids imitations or additions that are prejudicial to trademarks. Nicolas raised the parody defense in response to the allegations leveled against him. The issue before the court was whether the parody exception set forth in the Intellectual Property Code was applicable to trademark parody. The High Court of Paris held that it was not. The court ruled that parody was not applicable to trademark law. The court stated that though the welcome page of "OneTelFuck.fr" claimed that the website was a parody, a close examination of its content revealed that many of its highly indecent and malevolent statements were of a sexual nature, and were intended to harm One.Tel and disparage its services. Therefore, the parody exception set forth in article L.122-5 of the Intellectual Property Code was not applicable. The court issued a restraining order against publication and hosting of "OneTelFuck.fr." and fined Nicolas M. 100,000 French Francs (about $25,000) for intellectual property violation.[74] This case clearly reiterated French judicial hostility towards trademark parodies, as well as "gripe" websites that have pejorative epithets.

Olivier Malnuit, Réseau Voltaire v. Compagnie Gervais Danone and the Danone Group

Despite the refusal of French courts to recognize a parody exception in trademark law, French citizens continued to test the applicability of the parody exception to "gripe" websites. French journalist, Olivier Malnuit, and his organization, *Réseau Voltaire pour la liberté d'expression* (The Voltaire Network for Freedom of Expression), created two "gripe" websites, "*j eboycottedanone.com*" and "*jeboycottedanone.net*" (I boycott Danone.com and I boycott Danone.net) that were critical of French multi-national yogurt and soft-drinks manufacturer, *Compagnie Gervais Danone*. *Réseau Voltaire* and Malnuit's website, "jeboycottedanone.net," presented information on a corporate restructuring plan proposed by Danone, and started a highly critical discussion forum that highlighted the negative impact of the restructuring plan on Danone workers. The websites also called for a boycott of Danone products. *Compagnie Gervais Danone* sued Malnuit and *Réseau Voltaire* claiming that the complaint or "gripe" websites constituted counterfeiting of its trademarks, contrary to a provision of the Intellectual Property Code, which criminalized the reproduction, use, apposition or imitation of a mark or use of an imitated mark for products and services similar to those of a legally registered trademark, "if there is a likelihood of confusion in the mind of the public."[75] *Compagnie Gervais Danone* further claimed that the websites in question disparaged the Danone Group of companies, and tarnished the registered trademarks of the *Compagnie Gervais Danone*.[76] Malnuit and the *Réseau Voltaire* advanced a freedom of expression defense, claiming that their complaint websites were constitutionally protected forms of speech.

The High Court of Paris was not persuaded. It ruled that Malnuit and the *Réseau Voltaire* had, through the two websites, committed acts of trademark counterfeiting against Compagnie Gervais Danone and the Danone Group of companies. The court ordered Malnuit and the *Réseau Voltaire* to pay damages to the plaintiff, and cease counterfeiting Danone's marks (this essentially meant taking down the complaint websites). Malnuit and the *Réseau Voltaire* appealed to the Paris Court of Appeals. The issue before the court of appeals was whether the two websites, "jeboycottedanone.net," (I boycott Danone.net), and "*jeboycottedanone.com*" (I boycott Danone.com), were protected under French laws of freedom of expression. The Paris Court of Appeals said they were. The court reversed the decision of the High Court of Paris, and ruled that the websites were not expressly designed to promote the commercialization of products or services that competed with those of the Danone Group of companies.[77] The court held that the website had a purely polemical purpose that had nothing to do with [Danone's] business, and that reference to the registered trademark of the company "was necessary to explain the political and polemical nature of the campaign [against the restructuring], and contrary to the allegations of Danone Groupe and the Compagnie Gervais Danone, their products were neither disparaged nor targeted."[78]

The court said there was no likelihood of confusion on the part of the public between Danone's websites and the complaint websites in question. Danone could therefore not forbid the use and imitation [parody] of its trademark in a political and polemical context.[79] In this landmark case, for the first time, the Paris Court of Appeals applied freedom of expression law designed for real space to complaint websites in cyberspace. The court gave freedom of expression precedence over trademark law—at least in the area of politics and polemics—when it ruled that unauthorized registration and use of a trademark or service mark as a domain name may be justified under the constitutional protection of freedom of expression, on condition that the website in question be non-commercial in nature. That is, it must not promote competing products.

Escota v. Lycos, Lucent Technologies, & Nicolas Breil

While the Paris Court of Appeals enlarged the scope of freedom of expression on the Internet, in the same year, the *Tribunal de Grande Instance de Marseilles* (High Court of Marseilles) demonstrated that French complaint websites had, at best, a very narrow margin of maneuver in terms of the subject matter they are allowed to tackle. Nicolas Breil created a website, "www.multimania.com/escroca," that parodied "www.escota.com," the website and trademark of Escota, a French highway construction and toll collection company. Nicolas Breil's parody website "Escroca" was a clever play on the word *escroc*, French slang for "swindler or racketeer." The parody name, *Escroca,* had an uncanny resemblance—and sound—to the corporate trademark, Escota. Furthermore, Breil's Escroca parody website, www.multimania.com/escroca, had an identical look and feel as Escota's corporate website. In addition to suggestions of fraud, the parody website contained a number of gross, insulting, indecent and pornographic expressions directed at Escota and its employees.[80]

To complicate matters further, Breil's parody website was created largely in the offices of Lucent Technologies, France, the French subsidiary of the American multi-national telecommunications corporation, Lucent Technologies, Inc., where Breil was employed. Breil created the "gripe" website at his work place without the knowledge and approval of his employer. Escota sued Nicolas Breil, his Internet Service Provider, Lycos, and his employer, Lucent Technologies, in the High Court of Marseilles, claiming that the Escroca website constituted counterfeiting of intellectual property under the Intellectual Property Code, and disparagement under the defamation provisions of the Law of July 29, 1881 on Freedom of the Press. Escota further claimed that Lycos was responsible for hosting the objectionable website, and that Lucent Technologies, France, was responsible because the objectionable website had been created in a Lucent office, with equipment Lucent had put at the disposal of Breil.[81]

In his defense, Nicolas Breil claimed that his website was a humorous parody that was protected under the parody provision (article L122-5) of the Intellectual Property Code. He said the aim of the complaint website was to criticize the abuses of the highway construction, management, and toll collection company, and to expose its poor services to the public. The issue before the court was whether Nicholas Breil's Escroca "gripe" website was a protected parody. The court held that it was not, and ruled that Breil's reproduction of the trademark of Escota was so similar to the original that it was clearly an unauthorized "quasi-slavish reproduction of the trademark of Escota" that amounted to trademark counterfeiting. The court reasoned that the trademark parody defense advanced by Nicolas Breil was not persuasive in as much as "the imitation of the mark is not guided by an intention to amuse without causing harm but [it] was guided by hateful sentiments whose goal is to denigrate the company [Escota] and damage its reputation."[82] The court ordered Breil to pay the symbolic sum of 1 € (one Euro) in damages, ordered him to take down the offending website, and stop using Escota's trademark, or face a penalty of €1000 ($1,300) for every infringement ascertained.[83] The court reaffirmed the principle that the narrow parody exception set forth in the Intellectual Property Code, did not apply to malicious parodies in real space and cyberspace. Additionally, the court held Lucent Technologies, France, Breil's employer, vicariously liable under the Civil Code,[84] for providing its employee the technical means to create the objectionable satirical website, by not supervising what he did with official equipment. The Internet Service Provider, Lycos, was not held responsible for the content of the complaint website since it merely hosted the material.

On appeal, the *Cour d'appel d'Aix en Provence* (Court of Appeals of Aix en Provence) affirmed the ruling that the parody exception set forth in the Intellectual Property Code was applicable to author's rights (*droit d'auteur)* not to trademark law. The court said that even if the law of parody applied to trademark law, the intent to harm, sufficiently expressed in the objectionable gripe website, negates the pastiche or parody. The court also affirmed the lower court's ruling that Breil's website amounted to counterfeiting, and an imitation that had a likelihood of confusing the public. The court of appeals finally ordered Lucent Technologies and Breil to pay Escota the sum of €5000 ($6,500) each plus costs.[85] The escrota gripe website was ruled illegal because the subject matter was not overtly political, or polemical. The Court of Appeals of Aix en Provence essentially held that a gripe site whose intent was to harm the subject of its wrath was not protected under freedom of expression laws. Interestingly, the plaintiff was not required to show the harm caused by the parody.

The "Greenpeace affairs" and Trademark Parody: The Impact of European Policy Transfer and Legal Harmonization

So far, we have seen that from 1997 to 2003, French courts overwhelmingly rejected the parody defense in trademark parody and gripe website cases. There was one exception. Recognition of trademark parody as protected speech occurred only in *Danone*, a case with strident political, polemical, and class-based, anti-corporate ideology, consonant with the socialist orientation of the French state. Though two of the cases discussed above, *One.Tel*, and *Escota*, also involved corporations, the parodies involved were ruled illegal because of the blatantly indecent and pornographic nature of both websites. However, things took a different turn in two landmark cases, the so-called "*affaires Greenpeace*," (Greenpeace cases), namely, *Esso v. Greenpeace France,* and *Greenpeace France and Greenpeace New Zealand v. SPECIA*. In these cases, Greenpeace injected Euro-Communitarian freedom of expression claims into a French trademark parody case, leading to French judicial recognition of trademark parody and gripe websites as freedom of expression under European Community law.

As we saw above, the traditional parody standard in French intellectual property law is that to be legal, a parody must have a humorous intent that is unrelated to "an intent to harm" or injure the subject of the parody. Two parallel online trademark parody cases involving environmental protection groups—Greenpeace France and Greenpeace New Zealand—provided the French judiciary an opportunity to trace the contours of the law of parody in cyberspace, and in the process, resolve the tension between trademark parody and freedom of expression. The result was the transposition for the first time, of pan-European freedom of expression standards to French trademark parody law in general, and online trademark parody in particular.

The first of the two Greenpeace *affaires* was *Esso France v. Greenpeace France and Green Peace New Zealand.* This case was a parallel dispute—it erupted at the same time as the second case (discussed below)—that involved making a determination whether the time-honored general rules of parody could be applied to polemical, Internet-mediated trademark parody in the name of freedom of expression. The dispute in *Esso France v. Greenpeace France and Greenpeace New Zealand* (Greenpeace) arose over a parodic appropriation of "Esso," the international brand name and trademark of a subsidiary of the multi-national oil company, ExxonMobil. In effect, the defendant environmental protection organizations, Greenpeace France and Greenpeace New Zealand, launched an online denunciatory campaign against Esso from two websites: greenpeace.org, and "stopessofrance.org."

The groups claimed that the multinational oil company was using its financial muscle to sabotage implementation of the 1997 Kyoto Protocol of the United Nations Framework Convention on Climate Change. The Greenpeace campaign used dollar signs to deform and parody the trademark of the multinational company in its "STOP E$$O!" online campaign and urged the public to boycott the company's products.[86]

Esso France brought legal action against Greenpeace France and its Internet Service Provider, Internet.fr, at the *Tribunal de Grande Instance de Paris* (High Court of Paris) for trademark counterfeiting, an act criminalized by the French Intellectual Property Code.[87] Esso France asked the court to order Greenpeace to remove the distortions of its brand name from the Greenpeace website and from all its publications, and to hold Greenpeace liable for disparagement under Article 1382 of the French Civil Code.[88] In its defense, Greenpeace claimed that its online imitation of the trademarks of Esso was polemical, was done in parody, "unconnected to business interests," and was therefore protected freedom of expression.[89] The High Court of Paris did not find the Greenpeace argument persuasive. The court issued a preliminary injunction against the environmental organization.

On appeal, Greenpeace France injected European community freedom of expression law into the proceedings. In effect, under the procedural law of the Court of Justice of the European Communities, parties in legal disputes can invoke European community law to contest the validity of specific national rules of law that are being imposed on them as European Union residents. Litigants also have the right to challenge, as being contrary to a provision of European Union law, national rules of law that are being applied in their specific legal disputes. In such an eventuality, the national judge is required to issue a ruling on the challenge or refer the matter to the Court of Justice of the European Communities for its interpretation. The interpretation of the Court of Justice of the European Communities is binding on the referring national judge.[90]

Greenpeace France requested the *Cour d'appel de Paris* (Court of Appeals of Paris) to rule that it had not counterfeited the trademark of Esso, and subsidiarily, to refer the matter to the Court of Justice of the European Communities, for its interpretation of this matter, which touched on a European Union directive on freedom of expression. The Court of Appeals of Paris lifted the preliminary injunction against Greenpeace France and remanded the case to the High Court of Paris for a hearing on the merits. On remand, the issue before the High Court of Paris was whether the Greenpeace parody of Esso's trademark constituted trademark counterfeiting under the French Intellectual Property Code. The court held that it did not. The rationale for the decision was that the Greenpeace parody did not amount to trademark counterfeiting since the Greenpeace campaign was an environmental protection campaign, not a commercial campaign aimed at selling petroleum products, which were the stock-in-trade of Esso. The court ruled that the issue of a likelihood of confusion between the "products" of the two parties did not therefore arise.

The court concluded that though trademark law had no parody exception, the Greenpeace campaign did not disparage Esso's products and services and "did not exceed the limits of freedom of expression." The court said that imitation of a mark can be justified under the constitutional principle of freedom of expression as long as the public is not confused as to the identity of the author of the communication, and as long as the 'polemical usage' of the trademark was "unconnected to business matters."[91] In a *coup de théâtre* worthy of Molière, the court ordered the plaintiff, Esso, to pay the defendant, Greenpeace France, the sum of $2,600 plus costs. The higher freedom of expression standards of the European Communities clearly saved the day for Greenpeace in the light of the fact that in France, there is no parody exception in trademark law.

Greenpeace France and Green Peace New Zealand v. SPCEA

The second legal dispute involving the Greenpeace organization was *SPCEA v. Greenpeace*. This case also originated from the same online environmental protest campaign that led to the legal action undertaken by Esso. In effect, while Greenpeace France and Greenpeace New Zealand were protesting against Esso France, they ran a parallel online campaign of denunciation and complaints against La *Société de participations du commissariat à l'énergie atomique* (SPCEA), a joint-stock company of the French Atomic Energy Commission. The SPCEA did business in the nuclear industry under the commercial name of Areva. On their website, the Greenpeace groups denounced the nuclear industry and invited visitors to the website to sign a petition against the byproduct of the industry—radioactive waste. Additionally, Greenpeace reproduced the logo of Areva in the form of a pictogram of the symbol of death—a skull and cross bones—accompanied by the slogan "Stop Plutonium—*l'arrêt va de soi*" (Stopping it is self-evident). On the Greenpeace website, Areva's logo was also inscribed on a sickly-looking fish. In 2002, SPCEA, the parent company of Areva, sued Greenpeace France and its Internet hosting company for trademark counterfeiting, trademark imitation, and trademark dilution, in violation of Article 1382 of the Napoleonic Civil Code of 1804, which sets forth the general rule of French tort law. The general rule stipulates that anyone who, through his own fault, causes harm to another is required to pay damages to repair the harm done.[92] SPCEA claimed that the Greenpeace parody devalued the image and trademark of the company, and asked the *Tribunal de grande instance de Paris* (High Court of Paris) to ban the Internet-based, anti-Areva "caricature."

In its defense, Greenpeace France stated that its parody was protected expression under the Law of July 29, 1881 on Freedom of the Press, because it denounced the dangerous impact of the activities of Areva on the environment. The issue before the court was whether by associating Areva's trademark with the symbol of death, Greenpeace France was liable for trademark disparagement. The court answered in the affirmative and banned the Greenpeace campaign against Areva. The court ordered Greenpeace to pay Areva $20,000 in damages, and noted the Internet Service Provider's decision to discontinue hosting the website containing the offensive and illegal Greenpeace parody. This was a strict liability decision because the court did not require SPCEA to show either fault, or harm. That is, evidence that the Greenpeace parody had "devalued the image" of the public utility company in the marketplace.

Greenpeace appealed the decision to the Paris Court of Appeals. The environmental protection organization once more tried to contest the validity of the French rules of law that were being imposed on it. It also claimed that the strict liability rules that were being applied in the case were contrary to European Union law on freedom of expression. The issue before the appellate court was whether the Greenpeace campaign against Areva was protected by the Law of July 29, 1881 on Freedom of the Press. The court said that it was not. The court addressed the appeal to European Community law in its ruling. It said that by equating all the goods and services of Areva—including non-nuclear industry products—with death, the Greenpeace parody had disparaged and denigrated these products and services, thereby abusing the right of freedom of expression, and causing damage that it had to repair as a matter of law. The substance of the judgment of the High Court of Paris was therefore affirmed.[93] Interestingly, the Paris Court of Appeals did not also require SPCEA to show the harm caused by the trademark parody.

Greenpeace France appealed the decision to the *Cour de Cassation* (Court of Cassation), the French Supreme Court for civil and criminal matters. Greenpeace claimed that by holding both organizations liable for trademark disparagement, the Court of Appeal of Paris had violated their right of freedom of expression under the Law of July 29, 1881 on Freedom of the Press (as amended), and under Article 10 of the European Convention on Human Rights and Fundamental Freedoms of 1950. The issue before the court was whether the Greenpeace parody that associated Areva's logo with the symbol of death was an abuse of the right of freedom of expression. The *Cour de Cassation* held that it was not. The Court rejected the fault standard of the *Code civil* as not being applicable to this case. The rationale of the Court was that Greenpeace France and Greenpeace New Zealand had acted in the public interest:

> *ces associations agissant conformément à leur objet, dans un but d'intérêt général et de santé publique par des moyens proportionnés à cette fin, n'avaient pas abusé de leur droit de libre expression.*[94]
>
> these associations, acting in conformity with their objectives, in the general interest, and in the interest of public health, through means proportional to this end, did not abuse their right of freedom of expression.

The Court of Cassation therefore reversed the ruling of the Paris Court of Appeals in part, holding that the appellate court erred when it held that the environment protection organizations had abused the right of freedom of expression. However, the *Cour de Cassation* let stand the appellate ruling that the Greenpeace parody had disparaged and denigrated the products and services of Areva. Despite the fact that the appellate decision was reversed in part, SPCEA was ordered to pay the costs of the five-year litigation.

Greenpeace v. SPCEA was a landmark case in many respects. In its decision, the *Cour de Cassation* focused on the freedom of expression issues raised by trademark parodies and complaint websites, and rejected the application of the strict liability fault standard of the *Code civil* of 1804 to online trademark parody. The Court also applied, for the first time, the pan-European freedom of expression standard of Article 10 of the European Convention on Human Rights and Fundamental Freedoms to a French trademark parody case. This case therefore greatly enlarged the scope of freedom of expression with respect to trademark parodies on the Internet. Under the Article 10 (European) freedom of expression standard applied by the *Cour de Cassation*, a trademark parody may be legal even in circumstances where there is no clear, humorous, satirical intent, and where the parody may be prejudicial to the image of the owner or registrar of the trademark. The old standard was that in order to be legal, a parody had to have a clear, humorous, satirical intent. It could not be prejudicial to the subject of the parody or to others.[95] There also was no trademark parody exception in French trademark law. This case demonstrates that in matters of trademark parody and gripe sites, French courts have moved closer to the freer Euro-communitarian freedom of expression model.

American Exceptionalism, the French Exception, Trademark Parody and "Gripe" Websites: Comparative Analysis

This comparative study of trademark parody and Internet complaint websites in the United States and France was aimed at determining how the different freedom of expression and intellectual property regimes of both countries dealt with a similar problem—the clash between freedom of expression and the unauthorized appropriation and subversion of trademarks, and Internet domain names for purposes of political or social criticism. We have seen that though the United States and France have functionally equivalent legal means of protecting freedom of expression through parody or pastiche, while also protecting trademarks from unauthorized appropriation, dilution, or tarnishment, there remain a number of "irreducible specificities," to use the expression of Marc Ancel,[96] in the political and legal cultures of both countries. These specificities are grounded in the exceptional logics of both countries.

Trademark Parody and American Exceptionalism

In the United States, judicial attitudes toward trademark parody and "gripe" websites have evolved over time. American courts have held that the Trademark (Lanham) Act passes constitutional muster because its regulatory scope is limited to commercial speech, which has less protection than say, political speech, under the First Amendment.[97] Furthermore, the Trademark Act is circumscribed by fair use. Traditionally, the fair use provisions of the Copyright Act, which protect parodies—including trademark parodies—were designed for real space. With the development of cyberspace into a multi-communication platform, courts began to apply fair use to cyberspace. Both the Anti-Cybersquatting Consumer Protection Act (ACPA),[98] and the Trademark Dilution Revision Act of 2006 have fair use provisions.[99] Exceptional First Amendment values are therefore interwoven in the intellectual property regime and specifically in trademark law. This widens the scope of free speech on the Internet and ensures a wide latitude for social and political criticism. The only circumstance under which parody or "gripe" websites are stripped of First Amendment protection is when parodies of trademarks or domain names are used "in connection with the sale . . . or advertising of any goods or services." That is to say, the trademark parody loses protection if there is any commercial element in the "gripe" website or if the website is linked to content that could even remotely be construed as commercial or bad faith cybersquatting.

Though over the years American courts have become more and more skeptical of attempts by trademark and service mark owners to use trademark law to silence their cyber critics, they have to deal with the so-called law of unintended consequences. In effect, the Trademark Dilution Revision Act which granted Internet parodists greater latitude to criticize,[100] this has had an unintended effect—an increase in "trademark bullying."

In effect, when the TDRA granted owners of famous trademarks a cause of action "regardless of the presence or absence of actual or likely confusion, of competition, or of actual economic injury,"[101] it no longer required them to show actual damage to be successful in trademark dilution suits. This provision has become a weapon that owners of famous trademarks wield to effectively "bully" individuals and small businesses that are perceived to infringe on their famous trademarks. These corporate trademark bullies often employ litigation tactics that include "attempting to enforce trademark rights beyond a reasonable interpretation of the scope of the rights granted to the trademark owner."[102] In order to counter "trademark bullying," Congress inserted a provision in the Trademark Technical and Conforming Amendment Act of 2010 that instructed the Secretary of Commerce, in consultation with the Intellectual Property Enforcement Coordinator, to conduct a study of the extent to which small businesses were being harmed by trademark bullying.[103] Clearly, the balance between freedom of expression and the protection of trademarks needs to be re-examined.

Trademark Parody and the French Cultural Exception

As we noted above, the *Code de propriété intellectuelle* (Intellectual Property Code) has a parody exception intended to protect critical forms of expression from overzealous enforcement of proprietary rights in intellectual property. The French court decisions analyzed in this chapter defined the contours of trademark law in the context of parody and "gripe" websites. The analysis shows that French intellectual property law is at the confluence of two major politico-cultural currents—the centuries-old French cultural exception and its unique system of marks and gastronomic nomenclature, the *appellations d'origine controlées,* on the one hand, and post-World War II Euro-communitarian legal and regulatory harmonization, on the other hand. The cases analyzed above show how French courts mostly refrained from applying the parody defense designed for author's rights cases in real space, to trademark parody and complaint websites in cyberspace.

This posture was different from the demarche of the American courts and Congress, which applied exceptional First Amendment principles designed for real space, to trademark parody and complaint websites in cyberspace. Congress further expanded the fair use provisions of the Copyright Act to trademark law, thereby enlarging the scope of freedom of expression on the Internet. As for French courts, they routinely rejected parody defenses in trademark parody or "gripe" website litigation, stating that the parody defense was applicable only to literary works, not to trademarks, whether they be in real space or cyberspace. The non-applicability of the parody defense to criticism outside the domain of literary, or music criticism is part of the French cultural exception. France has a cultural stake in protecting the propriety interests of the vast, complex, culture of geographic, gastronomic, and fashion nomenclature.

However, the posture of the French judiciary towards online trademark parody and complaint website evolved from categorical rejection of the applicability of the parody defense to online content in the late 1990s, to tolerance, a decade later, of parody as a valid instrument of criticism within the framework of the judicial procedures of the Court of Justice of the European Communities. Courts also granted protection to certain types of trademark denigration under Article 10 (freedom of expression) jurisprudence of the European Court of Human Rights. The turning point was the so-called "*affaires Greenpeace*" (Greenpeace affairs). In these cases, the trademark parodists, Greenpeace France and Greenpeace New Zealand, availed themselves of the procedural law of the Court of Justice of the European Communities, which allow litigants in European national cases the right to invoke European Community law to contest the validity of specific national rules of law that are being imposed on them. The French national judges issued rulings that were consonant with European Community freedom of expression standards.

Conclusion

This chapter analyzed American and French application of trademark parody laws designed for real space to the reality of the cyberspace. It was found that the United States has amended trademark law and brought it within the ambit of the First Amendment by inserting a fair use provision in it. Thus, when it came to the clash between trademark integrity and trademark parody, Federal courts have generally held that trademark parody and gripe sites that are non-commercial may have a First Amendment protection that immunizes them from liability. The United States Court of Appeals for the 6th Circuit succinctly expressed the American position towards trademark parody and "gripe" websites when it ruled that: "The rooftops of our past have evolved into the internet domain names of our present. We find that the domain name is a type of public expression, no different in scope than a billboard or a pulpit."[104] The caveat is that direct or indirect commercial activity strips trademark parody and "gripe" websites of First Amendment parody protection.

This analysis shows that under the "blamable denigration" standard of French law, unauthorized registration of the trademarks of companies, institutions, geographic regions, municipalities, cooperatives, and individuals as domain names, for purposes of parody or satirical mimicry, can be legal only if the parody is found to be harmless. That is, it does not denigrate the subject of the criticism or cause "harm" to the trademark or its registrant. This standard is vague, overbroad and overly restrictive. It violates freedom of expression, given that one of the aims of parody is to cause some sort of psychic or tangible harm to the subject of the parody. A harmless parody is a contradiction in terms.

NOTES

1. This problem is also acute in other areas of law. See e.g. Orin S. Kerr, Applying the Fourth Amendment to the Internet: A General Approach, 62 Stanford Law Review 1005 (2010).

2. See Milton, Mueller, Ruling The Root: Internet Governance And The Taming Of Cyberspace 2 (2002)

3. See the Oxford English Dictionary 489 (1970).

4. See *Dr. Seuss Enterprises v. Penguin Books*, 109 F.3d 1394 (1997).

5. See the Oxford English Dictionary 489 (1970).

6. See *LL Bean, Inc. v. Drake Publishers*, 811 F.2d 26 (1987).

7. *Taubman Co. v. Webfeats & Mishkoff*, 391 F.3d 770, 775 (6th Cir. 2003).

8. *Bosley Medical Institute, Inc. v. Kremer,* 403 F. 3d 672 (Court of Appeals 9th Circuit 2005).

9. See generally, Michael Ignatieff, Introduction: American Exceptionalism and Human Rights. In American Exceptionalism And Human Rights, Michael Ignatieff (Ed.) 26 (2005). See also Jacques Rigaud, L'exception Culturelle: Culture Et Pouvoir Sous La Ve Rèpublique (The Cultural Exception: Culture And Power Under The Fifth Republic) 26-27 (1994).

10. See David L. Lange And H. Jefferson Powell, No Law: Intellectual Property In The Image Of An Absolute First Amendment 171 (Stanford Univ. Press 2009).

11. For a discussion on functionalism in comparative law, see Ralf Michaels, The Functional Method of Comparative Law. In Mathias Reimann and Reinhard Zimmermann (Eds.), The Oxford Handbook of Comparative Law, 339-382 (2006).

12. See generally, Louis Hartz, The Liberal Tradition In America: An Interpretation Of American Political Thought Since The Revolution. See also Ronald J. Schmidt, Jr. In the Beginning, all the world was America: American Exceptionalism in New contexts, in Oxford Handbook Of Political Theory 281-296 (2006).

13. See Frederick Schauer, The Exceptional First Amendment, in American Exceptionalism And Human Rights 29, 56 (Michael Ignatieff, Ed. 2005).

14. U.S. Constitution, Art. 1 §8, cl.8.

15. *Community for Creative Non-Violence v. Reid,* 490 U.S. 730, (1989) ("As a general rule, the author is the party who actually creates the work, that is, the person who translates an idea into a fixed, tangible expression entitled to protection. . . . If the work is for hire, 'the employer or other person for whom the work was prepared is considered the 'author' and owns the copyright unless there is a written agreement to the contrary").

16. See *Fogerty v. Fantasy, Inc.,* 510 U.S. 517, 524 (1994) (Holding that "the primary objective of the Copyright Act is to encourage the production of original, literary, artistic, and musical expression for the good of the public.").

17. See David L. Lange And H. Jefferson Powell, No Law: Intellectual Property In The Image Of An Absolute First Amendment X, XI, 171 (Stanford Univ. Press 2009).

18. *Eldred v. Ashcroft*, 537 U.S. 186, 219 (Ginsburg, J., quoting *Harper and Row, Inc v. Nation Enterprises, Inc.*, 471 U.S. 539, 558 (1985) and asserting that "copyright's purpose is to promote the creation and publication of free expression").

19. Copyright Act of 1976 (as amended) 17 U.S.C §107.

20. *Campbell v. Acuff-Rose Music*, 510 U.S. 569 (1994) (Holding that a commercially successful music parody was fair use); see also *Warner Brothers, Inc. v. American Broadcasting Corporation, Inc.*, 720 F.2d 231, 242 (2d. Cir. 1983) (Holding that a TV show parodying Superman is protected); and also *Elsmere Music, Inc. v. National broadcasting Company, Inc.*, 623 F.2d. 252, 253 (2d. Cir. 1980) (Holding that *Saturday Night Life* TV parody of the song, "I Love New York" was protected).

21. See David L. Lange And H. Jefferson Powell, No Law: Intellectual Property In The Image Of An Absolute First Amendment 52 (Stanford Univ. Press 2009).

22. Copyright Act of 1976 (as amended) 17 U.S.C §107.

23. See Nick Hewett, France and Exceptionalism, in The French Exception, Emmanuel Godin And Tony Chafer (Eds.) 3 (2005).

24. See Jacques Rigaud, L'exception Culturelle: Culture Et Pouvoir Sous La Ve République (The Cultural Exception: Culture And Power Under The Fifth Republic) 113, 127 (1994).

25. See *Claude M'Barali (MC Solaar et autres v. Société Media Consulting et autres) Claude M'Barali* (MC Solaar and others v. Société Media Consulting and others) Tribunal de Grande Instance de Paris, 3ème chambre, 2ème section (High Court of Paris) Jugement du 7 novembre (Judgment of November 7, 2003). Available at http://www.legalis.net/jurisprudence-decision.php3?id_article=1032 Last visited September 28, 2008. (Holding that a media company which licensed a musician's compositions from a copyright clearing house for use as cell phone ring tones violated the musician's moral rights because the musician did not authorize modification of the quality of the music).

26. See François Azouvi, Descartes in Pierre Nora (Ed.) Lieux De Mémoire (Tome 3) (Sites Of Memory) (Vol. III) 4475 Paris: Quarto Gallimard (1997) (Stating that French Philosopher, Réné Descartes is a "site of memory").

27. See *Code de la propriété intellectuelle, version consolidée au 22 décembre 2008*. (Intellectual Property Code, Consolidated version). Available at LegiFrance, http://www.legifrance.gouv.fr/affichCode.do?cidTexte=LEGITEXT000006069414&dateTexte=2008030 (Last visited March 24, 2009).

28. 15 U.S.C. § 1125(d) (1999).

29. The Anti-Cybersquatting Consumer Protection Act, 15 U.S.C §1125 (D) (1999).

30. The Anti-Cybersquatting Consumer Protection Act, 15 U.S.C §1125 (D) (1999).

31. 15 U.S.C. § 1125(d) (1) (B) (4) (1999).

32. *SNCF c/ Benoît* M. Tribunal de Grande Instance de Paris, 3ème chamber, 2ème section, Jugement du 29 octobre 2010. (*SNCF v. Benoît M.*, High Court of Paris, 3rd Chamber, 2nd Section, Judgment of October 29, 2010).

33. See WIPO, Brands Tackle Cybersquatters in 2009, UDRP becomes Eco-Friendly (2010). Available at: http://www.wipo.int/pressroom/en/articles/2010/article_0007.html.

34. Cliff Notes, Inc. v. Bantam Doubleday Dell Publishing, 886 F.2d 490, 494 (1989).

35. 15 U.S.C. §§ 1114, 1125(A); See Also Robert Trager, Joseph Russomanno & Susan Dente Ross, The Law Of journalism And Mass Communication (2nd Ed.) 590 (2010).

36. 263 F.3d 359 (4th Cir. 2001).

37. Id.

38. *PETA v. Doughney*, 113 F. Supp.2d 915 (E.D. Va. 2000).

39. 263 F.3d 359 (4th Cir. 2001).

40. 263 F.3d 359 (4th Cir. 2001).

41. See Alicia Montgomery, PETA on the Spot, *Salon.com,* August 30, 2000. Available at: http://www.salon.com/news/politics/feature/2000/08/30/giuliani_peta

42. *New York Times v. Sullivan*, 376 U.S. 254 (1964).

43. 42 U.S.P.Q.2d 1430 (S.D. NY, 1997).

44. 42 U.S.P.Q.2d 1430 (S.D. NY, 1997).

45. 42 U.S.P.Q.2d 1430 (S.D. NY, 1997.

46. 15 U.S.C. § 1125(c).

47. 34 F.Supp.2d 1145 (1999).

48. 34 F.Supp.2d 1145 (1999).

49. 34 F.Supp.2d 1145 (1999).

50. 319 F.3d 770, 778 (6th Cir. 2003).

51. 15 U.S.C. § 1114.

52. 319 F.3d 770, 778 (6th Cir. 2003).

53. See Jews for Jesus. Available at: http://www.jewsforjesus.org/

54. 993 F.Supp. 282 (D. NJ. 1998).

55. 993 F.Supp. 282 (D. NJ. 1998).

56. 993 F.Supp. 282 (D. NJ. 1998).

57. Trademark Dilution Revision Act of 2006 (TDRA), 15 U.S.C. § 1125(c) (2) (B-C).

58. Trademark Dilution Revision Act of 2006 (TDRA), 15 U.S.C. § 1125(c) (3) (A–C).

59. See *Décision n° 2006-540 DC du 27 juillet 2006—Loi relative au droit d'auteur et aux droits voisins dans la société de l'information*, journal Officiel du 3 août 2006, p. 11541 (Non conformité partielle).

60. See Art. L112-2, *Code de la propriété intellectuelle, version consolidée* au 22 mars 2011. Available at LegiFrance, http://www.legifrance.gouv.fr/affichCode.do?cidTexte=LEGITEXT000006069414&dateTexte=2011010 (Last visited January 10, 2011).

61. These products are covered mostly by the Code rural. See e.g. *Loi n° 57-1286 du 20 décembre 1957 interdisant la fabrication de vins mousseux autres que la "Clairette de Die" à l'intérieur de l'aire délimitée ayant droit à cette appellation d'origine contrôlée J.O. du 12 décembre 1957* (Law No. 57-1286 of December 20, 1957 forbidding the manufacture of sparkling (frothy) wines other than *"Clairette de Die"* within the area demarcated as having this protected designation of origin, J.O. of December 12, 1957).

62. See Philippe Roger, *L'ennémi Americain*: Génélologie De L'antiamericanisme Français (The American Enemy: Genealogy Of French Anti-Americanism) 442 (2002).

63. See Art. L623-1, *Code de la propriété intellectuelle, version consolidée* au 22 mars 2011. Available at LegiFrance, http://www.legifrance.gouv.fr/affichCode.do?cidTexte=LEGITEXT000006069414&dateTexte=2011010 (Last visited January 10, 2011).

64. See Lyombe Eko, Many Spiders, One World Wide Web: Towards a Typology of Internet Regulation 6 Communication Law and Policy 445, 471 (2001).

65. *Commune de Saint-Tropez c/ Eurovirtuel, Quadra Communication, Nova Développement, Tribunal de grande instance de Draguignan 1ère chambre civile jugement du 21 août 1997. (*Commune of Saint-Tropez v. *Eurovirtuel, Quadra Communication, Nova Développement, High Court of Draguignan, 1st Civil chamber, Judgment of August 21, 1997).*

66. See Art. L122-5 *Code de propriété intellectuelle* (Intellectual Property Code). Available at LegiFrance, http://www.legifrance.gouv.fr/affichCode.do;jsessionid=7F38B2FCEFC1D2AC2BAD445E7106D127.tpdJ.O.14v_3?cidTexte=LEGITEXT000006069414&dateTexte=20110107 (Viewed January 6, 2011).

67. See Art. L122-5 (4), *Code de la propriété intellectuelle, version consolidée* au 22 mars 2011. Available at LegiFrance, http://www.legifrance.gouv.fr/affichCode.do?cidTexte=LEGITEXT000006069414&dateTexte=2011010 (Last visited January 10, 2011).

68. Loi No. 64-1360 du 31 décembre 1964, JORF 1er janvier 1965 (Law No. 64-1360 of December 31, 1964, J.O. of January 1, 1965).

69. See *RATP c/Laurent M. & Valentin Lacambre, Tribunal de Grande Instance de Paris,* No. 99/3857 *RATP v. Laurent M. & Valentin Lacambre, High Court of Paris* (2000). Available at http://www.legalis.net/jurisprudence-decision.php3?id_article=393# Last visited January 3, 2011.

70. See *RATP c/Laurent M. & Valentin Lacambre, Tribunal de Grande Instance de Paris,* No. 99/3857 *RATP v. Laurent M. & Valentin Lacambre, High Court of Paris* (2000). Available at http://www.legalis.net/jurisprudence-decision.php3?id_article=393# Last visited June 3, 2010.

71. See *RATP c/Laurent M. & Valentin Lacambre, Tribunal de Grande Instance de Paris,* No. 99/3857 *RATP v. Laurent M. & Valentin Lacambre, High Court of Paris* (2000). Available at http://www.legalis.net/jurisprudence-decision.php3?id_article=393# Last visited June 3, 2010.

72. Tribunal de Grande Instance de Paris 3ème chambre, 3ème section jugement du 29 mai 2001 (High Court of Paris, Judgment of May 29, 2001).

73. Art. L713-2, *Code de la propriéte intellectuelle* (Intellectual Property Code). Available at LegiFrance, http://www.legifrance.gouv.fr/affichCode.do?cidTexte=LEGITEXT000006069414&dateTexte=2011010 (Last visited January 10, 2011).

74. Tribunal de Grande Instance de Paris 3ème chambre, 3ème section jugement du 29 mai 2001 (High Court of Paris, Judgment of May 29, 2001).

75. Art. L713-3, *Code de la propriéte intellectuelle* (Intellectual Property Code). Available at LegiFrance, http://www.legifrance.gouv.fr/affichCode.do?cidTexte=LEGITEXT000006069414&dateTexte=2011010 (Last visited January 10, 2011).

76. *Olivier Malnuit, Réseau Voltaire c/ Compagnie Gervais Danone, Groupe Danone* (*Olivier Malnuit and Réseau Voltaire v. Compagnie Gervais Danone and the Danone Group*) Cour d'appel de Paris 4ème chambre, section A Arrêt du 30 avril 2003 (Appeals Court of Paris, 4th Chamber, Section A, Judgment of April 30, 2003). Available at: http://www.legalis.net/spip.php?page=jurisprudence-decision&id_article=253

77. *Olivier Malnuit, Réseau Voltaire c/ Compagnie Gervais Danone, Groupe Danone* (*Olivier Malnuit and Réseau Voltaire v. Compagnie Gervais Danone and the Danone Group*) Cour d'appel de Paris 4ème chambre, section A Arrêt du 30 avril 2003 (Appeals Court of Paris, 4th Chamber, Section A, Judgment of April 30, 2003). Available at: http://www.legalis.net/spip.php?page=jurisprudence-decision&id_article=253

78. *Olivier Malnuit, Réseau Voltaire c/ Compagnie Gervais Danone, Groupe Danone* (*Olivier Malnuit and Réseau Voltaire v. Compagnie Gervais Danone and the Danone Group*) Cour d'appel de Paris 4ème chambre, section A Arrêt du 30 avril 2003 (Appeals Court of Paris, 4th Chamber, Section A, Judgment of April 30, 2003). Available at: http://www.legalis.net/spip.php?page=jurisprudence-decision&id_article=253

79. *Olivier Malnuit, Réseau Voltaire c/ Compagnie Gervais Danone, Groupe Danone* (*Olivier Malnuit and Réseau Voltaire v. Compagnie Gervais Danone and the Danone Group*) Cour d'appel de Paris 4ème chambre, section A Arrêt du 30 avril 2003 (Appeals Court of Paris, 4th Chamber, Section A, Judgment of April 30, 2003). Available at: http://www.legalis.net/spip.php?page=jurisprudence-decision&id_article=253

80. *Escota / Lycos, Lucent Technologies, Nicolas B.,* Tribunal de Grande Instance de Marseilles, 11 juin 2003 (High Court of Marseilles, Judgment of June 11, 2003) Available at: http://www.legalis.net/breves-article.php3?page=jurisprudence-decision&id_article=234

81. *Escota / Lycos, Lucent Technologies, Nicolas B.,* Tribunal de Grande Instance de Marseilles, 11 juin 2003 (High Court of Marseilles, Judgment of June 11, 2003) Available at: http://www.legalis.net/breves-article.php3?page=jurisprudence-decision&id_article=234

82. *Escota / Lycos, Lucent Technologies, Nicolas B.,* Tribunal de Grande Instance de Marseilles, 11 juin 2003 (High Court of Marseilles, Judgment of June 11, 2003) Available at: http://www.legalis.net/breves-article.php3?page=jurisprudence-decision&id_article=234

83. *Escota / Lycos, Lucent Technologies, Nicolas B.,* Tribunal de Grande Instance de Marseilles, 11 juin 2003 http://www.legalis.net/breves-article.php3?page=jurisprudence-decision&id_article=234

84. Art. 1384, *Code civil* (Civil Code) (stating that one is not only responsible for damages one causes, but also for damages caused by persons under one's supervision). Available at: http://www.legifrance.gouv.fr/affichCodeArticle.do?idArticle=LEGIARTI000006438840&cidTexte=LEGITEXT000006070721

85. *Lucent Technologies v. Escota, Lycos France, Nicolas B.*, Cour d'appel d'Aix en Provence, 2ème chambre Arrêt au fond du 13 mars 2006. (Appeals Court of Aix en Provence, 2nd Chamber, Substantive Judgment of March 13, 2006). Available at http://www.legalis.net/spip.php?page=jurisprudence-decision&id_article=1611

86. *Esso v. Greenpeace France and Internet.fr.*, Tribunal de Grande Instance de Paris (High Court of Paris), Judgment of January 30, 2004 Available at http://www.legalis.net/jurisprudence-imprimer.php3?id_article=1024

87. Esso France claimed that Greenpeace violated articles L 713-3 (a) and L 713-3 (b) which forbid trademark counterfeiting.

88. See Article 1382, Code Civil, Law 1804-02-09 promulgated on February 19, 1804. ("Anyone who, through his own fault, causes harm to someone else is required to pay damages to repair the harm done.") Available at: http://www.legifrance.gouv.fr/affichCodeArticle.do;jsessionid=4F3C44EF96625C18449E7480235A460C.tpdJ.O.12v_1?cidTexte=LEGITEXT000006070721&idArticle=LEGIARTI000006438819&dateTexte=20081119&categorieLien=cid

89. *Esso v. Greenpeace France and Internet.fr.*, Tribunal de Grande Instance de Paris (High Court of Paris), Judgment of January 30, 2004 Available at http://www.legalis.net/jurisprudence-imprimer.php3?id_article=1024

90. See Court of Justice of the European Communities, Presentation. Available at: http://curia.europa.eu/jcms/jcms/J.O.2_7024/. Visited January 10, 2011.

91. *Esso v. Greenpeace France and Internet.fr.*, Tribunal de Grande Instance de Paris (High Court of Paris), Judgment of January 30, 2004 Available at http://www.legalis.net/jurisprudence-imprimer.php3?id_article=1024

92. See Article 1382, Code Civil, Law 1804-02-09 promulgated on February 19, 1804. Available at: http://www.legifrance.gouv.fr/affichCodeArti-

cle.do;jsessionid=4F3C44EF96625C18449E7480235A460C.tpdJ.O.12v_1?cidTexte=LEGITEXT000006070721&idArticle=LEGIARTI000006438819&dateTexte=20081119&categorieLien=cid

93. See *Greenpeace v. SPCEA, Cour d'Appel de Paris* (Court of Appeal of Paris) Judgment of November 17, 2006. Available at http://www.legalis.net/jurisprudence-imprimer.php3?id_article=1838

94. *Greenpeace France and New Zealand v. SPCEA, Cour de Cassation (Supreme Court).* Judgment of April 8, 2008. Available at http://www.legalis.net/jurisprudence-decision.php3?id_article=2275#

95. See *Ministère de Culture: réponse* (Minister of Culture: Response), J.O. Senate of 18/09/2003 page 2837 (Reporting the decision of the High Court of Nanterre, which concluded that a humorous parody of a magazine's registered name and trademark was protected freedom of expression).

96. See Marc Ancel, *Le Problème de la comparabilité et la méthode fonctionelle en droit comparé* (The Problem of Comparability and the Functional Method in Comparative Law) in Festschrift Für Imre Zajtay 2 (1982).

97. See *Semco, Inc. v. Amcast, Inc.*, 52 F.3d 108, 111-12 (6th Cir.1995); *see also Seven-Up v. Coca-Cola Co.,* 86 F.3d 1379, 1383 n. 6 (5th Cir.1996).

98. 15 U.S.C. § 1125(d) (1999).

99. 15 U.S.C. 1125 § 43(2) (3) (2006).

100. *Taubman Co. v. Webfeats*, 319 F. 3d 770 (6th Cir 2003).

101. Trademark Dilution Revision Act of 2006 (TDRA), 15 U.S.C. § 1125(c) (2) (C).

102. Trademark Technical and Conforming Amendment Act of 2010, Pub. L. No. 111-146, 124 Stat. 66 (2010).

103. §4. Trademark Technical and Conforming Amendment Act of 2010, Pub. L. No. 111-146, 124 Stat. 66 (2010).

104. *Taubman Co. v. Webfeats & Mishkoff*, 391 F.3d 770, 775 (6th Cir. 2003).

Selected Bibliography

Abrams v. U.S. 250 U.S. 616 (1919).

Ancel, Marc (1982). Le Problème de la comparabilité et la méthode fonctionelle en droit comparé (The Problem of Comparability and the Functional Method in Comparative Law), in Festschrift für Imre Zajtay (Festschrift for Imre Zajtay) pp. 1-6, Tübingen, Germany: J.C.B. Mohr (Paul Siebeck).

Bellanger, C., Godechot, J., Guiral P. & Terrou, F (1969). *Histoire général de la presse française* (Tome III) [General history of the French press (Volume III)]. Paris: Presses universitaires de France.

Bellanger, C., Godechot, J., Guiral P. & Terrou, F (1975). *Histoire général de la presse française* (Tome IV) [General history of the French press (Volume IV)]. Paris: Presses universitaires de France.

Bennett, William (1998). The Death of Outrage: Bill Clinton and the Assault on American Ideals. New York: Simon and Shuster.

Beriss, D. (2004). "Culture-as Race or Culture-as-Culture: Caribbean Ethnicity and the Ambiguity of Cultural Identity in French Society," in Herrick Chapman and Laura Frader (Eds.), *Race in France*, pp. 111-140. New York: Berghan Books.

Berkowitz, D. & Eko, L. (2007). "Blasphemy As Sacred Rite/Right: 'The Mohammed Cartoons Affair' and Maintenance of Journalistic Ideology." *Journalism Studies* 8 (5), 779-797.

Bernand, C. (2006). The Right to be Different: Some Questions about the "French Exception." In Kathleen Perry Long (Ed.), *Religious Differences in France*. (p. 201-219). Kirksville, Mo.: Truman State University Press.

Bleich, E. (2004). "Anti-racism without races: Politics and policy in a color-blind state," in H. Chapman and L. Frader (Eds.), *Race in France*,Oxford: Berghahn Books, pp. 162-172.

Bloch, Ruth (2007). Religion and ideological Change in the American Revolution, in *Religion and American Politics*, pp. 47-63, Oxford: Oxford University Press.

Buchanan, Allen & Golove, David (2002). Philosophy of International Law, in *The Oxford Handbook of Jurisprudence and Philosoophy of Law*, 868-934. Jules Coleman and Scott Shapiro (Eds.), Oxford: Oxford University Press.

Burnett, Robert & Marshall, David. 2003. *Web Theory*. London: Routledge.

Borgwardt, Elizabeth (2005). *A New Deal for the World: America's Vision for Human Rights.* Cambridge, MA: Harvard/Bellknap Press.

Chapman, H. & Frader, L. (2004), Race in France. In Herrick Chapman and Laura Frader (Eds.), *Race in France* 1-22. New York: Berghan Books.

Clausen, Bente (2007). For God's Sake? American Religion and Politics viewed from Denmark, in *Religion and American Politics* (pp. 406-413). Oxford: Oxford University Press.

Clinton, William & Gore, Albert. (1997). *A Framework for Electronic Commerce.* Washington D.C.: United States Printing Office.

Corfield, Penelope (2007). *Time and The Shape of History*. New Haven: Yale University Press.

De Tocqueville, Alexis (1843). *De la démocracie en Amérique* (tome II) [Democracy in America. (Vol. II)]. (H. Reeve, Trans.). New York: J.H.G. Langley. (Original work published 1835).

Eko, Lyombe (2001). Many Spiders, One World Wide Web: Towards a Typology of Internet Regulation. *Communication Law and Policy*, 6 (448-460).

Eko, Lyombe (2006). New Medium: Old Free Speech Regimes: The Historical and Ideological Foundations of French and American regulation of Bias Motivated speech and Symbolic Expression on the Internet. *Loyola of Los Angeles, International and Comparative Law Review*, 28 (1) pp. 69-127.

Eko, Lyombe (2012). New Media, Old Regimes: Case Studies in Comparative Media Law and Policy. Lanham, MD: Lexington Press.

Feldblum, M. (1991). Reconstructing Citizenship: The Politics of Nationality reform and Immigration in Contemporary France. Albany, N.Y.: SUNY Press.

Foucault, M. (1994), *Dits et Ecrits* (Tome III), Sayings and Writings (Vol. III). Paris: Editions Gallimard

Foucault, M. (1994*). Dits et Ecrits (*Tome II*).(Sayings and Writings,* Vol. II*).* Paris: Gallimard.

Friedman, Lawrence (1990). *The Republic of Choice*. Cambridge, MA.: Harvard University Press.

Gordley, James (2003). The Universalist Heritage. in Pierre Legrand and Roderick Munday, (Eds.), *Comparative Legal Studies: Traditions and Transitions.* Cambridge, UK: Cambridge University Press, 31-45.

Graziplene, Leonard (2000). *Teletext: Its Promise and Demise*. London: Associated University Presses.

Griffiths, David & Harrison, Joel (2005). European Union, *in E-Commerce and the Law of Digital Signatures* (Dennis Campbell, Ed.) pp. 733-762. Dobbs Ferry, N.Y.: Oceana Publications.

Guerrin, Michel & de Roux, Emmanuel (2005). *Premiére victoire pour l'exception culturelle à l'unesco* (First Victory for Cultural Exception in UNESCO), *Le Monde*, June 11, 2005, p. 27.

Guice, Jon. 1998. Looking Backward and Forward at the Internet. The Information Society. 14 (3) 201-211.

Harrison, Jane. (1912). *Themis: A Study of the Social Origins of Greek Religion.* Cambridge, UK: Cambridge University Press.

Hewlett, Nick (2005). France and Exceptionalism, in *The French Exception*, Emmanuel Godin and Tony Chafer, (Eds.) 3-15. Oxford: Berghahn Books.

Higgott, Richard (2006). International Institutions, In *The Handbook of Political Institutions*, pp. 611-630, R.A.W Rhodes, Sarah Bender and Bert Rockman (Eds.), Oxford: Oxford University Press.

Hollander, P. (1995). *Anti-Americanism: Irrational and rational.* New Brunswick, N.J.: Transaction Publishers.

Hudson, Heather (2006). *From Rural Village to Global Village: Telecommunications for Development in the Information Age*. Mahwah, N.J.: Lawrence Earlbaum.

Ignatieff, Michael (ed., 2005). *American Exceptionalism and Human Rights.* Princeton, N.J.: Princeton University Press.

Ignatieff, Michael (2005). Introduction: American Exceptionalism and Human Rights. In *American Exceptionalism and Human Rights* pp. 1-26. Princeton, N.J.: Princeton University Press.

Ives, Greg (2002). *American Constitutional Law: Power and Politics* (Vol. II). Boston: Houghton Mifflin.

Kagan, Robert A. (2001). *Adversarial Legalism: The American Way of Law*. Cambridge, MA : Harvard University Press.

Kagan, Robert (2002). "Power and Weakness," *Policy Review*, No. 113 (June and July).

Kalathil, Shanthi & Boas Taylor (2003). *Open Networks, Closed Regimes: The Impact of the Internet on Authoritarian Rule.* Washington D.C.: Carnegie Endowment for International Peace.

Kaldis, Byron (2002). World Justice, Global Politics and Nation States: Three Ethico-Political Problems. *The European Legacy* 7 (2) pp. 167-194.

Kant, Immanuel (1991). Political Writings, Hans Reiss, (ed,); H.B. Nisbet, trans. Cambridge; Cambridge University Press.

Karsh, E. (2006). *Islamic Imperialism: A Short History.* New Haven, Ct.: Yale University Press.

Kauffmann, S. (2006). *Les fractures de l'affaire Mahomet* (The Rifts of the Mohammad Affair). *Le Monde*, February 21, p. 2.

Klein, Ernst (1967). *A Comprehensive Etymological Dictionary of the English Language* (Vol. II). Amsterdam, Netherlands: Elsevier.

Kuisel, Richard (1993). *Seducing the French: The dilemma of Americanization.* Berkley, CA.: University of California press.

Laurence, J. & Vaisse J. (2006). Integrating Islam: Political and Religious Challenges in Contemporary France. Washington D.C., Brookings Institution.

Legrand, Pierre (2003).The Same and the Different. In Pierre Legrand and Roderick Munday (Eds.), *Comparative Legal Studies: Traditions and Transitions*, pp. 240-311. Cambridge: Cambridge University Press.

Legrand, Pierre (1999). *Fragments on Law-as-Culture.* Deventer, Netherlands: W.E. J. Tjeenk Willink,

Lessig, Lawrence (1999). *Code and Other Laws of Cyberspace.* New York: Basic Books.

Lessig, Lawrence (2006) Code Version 2.0. New York: Basic Books. LICRA & UEJF v. Yahoo! & Yahoo! France, *Tribunal de Grande Instance de Paris* (High Court of Paris), 2000.

Lionnet, F. & Shih, S. (2005). Introduction, in *Minor Transnationalism*, Françoise Lionnet and Shuh-mei Shih (Eds.), pp. 1-23. Durham, N.C.: Duke University Press.

Lipsett, Seymour, Martin (1996). *American Exceptionalism: A Double-Edged Sword.* New York: W.W. Norton and Company.

Lipsett, Seymour, Martin (1991). American Exceptionalism Reaffirmed. In Byron Shafer (Ed.). *Is America Different?* Pp. 1-45. Oxford, U.K.: Oxford University Press.

Macridis, Ray & Burg, Steven (1991). *Introduction to Comparative Politics* (2nd Edition). New York: HarperCollins Publishers.

Majumdar, Margaret (2005). Exceptionalism and Universalism: The Uneasy alliance in the French-Speaking World, in *The French Exception*, Emmanuel Godin and Tony Chafer, (Eds.) 16-29. New York: Berghahn Books.

Marsh, David (1998). *Comparing Policy Networks.* Buckingham: Open University Press.

Mattelart, Armand, (2002). *La Mondialisation de la Communication (Globalization of Communication).* Paris: Presses Universitaires de France.

McBrien, Richard (1987). *Caesar's Coin: Religion and Politics in America.* New York: Macmillan.

Michaels, Ralf (2006). The Functional Method of Comparative Law, in *The Oxford Handbook of Comparative Law*, 339-382. Mathias Reimann & Reinhard Zimmermann (Eds.), New York: Oxford University Press.

Morin, E. (1990). *Le trou noir de la laicité* (The black hole of secularism). *Le Débat* No. 58, p. 38.

Mueller, Milton (2002). *Ruling the Root: Internet Governance and the Taming of Cybersapace.* Cambridge, MA: MIT Press.

Murphy, Jeffrie & Coleman, Jules (1990). *Philosophy of Law*: An Introduction to Jurisprudence. Boulder, CO., Westview.

Murrin, John (2007). Religion and Politics in America from the First Settlements to the Civil War, in *Religion and American Politics* (pp. 23-46). Oxford: Oxford University Press.

Nelken, David (2003). Comparatists and transferability, in Pierre Legrand and Roderick Munday (Eds.), *Comparative Legal Studies: Traditions and Transitions* pp. 437-466. Cambridge, UK: Cambridge University Press.

Nelken, David (1996). *Law as Communication*. Aldershot: Dartmouth University Press. Nora, Pierre (1989). Between Memory and History: Les Lieux de Mémoires (Sites of Memory). *Representations,* 26 (Spring) 7-24.

Osborne, Thomas (1998). Aspects of Elightenment: Social theory and the Ethics of Truth. Baltimore, MD., Rowman and Littlefield.

Perry, Ralph (1944). *Puritanism and Democracy*. New York: The Vanguard Press.

Reimann, Mathias & Zimmermann, Reinhard (Eds. 2007), *The Oxford Handbook of Comparative Law*. New York: Oxford University Press.

Reno v. American Civil Liberties Union, 521 U.S. 844 (1997).

Rey, A. & Re-Debove (Eds. 1992), *Le Petit Robert 1* Paris: Dictionnaires Le Robert.

Ricœur, Paul. (1991). *Lectures 1:Autour du Politique*. (Readings 1: On Politics). Paris: Éditions du Seuil.

Rigaud, Jacques (1995). *L'Exception culturelle: Culture et Pouvoir Sous La Ve République*. (The Cultural Exception:Culture and Power Under the Fifth Republic). Paris: Bernard Grasset.

Safa, Rachid (2005). France, in *E-Commerce and the Law of Digital Signatures* (Dennis Campbell, ed.) .pp. 203-219. Dobbs Ferry, N.Y.: Oceana Publications.

Sassoon, Donald, The Culture of the Europeans from 1800 to the Present (2006). London: Harper Press.

Saunders, David (1992). Approaches to the Historical Relations of the Legal and the Aesthetic. *New Literary History*, 23 (3) 505-521.

Scarpetta, G. (November 5, 1980). *L'anti-américaine primaire*. (Primary anti-Americanism). *Le Monde,* p. 2.

Schauer, Frederick (2005). The Exceptional First Amendment. In *American Exceptionalism and Human Rights* pp. 1-26. Princeton, N.J.: Princeton University Press.

Scoles, E., Hay, P., Borchers, P. & Symeonides, S. (2000). *Conflict of Laws* (3d. Ed.). St. Paul, Minnesota: West Group.

Sifaoui, Mohamed (2006). *L'Affaire des Caricatures: Déssins et Manipulations* (The Caricatures Affair: Drawings and Manipulations). Paris: Broché.

Tchikaya, Blaise (1998). *Le Droit International des Télécommunication* (The International Law of Telecommunications. Paris: Presses Universitaires de France.

Timmermann, Jens (2007). *Kant's Groundwork of the Metaphysics of Morals: A Commentary.* Cambridge, UK.: Cambridge University Press.

Van Gerven, Walter (2005). *The European Union: A Polity of States and Peoples.* Stanford: Stanford University Press.

Vick, Daniel. 2001. Exporting the First Amendment to Cyberspace, in Nancy Morris and Sylvio Waisbord, *Media and Globalization: Why the State Matters*. Boulder, CO.: Rowman and Littlefield.

Walker, Samuel (1999). *In defense of American liberties: A history of the ACLU.* Carbondale, Il.: Southern Illinois University Press.

Wallerstein, Immanuel (1979). *The Capitalist World Economy*. Cambridge, UK: Cambridge University Press.

Watson, Alan (1993). *Legal Transplants* (2nd ed.). Athens, Georgia: University of Georgia Press.

Webster, Frank (2006). *Theories of the Information Society* (3rd. ed.). London: Routledge.

Webster's Revised Unabridged Dictionary. Retrieved August 8, 2007 from Dictionary.com website: http://dictionary.reference.com/browse/Re-presentation

Webster's Third New International Dictionary (1986). Springfield, MA.: G&C Merriam Co.

Weinstein, Michael (2005). Introduction, in Michael Weinstein (ed).

Globalization: What's New? New York: Columbia University Press, 1-18.

Zweigert, Conrad & Korn, Hein (1998). *An Introduction to Comparative Law* (3rd. Ed). (Tony Weir, trans.). Oxford: Clarendon Press.

Index